THE VITALITY OF CONTRADICTION

THE VITALITY OF CONTRADICTION

Hegel, Politics, and the Dialectic of Liberal-Capitalism

BRUCE GILBERT

McGill-Queen's University Press
Montreal & Kingston • London • Ithaca

ISBN 978-0-7735-4257-0 (cloth)
ISBN 978-0-7735-4258-7 (paper)
ISBN 978-0-7735-8949-0 (ePDF)
ISBN 978-0-7735-8950-6 (ePUB)

Legal deposit fourth quarter 2013
Bibliothèque nationale du Québec

Printed in Canada on acid-free paper that is 100% ancient forest free (100% post-consumer recycled), processed chlorine free

This book has been published with the help of a grant from the Canadian Federation for the Humanities and Social Sciences, through the Awards to Scholarly Publications Program, using funds provided by the Social Sciences and Humanities Research Council of Canada. Funding has also been received from Bishop's University.

McGill-Queen's University Press acknowledges the support of the Canada Council for the Arts for our publishing program. We also acknowledge the financial support of the Government of Canada through the Canada Book Fund for our publishing activities.

Library and Archives Canada Cataloguing in Publication

Gilbert, Bruce, 1963–, author
The vitality of contradiction : Hegel, politics, and the dialectic of liberal-capitalism / Bruce Gilbert.

Includes bibliographical references and index.
Issued in print and electronic formats.
ISBN 978-0-7735-4257-0 (bound).
ISBN 978-0-7735-4258-7 (pbk.).
ISBN 978-0-7735-8949-0 (ePDF).
ISBN 978-0-7735-8950-6 (ePUB)

1. Hegel, Georg Wilhelm Friedrich, 1770–1831 – Political and social views. 2. Political science – Philosophy. 3. Dialectic. 4. State, The. 5. Capitalism. 6. Social movements. I. Title.

JC233.H46G54 2013 320.01 C2013-906434-6
C2013-906435-4

For John Russon

It is the nature of the real lover of learning to strive for what is; and … not lose the keenness of his passionate love nor cease from it before he grasps the nature of each thing.

Plato, *Republic*, 490a–b

Contents

Abbreviations of Hegel's Works

In all cases but those specifically noted, notes are to the pagination or paragraph number of an English edition, followed by a backslash and the pagination from the German edition. In cases where the paragraphs are numbered identically in the German and English editions, only one number will be cited, e.g., §45. Unless otherwise noted, German citations are taken from *Hegel: Werke: Theorie Werkausgabe*, cited by volume number, e.g., *Werke* 4.

With respect to Hegel's lectures, in all cases Remarks (*Anmerkungen*) are marked by the paragraph number with an R, and Additions (*Zusätzen*) by the paragraph number with an A, e.g., §45R.

A	*Aesthetics: Lectures on Fine Arts/Werke* 13–15
EL	*Encyclopedia Logic/Werke* 8
HP	*Lectures on the History of Philosophy/Werke* 18–20
JR	*Jenaer Realphilosophie*
NR	*Lectures on Natural Right and Political Science: The First Philosophy of Right*
PH	*Philosophy of History/Werke* 12
PM	*Philosophy of Mind/Werke* 10
PN	*Philosophy of Nature/Werke* 9
PR	*Elements of the Philosophy of Right/Werke* 7 Only the preface is not organized into numbered paragraphs, and thus the references are to the English edition and then the German, e.g., 21/14.
PRel	*Lectures on the Philosophy of Religion/Werke* 11–12
PS	*Phenomenology of Spirit* Citations are to paragraph numbers preceded by M, e.g.,

M19/*Phänomenologie des Geistes*.
Note: All citations from chapter 6, "Spirit," of *PS* are taken from *Spirit*, translated by the Hegel Translation Group. Citations are to paragraph numbers, preceded by H, e.g., H495.

SL *Science of Logic*/*Werke* 5–6

VPR 1817 *Die Philosophie des Rechts: Die Mitschriften Wannenmann* (Heidelberg 1817–1818) *und Homeyer* (Berlin 1818–1819). Page numbers are cited. After the slash is the page reference to the endnote in which Allen Wood's English translations of passages from *VPR* 1819 appear in the Nisbet/Wood translation of the *Elements of the Philosophy of Right*.

VPR 1819 *Philosophie des Rechts: Die Vorlesung von 1819–1820*. Page numbers are cited. After the slash is the page reference to the endnote in which Allen Wood's English translations of passages from *VPR* 1819 appear in the Nisbet/Wood translation of the *Elements of the Philosophy of Right*.

Preface

Denys Arcand's film *The Decline of the American Empire* prophesies the collapse of Western civilization not by dramatic means – not by following, for example, the trail of greedy adventure-capitalists, nor by showing the extrajudicial assassination of alleged "terrorists" by robot drones, nor indeed anything else of this sort.[1] Instead, Arcand cheekily explores how the decline of Western civilization is revealed in the intellectual class, among the people who read academic books like this one – university professors and their students. The erstwhile serious academics in Arcand's film actually live their lives in a kind of pleasant if disturbing malaise, spending all their time cooking and having sex with each other and their students (or talking about it). Arcand, of course, plays with the tradition most famously associated with Gibbon that moral weakness and decadence inaugurate the decline of civilizations.[2] Perhaps it is indeed the case that civilizations rise on the wings of principled conviction and collapse into the tedious anomy of material and erotic pleasure. In fact, Hegel sometimes seems to suggest this. However, Hegel also gives a far deeper analysis of how civilizations emerge and why they collapse into lassitude or terror. Humanity must slowly and painfully learn the character of its own freedom in a history of "wrecks confusedly hurled."[3]

There is an odd congruence between the notion of decline posited by Arcand in *Decline of the American Empire* and intellectuals in today's universities. I refer to a consensus that we are no longer supposed to speak of reason in history, with the result that the play of ideas becomes just one more (decadent?) pleasure. Of course, Hegel makes no concessions to the pleasure of his readers. His books are infamously difficult, even if enticingly so, but because his insights are profound and usually compelling, they are worth the work. A key goal of this text, then, is to show that there *is*, in spite of recent trends that argue to the contrary, reason in history, in the sense that human beings have to learn to be free.

This text is as much a Hegelian book as it is a book about Hegel. This is demanded by Hegel himself since Hegel thinks that philosophy's most important engagement is always with the philosopher's own time. For this reason I will speak as often about contemporary liberal-capitalism as about Hegel's books. Moreover, I do not hesitate to criticize Hegel's arguments when dialectical philosophy, as I understand it at least, so demands.

We human beings create worlds and, on rare occasions, these worlds collapse around us. We are the being that transforms nature and ourselves such that we feel *at home*, and yet there are dramatic moments or protracted epochs in which these worlds fall apart. Some of the most important historical moments of destruction – such as those marked by the storming of the Bastille, the Haitian Revolution, or the formation of the Petrograd Soviet – are not embodiments of some instinct to break apart what we have built or to transgress otherwise necessary systems of law and morality. Perhaps such impulses exist and make a difference in history, but the destruction of worlds that matters most happens when the very resources that one world has painstakingly built up throws humanity beyond it.

In our individual lives we tend to take this for granted. In learning, in self-transcendence or ek-stasis, the key changes we undergo are not contingent. We move toward more sophisticated ways of being human by standing on the less sophisticated ways that heretofore carried us along. There were times for all of us, long gone now, in which we couldn't yet walk or speak a language. Yet the nascent power in our struggles to move or communicate was the basis for our learning to walk and talk. Here we have the key to dialectics. The criteria for our own self-transformation emerge immanently from within our experience. We go forward by pushing against ourselves. This is the vitality of contradiction, and it exists too at the level of societies. We learn as a species.

Indeed, our being is temporal, so there is no transcendental, unchanging standard of the good. However, there is better and worse, and the standards by which we know the difference can emerge from nowhere other than our own experience. By those standards we negate our previous way of being and create something we trust to be new and better. The power of negation, Hegel observes, is characterized as *restless*,[4] and this restlessness is the *vitality*, the *creativity of freedom*. In all the most important spheres of human activity – love, friendship, art, religion, science, politics, philosophy, and others – the creativity of our freedom promises something better.

This book is a study of the self-exceeding character of human being as it has revealed itself to the philosophical study of the political. We have created many political structures for ourselves over the millennia – the tribal clan, the Greek polis, the Christian state, liberal-capitalism, and many others. Some of these were *at first* achievements of new and more sophisticated forms of being human. They revolutionized not just a political regime but human identity itself. Indeed, political revolution, in its most important moments, goes hand in hand with ontological revolution. Yet, what was once a creative advance later may become a limitation. As Kant says in "Idea for a Universal History with a Cosmopolitan Purpose," humanity is the species that learns, but this learning is the task of *history*, for the school of humanity requires much more than is possible in a single human lifetime.[5] We outgrow the very political structures that were at one time necessary to achieve our freedom in the first place. We outgrow them by standing upon them, by learning from them. This does not mean, of course, that the people who make historical change happen are all students of history. The development of freedom in history is far more subtle, but no less rational.

Consequently, humanity may not be content within the confines of liberal-capitalism forever. It has bestowed on (some of) us what is, from the point of view of earlier epochs, unimaginable wealth and prosperity, and it is the system by which we institutionally confer a certain dignity on each individual person by virtue of his or her universal rights as a free being. The conflicts endemic to the nature of liberal-capitalism, however, awaken the longing to go beyond it. And even if liberal-capitalism cannot itself endow a new world with the terms in which this "beyond" will come into being, it will nonetheless be its crucible. Or again, the vitality of our freedom creates powers in us that contradict those of liberal-capitalism, and we will be motivated to move beyond it toward that which carries our freedom to a more sophisticated place.

We first really said to ourselves that *we are free* barely more than two centuries ago, so it should not be a surprise that we still have much to achieve and much to learn. The failure of the first attempts to overcome liberal-capitalism – the communist revolutions of the Soviet Union, China, and others – are themselves moments in the learning of freedom and not sanctifications of the current state of affairs. They arose because of the contradictions of liberal-capitalism and these contradictions do not disappear just because state socialism failed to be a viable alternative. Thus, no matter how comforting and secure this liberal-capitalist world of ours seems to be, do we believe that we will settle for it in one hundred years? In a thousand? In ten thousand?

This book sets out to sketch an answer to that question. In order to do so, it draws on the philosophy of Hegel, the first philosopher to explore in a systematic way the thesis that freedom is a restless process of self-cultivation that discloses itself only in history – in the vitality of contradiction. I will attempt to show the origins of our liberal-capitalist world in the proto-free societies that were preconditions to its development. I will also identify the great achievement of our own socioeconomic and political world. However, this book will ultimately side with the future, by pointing to the emerging contradictions within liberal-capitalism that invite its downfall and suggesting the terms of its surpassing. Granted, this downfall might well be a calamitous destruction in which nothing new or better is created, but it also might be the moment that inaugurates a world in which freedom moves into a richer and more sophisticated encounter with itself.

If Hegel asks anything of us, as thoughtful people, it is that we attend with the utmost care to allowing a given world to tell us who and what it is, and thus let *it* disclose *on its own terms* where it might be heading. Hegel's philosophy is the cultivation of an attitude toward being in which we allow it, in its own way, to guide our thinking and our action. But beyond that, this philosophy is not *a method*, precisely because the attitude of attending to things on their own terms is itself a product of the development of those very things.

In the process I not only explore the sense in which the human journey has the "infinite" power to surpass itself, to become "other" to itself, to contradict itself. But I also explore how this journey itself generates configurations that it constantly relies on and thus that require perpetual nurturing, for in neglecting them we undermine the very project of freedom itself. For example, the family, civil society, and the state are essential institutions of freedom. Western philosophy in the late twentieth century has become very preoccupied with the open-endedness of the human future and thereby has obscured or even denied the ways in which human beings rely on and thus must nurture the forms of institutional sociability we have painstakingly developed in the past and that are utterly indispensible to our self-determination.

I could not have written this book without the support of many people. John Russon opened the world of philosophy to me with an extraordinary gift of his pedagogical wisdom and dedication to my education. John's commitment to cultivating philosophical communities is remarkable and has enriched my life and the lives of many others. This book is dedicated to him with deep gratitude. My philosophical development was also richly nurtured by other professors at the Pennsylvania State University, especially Alphonso Lingis, Daniel Conway, John Sallis, Doug Anderson, Vincent Colapietro, and Charles Scott. I have had the great privilege of working for nearly my entire philosophical career at Bishop's University. Jamie Crooks has been a very dear friend and fellow lover of wisdom that whole time. Everyone who knows Jamie will agree that I couldn't have a better colleague and friend. I also cherish my working relationships and friendships with my many colleagues at Bishop's, but would like to extend special thanks to Dale Stout, Don Dombowsky, Jenn Cianca, Jean Klucinskas, Benoit-Antoine Bacon, Harvey White, Don Beith, Noah Moss Brender, Cristiana Furlan, Michael Childs, George Rideout, Claude Charpentier, and Justina Browne. I have taught really wonderful students over the years, and I cherish the philosophy and liberal arts communities at Bishop's. I also have a stimulating and supportive philosophical community of friends beyond Bishop's, and take great pleasure in thanking David Ciavatta, Kym MacLaren, Eric Sanday, Jill Gilbert, Jim Gilbert-Walsh, Greg Recco, Susan Bredlau, Nathan Anderson, Pete Costello, Maria Talero, David Morris, Shannon Hoff, Kirsten Jacobson, Laura McMahon, Patricia Fagan, Karen Robertson, Eve Rabinoff, Greg Kirk, Tim Brownlee, Whitney Howell, Jesse Bailey, Cherilyn Keall, Michael Pelias, and Joe Arel. I would also like to thank the two McGill-Queen's reviewers of the original manuscript of this book: their suggestions were of great help. Indeed, it has been great to work with McGill- Queen's University Press, and I would like in particular to thank Mark Abley, Kate Merriman, and Ryan Van Huijstee.

This work draws not only from the philosophical tradition but also from my work in Latin America and, particularly, in Brazil. The Movement of Landless Rural Workers of Brazil has welcomed me as a researcher and friend of the movement, and I would like to especially thank Aldiva Sales Diniz, Ana Justo, Geraldo Gasparims, Maria Gorete Sousa, and the coordinators of the Escola Nacional Florestan Fernandes, as well as my fellow students in the Dirigentes de Movimentos Sociais course of January and February 2009. Emily Burton, Dave McKee, Elina Vuola, and other members of the Student Christian Movement of Canada created the community in my life in which my interest in politics and social justice was first born.

Alison Carpenter, my former partner and now dear friend, accompanied and supported me in so many ways, including the difficult years of my doctoral work, and I am very thankful to her. Ben and Abby, our wonderful children, are at the core of my life, my happiness, and are even the inspiration for much of my philosophical work. I thank them for tolerating the absences and stresses required to do a doctorate and this research and writing. None of this would have been possible without the great love, support, and constant encouragement of my parents, Ann Morwood and Alex Gilbert, as well as my two sisters, Jennifer and Jill, and their families – and thanks too to Betty Murray. This book is the product of a vital community of people: Deep thanks to all of you.

Contradiction is the root of all movement and vitality; it is only insofar as something has a contradiction within it that it moves, has an urge and activity.

– *Science of Logic*

Each individual is ... a *child of his time*; thus philosophy, too, is *its own time comprehended in thoughts*.

– *Philosophy of Right*

Introduction

The argument of this book is built on two claims by Hegel. The first:

> Contradiction is the root of all movement and vitality; it is only insofar as something has a contradiction within it that it moves, has an urge and activity.[1]

Hegel asserts that "There is no proposition of Heraclitus which I have not adopted in my Logic."[2] One in particular is important here. Heraclitus states, "They do not apprehend how being at variance, it agrees with itself: there is a back-stretched connexion, as in the bow and the lyre."[3] For Hegel the world is in constant motion and does not fit together in a peaceful, static harmony. Thus Hegel reads Heraclitus here as making an ontological statement about a founding tension, a transcendental antagonism, a vital contradiction. The only reason we feel passion, anxiety, longing, desire, fear, joy, love, and terror is because our existence is always suspended in the tension of a perpetually self-elaborating drama. This does not mean that our lives cannot at times be relatively peaceful, harmonious, and stable, but that peace, harmony, and stability are either false attempts to try to escape from the vitality of contradiction or, much better, the result of abiding in it.

Western philosophy often falls short of this vitality, Hegel thinks, because it succumbs to the temptation to separate, isolate, and freeze the terms of vital contradiction, as though Heraclitus's bow could be reduced merely to wood, to string, or to their simple combination. Much Western philosophy reduces reason to one of its essential, albeit lower forms – what Hegel calls the understanding (*Verstand*). We "understand" by separating, isolating, and holding propositions in stable, definable, and mutually exclusive identities. This is a necessary and important faculty of reason but, left on its own, it is terribly inadequate to life. For example, the liberal ontology that posits a multitude of individual free wills reduces the constitutive drama of human life by failing to recognize that we are at once irrevocably bound to other people and yet, at the same time, unsurpassably alien to them. Plato, in his *Symposium*, follows Eryximachus's misinterpretation of this same Heraclitus fragment with Aristophanes' humorous, touching, and even tragic embodiment of it. We are, Aristophanes says, the severed remnants of an original unity, bound in love to the impossible task of reuniting. This is vital contradiction. There is more existential truth in Aristophanes' comic speech than in the fundamental ontological stances of Hobbes, Locke, Rousseau, and Mill. Our thinking is thus prone to fall as flat as a poorly strung bow and our relationships with other people end up having far more vitality than do our theories. The form of reason that lives up to Heraclitus Hegel calls "reason" (*Vernunft*). It is reason that acknowledges that we are in constant flux and "self-negation," and reason recognizes this about reason itself. To think motion and change is to embrace what appears, from the point of view of the understanding, to be illogical – as in Zeno's paradoxes.

As thought recognizes its failure to keep up with the world, it starts to point out the places it itself cannot reach. New interpreters of Hegel are thus anxious to find in him an acknowledgment of the opaque, the unconscious, the unassimilable, and the incomprehensible. Judith Butler writes, "The assimilation of the particular into the universal leaves its trace, an unassimilable remainder, which renders universality ghostly to itself."[4] Slavoj Žižek, in an interpretation inspired by the Lacanian "Real," says that Hegel's "'absolute knowledge' denotes a subjective position which finally accepts 'contradiction' as an internal condition of every identity. In other words, Hegelian 'reconciliation' is not a 'panlogicist' sublation of all reality in the Concept but a final consent to the fact that the Concept itself is 'not-all' (to use this Lacanian term) ... 'absolute knowledge' itself is nothing but a name for the acknowledgment of a certain radical loss."[5]

Yet I will argue that even these authors don't quite live up to the vitality of contradiction. A "radical loss" presupposes a plenum, and a "shadow" presupposes light. That is, it is the "understanding" that posits pure and perfect concepts which, in their failure to grasp the vitality of being, might be said to disclose a radical loss or to cast an unacknowledged shadow. We find the same mistake in Levinas (at least in *Totality and Infinity*), for whom the discrete, self-same identity of the totality must be constantly interrupted by the Other. Levinas' subject here is modernist and thus it should come as no surprise that we feel the need for its transgression.[6] For Hegel, "same" and "Other" are abstractions of the understanding. What is original is being-in-relation, such that the need to hive off, dominate, or avoid the Other is a strategy to cope with ontological vulnerability and not at all the original modality of being.

Radical loss and the shadow may haunt the understanding (*Verstand*), but they are positive terms in the vitality of reason (*Vernunft*). The self of the understanding thinks it can preserve itself by holding fast to its identity, but this is to preserve one's life by killing it. "Identity," Hegel says, "is merely the determination of the simple immediate, of dead being."[7] To live fully we must, instead, be "grounded" or "resolved" in our vital contradiction. Hegel says, rather flatly, that "The resolved contradiction is therefore ground";[8] but what is this "ground" and this "resolution"? While the understanding tries to hold back the ceaseless motion and founding tensions of being and thus tries to deny our finitude by fortifying it, for reason, "Self-subsistence is ... through its own negation a unity returned into itself."[9] That is, our vitality is "our own negation" and the ground and the resolution thus demand the wholehearted affirmation of life's vitality, with all its consequences – including and especially our deaths. Indeed, to be grounded and resolved is "the power to be able to hold and endure" the contradiction within oneself.[10] For Hegel, then, one cannot affirm the vitality of contradiction – one cannot affirm *life* – without "letting go" or "renouncing" the understanding and with it the everyday way in which we act, know, and live. "[One] must consequently renounce [*entsagen*] [one's] natural will, knowledge and existence."[11] On the far side of the renunciation of the understanding is *love* – including the love of wisdom.[12] For Hegel, love is the highest power that abides the contradiction that otherwise causes one to fall to pieces. "Love is a distinguishing of two, who nevertheless are absolutely not distinguished for each other. The consciousness or feeling of the identity of the two – to be outside of myself only in this other – this is love. I have my self-consciousness not in myself but in the other. I am satisfied and have peace with myself only in this other and I am only because I have peace with myself; if I did not have [love], then I would be a contradiction that falls to pieces."[13]

To love being is to let being tell us about itself – to be phenomenologists. But this is no easy task. Indeed, Hegel would say that even the proposition in question, "Contradiction is the root of all movement and vitality," betrays the truth it articulates. The propositional form fails its content precisely because all propositions freeze time and solidify identities. If thought must freeze, kill, or hold being at rest in order to "know" it, then this supposed knowledge is violation rather than truth. Not surprisingly, on the other hand, we only get to the truth through violation. Following the clues left by thinkers like Heraclitus and Plato (especially in the *Parmenides*) Hegel called the world's attention to the dynamism of thought and the temporality of truth.[14] Thus the key to Hegel's philosophy is not to learn important Hegelian propositions like "Contradiction is the root of all movement and vitality," but to enter into this movement and vitality oneself. Or, rather, one has always already entered into it; the point is that one be able to think in terms that are at least as sophisticated as the life one is living.

Indeed, Hegel not only articulates self-moving concepts that "correspond" to self-moving being, but recognizes that the dynamism of human thought is the fulfillment of the history of transcendental antagonism. How odd and erroneous is the notion that dialectical philosophy comes to rest in its so-called "sublations" – the putative unification of opposing terms. Usually and for the most part, the sublation of a contradiction is the moment in which one relents in the stubborn attempt to reduce being to one of its parts or to force the dynamic to sit still. Sublation, in other words, is typically the recognition of the abiding terms of a ceaseless drama. Dialectics, which I spell out slowly and carefully in chapters 1 and 2, is not an a priori science but the momentum created by a history and a restless leaning toward the future. Dialectics is the logic, better still, the logics, of change and self-development. Plainly, Hegelian philosophy does not end with the cholera epidemic of 1831 that cost Hegel his life, but names what Catherine Malabou calls dialectical philosophy's eternal "plasticity."[15] The insights of Marx, Nietzsche, Heidegger, Sartre, Merleau-Ponty, Deleuze, Derrida, and others tend, sometimes in spite of these authors' intentions, to enrich dialectics rather than to challenge it.[16]

Perhaps the key difference between Hegel's notion of the restlessness of being and, say, its deconstructive cousin, is that Hegel unreservedly and wholeheartedly works within the light cast by Plato's idea of the Good. Dialectical development, seen on the largest scale, is a transition from the worse to the better. Hegel readily admits that change is sometimes or even usually random, repetitive, or even regressive. But at other times change takes place, quite literally, for the qualitatively *better*. Dialectics names the fact that being inaugurates new forms of human life that are more sophisticated than their predecessors. Of course, the burden of proof for the claim of greater sophistication, especially in an era in which the everyday skepticism and relativism of liberal culture has an array of postmodern allies in the academy, lies squarely with dialectics itself. This criterion for sophistication can come from nowhere other than the surpassed form of being itself which, on its own terms, falls short of that which it itself posited to transcend it.

This book thus defends the Hegelian claim that freedom and justice are properly human, that is universal, aspirations and that these aspirations have an intelligible history. Even if progress is rare and difficult, and even if regression is sometimes as or more plausible than progress, the vitality of contradiction leans us not just toward the future but toward the good.

The character of contradiction and historical change is particularly important in Hegel's political philosophy, concerned as it is with justice and the good society. As we shall see, the vital contradictions that animate human freedom give rise to varying historical notions of the just and the good. Before Hegel, Kant also seemed to point toward something of a transcendental contradiction. He says in the *Idea for a Universal History*, "The means which nature employs to bring about the development of innate capacities is that of antagonism within society, in so far as this antagonism becomes in the long run the cause of a law-governed social order."[17] For Hegel, however, the vitality of antagonism is not merely a means to the universality of law but is the constitutive contradiction of life *as such* – and, a fortiori, of political life.[18] Law does not so much settle the issue as give structure to a specific historical moment of its unfolding drama. That is, according to Hegel, the vitality of contradiction in the political realm (and any other, for that matter) is not that which generates a world of peaceful lawfulness as a response to a world of conflict (as Kant seems to suggest), but the process by which we come to realize that freedom exists only as the ongoing negotiation of ontological antagonisms, conflicts, and tensions. Hegelian politics, like Hegelian philosophy in general, does not seek the final resolution of all conflict, but the recognition that it is only in and through vital contradiction that freedom exists at all. Most of the time this process of vital contradiction unfolds behind our backs, as Hegel puts it.[19] Indeed, he says that our freedom "is liable to an infinity of misunderstandings, confusions and errors."[20] Our freedom does not, most of the time, require our self-conscious direction and, indeed, may suffer because of it. All the same, we are most free, most autonomous, when we are self-conscious – when we recognize that vital contradiction governs our existential predicament.

Politics, in other words, is always animated by exclusion, power, and domination as well as by protest, struggle, and liberation. Since full and equal democratic participation is never possible, privilege, control, power games, and corruption are always present, but so, too, are regulation, protest, resistance, and rebellion. In some cases, these struggles attempt to ameliorate problems within a given framework of social and political life. In other cases, these fundamental frameworks themselves become so self-contradictory that protest movements must become revolutionary. Vital contradiction is that in and through which we can cultivate for ourselves more and more sophisticated forms of thriving in history, but vital contradiction also names the fact that we will never be free of the fundamental antagonisms that make thriving an issue in the first place. Both these forms of vital contradiction are essential to Hegel – those that move history to more and more sophisticated forms of social life and those that always leave something at stake even in the most just of societies. Justice is not vital contradiction resolved, but vital contradiction recognized.

Thus, the great achievement of Hegel's philosophy is the recognition that these constitutive conflicts in human experience are not unsurpassable obstacles to our freedom and happiness, but dynamic conditions that make freedom and happiness meaningful in the first place. To be human, to be free, is always to have something at stake, to be in a life in which our vulnerability and our creative power are the constitutive poles of a founding difference, an original antagonism, without which freedom would quite literally not be. For Hegel, contradiction is the very vitality that makes it possible for the things that matter most to matter at all.

The second of Hegel's statements that animates this book is better known:

> Each individual is … a *child of his time*; thus philosophy, too, is *its own time comprehended in thoughts*.[21]

For Hegel, as we have begun to see, the truth unfolds only in history. His philosophy is a direct challenge to the tradition before him, which took truth to be eternal and unchanging, and Hegel is the first great philosopher of temporality. For political philosophy, freedom and the institutions of a just society thus emerge only in time and they do so in answer to questions that humanity poses to itself. The task of the philosophical historian is not merely to tell the story of Europe, Latin America, or anywhere else as a series of events, but to perceive how the character of certain forms of society become self-contradictory in such a way that it is almost impossible for them to sustain themselves. Moreover, the task of a philosophical history is to perceive the failures of these self-contradictory societies as themselves inviting solutions.

While Hegel's philosophy of history is known for his claim that a "cunning of reason" operates implicitly or "behind the backs" of its agents, his pre-eminent argument is that we become self-conscious about the demands of freedom. Indeed, his *Philosophy of Right* is itself an enormous contribution to that task and was written, at least in part, with the express intent of influencing German political figures who had the real possibility of writing and administering a new Prussian constitution. The vocation of human beings is to make the rationality of our freedom explicit so that we become the self-conscious authors of our history. Hegel says that freedom in truth demands that "human insight and conviction ... correspond with the Reason which it embodies."[22]

In his own time Hegel was gravely worried about liberalism and its "atomistic principle" – its championing of "the mere contingent will." As we shall see in some detail, Hegel thinks that societies that are predicated on atomistic individualism lead almost inevitably not only to "agitation" and "unrest" but to the concentration of wealth and power. A liberal society, in other words, faces a *contradiction* between the form of freedom it embraces, atomistic liberty, and the truth of freedom itself. "This collision," Hegel asserts, "this nodus, this problem is that with which history is now occupied, and whose solution it has to work out in the future."[23] We are that future, even if we may be unable to claim that we have found its solution.

Indeed, we may well worry that the situation has gotten far worse (or better) – and thus it is incumbent upon us as philosophers working in the spirit of Hegel to comprehend *our own time* in thoughts. Liberal-capitalism has developed a great deal since Hegel wrote and therefore, even if it is necessary to draw heavily on Hegel's writings, we must be devoted to understanding *our time* with the same rigour with which he attempted to understand his own. This book, then, not only delves into careful exegesis of Hegel's texts (as well as those of other philosophers from time to time), but also, by the end, devotes itself to understanding the vital contradictions of life in contemporary liberal-capitalism. The ultimate goal of this book is to show how Hegelian philosophy – dialectics – is essential to understanding political philosophy in general and liberal-capitalism in particular. The considerable exegetical work it embodies is a means to that end. Indeed, at key moments I give Hegelian arguments against Hegel's own conclusions – as he himself did in the many serious revisions he made to his philosophical arguments. For example, I will need to posit the priority of common property, a Hegelian theory of exploitation, and the imperative to democratize the economy.

Much has been made of Hegel's political philosophy. It has been condemned as obsolete or obscure, as proto-fascist and thus an enemy of the free society, and as hopelessly idealistic, both in the sense of claiming that history is driven by ideas and in the sense that it inherits the false optimism of the Enlightenment. It has been praised by communitarians for its capacity to recognize the embeddedness of the free self in his or her community, by scholars of civil society as its first great theorization, and by Marxists as the great dialectical system that needed only to be stood on its head for dialectical materialism to make its first strides. There are also many excellent commentaries and studies on *The Philosophy of Right*. My own book rarely enters into these interpretive polemics (although it has implications for many of them) and, as I say, it is certainly not a commentary on the *Phenomenology of Spirit* and the *Philosophy of Right* (although I delve into certain of Hegel's arguments and their commentators in some depth). I explore Hegel's texts in order to better engage with our own political time.

This book has three sections. In the first, "The Dialectic of Political Life" (comprising the first six chapters), I begin (in chapters 1 and 2) by establishing some key concepts in Hegel's political philosophy – *dialectic*, *mutual recognition*, *freedom*, and *domination*. Each concept, in turn, will be articulated in terms of *vital contradiction*. I argue that Hegel uses two forms dialectic – an *empirical dialectic* that follows the self-development of specific, existing forms of being in history, and a *conceptual dialectic* that follows the immanent self-elaboration of the abstract concepts whose concrete life is the very intelligibility of the world. We will see that our freedom arises and is best cultivated in our engagements with other people – in and through *mutual recognition*. We will also see that the vitality of our freedom permits us not only to fulfill ourselves in and through mutual relation but to make the mistake of thinking we can achieve that end by dominating over or even by submitting to other people. We will see that freedom for Hegel is thus a development of the Kantian notion of autonomy, except insofar as it is only in and through the necessary structures of human relationship that freedom is cultivated.

I then turn what we have learned about the dialectic of freedom explicitly to the political sphere (chapter 3). This is a study of the general philosophical terms we need to discover the necessary institutions of a free society. In the remaining three chapters in this first section, I study three forms of sociopolitical life analysed by Hegel in the *Phenomenology of Spirit* – the Ethical Society (*Sittlichkiet*), the Condition of Right (*Rechtszustand*), and Absolute Freedom (*absolut Freiheit*) – each of which posits a determinate form of society as fulfilling the human project. I explain Hegel's arguments that each of these forms of society develops a contradiction that is its downfall. In this context, vital contradiction moves us through a series of failed societies but also teaches us the necessary conditions for the fulfillment of our freedom.

In the second section, "Freedom and the Just Society" (chapters 7 to 9), I show that the failure of the three societies just outlined is itself the process in and through which we learn what institutions are necessary for freedom to thrive. The logic of each of the failed societies roughly articulates the structure of one of the three institutions – *family*, *civil society*, and *state* – that make up any and all free societies. Each of family, civil society, and state will be shown to be in vital contradiction with the other two, and thus the success or failure of freedom will rest in the ways in which we are able, or unable, to cultivate the conditions of freedom in and through these contradictions.[24] In this context, vital contradiction names the inherent and unsurpassable tensions that animate even the most just society.

In the third section, "Liberal-Capitalism and Democracy" (chapters 10 and 11), I apply the concepts developed in the first two sections to a study of liberal-capitalism. Like Hegel and Marx, I defend the idea that liberalism and capitalism have been necessary to the development of freedom, but argue that they also prevent the emerging of yet more sophisticated forms of self-determination. I explore how the democratic essence of political life demands that we break the ceiling on democratic participation created by wage-labour and certain forms of representative democracy. This requires positing a dialectical criticism of private property and wage-labour. I argue, instead, that Hegelian philosophy must institutionalize a regime of common property and the democratization of the economy. This also requires a Hegelian theory of exploitation. In each of these three cases, I give Hegelian arguments against Hegel's texts since he defends the priority of private property, the justice of wage-labour, and a hierarchical, non-democratic civil society.

I conclude, in the last chapter, by outlining the terms of a non-utopian critique of liberal-capitalism. This requires summarizing the reasons why liberal-capitalism, even if it is responsible for inaugurating many decisive institutions of human freedom, has come to be in contradiction with the further development of freedom. Moreover, I posit the institutional outline of a regime, which I call socialist civil democracy, that can sustain and cultivate the vitality of freedom in ways that are impossible for liberal-capitalism.

The task of philosophy in the political realm is to criticize the structures which constrain freedom – even if these same structures *were*, heretofore, necessary to its cultivation. Moreover, this task then elaborates itself into concrete proposals for the new institutions that must be created for freedom to flourish in yet more comprehensive ways. However, the creative acts needed must not be understood as requiring that we wipe the slate clean and build from scratch. On the contrary, they require recognizing that the process of cultivating freedom is already long underway; in a sense, this is the task of human history itself. However, it is also our responsibility to elaborate on that momentum – to cultivate much further what has already been developed. This book is my attempt to contribute to this project.

PART ONE

THE DIALECTIC OF POLITICAL LIFE

1

Empirical and Conceptual Dialectic

I DIALECTICAL PHILOSOPHY

Dialectic is the process by which *being*, and a fortiori, *human being*, elaborates, develops, and embellishes itself into more sophisticated forms of self-determination. Life lives out this self-elaboration as the *vitality of contradiction*. Thus the life of a plant is dialectical: a plant develops itself as it becomes a flower. Each stage of this development demands that the previous stages be realized, but then opposed and surpassed. That is, when the seed germinates and sends out a shoot, the original seed is negated. Hegel states in the *Science of Logic*, as we saw in the introduction, that "Contradiction is the root of all movement and vitality; it is only insofar as something has a contradiction within it that it moves, has an urge and activity."[1] Dialectical contradiction, then, is far from simply a mode of refuting bad arguments (as in the principle of non-contradiction), but is the kind of opposition by virtue of which something is at stake in life – by virtue of which, as Plato puts it in the *Phaedo*, all things appear to be "striving."[2] In due course I will explore dialectic in a technical way, but I begin that study by discussing dialectic more informally.

The human journey is also sometimes dialectical, but in a different way from other kinds of being. While the end toward which the plant strives is present within it at the very beginning of its life as a seed, the process by which a human life develops is not determined in advance.[3] The motion of dialectic in human life, then, cannot be reduced to the drive toward a predetermined telos or final cause, as one finds, for example, in Aristotle's notion of *substance*. The process by which a human life develops is always open to creative self-transformation and constantly leads to new and unexpected places. The dialectic of human freedom is the story of anxiety and allure, curiosity and fear, delight and trepidation – indeed, all the feelings that typically accompany encounters between the familiar and the unknown. The human dialectic, Hegel says in the *Phenomenology of Spirit*, is sometimes a "way of despair,"[4] while at other times it is like the glorious "sunburst, which, in one flash, illuminates the features of the new world."[5]

The elegance and smoothness of the dialectical transition by which a seed becomes a plant and the plant flowers differs from the dialectical development of, say, a young man who is reluctant to question the beliefs and relationships within which he grew up and which he holds dear. His own hesitation, anxiety, and fear grind up against the voice within him that seems to whisper, in an oracle-like way, the promise of something beyond his familiar world. For him to answer that voice requires a kind of self-violation, for he must criticize the common sense of the very beliefs that have sustained him, that have made him who he is. This act of listening to the oracle-like voice is, as Hegel puts it, a violence done *at his own hands*.[6] And violence it really is, for those cherished relationships and beliefs are the very things that gave him the psychological confidence, the basic respect for himself, the intellectual know-how, and the moral courage by which he stands on his own two feet and is able to face the unknown at all. The very structures of life that generated the strength by virtue of which he can respond to this longing suddenly disclose themselves as in vital contradiction: He would not be able to face the unfamiliar to which the oracular voice calls him without the strength those relationships and beliefs have given him, and yet it is precisely *those* relationships and beliefs which he is called to surpass and repudiate.[7] He is literally called by those very strengths to turn their power against what created them in the first place, in order to sever himself from his old ways and follow that voice *elsewhere*. Where is this "elsewhere"? He doesn't really know. It may be like a kind of promised land, erotic in its allure, bathed in sunshine, and yet too glaring and beset with anxiety and excitement to reveal itself to him with any clarity. Its indeterminacy may well combine with fear and anxiety to make him say *no* to this calling. But if he says *yes* he will leap out of himself into what could well be, at least in some respects, a richer and more sophisticated way of being. This young man's experience is, in an important sense, what life is like for all of us: it is the story of *learning*. This learning life is the dialectical life, and this young man's sunburst of development is dialectical excess, the prodigality of a freedom that gives us hope in the possibility of an always richer and more sophisticated life.

Having taken the leap, this man may look back on his previous life with nostalgia, but he will have left it behind for good. He could not go back even if he wanted to, for once the spell is broken it can no longer be conjured again. He may take this moment of self-transformation into yet other new worlds, some of which might themselves become all-too-familiar and give rise to their own voices-from-elsewhere, which he might once again either refuse or follow. One such voice might even call him into a fascination with this ecstasy of learning itself, such that he might turn his gaze toward grasping how it is that we transcend ourselves. He might well discover echoes of his own sunbursts in Socrates' account of his education in Plato's *Phaedo*, in Descartes' skeptical method in the *Meditations,* in James Joyce's recognition of his artistic vocation in *Portrait of the Artist as a Young Man*, or in Simone de Beauvoir's insight that her philosophical raison d'être lay in exploring the exclusion and exploitation of women – an insight that would lead her to write *The Second Sex*. By studying these texts about learning, he will learn much about his own journey of learning.

Moreover, the young man's experience of learning has led him to adopt not just a different but a more sophisticated stance toward the world. As a naive believer in his familiar credos and forms of relationship, he saw the unfamiliar world beyond as a limitation, a barrier, and perhaps even as a strange combination of allure and threat. That he then moved past the realm of his familiar beliefs made him a more sophisticated participant in the world, more intellectually supple and welcoming of those different from him, more insightful in understanding how others identify themselves and how they are motivated, more courageous about taking similar leaps in the future. He thus became *more free*, not because he satisfied some arbitrary moral standard or because he simply made a choice, but because he was able to overcome a stance, a way of living, that he had come to experience as an impediment or obstacle.[8] Indeed, what was once the means and indeed the embodiment of his freedom (his own beliefs) then became a barrier to his freedom (because those beliefs closed him to the unfamiliar), and, from there, became a passageway, a door, to a more sophisticated world (insofar as the original beliefs now disclose themselves as rungs on his ladder of education). He is now more autonomous, more *at home in his world* – more free.[9]

Of course, not just any change of perspective is more sophisticated than its predecessor. There are transitions, some even experienced as epiphanies, that actually lead us to be self-destructive, to undermine the necessary structures of our freedom, and to adopt what are in fact less sophisticated ways of being. The criteria for determining if we have made progress or have regressed, become more free or less, lie in the character of human freedom itself.

In this context, then, dialectic names our capacity to overreach ourselves with nothing other than the resources that our self-transcendent character gives to us. More generally, dialectic is the immanent self-development of being, where being has disclosed itself to us as self-elaborating and self-unfolding in ways that cannot be predicted ahead of time, but that are nonetheless intelligible. Of course, the standards of by which we can say they are "intelligible" at all are themselves dialectical since the character of "reason" is not established in advance of change in the real world. Reason is not an external standard allowing us to say whether this or that is rational or irrational. Reason is the structure, the logos, of the change itself. The fictitious phenomenology of the young man's moment of self-transformation is as much dialectic as are the great arguments of Plato's *Parmenides*, the conceptual transitions of Hegel's *Science of Logic*, or the revolutionary upheaval that displaced feudalism and ushered in the modern liberal-capitalist world.

This book is a *political* dialectic – an exposition of the institutions that are necessary if we human beings are to create a community for ourselves that most fully cultivates our freedom. I think through Hegel's arguments about how our communal life must be structured to achieve this goal. In most respects this will be a study of *recollection* (*Er-Innerung*) – a study of what we have learned (often the hard way) about the cultivation of freedom in history. More concretely, I examine three forms of society that are contradictory and that thus collapse upon themselves precisely because of their antipathy to emergent aspects of human thriving. The failure of each is, however, an invitation to insight – an invitation to the possibility of a social and political form that has learned from its mistakes and that thus creates a different and better set of institutions. The essence of a dialectic is found not in formulas like the infamous thesis/antithesis/synthesis, but in understanding what it is like *to learn*, to cultivate oneself into the flourishing of freedom.[10]

2 EMPIRICAL DIALECTIC

However, before I get into the details of the study of political life, I want to take this introductory study of dialectic a good deal further – in order both to gather together the insights arising from the brief and informal explorations made above and to extend and elaborate our understanding of the character of dialectic itself. In order to do so, I adapt an example based on John Russon's study of *neurosis* in *Human Experience*. Russon gives a phenomenology of the emergence of neurosis which I use as the basis for a somewhat more detailed study of dialectic.[11]

Consider the case of a teenage girl who has discovered that she can cope best with a dysfunctional home environment by adopting certain strategies. For example, she adopts the attitude of stoic indifference to a father who is often angry. She learns to tune him out: she pretends to listen to his tirades and withdraws to her room or out of doors as quickly as possible. Her stoic attitude is part of what I call her "know-how of freedom" – the resources of practical reason that she draws on to navigate in her (unfortunately dysfunctional) world.

This stoic indifference is the appropriate strategy of self-determination in her home, and so she has become habituated to it. She automatically responds stoically when faced with anger because years of experience have taught her that this is the best means of dealing with it. Indeed, the stoic response to anger is so fully habituated that she unconsciously brings it with her when she moves away from home and begins to live in residence at university. But in her new relationships on campus her stoic indifference, which was the very solution to the problems presented by her abusive father and thus the very means that best promoted her freedom, now creates problems in her relationships with her friends. In situations where she needs to devote herself to the resolution of a conflict, for example, when a friend or lover is angry with her for some reason, she withdraws into herself rather than engaging with the challenge constructively. Of course, what worked well with her abusive father fails miserably with her friends. Her withdrawal allows the conflict to fester and thus works to undermine the relationship. This woman might well be plagued by these forms of conflict her whole life, with the result that she will constantly alienate her friends and find that she is happiest when she is alone.

On the other hand, these conflicts and the loneliness that follows yet another broken relationship might provoke her to seek therapy, either informally with friends or formally with a psychotherapist. If this counselling goes well, her friends or psychotherapist will help her to rehabituate herself into new modes of behaviour appropriate to the maintenance and development of good friendships in her new world. Moreover, she may even retain her attitude of stoic indifference as a helpful tool to cope with her father and with other problematic people she might encounter, but when it matters most she is constructive rather than stoic in the face of anger.

In so doing, this young woman has reached a point of transcendence not unlike the man in the earlier story who questions his familiar beliefs. Her neurosis (her stoic stance, which is out of place at university) is *dialectically* criticized insofar as it was this woman's own project of self-determination that disclosed both the conflict (the contradiction between her habituated attitude toward anger and her relationship with her friends at university) and its solution (therapy, leading to more constructive ways of relating). This account is dialectical because determinate modes of being disclose their own criteria for self-criticism and thus also for their self-transformation and development.

Dialectic is, then, *immanent critique* practised in the most rigorous way. Dialectic in Hegel is also phenomenology in the sense typically given by twentieth-century philosophers – a sensitive descriptive study of things as they are in themselves. A sensitive description recognizes the characteristic ways in which things develop themselves. Dialectics should never be construed as a method one can isolate from experience and thus never as a priori in the traditional, rationalist sense of the term, but as an observation of the character of becoming by means of which determinate realities show themselves as unable to fully sustain or explain their character. They make necessary reference to or develop into other realities.

To further clarify dialectic, the example of the stoic young woman can be reconfigured. Her example reveals four general elements of dialectical self-criticism and transformation:

1 The original stance (the stoic attitude of the woman) is a strategy of self-determination, of freedom. That is, it is the best strategy for coping with her dysfunctional home environment. She "determines herself" as stoic because it is the best way, in her judgment, to deal with the world in which she lives.
2 There is a decisive change that makes the original stance problematic such that it is now in contradiction with this woman's own projects of freedom and self-determination. The woman's stoic attitude contradicts

her new situation, her new community of friends at university, because it now fails to forward her projects. What once worked as a project of self-determination now impedes that same freedom.

3 The resulting conflict, although it could go on forever, invites a resolution, a surpassing, by which a new stance may be adopted. On her own or with the help of a psychotherapist, the young woman develops new skills in relating to others, specifically, some kind of constructive engagement with anger. Hegel calls this the moment of *Aufhebung* or *sublation*. She has chosen a more sophisticated way of relating to others.
4 The original stoic stance is reincorporated into her projects of self-determination, but no longer as the definition of her most fundamental comportment with others. It is now but one of her modes of coping with others, which she can rely on in situations that may call for it. The young woman is no longer a fundamentally stoic person, but can use stoicism or features of it in certain situations that call for it as the best comportment of self-determination. Meanwhile, her attitude toward the world is now fundamentally defined by what I have been calling, to simplify matters a bit, "constructive engagement."

These four elements of dialectic can now be generalized and named:

1 Original self-determination
2 Emergence of contradiction
3 Invitation to surpassing, or "sublation"
4 Incorporation of a more sophisticated form of self-determination

My working example here has been *empirical* – a hypothetical young woman who has developed a neurotic mode of behaviour. An *empirical dialectic*, then, is a study of a given determinate existence of freedom – a concrete plant, animal, person, relationship, community, society, country, or historical period. Hegel called this kind of study "Real Philosophy" (*Realphilosophie*)[12] and he sometimes uses Real Philosophy, empirical dialectic, in his philosophical work, for example, in is his *Lectures on the Philosophy of History*. Hegel has, of course, been widely criticized for his historical scholarship in the two centuries that have passed since he gave these lectures – during which time methods and findings of historical research have developed enormously. However much we might need to take issue with specific historical claims in the text itself, the key for the philosophical reader is not whether Hegel was right or wrong about certain points of the historical record or certain interpretations of specific historical events, but how we can discern the dialectical character of change taking place within history. More specifically, as we study history, how can we see that humanity has slowly and painfully developed, or sometimes failed to develop, more and more sophisticated forms of freedom? Indeed, sometimes we have regressed and tumbled into much less sophisticated forms self-determination – and the same can be said, of course, of individuals. It is not easy to determine precisely what "more sophisticated" means, but I return to this issue more than once below.

Furthermore, the young woman's psychotherapist might seek to help her sort out the "reasons" for her stoic attitude and the problems it creates by going through the great mass of empirical details in her life and, in the process, create a sketch of the "rationality" of how she came to have this neurosis and how it might be overcome. Her old stance and its contradictions invite the new stance as a solution to the problem that it, the first stance, poses. This provides a clue about what "reason" means for Hegel. Just as dialectic is never an abstract method applied on top of various forms of reality, so too reason must never be construed as merely the abstracted universals of knowledge, as a priori categories or any such thing. Abstract universals, like "All humans are rational," have their place in our project of knowledge, but philosophy can never be reduced to this form of rationality. A preliminary notion of reason might then be the following: reason is the immanent intelligibility of self-determination. This rationality is typically lived implicitly but it can also be known explicitly. My cat Emily is self-determining, but in a completely unselfconscious or implicit way. When we disclose the immanent character of self-determination to ourselves, the implicit becomes explicit. It is thus hard to overestimate the importance of self-consciousness to the human experience of self-determining reason. The philosophical historian of political life seeks the same patterns of intelligibility not with respect to the history of an individual person, but with respect to the history of civilizations, indeed (most ambitiously) the history of humanity itself.

Empirical dialectic, then, is the study of a given mode of self-determination in everyday experience. It is constituted by four steps: an original stance of self-determination, the emergence of a contradiction, an invitation to sublate the old stance and move to a more sophisticated stance of freedom and, finally, an incorporation of this new stance. It is rational in the sense that it embodies a living intelligibility that can be implicitly experienced as well as, sometimes, explicitly known.

Of course, there are many contingencies in any empirical dialectic. In either of our hypothetical examples, the young man who comes to doubt his traditional beliefs and the stoic woman, the course of events could have turned out any number of different ways. But the key to a dialectical reading of these situations is nonetheless to discern their intelligibility – how a given diversity over time makes sense. Indeed, given that freedom is the key to all of Hegel's dialectic, even contingency itself is necessary to the dialectic of freedom. Even a chance encounter between me and a stranger that sets my life in a whole new direction is a complex web whose intelligibility includes even the fact that randomness is inevitable (necessary) and indeed a rich part of our freedom.[13] Contingency should never be construed as that which undermines the intelligibility of life. It does not create aporias or gaps in the intelligibility of things. To arrive at such a conclusion is to already be using a notion of reason and intelligibility that is not dialectical, but the stubborn application of certain abstract canons of reason typically derived (correctly) from one mode of freedom and then applied (incorrectly) to other modes of freedom. It is a correct phenomenology of geometrical rationality to conclude that there are only three species of triangle (equilateral, isosceles, scalene), that each of these species fully excludes the others (a triangle can never be both equilateral and scalene), and that no one form of triangle is better than another (a scalene triangle does not more fully fulfill what it means to be a triangle than does an isosceles triangle). But to then apply this notion of rationality to the study of friendship will create grave problems. Friendship, if we take up Aristotle's lead, also has three species: friendships of utility, friendships of pleasure, and friendships that seek the good. However, unlike triangles, the species do not exclude each other – good friends can and indeed should also be useful and pleasurable. Even more importantly, and also unlike the triangle, the good friend is a *better* friend than the useful friend. That is, the good friend more fully realizes what it means to be a friend. The useful friend, in a way, fails to live up to what friendship most fully is, while the good friend is precisely the one to recognize and live out what it would mean to fully realize friendship. In this case, the highest species of the genus is itself equivalent to the genus, while the other species are failures to live up to that standard. The intelligibility of dialectic, then, may sometimes break into species of a genus, but these species will usually overlap and, more importantly, some species will fail to fully live up to their own character, while others will fulfill it.[14] In our case, the *stoicism* of the young woman is a species of the genus "self-determination," but not as sophisticated a species as what I call *constructive engagement*.

I have emphasized the everydayness of dialectical intelligibility in my opening discussion, but would like now to place this discussion within the technical terms of dialectic in the history of philosophy. When we speak of, say, the young woman's initial stance of stoicism, which is followed by her later stance of engagement, the intelligibility of each stance and their relationship to each other requires the notion of *synthesis* – the unification of difference. There are many forms of synthesis,[15] but a synthesis is dialectical, to use Jay Lampert's very precise articulation, when it has three features: "First, a synthesis of two theses is a dialectical one only if the synthesis becomes both possible and necessary in the context of the synthetic activity of a larger system. Second, in a dialectical synthesis, the theses are individuated in the same processes in which they are combined. Originary units would thus not in the final analysis be prior to the totalities which result from their synthesis. Third, the motivation for a dialectical synthesis must be inherently present in each of the synthesized determinations themselves. The meaning of each thesis must include a requirement to submerge its independence in a unity with others."[16]

A system (criterion 1) is itself nothing other than a comprehensive unity – a synthesis of syntheses. The life of the young stoic woman is thus a system in this sense; it is a whole intelligible in terms of its parts and their relationships to each other. The therapist and the woman, as they talk, would try to grasp this whole. However, this "whole" is complete not when the woman eventually dies, but when her process of learning has led her to the most sophisticated possible stance of relating to others. Aristotle might call this something like the "good friendship." (See the discussion of what I will call "conceptual dialectic" below). Of course, in another sense, this "whole" is always incomplete, insofar as contingencies and other events in the woman's life could change in subtle or in dramatic ways.

Each of these parts (criterion 2) – the *original stoicism* and then the *constructive engagement* – are *parts* (particulars) that fully make sense only as parts *of her self-determining life* and yet, reciprocally, her life is nothing but *the whole of these parts* (and others). That is, to speak of stoicism and constructive engagement is to speak of species of the genus "self-determination," so the character of each makes sense only in light of the whole. And yet it is just as true that the whole, the genus self-determination, is made up of nothing more than these particulars. The identity of the genus depends on particular species, and the identity of the species depends on the genus. The genus is the *universal* (the truth of them *all*), while the species are the *particulars* (the truth of *this* rather than *that* species of the all). That is, as Lampert puts it, the "theses are individuated in the same processes in which they are combined."

Moreover, (criterion 3) it is the very nature of the conflict engendered by her stoicism to invite the possibility of its resolution, its sublation, by a *specific* solution – her new stance of constructive engagement. That is, she will see that the conflicts created by her stoic attitude are addressed *if* she adopts the attitude of constructive engagement. Reciprocally, the attitude of constructive engagement itself makes sense, is fully intelligible, only as the solution to the problem presented by her stoicism. Even more generally, the attitudes of both constructive engagement and stoicism are intelligible as motivations at all only within the intelligibility of "self-determination." That is, the "motivation" for the synthesis, the transition from stoicism to constructive engagement, is present in each of the two parts, in the first as "problem" and in the second as "solution."

Two intelligent and common rejoinders to my claims here might go as follows. First, surely the young woman could have done any number of different things about her conflicts with friends. It was good that she went into therapy and developed a stance of constructive engagement, but she also could have become a recluse, a psychotic, or lived her entire life in a constant state of flight from others. Certainly each of these is an intelligible course of action, but since none of them is *necessary*, the challenge would go on to say, we cannot call this a dialectical synthesis. To generalize, the rejoinder holds that the terms of the synthesis must strictly *necessitate* each other. Such a definition of dialectic finds its exemplars in oppositional relatives – to think "big" I must think "small" (rather than think "blue," "pencil," or "Joni Mitchell"). While such oppositions play an important role in dialectical philosophy, dialectic certainly cannot be reduced to this mode of synthesis. This objection, in other words, is an example of imposing the intelligibility of one form of being on another, as in the attempt to understand friendship with the intelligible structures of triangles examined above.

All the same, the "necessity" of the second stance emerges in another sense. In the case of the young stoic woman, "constructive engagement" is not the only possible attitude, but it is the *best one*. On what grounds is it the *best*? It is the best on the grounds of nothing other than the self-determining projects of the woman *herself* determined by the context in which she lives. Once again, dialectic is immanent development of each thing such that to impose a dialectic of relational opposites (as the objector would have it) on a free being is not to attend to the determinate intelligibility of that form of being *on its own terms*. The only form of intelligibility appropriate to that young woman is the intelligibility of her life. She will have greater powers of self-determination, she will be *more free*, if she adopts the stance of constructive engagement because she will be able to be more "at home in her world."

The logic of her life answers to and informs broader logics – such as, in this case, the logic of *better* and *worse*. It is *better* that she engage constructively and *worse* that she become a recluse. Necessity thus emerges here in a different from. It emerges as the *hypothetical necessity* that can be articulated as follows: *If* the young woman is *best* to forward her projects of self-determination, *then* it is *necessary* that she adopt the stance of constructive engagement. Of course "better" and "worse" are themselves oppositional relatives that structure projects of self-determination in general. Retrospectively (or, "in the final analysis"), once this deed is done, it is, *in truth*, necessary.[17] It is not my goal to articulate the relationship of the basic categories of intelligibility developed in Hegel's *Science of Logic* to the empirical world of this woman, but suffice it to say that even though the intelligibility of her life is no simple matter, its complexity is not a mark against its intelligibility.

A second challenge might unfold as follows. Lampert's second criterion included the claim, "Originary units would thus not in the final analysis be prior to the totalities which result from their synthesis." Surely, the young woman's original stance of stoicism is prior to the later stance of constructive engagement. Indeed, this is, once again, why Hegel's dialectic is always, empirically speaking, a form of recollection (*Er-Innerung*). Before she adopted her stance of constructive engagement, her stoicism was the definitive stance of her life. It was itself the dialectical response the intelligibility of which is established only in terms of yet earlier stances she would have had as a young girl. Indeed, if she had died before going into therapy, or remained stoic her whole life, then stoicism would be the last and definitive term of her "system" – of her life. But the identity of her stoicism *changes* once she adopts the stance of constructive engagement. It changes from being the definitive attitude of this woman's personality to that attitude identified in terms of the question to which *constructive engagement* is the answer. Or again, the identity of stoicism prior to therapy was defined in terms of *answers* to the questions of earlier struggles, but once therapy starts, its identity changes from the logic of "answer" to the logic of "question." According to the logic of the intelligibility of human freedom, the most recent stance in someone's life in a way defines or summarizes the terms of that whole life, but it is always possible that it will not remain the most recent term. This is perhaps a clue to why Aristotle states that, in a way, we cannot say that a man is happy until he is dead.[18] The dialectical synthesis of a human life, then, is always a *recollective* one. That is, even if her stoicism is empirically prior to constructive engagement, in the realm of their intelligibility after the emergence of the latter, each implicates the other and they cannot be spoken of intelligibly in isolation. When Lampert says "in the final analysis" he means that once we recognize the greater sophistication of "constructive engagement" over "stoicism," the temporality of the succession in empirical experience is no longer a directly relevant premise. "Constructive engagement" is a more sophisticated attitude whether it emerges before or after stoicism in any empirical experience. But to better comprehend this claim, I move on to a study of what I call "conceptual dialectic."

3 CONCEPTUAL DIALECTIC

Empirical dialectic is a very fruitful method of analysis, and I put it to work in this text, especially in chapters 10 and 11 when I discuss contemporary liberal-capitalist society. But Hegel also employs another form of dialectical analysis, which I call *conceptual dialectic*.[19] Instead of tracing the empirical history of a given society, person, or relationship, conceptual dialectic traces the history of a certain kind of unification (synthesis) of a multiplicity – a concept – *on its own terms*. Such a history, then, is not the history of how people have actually used a concept over time or of how it developed in the course of its history (that would be the empirical dialectic of the concept), but a study of the concept taken in abstraction from empirical history and studied *as such*. For example, when Hegel begins his *Science of Logic*, he begins not with how certain thinkers from the past have considered "being," but with the concept of "being" itself.[20] He shows that to think "being" immediately demands the thought of "nothing."

And, in turn, to think "nothing" demands that we once again think "being." But if to think "being" is to think "nothing" and to think "nothing" is to return once more to "being," we find ourselves in a cycle of that which moves from *what is* to *what is not*, and vice versa. But such a cycle is familiar to us as the concept of "becoming" – as *coming to be* and as *passing away*.

That is, engagement with a certain concept will itself generate a motion in thought that leads it toward more sophisticated concepts. It is not merely that living beings think, but that thinking itself is self-determining. Hegel learned conceptual dialectic from Plato and many others, and then developed it in a most sophisticated way. But it is also present in various ways in many philosophers, even if that was not their intention. These include, for example, the great social contract thinkers. Locke and Hobbes, to take two prominent examples, select the concept of an individual free will in a state of nature. Such an individual is thus in a state prior to the formation of society and its laws and morality. That is, neither the state of nature nor the individuals within it are empirical realities. The "state of nature" is a concept. The goal of Locke and Hobbes is to show that a plurality of such free wills will generate new intelligible insight – new concepts. In this case, the individuals imagined to be in the state of nature enter into conflict with each other in such a way as to require the formation of a society.

A conceptual dialectic, then, is a certain specific form of counterfactual argument. When Locke and Hobbes use this technique, they abstract from the concrete conditions of individuals with free wills (like you and me) and from empirically existing societies in order to isolate the determinate, abstract concept of, in this case, a free will.[21] Having imagined this counterfactual concept, they then "let go of it," so to speak. This "letting go" is the act of allowing the specific logic of the concept itself to show the observer where it will go *on its own terms*.[22] As an observer, one does not intervene in any way – one does not stop the process where one wants, nor does one import any criticism based on premises from outside the dynamic itself: one simply watches the immanent motion of the concept itself. When we do this, Locke and Hobbes argue, we learn something of great importance to human experience: we learn that human freedom (so their story goes) demands the constraint of law and morality. A naive reader who wistfully longs for a life in which he can do anything he wants comes to see that such a desire ultimately educates itself to accept the necessity of law and morality. Locke and Hobbes, by means of their "conceptual dialectic," show that this aspiration is predicated on an ignorance of what such a life would actually be like. As a result, the formerly naive individual ceases resisting law and morality and accepts them as necessary conditions of his or her liberty. John Rawls also carries out a conceptual dialectic in his *Theory of Justice*. We imagine ourselves behind a "veil of ignorance" (of our gender, race, family income, and other particularities) in the "original position" as free subjects. From this conceptual rather than empirical starting point Rawls derives the fundamental structures of justice.[23]

Although Hegel rejects the notion that society can be understood as a contract arising from a state of nature, as Locke and Hobbes argue, and he would take issue with some of Rawls's conclusions, he makes effective use of the counterfactual structure of conceptual dialectic in his philosophy. Indeed, he develops it to a degree of sophistication and breadth unprecedented in Western philosophy. This is the strategy Hegel predominantly uses in his most famous works, *The Phenomenology of Spirit* and *The Science of Logic*,[24] and I put it to use especially in chapters 2 to 6 of this work. My goal is to articulate Hegel's conceptual dialectic of social and political life.

Hegel's dialectic of mutual recognition in chapter 4 of the *Phenomenology* is a very helpful example of conceptual dialectic. To put it somewhat simply, the dialectic that leads to mutual recognition explains the dynamics of *human relatedness*. There are three ways one could develop a philosophical study of "relating to others":

1 One could observe human behaviour in general and make a list of all the different ways of relating and the repercussions these modes of behaviour tend to have. This methodology is used with great subtlety and insight, for example, by David Hume in his *Enquiry Concerning the Principles of Morals* and by John Stuart Mill in *Utilitarianism*. This is empiricism. We know on the basis of a posteriori observation.
2 One could develop a kind of developmental history of human relationships. This would be a historical and societal version of the same kind of study we have already seen at work in our example of the stoic young woman. It is like empiricism insofar as it is based on a posteriori observation, but it is different because it posits a process of education or development toward more and more sophisticated stances. This method is found in Freud's case studies and in the philosophically informed historical studies carried out by writers like Hegel or Karl Marx – indeed frequently in Hume and Mill as well. Marx shows, for example,

how modes of production increase in sophistication as we learn both to transform nature and elaborate our needs. It is a story of the development or cultivation of relating-to-others and to nature. This is, of course, *empirical dialectic*.

3 One could ask what is the most primitive possible form of relating to others, show why it fails on its own terms as a strategy of self-determination, and, in so doing, show how it invites the creation of a more sophisticated attitude toward others. Hegel calls the failure of any stance a "determinate negation" – the failure of a given stance is simultaneously the exposition of a new and more sophisticated stance.[25] This is, as with empirical dialectic, the process of sublation (*Aufhebung*). One could then carry out the same kind of analysis of this more sophisticated attitude until one arrives at a stance that can sustain itself, a stance that, *in the last analysis*, would not itself give rise to a yet more sophisticated stance. Such a stance would arguably be the most sophisticated possible attitude one could have toward other human beings. This procedure is *conceptual dialectic*. It might be tempting to say that if the other two categories were a posteriori, then the conceptual dialectic is a priori, but this is not the case. It involves the abstraction of concepts from experience and thus is, in its own way, also a posteriori.[26] We have noted already that Hegel uses conceptual dialectic in, for example, the *Phenomenology of Spirit* and the *Science of Logic*. It is also used by Karl Marx in *Capital*.

The hallmark of the strategy of conceptual dialectic is to identify how, in the case of our example of human relatedness, each form of relating to other people is itself connected to more and less sophisticated forms of relating. It is a mode of analysis that, should it be successful, promises to be superior to the empiricism of philosophers like Hume and Mill because their lists could potentially be partial (we might have failed to observe certain strategies) and, moreover, their strategy does not methodically show why and how certain forms of relationship relate to and are superior or inferior to others (although by virtue of their careful observational skills they may well have pointed these kinds of things out most of the time). After all, if Hegel is right, dialectic is not a method, but the structure of freedom itself which is in large part revealed to the perceptive empirical observer. More emphatically, I want to show how we can learn to have more and more sophisticated relationships with other people, and chart the course taken by this dialectical process of self-education.

And yet, how would I begin such a process? What is its starting point? Surely there is the danger of positing a starting point that is itself already presupposed by the concluding stance. If that were so, the supposedly dialectical argument is merely circular. How can this danger be avoided, if at all?

The starting point of the conceptual dialectic of relating to others should, of course, be the "first," the "primary," way of relating to other people. To be *prim*ary means also *prim*itive, for conceptual dialectic promises to offer a kind catalogue of progressively more sophisticated forms of relating, such that the logical starting point must be that stance of relation that is the least sophisticated of all. A stance would be the most primitive, or primary, if it were literally *impossible* to conceive of a yet more primitive stance. This is the same as saying that the primitive stance does not presuppose any other stance within the same general concept.[27]

I offer a simple example to show how the starting point for the conceptual dialectic of "relating to others" can be derived. As parents, we frequently tell our children not to be selfish, and we do this not only because we think generosity and concern for others are simply good but because we know that selfishness will create innumerable problems for our children later on. If a child becomes a selfish person, he will constantly be in conflict with others or will also be chronically lacking the friendship, love, and intimacy that unselfish forms of relating typically generate. We thus council sharing, respect for others, and so on. Notice that this parenting attitude already presupposes the less and more sophisticated forms of relating to other people identified as essential to dialectical analysis, and it indeed presupposes that we can learn to move from the less to the more sophisticated.

Here, then, we have a nice clue to what would constitute the "primitive" form of human relating with which we can start our dialectical analysis. Selfishness constitutes a kind of refusal to acknowledge and respect the fact that other people have legitimate claims of their own. Indeed, if we take selfishness in its purest and most radical possible form (that is, if we try to identify its *pure concept*), it reveals itself as something like the stance that *Only my desires are real and worthy of satisfaction.* I might perceive others, but I perceive them only in terms of how they might facilitate or obstruct my getting what I want. Indeed, selfishness in its *absolutely purest form* is the claim that there really is only one "I" in all of being – *me* – and that *my* attitudes determine how the rest of the world should be ordered. This is, I suggest, our primitive starting point, for how could we possibly have a more primitive attitude toward other selves than that they have no independent reality at all, and that they are merely modes of my own desires and projects?

This argument would appear circular because we have started out claiming that "relating to others" is the concept we are studying and yet have posited the *refusal* of relation as our first stance. But the claim is not circular for two related reasons. First, our goal all along is to find the most primitive possible stance, and if we are asking ourselves that question, presumably we are already well beyond that stance ourselves. Dialectic is, as I suggested earlier, most often a *recollection* of the steps that explain how we achieved a certain view that we hold already – say the moral notion that "one should respect the dignity of other people as ends in themselves rather than just as means" or the political notion that "all human beings are endowed with equal rights." That is, dialectical philosophy is usually a kind of retrospective, a posteriori "look back" at the conceptual route to a stance that we currently affirm. As we saw briefly above, Hegel explicitly calls it *recollection* (*Er-Innerung*) in the *Phenomenology of Spirit* in a way that plays off Plato's notion of recollection, but that simultaneously does not claim that what is recollected is a priori.[28]

Second, even if the primitive stance we identify is defined as the absolute negation of the very affirmation we are studying (pure selfishness is the negation of the moral commandment to respect others as ends rather than just as means), there is no guarantee that this primitive starting point will lead us to the moral notion of respect for others. The decisive thing about dialectical analysis is that it eschew any external criteria. A given stance must come to negate *itself on its own terms*. Thus, just because we posit pure selfishness as the beginning of the conceptual dialectic of "relating to others," we in no way presuppose that we can derive the moral commandment to respect others from this starting point. We might discover, upon examining the stance of pure selfishness, that it is perfectly capable of sustaining itself as a viable way of living, and that the notion of "respecting others" is but a competing attitude that has no internal connection with selfishness whatsoever. We might know by reading ahead in the *Phenomenology* that the pure selfishness of desire leads dialectically to what

Hegel calls *mutual recognition*, but as readers we do not grant this conclusion until we follow the dialectic *for ourselves*. Conceptual dialectic, in sum, is not circular, but is recollective and strictly self-cultivating. I return to this decisive point once more in the next chapter when determining the primitive starting point of the conceptual dialectic of "society."

I have introduced the basic structure of empirical and conceptual dialectic. In the next chapter I examine the three key concepts of Hegel's political philosophy: mutual recognition, freedom, and vital contradiction. This will require engaging in a conceptual dialectic of self-consciousness which, Hegel surprisingly says, is *desire*. In other words, we can simultaneously strengthen our grasp of Hegel's strategy of conceptual dialectic and introduce decisive terms in his political philosophy.

2

Mutual Recognition, Freedom, and Vital Contradiction

I THE CONCEPTUAL DIALECTIC OF DESIRE

With the introduction to conceptual dialectic in the previous chapter, I turn to Hegel's dialectic of human relationships in chapter 4, "Self-Consciousness," of the *Phenomenology of Spirit*. His argument is complex, multi-dimensional, and, unfortunately, extremely condensed. I certainly do not try to do justice to its full breadth and depth here, but study Hegel's argument with three goals in mind. First, as our initial study of conceptual dialectic in Hegel's texts, it teaches us much about the formal structure of most conceptual dialectics. Second, the study allows me to examine not only the form of dialectic but its content – in this case the concept of social relationships. And third, it allows me to introduce and define Hegel's two most important terms of social and political analysis, *freedom* and *mutual recognition*.

Hegel claims, at the beginning of this conceptual dialectic, that "self-consciousness is *Desire* [*Begierde*] in general."[1] A being with desires (at least the kind of desires discussed here) is always dependent on something other than itself. In other words, it is always in a state that it cannot control simply on its own terms. Recalling Socrates' examination of Agathon in the *Symposium*, we see that desires of this kind lack that which they desire.[2] The overcoming of this lack is the achievement of satisfaction. In his introduction to the *Philosophy of Nature*, Hegel calls this lack the "negation of myself": "The negation of myself which I suffer within me in hunger, is at the same time present as an other than myself, as something to be consumed; my act is to annul this contradiction by making this other identical with myself, or by restoring my self-unity through sacrificing the thing."[3]

We see plainly here a key example of what Hegel means by the vitality of contradiction. Like Heraclitus's bow, to have desire is to be suspended in a tension that demands action. More contemplative forms of self-consciousness, we can begin to anticipate, have their roots in a vital contradiction between the self of desire and its object. I will follow the conceptual dialectic of this form of desire.[4]

This is to say, however, that the identity of the self is established only in relating to others. The self can achieve "self-certainty"[5] not by merely laying a claim to its autonomy opposed to others, but in and through some successful negotiation of its inevitable relatedness to others. Yet this is to say that the self-certainty of each human being is constituted by an original, ontological vulnerability to others. Thus, the most primitive possible stance of self-consciousness is that desire which seeks to achieve the unity of self-certainty by denying any ontological status to the other (cf. the pure selfishness discussed near the end of chapter 1). It seeks to deny its ontological vulnerability by insisting that all reality conform to its desire. Hegel describes the primitive stance in this way: "Self-consciousness is, to begin with, simple being-for-self, self-equal through the exclusion from itself of everything else. For it, its essence and absolute object is 'I' ... What is 'other' for it is an unessential, negatively characterized object."[6] The (supposed) unity of this primitive form of self-consciousness is achieved only by overcoming a kind of self-contradiction by virtue of which what is essential to desire is outside it and indeed resists it. This alienated situation must be addressed in the act that *sublates* it. That is, to achieve self-certainty, in this most primitive form, the other, which challenges the certainty of the self, must be destroyed. "Certain of the nothingness of this other, it explicitly affirms that this nothingness is *for it* the truth of the other; it destroys the independent object and thereby gives itself the certainty of itself as a *true* certainty, a certainty which has become explicit for self-consciousness itself *in an objective manner*."[7]

Hunger is an excellent example of this kind of desire and eating an excellent example of its satisfaction.[8] The unity of self-certainty is achieved, as we have seen, by simply destroying the object. Desire must transform that which is other than it and that upon which it depends for its ability to unify itself (to satisfy its desire) into that which will satisfy it. When I am hungry I lack what will satisfy me. The food I long to eat is, at first, other than me. And yet it is not so alien that I cannot perceive it as precisely what

I need. However, in the case of appetite, what it means to satisfy my hunger is to transform this other quite literally *into me*. When I eat the food its otherness is negated and it comes to be the very substance of my body.

Moreover, this kind of desire is a form of *vulnerability*. After all, the desiring self is dependent on the other and yet must overcome this otherness in order to thrive, indeed survive. This vulnerability to the other, in short, must be allayed by my exercise of *power*. Here it is helpful to use words from Latin-based languages. *Pouvoir* and *poder* mean, in French and Portuguese respectively, not only "power" as a noun, but "to be able to" as a verb. Human desire (indeed, human relating), then, is always suspended in the vital contradiction between *vulnerability* and *power*. Without air, water, and food I will die, and yet I also have the power, the capability, to transform these elements from that which is other than me into that which *is* me. We are never purely vulnerable (purely passive or receptive) nor purely powerful (purely active or efficacious). It is, rather, the vital contradiction between activity and passivity, vulnerability and power, that animates *all* of our experience. It is impossible, in other words, to experience *anything* outside this constitutive contradiction. Friendship, love, hunger, and political life only ever arise as suspended between the two poles in irreducible ontological tension. We can also now anticipate that the "self-certainty" of the self can be achieved not by denying or destroying the other, but by seeking his or her *recognition*. We can never fully connect with each other, nor ever fully understand or trust each other. And yet it is precisely this unbridgeable gap between us that makes something to be at stake in human relationships at all. Friendship and love have meaning only in and through the impossibility of ever being completely united with others. Presumably Plato intended something like this when he had Aristophanes define love in the *Symposium* as the impossible attempt to unite with one's severed other half.

The ontological tension between vulnerability and power means that domination and submission are always possible outcomes for human relationships. There will always be people and classes who attempt to achieve certainty and security by using their power to dominate or exploit others. Meanwhile, there will always be those who do not have the strength (of whatever kind) to resist this power, and must then submit. There will even be those who get a kind of pleasure in submission, since it absolves them of responsibility.

When we breathe, drink, or eat, we implicitly engage in the activity of exercising our power by denying air, water, and food their autonomy. When we literally *incorporate* these elements, we do not permit them to retain their identity, but violate that identity such as to literally give them *our own* identity. The wheat that grows in the field and the deer that runs in the forest never intend to be my food, but when I eat them I have overcome the resistance they might offer and have literally destroyed their identity to strengthen my own. That is, we not only fail to recognize and respect the identity of these others, we must confess that we actively seek their destruction. At the same time, we alleviate the anxiety of our own vulnerability, for we have proved that, in fact, we have the power to overcome the threat that gave us anxiety in the first place. Appetite as such, again, is the pure selfishness discussed above in considering the most primitive stance of the dialectic of relating to others.[9] Indeed, Hegel himself explicitly links appetitive desire and selfishness: "Thus appetite [*Begierde*] in its satisfaction is always destructive, and in its content selfish: and as the satisfaction has only happened in the individual (and that is transient) the appetite is again generated in the very act of satisfaction."[10]

Conceptual dialectic can now get underway in earnest. We have found the most "primitive" stance of relating to others in pure selfishness – the attitude in which we treat the identity of another as nothing but a mode of our own desires. Air does not simply go into my body on its own: it must be sucked in by my lungs. The same dynamic is true of food: what we eat does not on its own present itself as *my food* but as its own autonomous form of life, a plant that grows or animal that wanders around, both of which seek their own end and not mine. In a sense, then, to be air, plant, or animal is have a certain identity whose very nature is *to refuse* to be a mode of *my identity*. It is precisely this refusal to be me that makes me vulnerable to these elements, for even if I absolutely need them in order to survive, they manifest themselves as involved thoroughly in their own identity and not in mine. It is precisely this refusal to be me, and the *vulnerable* position in which this puts me, that must be overcome with my power – my *pouvoir*. Indeed, we are able to marshal some very sophisticated powers in order to overcome our vulnerability. Our lungs are highly evolved mechanisms for sucking in, processing, and exhaling air – so sophisticated that we rarely need even notice their functioning. With respect to our nutrition, we work hard to overcome our vulnerabilities so that we (privileged people at least) now eat with almost the same absent-mindedness that we breathe. The domestication of plants and animals and the food industry make eating a casual and unpreoccupying activity for those who do not live in poverty. We have so thoroughly stamped our identity on food that we often never stop to consider that it was at one time an autonomous being pursuing its own nature and interests. The reason our projects succeed in determining which identity wins out here is that we are capable of over-*powering* these other identities. We have, for example, literally tricked wild animals into domestication and, with respect to this issue at least, all but eliminated our vulnerability. We have succeeded in this so well that we often forget that it was ever a struggle.

Two of Hegel's technical terms, the finite and the infinite, help us to understand desire and are essential to further developments below. If a finite or determinate thing sustains its identity only by negating what is not it (this cat is not that dog), it constitutes a "bad infinite," an endless series of finite things, as in the set of integers – the perpetual repetition of quantitative units. Appetitive desire fails, in part, because it is a bad infinite. The attempt to eradicate vulnerability by consuming the other just leads over and over again to renewed hunger. What Hegel calls a "good infinite," however, is a structure that is at once differentiated and yet internally unified. The pure selfishness of desire is a failed attempt to be a "good infinite." The being with desires is finite insofar as it is distinct from all that is not it, and yet it takes itself to be the governing unity of a good infinite because it interprets, as we have seen, all otherness only in terms of its own project of self-affirmation. The food that it wants to eat, for example, appears to it not as an independently subsisting reality, but as "that-which-will-satisfy-my-hunger." Indeed, all determinations in the world are ascribed an identity by desire in keeping with its own projects. This process helps to disclose the conflicted structure of desire since, when an object appears to be resisting the desiring self, desire must prove this to be a false appearance by overcoming the resistance. As we have just seen, desire can generally be successful with the objects of nature in this regard. Each presents itself as insisting on its own autonomous identity, but this claim is rebutted when desire destroys it and thus proves that it is the governing unity or the "infinity" of what it perceives. However, this process is repetitive and thus itself a bad infinite, for each and every return of desire presents new challenges each of which must, in turn, be overcome. There is no termination to this desire-satisfaction-desire structure: in principle, it could go on forever, with desire winning each battle but never the war.[11] Because it structures capitalism – the (bad) infinite project of constantly increasing profit, this form of desire will be decisive later in this text.

If the pure selfishness of desire can maintain its perceptual field as an infinite unified by its own project when confronted by the beings of nature, what happens if it tries to relate to other human beings with the same attitude? When we domesticate animals in order to eat them, they resist, if they resist at all, in rather impotent ways. But if I attempt to reduce another human being to my desires, her power to resist me is in principle equal to my ability to overcome that resistance. Indeed, if my attitude *and hers* see others as simply modes of desire, just like food or air, then we cannot help but be in violent conflict with each other. If we both have the attitude of what I have called pure selfishness and what Hegel calls appetitive desire, then a "struggle to the death" cannot help but emerge in the conceptual dialectic. "Thus the relation of the two self-conscious individuals," Hegel explains, "is such that they prove themselves and each other through a life-and-death struggle."[12] The pure form of "selfishness," then, when sustained to the very end, can only result in a struggle to the death with another similar self, since both selves are determined to prove the same thing – that each one is the sole determining reality of being, the only "I."[13]

The emerging conceptual dialectic can now be summarized. Potentially, the same four key steps of dialectic that I identified in my analysis of the young neurotic woman above are also involved here. With this in mind, the conceptual dialectic of the absolutely selfish individual in her battle with another such selfish being can be analysed in four steps.

1. *The original stance of self-determination*: The original stance of self-determination is a radical selfishness defined by its failure to perceive others as anything other than modalities of its own desire. I have called this, with Hegel, appetitive desire (*Begierde*). Pure selfishness attempts to unify all that is different from it within an infinite system governed by its own desires.
2. *The emergence of contradiction*: This stance of appetitive desire, as soon as it encounters another such self, becomes contradictory. This happens because the other self insists with every bit as much conviction and power that it is the determining centre of reality. The logic of the situation is

contradictory: two different selves each claim to be the unique and sole determining centre of reality. If they are both fully committed to their stance, then they have no other option than to fight to the death.

3 *Invitation to surpassing*: This situation could continue ad infinitum, as a bad infinite, with each selfish self battling as best it could against all comers. Winners and losers would come and go forever. The only solution to this situation would require that the beings in question be able to change their attitude – surpass their original stance of selfishness and adopt another (more sophisticated) one. It might be tempting to rush in and suggest *co-operation* (constructive engagement), but in conceptual dialectic one must find not just any solution to the struggle, but the one that is logically *the next most sophisticated*. Or again, the question is this: Given the failure of the pure selfishness of desire, what is the second most primitive stance one could have toward others? The stance will have to be a relating, since it is relationship itself that the first stance rejects, but it could be a relating in which one self gives in and recognizes the other's selfish desire as the real determining centre of the world. Indeed, Hegel calls this new form of relationship "lordship and bondage" (*Herrschaft* und *Knechtschaft*), although it is frequently called "mastery and slavery." The slave resolves that his own desires shall be none other than those of the master, and the master treats the slave as nothing other than a modality of his desire. That is, the master retains the attitude of appetitive desire or pure selfishness, and the slave agrees to go along with this. The world of the master and slave is now still a (good) infinite, because the master's desire unifies all difference in answer to his projects such that the slave must assiduously conform himself to that desire. The two self-consciousnesses now "exist as two opposed shapes of consciousness; one is the independent consciousness whose essential nature is to be for itself, the other is the dependent consciousness whose essential nature is simply to live or be for another."[14]

4 *Incorporation of the more sophisticated stance of self-determination*: The slave in question now has two basic options in relating. With respect to his master he will recognize nothing other than pure subordination. Yet he might still find occasions to use a kind of pure appetitive desire. The slave says that the master's desire is the determining centre of reality but, when the slave eats, he asserts the dominion of the remnant of his appetitive desire over the food. That is, even the

more primitive stance (struggle to the death) is folded into the more sophisticated stance (mastery and slavery).

Thus unfolds Hegel's deservedly famous dialectic of self-consciousness in the *Phenomenology of Spirit*.[15] It is a dialectical analysis like that of my study of the stoic young woman, and yet it is not an empirical dialectic. Hegel has not taken up a dialectic of some specific history, but of the "concept" of "relating to others" or, more accurately, of "self-consciousness." We could even say, if we like, that this concept is a dialectical genus, an abstract universal, for which we have determined the first two species (appetitive desire and mastery/slavery).[16] There are more species of this genus to come, and I will return to this story shortly. In summary, conceptual dialectic, like the dialectical analysis of a determinate "history," has the four points of

a original stance of self-determination;
b emergence of contradiction;
c invitation to surpassing, sublation; and
d incorporation of a more sophisticated stance of self-determination.

However, in a conceptual dialectic there are new features above and beyond what was necessary in empirical dialectic:

1 In a conceptual dialectic, the first step is the one that is most logically *primitive*, in both senses of the term. It comes *first*, but is also the *least sophisticated*. We have found the first step when we have found that stance that *must* be the first step: it is literally *impossible* that it be otherwise. Later steps are elaborations of this first, primordial step.
2 In conceptual dialectic one must move systematically through the least to the most sophisticated stance, without skipping any steps. Empirical dialectic has no such restriction. Once one moves systematically through all possible steps in conceptual dialectic, the result is the complete dialectical elaboration of that concept.
3 Each step is itself a pure "concept" – a generalized (universal) mode of being. We know, however, that no empirical experience reproduces that concept in its purity. There are no perfectly selfish people. Thus, the pure concept is not a posteriori in the traditional sense of the term. However,

it is also not a priori, for we are in a sense reconstructing the conceptual ways of relating to other people – a project in which we are all always already committed and experienced. Thus the concept is empirical in the *phenomenological* (not Humean or Ayerian) *sense* – it is the rational coagulation of an infinite multiplicity of experiences of relation. And thus the concept is rational as well, but also in the *phenomenological* (and not the Platonic or Kantian) sense of rationality. That is, the concept is rationally true, and gives rise to what we might call performative or dialectical developments. The concept (*Begriff*) here is always related to an infinitely differentiated empirical experience which Hegel calls "existence" (*Dasein*, sometimes *Existenz*). In existence, cases of selfishness are interwoven in vastly complex webs of experience that have a potentially infinite (in the "bad" sense) array of variations. "Concepts" are the intelligible structures that are drawn from and relate to this objective existence. Hegel calls the unity of concept and its objective existence the "Idea" (*Idee*).[17] Thus, truth – intelligibility – arises only as Idea, as the relationship of dialectical concepts with infinitely variable forms of objective existence. Actual experiences will arise in such a way as to be closer to or farther from their concept.

4 Since the dialectical development is driven by contradictions within the structure of self-determining life, it is at least possible to posit a stage in the dialectic in which contradiction is eliminated such that the dialectic stops at what must be described as the most sophisticated step. For example, we can say that Heidegger's claim that humans are *ekstatic* is true in this sense of sophistication, because any possible future change in human life will itself presuppose the ecstatic mode of our being (and, indeed, we will see that Hegel says precisely that as well).

5 The unity and diversity of the structures in a conceptual dialectic are interdependent. Hegel's articulation of the structure of truth uses the metaphor of *unfolding*, but the unfolding of the conceptual dialectic reveals what he calls a "totality" – good infinite. For example, he says in the *Lectures on Fine Art*, "The true has existence and truth only as it unfolds into external reality; but, on the other hand, the externally separated parts, into which it unfolds, it can so combine and retain in unity that now every part of its unfolding makes this soul, this totality, appear in each part."[18] If we take our example of the concept of "relating to others," and the forms we have found so far, appetitive desire

and mastery and slavery, we can see how they illustrate Hegel's point. There is no pure abstraction of "relating to others": one always relates to others in this way or that. Or again, the pure unity, the universal, "relating to others" (self-consciousness), is always particularized and exists only *as particularized*. And yet these particularities, appetitive desire and mastery and slavery, are intelligible only in terms of the universal – that is, they are intelligible only as ways *of relating*. The universal concept is unified with all the particular unfoldings as this unique, or *singular*, form of being. No one of the terms of universal, particular, or singular could exist without the others. (This was, once again, the second of Lampert's criteria above.)

6 But even if the terms of the conceptual dialectic can reach a most sophisticated possible state, in many other senses the philosophical analysis could never end – because existence and the concepts that lurk within it are always open to historical change. That is, even if the conceptual dialectic (dialectic of the *concept*) provides the terms for the intelligibility of the empirical dialectic (dialectic of *existence*), their unity (*Idea*) is open to a (bad) infinite number of variations. Moreover, these variations are not just random instances; they are the very stuff of our lives – what matters most to us, the selfishness of my lover, the enslavement of Haitian sugarcane cutters in the Dominican Republic, the struggle of my daughter with her vain friends, and so on.[19]

With a relatively solid sense of what constitutes conceptual dialectic, I now follow the conceptual dialectic of self-consciousness a little further.

2 SLAVERY AND WORK

I began the conceptual dialectic with a kind of absolute selfishness, appetitive desire, and saw how this stance led dialectically to a struggle to the death and then the institution of master and slave. The attitude of the slave is a kind of unilateral recognition of the master: the slave holds the view that the master is the determining centre of reality (the unity of a good infinite). The attitude of the slave is a form of self-determination – the slave perceives that his best mode of comportment is to recognize the will of the master as determining. Yet, as one moves to step two of the dialectic, the emergence of contradiction, an internal conflict in the slave's strategy becomes apparent. The slave has determined that the master's will is the determining centre – plainly a contradiction. In the very act of renouncing himself as desiring centre, the slave implicitly affirms that he is, in fact, a desiring centre. Self-renunciation is a self-contradictory act of self-consciousness. In this act of self-renunciation, he must exercise precisely that faculty that he claims not to have. He has attempted to alienate his self-determination, but has merely contradicted it.

However easily this contradiction can be observed from outside, it is not one the slave himself grasps. The slave really believes that the master rules reality. Empirical versions of this kind of submissiveness can be found in many historical and contemporary forms that are not far from the pure concept, from the loyal and obedient slaves of history to those women that Simone de Beauvoir identifies as *enjoying* a child-like station in a world dominated by men.[20] Although it is easy to find examples of slave-like submissiveness in everyday experience, it is important to recall that the conceptual dialectic, just as it considered the pure concept of appetitive desire, considers the *pure concept* of mastery and slavery. Actual situations will embody this concept only to certain degrees.

Although the slave's situation is contradictory, it is a contradiction only "for us" (as Hegel often puts it). Indeed, it is not really a contradiction at all until the slave himself experiences it as such. Yet for that to happen, the slave must be transformed from within the demands of living out a slave's life. How can a radically submissive slave learn to make a claim to be free?

The stance of the slave is that the master's desire rules all, such that everything in reality, including the slave, appears only in the light of what facilitates or obstructs the desire of the master. The appetitive desire of the slave, therefore, "is held in check," for the slave simply cannot satisfy his own desires as he sees fit.[21] Indeed, we might even go so far as to say that the slave does not even initially experience his own desire as "his own": everything in reality is an expression of the will of the master. When the slave works for the master, each and every object the slave transforms belongs *to the master*.

Indeed, in a way, the master's domination liberates the slave from the bad infinite of his desire. Appetitive desire is a constantly repetitive structure for which there is no full or lasting satisfaction. "Desire," Hegel says, "has reserved to itself the pure negating of the object and thereby its unalloyed feeling of self." However, this satisfaction is "a fleeting one, for it lacks the side of objectivity and permanence."[22] The primitive form of desire, once again, has the logical form of lack-temporary satisfaction-lack.

The very attempt to attain self-certainty by destroying the object lasts for a moment, only to return over and over again. Since appetitive desire is, in this way, a bad infinite, it is possible, as I put it above, to win battles but never the war itself. It thus lives in a continual state of renewed dependence and renewed vulnerability and its goal of self-certainty is actually defeated.[23]

This form of desire is very familiar to us in experiences of pleasure like eating, sexual desire, consumerism, and what have come to be called "cheap thrills." Indeed, the intensity of these pleasures, and the fact that they frequently answer to real needs, make it tempting to organize one's life around their satisfaction. I will maintain in chapters 9 and 10 that one of the great dangers of capitalism is that it incarnates an entire economy in terms of the logic of appetitive desire. I will also outline a form of society, the "Condition of Right," which tends to privilege appetitive desire (chapter 4). However, Hegel's view is that this temptation never fully satisfies us because we ultimately want the lasting satisfaction of mutual recognition (as we shall see shortly).[24]

By holding this desire in check, by repressing it, the slave is opened up to a new and potentially more sophisticated and satisfying form of experience.[25] The product of the slave's labour, after all, is not consumed by (the slave's) desire, but remains independent. "It is in this way," Hegel explains, "that consciousness, *qua* worker, comes to see in the independent being [of the object] its *own* independence."[26] Hegel goes into somewhat more detail about this process. The power of the master, which causes fear in the slave, is the "negation" of the slave's independence, but, "In fashioning the thing, the bondsman's own negativity, his being-for-self, becomes an object for him only through his setting at nought the existing *shape* confronting him." That is, the negation of the slave's independence is counteracted by the slave's own power to negate the existing shape before him and transform it into something else. Thus, the slave "destroys this alien negative moment, posits *himself* as a negative in the permanent order of things, and thereby becomes *for himself*, someone existing on his own account." The power to negate is the power of mind, for mind can always extend past, and thus negate, any finitude that it encounters. But this power is made particularly manifest in work, for work negates an existing state of affairs and then creates a new one by using nothing other than the worker's creative powers. Work, then, gradually teaches the slave that he is a free, infinite mind – that he is the *power* of negation, and thus is free to determine the world in *his own* image. The slave realizes, Hegel continues, "that it is precisely in his work wherein he seemed to have only an alienated existence that he acquires a mind of his own."[27]

I will extrapolate on Hegel's unfortunately terse text by studying what he says in the *Philosophy of Mind*, and thereby posit four distinct forms of learning that take place in work. First, in order to transform an object, the slave must learn something like the "concept" of that object. As the slave learns the character of trees and houses when he builds, he must become a kind of proto-scientist of the world. Hegel is emphatic that no such thing as science can ever develop if human beings simply see nature in terms of their appetitive desire. Indeed, in the *Philosophy of Nature* he says, "The practical approach to Nature is, in general, determined by appetite, which is self-seeking; need impels us to use Nature for our own advantage, to wear her out, to wear her down, in short, to annihilate her."[28] Of course, the slave is not yet at the truly scientific attitude, which is "the method of regarding Nature as free in her own peculiar vital activity,"[29] but the repression of his appetitive desire is a decisive premise of stoicism (the next stage of the conceptual dialectic of self-consciousness) and thus of science as well.

Second, the slave must learn to abstract intellectually from a current state of affairs in order to posit in his imagination a new and different world. It might seem odd to claim that the slave seeks happiness when that happiness consists in little more than pleasing the master, but his happiness is thoroughly bound up in successfully doing the bidding of his master – in his work. Yet, not only is the theoretical attitude of science dependent on holding "desire in check" but so is the practical attitude of seeking happiness. For happiness to arise, the immediate impulses of desire cannot simply be allowed to carry the self in contradictory directions, nor can the self be governed by endlessly repeated, temporary pleasures. These desires must be subsumed under something of an organized plan such that they can be harmonized (turned into something like a good infinite), and this means positing a scheme in the imagination that "ought" to be realized.[30] This requires, Hegel says in the *Philosophy of Mind,* "the subordination of *particular* impulses [*Triebe*],[31] to a *universal* one – *happiness.*" This notion of happiness, when it is transformed in a harmonious unity in one's relations with others, is a preliminary sketch of *freedom*. The particularities of the impulses "come together in the will that wills the *concrete* universal, the Concept of freedom which … forms the goal of practical mind."[32]

Of course, our happiness is something we hope for more than we actually achieve, and thus Hegel says, "Happiness is the mere abstract and merely imagined universality of things desired – a universality which only ought to be."[33] However, it is precisely this ought, projected into a future, which thus negates the present as a kind of inadequacy, even a "should not be." The slave practises this over and over again as he works to transform things from their raw materials into their finished products. Indeed, the ultimate "finished product" here turns out to be, more and more, not so much the fashioned object but the happiness of the slave. Just as the work of the slave makes him a prototypical scientist of the objective world, it also makes him a prototypical agent of his own subjective freedom, realized as his own self-organized project of happiness.

Third, the slave learns by working that he can actively transform the world. His freedom is more and more *actualized*. Yet this requires precisely the harmonious development of the slave as both theoretical intelligence, which seeks to know the truth of the objective world, and practical intelligence, which seeks the happiness of the slave himself. "Actual free will," Hegel says, "is the unity of theoretical and practical mind: a free will, which realizes its own freedom of will, now that the formalism, fortuitousness, and contractedness of the practical content up to this point have been superseded."[34] As the slave works, he sees a reflection of his own capacities in every object he makes, and experiences the pleasure and satisfaction of these skills being developed and realized. In so doing he comes to recognize himself as free. At that point, "The will to liberty is no longer an *impulse* which demands its satisfaction, but the permanent character – the spiritual consciousness grown into a non-impulsive nature."[35] The work of the slave makes the slave come to recognize that his own truth is to be free, to be the autonomous author of his own happiness. But once this happens, the slave is no longer a slave, but is free.

Fourth, the slave will typically carry out his work in relationships with other people, and thus the emergence of his freedom is not merely a personal process, but the process by which a co-operating community learns of its freedom.[36] The slave learns to be a member of an emerging culture of people who recognize in the products of *their* work a reflection of *their* own constantly growing capacity to transform the world. The pleasures and satisfactions of work in this communal context give rise to the new terms of happiness. The most sophisticated kind of feelings, those that have to do with the character of relations between people, arise "when the substantial content of right, morality, ethics and religion, which originates in *thought*, is received into the feeling will."[37]

To summarize, the slave will come to see in the product of his work an image not of the master and his desire, but of the slave's own intellectual and practical abilities. The slave effectively wrests the object of nature from the oppressive shadow of the master and in the process sheds light on his own self-determination and that of the others with whom he co-operates. In objectifying his will in the object, the slave can come to conceive himself objectively as self-consciousness.[38]

Indeed, as I discuss in detail below, Hegel says that property arises when we put our "will in a thing."[39] Yet this is precisely what the slave and his co-workers do. If the product of work was originally recognized by the slave as the property of the master, it is the slave who manifestly has put *his* will into the thing when it is transformed by his work. The slave appropriates the product of labour from the master and, since it is his will that is "in the thing," it is simultaneously a mirror that reflects his own freedom back to him. Thus, Hegel argues that human work will gradually demonstrate the contradiction we observed above to the slave himself: in creating images of his own power to determine reality, the slave will come to recognize himself as self-determining.[40] When he does so he will no longer be a slave, for now it would indeed be a contradiction to will that he does not have a will, or to will that the master's will be the only self-determining will in reality.[41] Yet this reveals something decisive about the slave's work. The most important object of work is not the transformation of objects of nature, but the transformation of human relationships and thus of the self in relationships.

The dialectic of the slave's work can be expressed in terms of the steps of conceptual dialectic I have already identified. First, although it might not seem like it, the slave's original attitude is one of self-determination – even if a very primitive one. The slave fears the authority of the master and obeys every one of the master's commands. The pure concept of slavery at work here is not just that of a prisoner forced to work by the threat of violence but of a person so submissive that he really believes in the truthfulness of his subordinate position. In terms of the ontological tension between vulnerability and power, between passivity and activity, the slave represents the furthest possible extreme of using one's vulnerability and passivity to ensure survival. Yet this is, of course, still a strategy; in order to survive the slave embraces vulnerable passivity. As a strategy, however, it is also an expression, even if minimally, of the slave's "pouvoir"

– his power to actively engage in the world. The slave acts as the master's body, and thus recognizes the will of the master as that which literally determines its own reality.

The key to the argument, however, arises in the second moment of the dialectic – the emergence of contradiction. When the slave works, as we have seen, he creates images of his own creative power before himself. The slave's work will build up these powers to the point where the slave can claim his independence. That is, there is no contradiction in the mastery and slavery relationship until the slave literally teaches himself to lay a claim to his own freedom, which he does due to the intellectual and practical cultivation of the soul when he works. When the slave comes to recognize himself as a centre of creative power, as an independent will, he has already ceased to be a slave, since he now considers his own will, and not the master's, to be the determining centre of reality.

Most generally, Hegel is making a claim here about the pedagogical power of work and, even more broadly, of engaged human activity in general. Through work human beings not only transform external nature into that which satisfies their needs but transform themselves as human beings as well. For example, when the slave comes to recognize himself as free, one might think that this creates the conditions for a return to the struggle to the death. But Hegel recognizes that, having gone through this process of work, the slave has not only learned that he is free, but that each thing in the world has its own characteristic way of being. Recall that in order to carry out transformative labour, the slave must learn the concept of that which he transforms. If the primitive stance of human relationship is appetitive desire, which is marked by a failure to recognize the other as a self, then it is this "desire" that is "held in check" during the slave's work. The slave learns of the independence of things because he cannot simply reduce them to the status of usefulness for his own ends. The result of the slave's labour, then, is not a return to the struggle to the death, but a sublation (*Aufhebung*), an advance to what Hegel calls "stoicism."

If a contradiction has emerged between the slave's concept of himself and the slave's status as slave, then the invitation to surpass this contradiction (step 3 of the dialectic) is the possibility of, first, recognizing that freedom is found in one's own ability to determine one's *own* attitude toward the world; and, second, to recognize that every other person and object one encounters has its own independent concept. This power, which is the power of thought, is the core of the stoic's identity. "In thinking," Hegel says, "I *am free*, because I am not in an *other*, but remain simply and solely in communion with myself, and the object, which is for me the *essential* being, is in undivided unity my being-for-myself; and my activity in conceptual thinking is a movement within myself."[42] In sublating slavery and thus incorporating the new stance, the fourth step of the dialectic is reached. This is, however, not the final step of the development of the genus "relating to others," as I now go on to show.

3 MUTUAL RECOGNITION AND FREEDOM

I will not study the three forms of self-consciousness that directly follow slavery, "stoicism," "skepticism," and the "unhappy consciousness," since they all embody forms of the key to Hegel's notion of freedom, "mutual recognition." I focus instead on the dialectic of vulnerability and power that produces mutual recognition itself. Hegel gives his argument for this in the *Phenomenology* immediately after introducing desire and self-consciousness, but prior to all the other stages, including the struggle to the death and mastery and slavery. I want to show why the struggle to the death is plainly not a case of mutual recognition, while mastery and slavery is only unilateral recognition. I begin where I left off, with the stoic self.

As the stoic considers the other person, the one with whom she could re-enter the struggle to the death, she now recognizes that this other has a concept in and for itself, and this concept is that the other thinks of herself as determining centre, just as the stoic self does. Thus, if there is to be a step forward in the way they relate, it must be one which preserves the sense in which both selves are determining centres. Or again, the only possible solution will be one that satisfies the desire that both selves have to be that in terms of which reality is determined. Yet this seems impossible, for the same reason that it is impossible that a circle have two distinct centres. Reality, it would seem, cannot have more than one determining centre. We sublate this contradiction when we recognize the solution to this problem, Hegel argues, when we embrace co-operation in the form of "mutual recognition."

Recognition, the most sophisticated attitude with respect to the vital contradiction of human relationship, involves two key dialectical stages. By tracing these two steps, one can see why recognition addresses the puzzle of two determining centres. First, Hegel says, "On account of the independence of the object, therefore, it can achieve satisfaction only when the object itself effects the negation within itself; and it must carry out this negation of itself in itself, for it is *in itself* the negative, and must be *for* the other what it *is*."[43] The key in this passage is that each self that confronts the other must carry out a "negation within itself." And yet, Hegel continues, this is precisely what each self already is, "for it is in itself the negative, and must be *for* the other what it *is*." This power of self-negation is the primitive root of abstraction and choice. Most fundamentally, each self must choose to *negate* an original mode of its being, its own appetitive desire, and conceive of a new and different mode of being that will permit both selves, mutually, to be determining centres. Recognition can be mutual, however, only when each self does this at once. Indeed, the new stoic stance will accept nothing less. To be *self-determined* is to be *not predetermined*, but to choose one's future: this was a capacity that the slave developed as he worked.

Second, if both selves must negate themselves and choose a different attitude toward the other, then this attitude must be one in which the desire to be determining centre is satisfied. This is possible only in the following way: Any mode of co-operative activity involves a *shared notion* of determining centre. When we engage in a common project, each self can still say that she is determining centre, but it is the shared project of a "we" that is the determining centre. When we act in co-operation, there is also a sense in which we have become one, a unity, a new "I" that is the synthesis of two or more different selves. All modes of co-operation involve the mutual recognition of at least two different selves who can maintain their status as determining centres only through a co-operative or mutual centring. Anytime we say "we," we are both desiring centres co-operating together in a shared venture. "With this," Hegel says, "we already have before us the Concept of *Spirit*." Mutual recognition demands that the singularity of each be preserved, but most especially as the capacity of each to choose to co-operate with the other.[44] Recognition is thus "this absolute substance which is the unity of the different, independent self-consciousnesses which, in their opposition, enjoy perfect freedom and independence: 'I' that is 'We' and 'We' that is 'I.'"[45] We can now retrospectively understand that neither killing the other nor enslaving him satisfies the desire of the killer or the master, because it is only the mutual recognition from an equal other, in cooperation, that satisfies human desire, that responds satisfactorily to the vital contradiction of human social life.

Such mutual recognition, Hegel thinks, certainly happens in explicit agreements – contracts, law, love, and so on.[46] But it happens even more pervasively as the unconscious body of social life – in language and customs enacted unself-consciously as we engage with the world as societies, as systems of mutual recognition.[47] When we co-operate in the writing and reading of this text, for example, we call upon a deeply habituated, mutually recognized structure of the English language. Our differences, meanwhile, are preserved, and yet we reach across that difference in the creation of a jointly engaged project. There is no demand in Hegel's theory that we interpret these texts in identical ways; indeed, to do so would precisely be to deny the difference between singulars that is a necessary condition of their opposition. All the same, the very act of communicating happens in and through the fact of our difference. It happens, in other words, in the ontological tension between two selves who create a bridge across a gulf that is always in some important sense *different*.

A society, as an enormous web of co-operation, is a sophisticated system of mutual recognition – a "we."[48] By "co-operation" here I certainly do not mean necessarily to preclude competition and conflict. As for competition, such as that in a market economy, we can quickly recognize that competition in this sphere is marked by very well-organized systems of co-operation – the implicit and explicit rules of market activity, which nearly everyone follows, including the rule that each should try to make as much profit as possible and put one's competitors out of business. Even competition, then, is a co-operative activity of a "we" engaged in mutual recognition. I return to this issue in detail in chapters 9, 10, and 11.

A society enacts this "we" in its explicit constitution and formal laws, as well as in the religious and artistic texts and images in which it, as it were, tells itself who it is. Just as a constitution announces to its people what "we" most fundamentally have in common, so too does the singing of the national anthem or the recognition of especially virtuous leaders and heroes in literature and film celebrate the unified and unifying character of the people. I call this form of "we" *juridical-imaginative recognition*, for it establishes the formal, legal infrastructure of a society as well as projecting the images in and through which members of the society recognize themselves as such. The juridical-imaginative system of mutual recognition, for example, can be tightly defined as restricted to the specific members of, say, an ethnic group, or broadly defined as "we citizens who are unified by nothing other than our right to be different from each other as we see fit." I am not yet interested in *what kind* of unity is being explored here, but in the fact of *some kind* of unity. As I show below, there are very different ways of organizing a system of juridical-imaginative recognition, and the dialectic of these systems will teach us what a just and free society is.

The sphere of juridical-imaginative recognition must be distinguished from what I call the sphere of *concrete-lived recognition*. That is, mutual recognition also takes place at the mostly unconscious level of custom, language, and habituated daily practice. This sphere of concrete-lived recognition embodies the ubiquitous practices that make a society what it is.

Of course, there is no necessity that the spheres of juridical-imaginative and concrete-lived recognition harmonize. Indeed, the contradiction of these two spheres of society is precisely what may cause it to fail. When a society's juridical structures and most important images are out of step with how actual practice develops, then conflict will emerge, and this conflict will motivate (though not necessitate) resolution – a change in the juridical-imaginative and concrete-lived recognition that attempts to achieve their harmony. This is to say, in the process by which a society develops, it is very possible that changes at the level of concrete-lived recognition will create contradictions with that which the juridical-imaginative structures explicitly sanction. These contradictions can mount to the point that they motivate the collapse of the whole society. Indeed, we have already seen this in microcosm with the society of masters and slaves. A community of slaves, at the juridical-imaginative level, might really believe themselves to be slaves. However, when they work, which takes place at the level of concrete-lived recognition, their identity develops in the direction of free self-determination and thus comes to be in contradiction with the juridical-imaginative structures that deny them their freedom.

It is now possible to identify our first insights into the character of *freedom*. The familiar notion of freedom as choice has already appeared here as the "negation" in which each self recognizes that the satisfaction of its desire rests in recognition and not the struggle to the death or mastery and slavery. Indeed, it is for this reason that liberals like Isaiah Berlin have called this power to change our attitude toward things, to choose, "negative freedom."[49] However, for Hegel this negation happens only in the context of relationship and is in fact a strategy the self adopts with respect to the concrete demands of relating to others. It makes no sense, therefore, to abstract mere negation from the context in which it has meaning. Thus, for Hegel freedom is something more like the "know-how of flourishing." To learn is precisely to effect a series of self-negations in the name of gradually more and more sophisticated ways of engaging in the world – primarily with other people. This, indeed, is what we have just seen. The self-negation that leads slaves to deny their juridical-imaginative status as slaves is an experience of *education*; they have *learned* on their own that they are not slaves, such that the power of freedom is not merely to negate the proposition "I am a slave," but at the same to embrace the proposition, "I now see that I am free and recognize others also as free."

At first, the two selves in the struggle to the death experienced each other as obstacles, as aliens who challenged each other's claim to be that in terms of which reality is determined. But their mutual recognition has allowed each of these individuals to preserve their uniqueness and yet to do so precisely in the act of agreeing to co-operative action together. It is only by co-operating with the other, and recognizing this other on its own terms, that one is free. It is only by fulfilling this vocation to recognize the other on the other's own terms that freedom is experienced. "Only this way," Hegel says in his most concise definition of freedom, "is the spirit *at home* and *with itself* in ... *externality* as such."[50]

This formula strikes many people as an odd and indeed opaque notion of freedom. What, then, is the force of Hegel's claim? A child who has parents, family, and friends that love and support her and, indeed, very good teachers at school, does not primarily experience other people has impediments to her projects – very much the opposite. She perceives, implicitly, that others give her material support (the things she needs), psychological support (encouragement, help, conversation, and so on) and, indeed, they create an overall environment that cultivates a path for this child to thrive. Obviously a child's parents and teachers are external beings, they are others, and yet their otherness *cultivates* the flourishing of the child. Otherness, in this example, facilitates rather than impedes the project of the child – she is *recognized*. Her projects, we might then say, are "at home" in her relationships with "others." More generally, our experience is constituted by the vital contradiction of our vulnerable/empowered relations with others. We strive to overcome the conflicts of these relationships by "making ourselves at home in our world" – by creating relationships of mutual recognition. To be at home, then, is the experience that one's world, by and large, supports one's projects.

I note briefly four remarkable things about this freedom, all of which I analyse in detail throughout this book. First, Hegel's metaphor of "being at home" is an apt one, for everyone who has had a by and large loving family and good teachers and friends has had their own concrete experience of freedom in its basic form. To have others who feel love for us, *philia* in Aristotle's highly relevant notion of friendship in the *Nichomachean Ethics*, means precisely that they seek the good for us. Second, this notion of freedom is radically different from, say, Hobbes or Locke, for whom the freedom of each is necessarily a threat to the freedom of others. Each person experiences others as impediments, limits, or threats to freedom. This is, indeed, the very opposite of "being at home." Third, we must say that Hobbes and Locke are not purely and simply wrong, for there are many situations in human life, from nasty brothers who take one's toys to people in civil society who manipulate, obstruct, and violate us, in which others do not cultivate our flourishing. There are many situations, in other words, in which others really are impediments to our freedom and in which we are quite decidedly not "at home in externality" as such. Indeed, the passage from one's loving family to an environment of strangers in society is a difficult one, at least in part for this reason.[51] Fourth, these experiences of not being at home generate in us what we should rightfully call a "longing for the universal" – a longing to create harmonious systems of mutual recognition. Since we all have experiences of being at home among others, we will often find ourselves alienated and dissatisfied in those situations in which we are not at home. Of course, we can also accommodate ourselves to not being at home, and thus cultivate skills of competition, manipulation, mendacity, suspicion, defensiveness, stoicism, indifference, violence, and so on. Yet even this strategy, in a warped and contradictory sense, is an attempt to "be at home." If one's world is violent and competitive, the only way to be at home in it is to learn the skills of competition and violence, or to *change it*. To change it is to long to create a world in which we are truly at home among others. But if mutual recognition is a co-operative environment of a "we," it is also a "universal." The "we," after all, is a universal term – "we *all*." Human freedom, in short, is found only in the universal, which is the same as saying that human desire is fully satisfied only in the *commons* of communication and community. This is why Hegel says, in the preface to the *Phenomenology of Spirit*, "It is the nature of humanity to press onward to agreement with others; human nature only really exists in an achieved community of minds."[52]

Hegel is often accused of having a philosophy in which the self obscures, over-reaches, denies, or even colonizes the other. This is not the case. The only fully free attitude one can have toward the other is to respect and indeed cultivate the uniqueness and independence of the other person. Freedom is *not* when the other obeys my wishes such that I can do what I want, but when I let the other be herself on her own terms, and enter into a mutually supportive relationship with her on this basis. Our thought, Hegel says, rejects all "arrogance" and is "humble" in the "giving up of our *particular* opinions and beliefs and in allowing the matter [itself] to hold sway over us."[53] In the vital contradiction of power and vulnerability, precisely the *active* stance one should take up toward the other is the *humble vulnerability* of allowing the other to say on her own terms who or what she is. But this also means that freedom is the process of cultivation (*Bildung*), the *education* by which we seek out co-operative relationship with what is other. "*Education*, in its absolute determination, is therefore *liberation* and *work* towards a higher liberation."[54] Education, then, is the cultivation of more and more sophisticated forms of freedom. Hegel's categorical imperative, as I show in much more detail below, is thus *act in such a way as to cultivate freedom.* And yet freedom is itself cultivation, understood as the process by which we become more and more at home in, more and more capable of mutually recognizing, otherness as such. Thus one is most truly free when one participates wholeheartedly in relationships of learning. The political version of this imperative is that we create a world in which human beings co-operatively thrive.

For Hegel the cultivation of freedom in mutual recognition is also the creation of what I called above, following Hegel's logical categories, a "good infinite." As we have begun to see in our brief encounters with Hobbes and Locke, liberal individualists think of freedom in terms of the "bad infinite"; each free self is a finite being which, in its own freedom, poses a limit to the freedom of others. Since the freedom of each is a finite limit on the freedom of others, co-operative action is always, in these theories, a sacrifice of some freedom for the sake of the security to pursue others. Since, moreover, there is no logical limit to the number of these finite atomistic selves, the operative logic here is the bad infinite – an endless series of discrete units each of which is the external limit to the others. These theories of freedom are blind to the fact that it is only in and through others that freedom is realized, as Hegel has demonstrated in the dialectic of mutual recognition. Thus, for Hegel, the other is not a barrier to or limit on my freedom, but the condition of its possibility, and I play the same role for the other. In co-operation we see the logic of the good infinite at work, for each finite person devotes his or her finitude to the co-operative fulfillment of all, such that the success of each depends on the others. The overall unity of individuals, their community, animates each in their finitude. Or again, the community of friends is a self-differentiated unity in which each recognizes the others not as limits but as conditions for freedom. This notion of freedom as a good infinite was taken up by Marx, who described it as a state in which "the free development of each is the condition for the free development of all."[55] Though others can certainly act as barriers to my freedom, human beings thrive most when we act co-operatively together. Lest this notion seem overly sanguine or even utopian, I will explore how the vital contradiction of finitude and infinitude means that freedom is constituted only in and through fundamental tensions. Indeed, this has already been seen in a preliminary way in the vital contradiction between vulnerability and power.

I close this introductory study of mutual recognition and freedom by making three quick points. First, Hegel's notion of freedom can now be seen as very similar to the Socratic midwifery practised throughout Plato's dialogues, with the *Symposium*'s ladder of *eros* as perhaps its most definitive statement.[56] To practise Socratic midwifery is to act in such a way as to allow others to "[give] birth in beauty."[57] That is, it is to guide others in order that they give birth to ever more beautiful ways of living in which one graduates from love of beautiful bodies, to love of beautiful souls, to beautiful laws and customs and, finally, to beautiful wisdom. Each step articulates more inclusive experiences of "having in common" – of universals.[58] But this means, of course, that the greatest possible giving birth in beauty is precisely to demonstrate that this kind of midwifery is the most beautiful human vocation – and it is the Platonic portrayal of Socrates' educational practice that accomplishes this task.

Second, if freedom is the practice of education, then education is precisely *the engagement in dialectic*. When we learn, we outgrow a determinate way of being (enter into contradiction with it) and thus negate it such as to adopt a yet more sophisticated stance (we transcend it). In education, as in dialectic, each stance functions as a stair; it is a platform on which we can then engage the world so as to encounter new others and learn yet more sophisticated ways of co-operating with them. The imperative of freedom is to *cultivate* more sophisticated attitudes to the world in and through welcoming that which is other, but this is equivalent to saying, *practise dialectical education*.

Third, the Kantian notion of autonomy has been dialectically developed by Hegel in his argument for mutual recognition. Freedom, for Kant, is realized when we give ourselves the laws we will obey (*auto-nomos*), rather than allowing heteronomous forces to determine us. We achieve this autonomy by following the law of reason: we must act in such a way that the maxim of our action is a universal law. For Kant this means ignoring one's desire in favour of an abstract universal. Hegel's argument, however, shows that it is precisely the universals of shared action with others that are the only forms of behaviour that truly satisfy desire. We are most fully free, we are autonomous, when we self-consciously enter into mutual recognition with others, when we respect those others on their own terms, and when we cultivate the conditions of freedom through education. The formation of this kind of universal community is a concrete universal or, as we have seen already, a good infinite.

4 RECOGNITION, FREEDOM, AND THE VITALITY OF CONTRADICTION

The last task of this chapter is to gather what has been learned so far into the notion of "vital contradiction." In our study of empirical and conceptual dialectic in this chapter we have encountered Hegel's theory of the vitality of contradiction, especially in the relation of two selves culminating in mutual recognition. Hegel has a unique analysis of contradiction that has become quite controversial. Indeed, in distinction from the notion of contradiction found in traditional symbolic logic, in which contradictions arise only in the sphere of propositions, Hegel says that "everything is inherently contradictory."[59] We have already seen that, for Hegel, dialectic names the developmental and indeed historical character of being. This development, he thinks, is impossible without contradiction. "Contradiction is the root of all movement and vitality; it is only insofar as something has a contradiction within it that it moves, has an urge and activity."[60] Yet this notion of contradiction is not opaque, as some have taken it to be. Hegel articulates three forms of contradiction and sublation that are relevant to our purposes.[61]

First, Hegel shows in the *Science of Logic* that the principal of non-contradiction, by which something cannot be itself and its negation at the same time and in the same respect, applies to insights of a specific kind of reasoning – *Verstand* or the *understanding*. The understanding contributes to our intellectual engagement with the world by clearly grasping identities in distinction from other identities. The understanding, then, gives rise to the tradition of formal logic. The understanding is decisive to Hegel's philosophy and, to the extent that the insights of the understanding are necessary and valid, so too Hegel assiduously observes the principle of non-contradiction.[62]

However, Hegel shows the necessity of moving beyond this form of contradiction. First, he argues in the *Science of Logic* that the principle of non-contradiction cannot be grounded or otherwise demonstrated through positive argument. In one sense, this is not to argue anything different from Aristotle, who of course showed that the principle of non-contradiction could only be proved by negative or apagogic argument, insofar as any attempt to deny it makes all knowledge and, indeed, all language, impossible.[63] If a table cannot be clearly distinguished from a crocodile or a dangling participle, then any determinate thing is both itself and everything else. Hegel simply shows that the same argument holds for the principal itself – any attempt to ground it must presuppose it.[64] It is a first principle.

Second, and much more importantly, Hegel demonstrates that the validity of the understanding is realized only in relation to things that do not change, like propositions. But for Hegel, of course, the real world constantly changes and demands, therefore, a higher form of intellectual activity, *Vernunft* or *reason*. In the light of reason, the understanding's distinct role is to name the constituent, abstract parts of transformations and tensions which it must freeze in order to grasp. The understanding, for example, necessarily grasps that difference between "being" and "non-being" which, in light of reason, are seen as the abstract moments or parts of the single unity which is "becoming." The understanding grasps quite adequately the distinct, mutually exclusive stages in the blossoming of a rose and, by the principle of non-contradiction, it is quite justified in saying that the rose cannot both have and not have a blossom at the same time in the same respect. However, we have no difficulty realizing that the rose changes not in distinct, mutually exclusive stages but that it is an abiding unity in and through perfectly fluid change. Thus, it is not the case that reason insists that a rose both has and has not a blossom in the same respect and at the same time, but it does show that the understanding freezes, fragments, and thus violates fluid temporal change in order to establish what are really artificially stable propositions. Reason thus recognizes and retains the power of the understanding to identify the determinate stages in the growth and flowering of a plant, while simultaneously showing that we have the intellectual power to conceive the plant as a self-transforming, self-determining being the nature of which is to always fluidly move through its own stages of development.

In the process of clarifying this point, the second form of contradiction in Hegel has emerged. When the understanding insists that being can be clearly and once and for all distinguished from non-being, it is our power of reason that refutes it. If being is free of all determination, it becomes non-being, and it is easy to grasp that if the stages in the growth of a plant were mutually exclusive identities, we would not have one plant, but two (or more). Thus, the second form of contradiction, in the light of reason, emerges when we observe that a certain stage in the development of something tries but fails to provide the terms for the identity of the thing as a whole. The second form of contradiction, then, names the dynamic by which certain notions disclose their inadequacy in and through their own self-development. This form is familiar to us under the name of learning and development, but also "immanent critique." It is worth noting that this process of change need not be conflicted to be animated by the vitality of contradiction. Even in fluid development, a plant must "oppose itself to itself" – it must oppose and negate an earlier and less fulfilled form of itself.

The second form of contradiction has already come up several times in this text. I used this sense of the term contradiction when I said that the stoicism of the young woman, which was helpful with her angry father, entered into contradiction with her life among her friends at university. The contradiction between stoic comportment and the demands of friendship motivated a surpassing or a sublation (*Aufhebung*) toward a more sophisticated stance. In this case, the successful sublation resolves the contradiction; it eliminates the tension or conflict that emerged with the contradiction. The young woman's stoicism, after her successful therapy, no longer poses a difficulty for her. Once she has sublated her freedom by embodying a stance I called constructive engagement, her stoicism becomes one tool among others that she can use to negotiate her relationships with others. Moreover, it will never be her most important tool, which of course is constructive engagement. In sum, the second form of contradiction is sublated in a way that resolves the tension and conflict of the contradiction itself. However, it is "vital" because it is the oppositional dynamic that makes change take place. This form of contradiction, therefore, demands a change.

We will encounter this form of contradiction frequently, especially in the way that determinate forms of social and political organization claim to fully realize the project of human self-determination but demonstrate, on their own terms, the need to be surpassed. That is, a determinate claim about the character of human freedom reveals itself to be only a stage in the emergence of freedom and thus comes to contradict freedom itself, calling therein for its own surpassing. When Hegel speaks of the vitality of contradiction, we can see how growth and transformation rely on contradiction in this sense.

There is a third form of contradiction and sublation in Hegel which is discussed much less frequently in the literature. We saw this third form of contradiction in the unsurpassable ontological tension between vulnerability and power that animates self-consciousness and all human relationship. Mastery tries to resolve this tension through domination of the other, through the absolute exercise of power, and slavery attempts to resolve it through absolute passivity or vulnerability. Both plainly fail. However, the formation of a co-operative "we," such that both self-consciousnesses are determining centres, in mutual recognition, can abide the tension of vulnerability and power. This might well seem to be just another example of the second form of contradiction and sublation, for an inferior and contradictory stance is sublated in favour of a more sophisticated and thus, one would think, non-contradictory stance. However, this is not the case. Mutual recognition is the best way to live in a world of other human beings in which all are suspended in the tension of vulnerability and power, but when we adopt stances of mutual recognition, we do not totally abolish the anxieties, fears, and opportunities of vulnerability nor the kinds of pride, sense of self, and well-being that come from exercising our power. No matter how much we recognize others, no matter how much we love and are loved, we remain within the anxiety and opportunity of this founding ontological tension. That is, in the third form of contradiction, the tensions of the unsublated contradiction are not totally eliminated, but are transformed. Mutual recognition is the best way to engage with others in the context of vulnerability and power, but it is not the dissolution of vulnerability and power. It should be noted as well that in this form of contradiction, the contradictory terms are not marked out by a relationship of superiority and inferiority. Vulnerability is not dialectically superior to power in the way that recognition is superior to slavery. In sum, the third form of contradiction sublates the conflict or tension of a contradiction but not in a way that eliminates all the tension or conflict, nor in a way that posits the superiority or inferiority of the relative terms. As I suggested earlier, this form of contradiction names Hegel's great elaboration of the famous fragment by Heraclitus: "They do not apprehend how being at variance, it agrees with itself: there is a back-stretched connexion, as in the bow and the lyre."[65]

Slavoj Žižek discusses this form of contradiction frequently in his analyses of Hegel. He says, for example, that Hegelian dialectic is an "acknowledgment of antagonism" and that dialectic is not the story of the overcoming of antagonism, but "a systematic notation of the failure of all such attempts." Indeed, as already quoted in the introduction, Žižek says, "'absolute knowledge' itself is nothing but a name for the acknowledgment of a certain radical loss."[66] I have great sympathy for the core of Žižek's claim here, but as I began to suggest in the introduction, I do not believe that the notion of "radical loss" is adequate to vital contradiction. After all, we can only perceive that something is lost by comparing it to some unalienated, untransgressed state. But for Hegel the only faculty that conceives such pure states is the understanding, and its abstract universals by their very purity are utterly empty and thus non-actual. One must, in other words, privilege the understanding and its non-existent pure states to call something a loss (in this ontological sense of the term). For Hegel, the universals that matter most are not the perfect abstractions of the understanding that can then be "tainted" by particularity or marked by "loss," but the concrete universals that are nothing other than the immanent relationship of particulars. If ontological primacy lies in vital contradiction, in transcendental antagonism, "loss" and "alienation" are not primary terms but the result of failures or developments of self-consciousness in certain stages of its self-elaboration. To put it in psychological terms, it is only in fantasy that libidinal satisfaction is complete and thus it is only in light of this self-defeating fantasy that there is loss.[67] Of course, this third form of contradiction is typically the result of immanent development animated by the second kind – as will be seen in detail below.

The opening two chapters of this book have presented an analysis of foundation concepts in Hegelian philosophy – empirical and conceptual dialectic, recognition, freedom, and vital contradiction. We now have the tools we need to begin our study of Hegel's political philosophy proper. In the next chapter, I study Hegel's dialectic of political life in order to begin to demonstrate the necessary institutions of political freedom. That is, I must determine, through a conceptual dialectic, what institutions must be formed in order to create a society in which our freedom can flourish, in which the free development of each is a condition for the free development of all. This task is complicated by the fact that Hegel himself never carried out this conceptual dialectic. While the *Phenomenology of Spirit* speaks a great deal about political life, the political is considered in terms of its place in the ladder that an individual self-consciousness climbs toward the absolute standpoint of philosophy. All the same, I will show in the next chapter that we can use the dialectic of the *Phenomenology of Spirit* to teach us the conceptual dialectic of politics.

3

The Conceptual Dialectic of Political Life: First Steps

THE WAY OF DESPAIR AND THE SUNBURST OF LIBERATION

Dialectic, for our purposes, is the process by which we learn what it means to be free. We have already seen that freedom is much more than choice. It is most fully realized when we engage in relationships of mutual recognition such as to be "at home" in our worlds. Yet even the experience of being at home is characterized by an abiding tension, a vital contradiction. Our freedom is achieved only by developing the institutions of human co-operation and development that allow us to flourish in the midst of this constitutive drama. Like the tension that sustains the strength of Heraclitus's bow, there is always something at stake in human freedom. Freedom is an achievement that develops in time, both in our personal lives and in the history of humanity in general. As I will show in greater detail, if freedom requires learning, then the Hegelian imperative for autonomous action might be characterized as "cultivate the conditions for co-operative human flourishing." To be free, to be autonomous, is to be at home in what is other to oneself, which can only mean to *recognize* other people in such a way that the development of each is a condition for the development of all.

Hegel was highly influential among American pragmatists because he recognized that the process of learning is a struggle of trial and error. Indeed, the most straightforward way to introduce dialectic is, as we have just seen, to describe the everyday experience of learning. Our trial and error procedures are far from random – they involve informed hypotheses and strategies, indeed, creative self-transformation, which, even if unsuccessful, make us that much more sophisticated given what we learn. Our failures, then, typically do not simply involve despair, but are themselves the necessary conditions by which we posit new and qualitatively better ways to engage creatively with the demands of our existence. Learning, to repeat the Hegelian technical term, is a process of *determinate negation*; the negation of a failed stance may simultaneously afford insight into a new and more sophisticated one. Negation, that is, determines a new and better path. For example, any strategy for freedom that involves dominating others in an unequal system of mutual recognition (epitomized by mastery and slavery) is unstable because human action ("work") tends to teach the dominated that they are free. It was only a matter of time (even if a very long time) before humanity came to abhor the institution of slavery. Our engagement with the world and in particular with each other taught us something better. The process of education constantly requires that certain stances and attitudes be undermined and abandoned in favour of more sophisticated stances and attitudes – even when the original stance or attitude is interwoven with the whole identity of an individual or society, such that abandoning it is experienced as traumatic.

Indeed, in the *Phenomenology of Spirit*, Hegel writes that the dialectical ladder, which we considered in chapter 1, is, for the individual actually living through the experience of it, very often a "way of despair."[1] He says the same kind of thing about human civilizations. In one of his most moving statements Hegel states (and I quote this passage at length),

> When we look at this display of passions, and the consequences of their violence; the Unreason which is associated not only with them, but even (rather we might say, *especially*) with *good* designs and righteous aims; when we see the evil, the vice, the ruin that has befallen the most flourishing kingdoms which the mind of man ever created; we can scarce avoid being filled with sorrow at this universal taint of corruption ... Without rhetorical exaggeration, a simply truthful combination of the miseries that have overwhelmed the noblest of nations and polities, and the finest exemplars of private virtue – forms a picture of most fearful aspect, and excites emotions of the profoundest and most hopeless sadness, counterbalanced by no consolatory result ... we retreat into the selfishness that stands on the quiet shore, and thence enjoy in safety the distant spectacle of "wrecks confusedly hurled." But even regarding History as the slaughter-bench at which the happiness of peoples, the wisdom of

> States, and the virtue of individuals have been victimized – the question involuntarily arises – to what principle, to what final aim these enormous sacrifices have been offered.[2]

The final aim toward which these sacrifices have been made is, of course, *freedom*. That is, the final aim, the telos, is a system of mutual recognition that can sustain itself without fatally pitting itself against itself. But this is an unusual telos because, unlike the Aristotelian final cause, which is the realization of a pre-existing nature, a necessary condition of freedom is that there be no predetermined nature. Hegel is Aristotelian insofar as he agrees that a telos is present at the beginning of the dialectic of human freedom, but only in a very specific sense. I have already suggested that even the most primitive attitudes and stances are always types of self-determination, types of freedom. That is, the dialectic is an account of a form of being that determines itself – that gives its identity to itself. However, given that we are studying the determinations of freedom, we can see that the telos is not present at the beginning in another sense. We could never have known at the beginning of empirical history, nor indeed can we ever know, precisely where the dialectic of freedom will take us. We can determine which institutions will tolerate and promote freedom, but we cannot know in advance the new shapes of freedom or the particular opportunities and problems they will present to us.

Moreover, if freedom is our fundamental condition as human beings, a puzzling question is posed for dialectical philosophy. What would it be to institutionalize a society the essence of which is the cultivation of freedom if freedom, at least in part, refers to our inextinguishable capacity to supersede ourselves and thus, it would also seem, to supersede any institutions that we have created along the way? We can get a glimpse of what this society amounts to by reminding ourselves once more of what we have learned about freedom so far. If freedom is the capacity of human beings to educate ourselves into new and more sophisticated forms of encountering and recognizing others, then the only system of mutual recognition that can sustain itself is one that condones, indeed, promotes this process of self-development. It is one that welcomes the encounter with others and with the new, and does so by respecting the necessities of human social life. Indeed, human civilization's pathway of despair will be scattered with the wrecks of societies that postulate a given, determinate, and thus permanent essence to the human condition, since it is precisely given, determinate, and permanent essences that the process of dialectical education constantly destroys.

Hegel believed that the revolutionary developments of the late eighteenth century were decisive in the formation of certain of the "absolute" institutions – the institutions of human life that condone and indeed promote freedom, and that thus cannot, in their essence at least, be surpassed. Thus, even if Hegel is grimly depressed about the corruption, violence, and destruction in history, he is, at other times, sanguine about the human historical vocation in general and, in particular, of his own time.[3] Indeed, Hegel considers himself, at least in 1807, to be less under the clouds of this pathway of political despair than in the sunlight of a whole new age. "It is not difficult to see that our epoch is a birth-time, and a period of transition. The spirit of man has broken with the old order of things hitherto prevailing, and with the old ways of thinking, and is in the mind to let them all sink into the depths of the past and to set about its own transformation." This old world has been interrupted, he continues, by a magnificent "sunburst, which, in one flash, illuminates the features of the new world."[4]

This new, sunlit world is the revolutionary, modern civilization of the French and American revolutions, the era in which freedom as autonomy is posited as our most essential determination. From this moment in Western civilization nearly all political debates take for granted the premise of human freedom and toil over how exactly freedom is to be fulfilled. The first premise of political life, then, is not a certain nature or given state of affairs, but *freedom* itself. This moment will also present humanity with whole new problems, specifically those that follow from the formation of a society predicated on abstract, universal right – liberalism and capitalism. In the following three chapters I study not only what led to this sunburst, but develop its implications as a study of the new forms of freedom, domination, and exploitation found in liberal-capitalism. First, however, I trace the dialectic that leads to this sunburst in the first place.

As I tried to make clear in chapter 1, there are two ways to explore the dialectical emergence of political freedom. The first is an empirical dialectic which would have, among its greatest moments, we might well say, the English, American, French, and Haitian revolutions.[5] Surely, we would also discuss civil rights, feminism, Third World liberation movements, unionization, libertarianism, and so on. Such a dialectic would study the revolutionary defeat of slavery and serfdom, the emergence of the concept of human rights, and the new opportunities and forms of exploitation and alienation created by capitalism. This *empirical dialectic* would be a study much along the lines of Hegel's *Lectures on the Philosophy of History*, albeit one much revised in light of contemporary developments of our historical knowledge and methods. Indeed, writers like Karl Marx, E.P. Thompson, and many others would be indispensable for a Hegelian approach to this issue. I engage in this kind of empirical dialectic in chapters 10 and 11.

The second possible account of the emergence of freedom, and the one I undertake in this chapter and the three to follow, is what I have called a *conceptual dialectic*. Here we *recollect* the pathway of concepts of human political life as they develop from the most primitive possible to the sunburst of freedom itself and from there to a consideration of the institutions that allow freedom to flourish.

As I have said already, it was not Hegel's purpose to write a conceptual dialectic of political life in the *Phenomenology of Spirit*, and yet that text provides all the essential features of the argument. While I refer at times to the study of "Self-Consciousness" in chapter 4 of the *Phenomenology*, the key to the argument is in chapter 6, "Spirit." This chapter is divided into three broad sections, "Ethical Life," "Culture or Self-Alienated Spirit," and "Morality." These studies are essential to understanding how societies fail to be free, and thus also how they more and more fully realize freedom. However, the institutions of a fully free society are not discussed by Hegel in the *Phenomenology of Spirit*. At that point in the argument I turn to his *Philosophy of Right* and, from there, to a serious study of the socioeconomic and political structure in liberal-capitalism.

A conceptual dialectic must begin with the most primitive form of self-determination and attend to the emergence of contradiction within it. This contradiction will emerge between the *juridical-imaginative sphere* of mutual recognition – what a society believes itself to be and how it incarnates these beliefs in formal structures – and the *concrete-lived sphere* of mutual recognition – what a society is actually doing and how those actions create changes within it. The conflict that develops because of this contradiction will generate the possibility of a self-transcendence, a sublation: an invitation to a new stance that will address the contradiction. Finally, this new stance will be incorporated as a new way of living, while the old one will in a certain sense be retained as what might be called the body of freedom. Again, the first stage of the conceptual dialectic must not be just any particular form of self-determination; it must be the logically first one: that which is both *primary* and *primitive*.

2 MARX AND THE PRIMITIVE FORM OF SOCIETY

How do we determine what kind of society comes first logically? What is the most primitive society? We seek, moreover, to recollect the form of society that is the most *logically* primitive rather than (necessarily) the most temporally primitive. Since Karl Marx explicitly claims to be a dialectical philosopher, I approach the issue of the most "primitive" society by way of a discussion of his work. Establishing some of the key features of Marx's thought will also be very helpful in arguments I develop later on. Of course, Marx claims that his dialectic is the "opposite" of Hegel's, famously saying, "For Hegel the process of thinking, which he even transforms into an independent subject, under the name of the 'Idea,' is the creator of the real world, and the real world is only the appearance of the idea. With me the reverse is true: the ideal is nothing but the material world reflected in the mind of man, and translated into forms of thought ... With him [the dialectic] is standing on its head. It must be inverted, in order to discover the rational kernel within the mystical shell."[6]

It is thus tempting to claim that Marx rejects conceptual dialectic altogether in favour of an exclusive focus on empirical dialectic. However, as I briefly mentioned earlier, Marx himself writes books of conceptual dialectic, like *Capital.* Those books will not help us in our task, however, because the subject they analyse is capitalism, and thus the primitive starting point (in *Capital*) is the "commodity." One might have thought that Marx would begin *Capital* with a study of labour, indeed with the dialectic of production, distribution, exchange, and consumption which he outlines in the introduction to the *Grundrisse*,[7] but it is essential to remember that if the topic of *Capital* is capitalism, then even labour (production) is itself already a commodity. The primitive term of the conceptual dialectic, he thus concludes, is a study of the commodity, beginning with the dialectical tension, the vital contradiction, in a commodity between its use value and exchange value.

Marx, in fact, does not exactly write a conceptual dialectic of "society." On this topic he works more or less empirically. Nonetheless, he employs key features of conceptual dialectic in his analysis. To begin with, for Marx the term *society* is primarily analysed in terms of its "mode of production" and concomitant "mode of social relations."[8] A mode of production is made up of both "material" and "social" components. Its material components are the "productive forces," *labour-power*, combined with the *means of production* (raw materials and instruments of production), as well as the division of labour. Its social component includes its purpose (production for use or for exchange, etc.), the form of surplus value created by work (how it manifests itself in a society – the product of slave labour, rent, surplus value as money, etc.), and, most importantly, the mode of exploitation (slavery, serfdom, wage labour).[9] The mode of production is said to "determine" the character of society, including its ideological and legal superstructure, although Marxist scholars hotly debate what "determine" might mean.[10]

Given that modes of production determine history (in some sense at least), what would constitute Marx's dialectical starting point? In fact, he posits that the first mode of production is a kind of primitive communism. It is very interesting to note, however, that the philosopher who purports to stand Hegel on his head does not draw on empirical evidence to establish primitive communism as his starting point, but on a conceptual deduction. That is, he posits primitive communism as the starting point not on the basis of historical or anthropological studies of actually existing societies, but on the following conceptual claim. In any society in which an exploiting (and thus non-producing) class expropriates the surplus value produced by an exploited (and thus producing) class, there must be a surplus product in that society above and beyond what is needed to meet the basic requirements of survival, such that the exploiting class can seize this value and not have to work itself. If there were no surplus product to expropriate, there could be no exploitation and, indeed, everyone would have to work all the time just to meet basic needs. This surplus product is a historical achievement, the result primarily of developments in productive forces, prior to which everyone in the society had to work all the time to produce what was necessary to survive. The society prior to the creation of surplus product would thus be a society without exploiters – hence a primitive communism. Now, as is plain from reading the *Phenomenology of Spirit*, Hegel does not start with primitive communism, but with "ethical life" (*Sittlichkeit*), the example of which is the ancient Greek polis. How are we to decide who is right (if either) in determining the primitive stance of the dialectic of "society" between Hegel and Marx? I begin by exploring Marx's claim in more detail (not only to help with the problem at hand, but also to provide some familiarity with Marx's theories which will be helpful later in this work).

Marx states in the preface to the *Contribution to the Critique of Political Economy* and elsewhere that, as new productive forces are created, they come into conflict with existing "relations of production."[11] These contradictions take the form of class conflict. The mode of social relations that follows from the mode of production is in fact a class relation since in each mode of production (save the first), one class exploits the surplus labour of another. If we take capitalism as an example of a mode of production, we see that the capitalist class is endowed with private ownership of the means of production and its product, such that members of the propertyless proletariat class must sell their labour-power to survive. These two classes themselves emerged from the crucible of the contradictions created when developments in factory production (and so on) usurped feudal agriculture as the dominant mode of transforming nature. The capitalist class, which owned the new, technologically sophisticated means of production, increased in power to the point where it could challenge the dominant class of feudalism, the landed nobility, and so inaugurate the era of capitalism proper. The capitalist class (according to Marx) then proceeded to create a legal, political, and cultural system (generally *liberalism*) because it is this system that functions most consistently to promote capitalist production – that is, to promote the interests of the capitalist class. According to Marx, classes are in a hostile relationship since the dominant class exists in and through the exploitation of the surplus value created by the work of the subordinate class.

A feudal noble, for example, does not produce surplus value by working himself, but appropriates much or most of the surplus value created by his serfs. That is, the feudal noble lives (and lives well) by *exploitation*. The serf must work a determinate number of days on the noble's land, and the product of that work belongs exclusively to the noble. The noble is able to appropriate the serf's surplus value by two means. First, he uses ideological coercion since it is always the dominant class that sets the terms for what it means to be human, and thus, in this case, he and everyone else take it for granted that the blue-blooded nobles are ontologically superior to the serfs, whose very nature is (or, at least, should be) something akin to "loyal service." Second, failing ideological coercion, he uses sheer physical coercion – the threat or the use of violence. In sum, a mode of production produces classes because of the characteristic division between exploiting class and exploited class, such that Marx can say that "The history of all hitherto existing society is the history of class struggles."[12]

Marx's dialectic here matches the form of empirical dialectic I posited in chapter 1. A contradiction emerges within a given mode of production when technical developments create the possibility of a new and more sophisticated mode of production. An invitation to surpassing emerges in the revolutionary action of the class that stands to gain by this new mode of production – a surpassing that is institutionalized precisely in the (almost inevitable) success of this revolutionary project.

This means that the most primitive society, in a Marxist historical dialectic, will be the one with the most primitive techniques for transforming nature. The most primitive possible means of transforming nature is one so poorly developed that it cannot even produce surplus value. Thus, every member of the society must work all the time, or fail to meet even their most basic needs. Since this society has no surplus to expropriate, it cannot have exploitation and it cannot have classes (although it might still have a division of labour). Hence, the earliest or most primitive societies were forms of what Marx typically calls "primitive communism."

Even though Marx's claims about primitive communism are ultimately empirical, he begins not with the empirically but the conceptually most primitive possible mode of production. Note once more that no anthropological or historical research was necessary to make this claim. His only argument for primitive communism is the deduction just outlined. It deduces from the necessary conditions for the possibility of exploitation (in feudalism and capitalism, for example) the existence of a society so unsophisticated that exploitation is not possible. It is this kind of reasoning that forms the basis, the primitive starting point, of conceptual dialectic.

Marx then goes on to reason, with more empirical evidence in this case, that the eventual emergence of a surplus product, which is the result of technical advances in production (like more sophisticated tools) as well as the capacity to preserve food, means that for the first time in history the population will start to expand, the division of labour will become more complex, and, most importantly, not everyone in the society must produce. If initially this means that the elderly or infirm can be supported without working or that religious authorities need not produce, its eventual upshot is the formation of classes. A dominant class, according to Marx, comes to live off the surplus created by a subordinate class. This is a case of domination, since it is sustained only by force – ideological or physical.

By criticizing Marx's claims about primitive communism and the emergence of exploitation, it is possible to discern criteria very helpful in the determination of Hegel's own starting point. Oddly, Marxists do not say *why* domination and, in particular, exploitation, occur at the moment of the creation of a surplus. Even if we grant that class domination can arise only when the society can create a surplus product,[13] we have identified herein a necessary but not a sufficient condition of class domination since there is no reason why a surplus product even motivates, much less necessitates, the emergence of exploitation.[14] There are at least three other options for a society that produces more total product than it needs to survive. Such a society could a) share its surplus equally, b) cut down on the amount of work carried out each day and eliminate the surplus, or c) expend its surplus in potlatch-like festivals or on other forms luxurious living.[15] Indeed, it is possible to conceive every set of productive forces combined with a *co-operative* and non-exploitive mode of social relations *rather than* one based on domination and exploitation. Any form of hunting and gathering, of crop cultivation and herding of domesticated animals, of industry – indeed any set of productive forces we can imagine – could in principle be carried out by democratically organized co-operation that contains no exploitation whatever. Obviously most were not, but the key question before us is *why not*?

A Marxist might respond that co-operatively organized modes of production would not maximize production because exploitation (in a form corresponding to each mode of production) is the most efficient and productive way of generating wealth. This claim is probably not true even on its own terms (nearly all empirical evidence shows that co-operation may be at least or even more productive than exploitation),[16] but let us assume for the sake of argument that it is. Exploitation may well be the most productive form of social relations in general, but this argument only introduces a new undefended premise, and one that is even more difficult to justify than the first. On what grounds could we claim that humans always organize their entire social life around the priority of the maximization of production? The best possible answer to this question, it seems, is that conditions of *lack* will always motivate human beings to create as much product as they can. Marx himself uses something like this claim as a premise in his famous argument in *Capital*: "The realm of freedom really begins only where labour determined by necessity and external expediency ends; it lies by its very nature beyond the sphere of material production proper." That is, work is driven by the necessity of meeting basic needs in a context defined by a lack of adequate resources. Given that resources are fewer than needed, it is inevitable that some will have more than others. While capitalism is the first mode of production to create the means to eliminate necessity (by creating abundance), the alienation of private property artificially prolongs necessity. Thus, Marx continues, "Freedom, in this sphere, can consist only in this, that socialized man, the associated producers, govern the human metabolism with nature in a rational way, bringing it under their collective control instead of being dominated by it as a blind power; accomplishing it with the least expenditure of energy and in conditions most worthy and appropriate for their human nature."[17]

This argument, whatever its other merits, does not justify the premise that Marx needs here. While the working class may well experience its existence constantly in terms of material lack, this is certainly not true of the dominating class in most modes of production, which typically lives in luxury or at least at a level of comfort far beyond the realm of mere necessity. And yet it is this dominant class that sets the terms for production. If the dominant class is not driven by necessity, then neither is the mode of production in general. Moreover, as Marxist scholar Ellen Meiksins Wood claims, arguably the only mode of production that systematically seeks to maximize production is capitalism itself.[18] Thus, even if we grant the improbable premise that exploitation relations are the most economically productive, there are no grounds to claim that exploitation arises out of conditions of lack. Even more fundamentally, if the problem under consideration is what a society will do with its *surplus*, it is hard to imagine why it would be animated by a notion of *lack*.

It is possible that Marx made the following argument to justify the emergence of class exploitation in history:

A A fully developed communist society presupposes a state of material abundance, which itself arises only from highly developed productive forces.
B In order to develop the productive forces sufficiently to create this abundance, severe working conditions are necessary over a great period of time, especially during the period of industrial capitalism, such as to generate very high levels of productivity.
C Workers would never impose these severe working conditions on themselves.
D Therefore, class domination is necessary to create the abundance necessary for communism.[19]

Yet this argument is blatantly teleological in a way that dialecticians must reject. The conditions necessary for communist society (an abundance created by highly developed productive forces) compose the key premise used to explain why class domination emerged millennia before anyone even dreamed of communism. The argument literally claims that the first societies to create surplus product opted for class domination rather than co-operative common property, increased leisure, and/or potlatch festivals because the eventual goal of communism, many thousands of years in the future, demanded that they do so.[20] This is preposterous, and even if scholars have found certain passages in Marx that support it, the argument is so poor that I would at least like to think that Marx would never have entertained it.

Yet if this is so, Marxists are left with no explanation of why human beings dominate and exploit each other. Indeed, there appears to be nothing in the character of productive forces or their development that necessitates or even motivates domination and exploitation. Marx may well be one of the great theorists of how domination and exploitation take place, but he does not say *why* it takes place.

Interestingly, there are texts in Marx in which he seems to reject the idea that class exploitation is necessary, at least at the moment of its supposed emergence – the first creation of a surplus product. Following this lead will be of great service in determining our starting point in the conceptual dialectic of society. In the following passage, Marx charts the emergence of *rent*, the appropriation of a surplus value by a landowner. He says that "The natural productivity of [the direct producer's] labour must be great enough ... to allow him the possibility of surplus labour over and above the labour needed to satisfy his own indispensible needs. It is not this possibility that creates rent; only the compulsion makes the possibility a reality."[21] As Marx makes clear in the last sentence, the surplus that makes rent possible requires a further gesture not deducible from the surplus itself: a *compulsion* placed on some human beings by others. One of the most important Marxist theorists of the twentieth century, Ernest Mandel, also grants this point without then following up its implications. "As soon as a considerable surplus has been formed, the possibility appears for a part of society to give up productive labour, obtaining leisure at the expense of the remainder of society."[22] He goes on to confess, "This is obviously only a possibility: it is equally possible that the leisure thus won may reduce the working time of all the producers and be put to use for extra-economic activities by everyone." He then even cites some anthropological evidence that such sharing has indeed taken place in certain contexts.[23] Mandel goes further still: "Once there is a surplus of products

... then the conditions have been set for a struggle over how this surplus will be shared."[24] He implicitly recognizes, in other words, not only that there is nothing about the surplus itself or the development of productive forces that requires the formation of classes, but that there seems to be a temptation among certain members of the society to manipulate and indeed dominate others, which emerges in the "struggle" over how to divide the limited surplus. In conclusion, then, we must turn away from the human dialectic with nature (of productive forces within modes of production) and toward the dialectic between humans themselves. It is a struggle between people that leads to exploitation and class society.

That is, if the temptation to dominate others exists in the human condition, we must recognize three things, the third of which is most fundamentally important. First, this temptation to dominate could have and indeed likely did emerge in other forms prior to the formation of an economic surplus and exploitation. This may have involved, for example, the domination of one gender over the other (typically, though not necessarily, men over women), or it may have been a kind of political domination, by virtue of which a certain specific group monopolizes decision-making powers in the community. It could even function in terms of economic production, by which a certain group is forced to do the most tedious, arduous, boring, or dangerous work. Second, granted this first point, if the temptation to dominate others exists independently of and prior to economic surpluses, then the fundamental philosophical issue is not *class* domination, but *domination as such*. Or again, domination is a genus of which class domination, exploitation, is a species. Other species of the genus would include gender, political groupings, physical characteristics, outsiders, race, ethnicity, and so on.[25] Third, dialectical political philosophy requires an explanation of the emergence of the domination of some human beings over others as well as the character and prospects of its elimination. Marx's theory does not provide this explanation.

In sum, the dialectic of productive forces might reveal much about the struggle in which human beings have long engaged with nature, but since the dialectic of freedom and domination cannot be reduced to economic production, then we must look in the direction that Mandel points: to the *struggle* between people.[26] Now, problematizing Marx's starting point does not validate Hegel's, but gestures in its direction. The key issue at stake here is the domination of some people by others, and this is the clue I shall soon follow up.

Before doing so, however, I want to explore whether the state of nature theorists, Hobbes, Locke, and Rousseau, whom I discussed very briefly above, might help locate the starting point of our conceptual dialectic. After all, I suggested that their state of nature theories were also conceptual dialectics of sorts. But plainly their idea of the state of nature is not actually a society at all. And yet, why not start the conceptual dialectic of society with a non-society – with Hobbes's state of nature? To put this another way, the notion of "society," at least in some essential sense, is a *universal* – it is a community, a having-in-common. On what grounds do we then start the dialectic with the universal? Why not start with the singular self, as do Hobbes, Locke, and Rousseau? We have already encountered the answer to this question. Were we to start with the singular self, it would enter into the struggle to the death and come, by means of its own dialectical self-education, to recognize that the key to its freedom is the co-operative community of mutual recognition – a universal. The only satisfaction of singular desire is to be recognized, and thus to start with this abstraction refutes itself. Moreover, it refutes itself not because (as in the state of nature theorists) we come to recognize the need to compromise our freedom for the sake of security, but because the mutual recognition of a society is the realization of freedom and not its partial self-sacrifice. This argument, as I noted in chapter 1, appears in chapter 4 of the *Phenomenology*. Indeed, we are always already in community with each other, and the self-abstraction of the free will that is typical of liberal theory is derivative of the more original sociability of human experience. In other words, a differentiated universal, a community, begins the conceptual and empirical dialectic. We are, in other words, always already in societies – in modes of relating to each other. Yet if neither the liberal nor the Marxist accounts give us our starting point, where are we to begin?

3 NATURE, THE GODS, AND THE "FIRST" SOCIETY

An analysis of Marx's philosophy reveals that it is necessary to tackle not only the dynamics of our relationship with nature in work, but also the character of the ways in which we relate to each other. When I discussed the concept of "relating to others" in chapter 1, I asked what the most primitive, least sophisticated possible way of relating to others could be. The answer was *appetitive desire* or, more informally, "pure selfishness." This is the attitude that denies others any autonomous status at all and considers them solely in terms of how they might be useful or obstructive to the desires of the self. If we use this starting point as a clue and say that the dialectic of "relating to others" starts with the denial of relationship, then we should entertain the hypothesis that the conceptual dialectic of "society" begins with the definition of *a society that denies it is a society*. But what could this mean?

At the very least, any notion of a free society must acknowledge that it involves a plurality of individuals who develop norms and customs, written or unwritten, of relating to each other. One need not commit oneself to what it means to be an "individual," nor to the relative ways in which norms and customs form or are formed by individuals, nor even to the characteristic types of unity or disunity normally ascribed to societies in academic debates. For example, to say that a society is a plurality of individuals who have over time created laws, customs, and norms that structure their interaction does not presume that this society is unified merely as an aggregate of separate, atomistic individuals or, on the other hand, as an organic body-politic. We know as empirical historians that the norms, laws, images, and techniques of the many thousands of different societies that have developed over time did not appear out of the blue, but have evolved over time as people have worked out how to relate to nature and to each other in groups. By virtue of the variety of different societies we can observe in history and indeed in our own contemporary world, we know that the norms and customs that guide these societies were not determined in advance, but were, to a varying but always significant degree, contingent upon the circumstances and interpretations of the members of each society as it developed in time. Thus we can say that the concrete-lived experience of the formation of a society presupposes, at the very least, some interpretive and creative *action* – a society's members have made interpretations, deliberations, and choices about how to navigate within the world in which they find themselves. This does not mean that interpretive, creative action is the essence of society or its most important or prevalent feature, but is a minimum and common condition of anything that we would consider to be a society. A Marxist would claim that interpretive decisions with culture and politics are contingent upon the interpretive decisions that develop productive forces, but she nonetheless acknowledges the importance of interpretive choice. A methodological individualist or a Rawlsian would grant interpretive choice a greater significance than would a communitarian, but no one denies its importance. That is to say, we can posit that societies are to some significant degree autonomous; they give their character to themselves. Once again, we need not at this point debate what precisely this means, but content ourselves, for the moment at least, with the conclusion that the vast array of differences one finds in historical societies is clear evidence that autonomy is a necessary, if not a sufficient condition for understanding what a society is. Moreover, modern Western nations have typically adopted this rough and ready notion of autonomy as the key feature of their juridical-imaginative systems of recognition, such that individual citizens are guaranteed the right to autonomy – the right to determine their own lives as they see fit.

Even more importantly, these notions of autonomy and free choice are considered by most philosophers in our tradition to be the most important feature of contemporary Western society. There may be debates about precisely what freedom should be, about the institutions that would fulfill it, or the ways in which it might be undermined, but there is consensus that the central theme around which all debate revolves is the nature of freedom. The communitarian who values the distinctive cultural values of a specific ethnic group as equal to or greater than the importance of the free choice of atomistic individuals still makes a claim to the self-determination, the freedom, of that ethnic group. She claims that the distinctive tradition of interpretive, creative action that has made that culture what it is deserves the recognition of others since distinctive virtue lies in its being the result of interpretive, creative actions that are different from other cultures and are then valuable as ends in themselves.

The general concept of a society, therefore, might go something like this: A society is a collectivity of human beings who have agreed (implicitly or explicitly) over time to abide by norms (laws, written or unwritten) which they have *determined* by their own action, by their own interpretation, deliberation, and choice in light of the demands placed upon them by nature and their relations with each other and outsiders. We might add to this that as societies develop capacities in the various realms of social, economic, and political life, these capacities have become like habits – ingrained skills that people need not explicitly think about in order to live. Such habits would be found in the society's language, religious belief and ritual, economic abilities, technological capacities, customs of mutual relation, and so on.

More generally, we can say that the concrete-lived experience of all societies is to have determined themselves in these ways. Moreover, since these societies have so determined themselves, they are *self-determining* – they are instantiations of *freedom*. It might be objected that most, if not all, societies are not free; they have created systems of domination, manipulation, exclusion, and exploitation. The problem with this objection is that it articulates a certain kind of self-determination (one free of various kinds of domination) and not domination itself. This kind of objection is precluded by dialectical philosophy on the grounds that it introduces external and thus arbitrary criteria with which to criticize a certain society in the name of another one. We must not simply and arbitrarily posit that domination and exploitation are just or unjust, but observe how the dialectic of society determines their respective status. We are here presupposing not some particular form of self-determination or autonomy, but only the notion that human beings create their own societies such that modes of domination and exploitation are themselves just as much the result of dynamics of human relationship as are the legal, customary, and moral systems that sanctify or criticize them. We are not justified, in short, in imposing our own notion of self-determination on other societies and instead must consider self-determination to be nothing other than the claim that all societies have made themselves what they are.

These reflections on the general nature of society allow us now to determine the most primitive conceptual form of society and, thus, the starting point for our dialectic. Once again, if the most primitive form of relating to others was to deny that relationship altogether, then the most primitive form of society is a society that denies it is a society. This would amount to describing a society that denies that it is autonomous, that denies that it is self-determining. We may know that it has determined itself on the basis of its own interpretations, deliberations, and choices because other societies with which we can compare it made different interpretations, deliberations, and choices, but it does not know this about itself. In Hegel's technical language, the dialectic of social life of society *in general* is the study of that which is "*in and for itself*" – it is a self-created act of freedom. However, to determine the starting point of the conceptual dialectic, one needs a society that is not *for itself* what it is *in itself*: "But this being-in-and-for-itself is at first ... only *in-itself,* it is spiritual *Substance*." That is, the society that is only in-itself is not aware that it has created itself and is, indeed, only dimly aware, if it is aware at all, of the creative power of human freedom. "For itself" (according to itself, to its juridical-imaginative self-understanding) it is not free, autonomous, and self-determined, but thinks of itself as a reflection of the predetermined forces that it typically finds articulated by nature or the gods. Historically oriented philosophers can see that such a society is an embodiment of self-determining freedom, but the members of this, the most primitive, society do not know that about themselves. We must teach ourselves in history that we are free, such that the spiritual Substance "must also be this for itself."[27]

This is a society, then, that thinks of itself not as self-determined but as *predetermined* and indeed *other determined*. Or again, it is not a society that thinks of itself as autonomous, but as heteronomous. It is a society whose members understand that the laws and customs they follow were determined not by themselves but by some "other" – typically, something like "the natural order of things" or "the gods." These laws are not authored by humans, this society thinks, and thus they must necessarily be followed in a manner that precludes the interpretive dubiousness of anything like a skeptical consciousness – that is, precludes their own interpretation, deliberation, and choice as singular selves or collectivities.[28] Moreover, such a society will typically create cultural images that reinforce this belief and that warn of dire punishments for those who transgress them. We have thus outlined the juridical-imaginative structure of the primary or primitive society in our conceptual dialectic.

Indeed, such a society arguably "forgets" that it has authored itself precisely because the qualitative degree of its self-authorship is so slight. Such a society may take the biological differences among humans to be constitutive of the "natural order of things" and indeed to be the will of the gods. For this very reason, it may not even think of humanity as a single, unified form of being. It is the task of anthropologists and archaeologists to tell us the details of these societies, but suffice it to say that the most primitive society, the starting point of the conceptual dialectic of society, is the society that denies it is a society precisely by thinking of itself not as self-determined, but as predetermined by nature or the gods. Hegel calls this "ethicality" (*Sittlichkeit*) – it is the *Ethical Society*.

It is possible to get a better sense of what is most essential about the Ethical Society by returning to Marx's concerns about domination and exploitation. The Ethical Society denies it is a society precisely by not recognizing that its own interpretive choices, its own freedom, has informed its juridical-imaginative structure. It thinks it is determined by natural imperatives personified as the gods. As a matter of historical record, and from our point of view, these kinds of society are typically characterized by the domination and exploitation of some people by others, the subordination of women, for example, but this is not necessarily so. If an Ethical Society considers itself determined by something like the natural order, it may well use the categories of biological nature as that which it considers most fundamental – mothering, fathering, the satisfaction of biological needs of eating, keeping warm, sleeping. Indeed, it may well constantly fight against neighbouring peoples. For all these reasons, it is easy to imagine that those members of its society who are best endowed by nature with the capacities necessary for this society to meet its needs will be dominant within it, not just by virtue of their personal capacities, but by virtue of an ontological judgment that men by virtue of their superior physical strength (or, alternatively, women, by virtue of their magical powers to create life) are superior. Typically, it should not come as a shock that a society for which physical strength in the hunt or in war is of predominant importance would be patriarchal. It would not be in the least surprising, if the dominant members of this society successfully ruled others, that this dominance would be considered to be natural. That is, the gods will that some rule over others, and those who are naturally superior in physical strength are obviously the superior beings *by nature*. Indeed, some, like the barbarians for the Greeks, would be considered so inferior as to merit the status of nothing more than slaves because, as Aristotle says, "It is clear ... that some men are by nature free, and others slaves, and that for these latter slavery is both expedient and right."[29] The slave is not merely a captured free man who is forced to work at the end of a sword; he is ontologically inferior to his masters, and may well believe that of himself with as much conviction as do his masters. The Greek citizen thus does not consider that he is dominating his wife or exploiting his slaves, even if we would hold that to be manifestly obvious on both counts. To him, *citizen*, *wife*, and *slave* are natural categories ordained by the gods, and the status of each is not doubted even by the greatest minds of that cultural tradition.

However, it is not strictly speaking necessary that an Ethical Society be patriarchal or involve exploitation. It is possible indeed to find a huge variation, including ethical societies that are matriarchal, share common property, and involve various forms of proto-democratic governance. However, if they are an Ethical Society, they are not matriarchal because they are proto-feminists nor are they democratic because they grasp the demands of freedom, but because through their own (not recognized) interpretive acts, they have implicitly laid claim to the fact that the gods (nature) mandate matriarchy or some form of consultative decision-making. Indeed, a traditional society that is not threatened with war and that has plentiful food would have no particularly strong motivation to elevate male strength and bellicose virtue nor, given the abundance that surrounds it, to translate any form of superiority that it does posit (say of women, who hold the magical power of creating life) into forms of exploitation or domination. However, they are no less obedient to the will of the gods than the war-like, slave society, and even the members of a peaceful, egalitarian matriarchy may well come to see themselves as ontologically inferior should they have the misfortune of being enslaved by a far more aggressive group of human beings with more sophisticated weaponry and the capacity to exercise domination.

The key to the Ethical Society, then, is that its members are dominated "by the gods," by the natural order that they themselves, unwittingly, have posited as their own authority. They are very likely to have forms of domination and exploitation because there is little in the character of nature, saturated as it is with competition, violence, and hierarchy, that would make them think that the gods willed anything different. Indeed, the natural differences between human beings correspond in many ways to the hierarchies of nature. Or again, on their own terms, these societies do not dominate or exploit at all, but are obedient to the imperatives of nature as expressed in the commands of the gods in which it is mandated that some control the destinies of others. Some might well be slaves to others, but in a broader and more important sense they are all slaves to the gods and, as such, the logical structure of mastery and slavery that I outlined in chapter 1 applies to the society *in toto*.

Since categories like domination and exploitation emerge in history, which we then retrospectively apply to ethical societies, our task is not to engage in anachronistic slander against ethical societies, but, as good dialecticians, to study ethical societies in order to see if and how our own categories of freedom, domination, and exploitation emerge from within the crucible of the Ethical Society itself (and, indeed, other forms of society further down the road of the conceptual dialectic).

I will shortly delve into the logic of this "Ethical Society," but I want to quickly return to a philosophical objection to conceptual dialectic that I discussed briefly in chapter 1. That is, by seeking a "primitive" starting point for the dialectic, are we not creating a circular argument? It seems that we have defined a society on the basis of (something like) *our own notion* of what society is – a collectivity of individuals who create their own laws and customs. We have then, on the basis of this, chosen to condemn its contrary as "primitive." We should thus not be surprised, this criticism would proceed, if this argument ends up affirming our own notion of society as its conclusion if only because it presupposes this definition from the beginning. Surely this is the hallmark of the circular argument.

Yet, I have said from the beginning that dialectics is a kind of *recollective* history. This history would, without a doubt, need to be empirical, but Hegel gives us another form of historical method as well – a conceptual history. It is true that we consider ourselves to be free interpreters, deliberators, and choosers. We read and write books such as this one and we raise skeptical doubts about the arguments we find therein (one such skeptical doubt I am addressing at this moment). The fact that we do this is proof that we are, at least in some important sense, right to say that we are interpreters, deliberators, and choosers. Moreover, we have built a whole society, more or less, on these principles. We have juridically enshrined the right to free thought and action in our constitutions, and our cultural imaginary is full of poems, novels, films, television, and so on that affirm the importance of free thought and that criticize infractions against it. So our task here is not some kind of a priori philosophy, but the study of the conceptual (rather than empirical) history of the stance that we undoubtedly already hold. We are searching for the philosophically informed route that has allowed us to reach the point that we now inhabit. Once more, the dialectic is recollective.

But this is not enough of a response to the objection, for even if there is a kind of circular reconstruction to conceptual dialectic, this kind of argument is emphatically not circular in another and more directly relevant sense. What we have done here is establish where we should start our argument; we have identified its primordial point of departure. But we have not decided in advance where this argument will take us. We may well postulate that the Ethical Society is very different from our society, and that we should start with a study of it, but this in no way predetermines how this analysis will unfold. The argument is only circular in the traditional sense if we literally import our definition of society as a premise in some kind of refutation of the Ethical Society. But this strategy not only violates the traditional canons of argumentation, it also violates the canons (if we may call them that) of dialectical argumentation. As we saw above, the principle of critique in dialectic can only be immanent: a society, or anything else involved in a dialectical examination, can generate the terms of its criticism only from within itself. We import no foreign criteria of any kind, and simply look at the society itself to see if any contradictions emerge from within it. If the society proves itself capable of sustaining itself without contradiction, then the dialectic stops. Were this to happen with the Ethical Society, we would simply conclude that there are (at least) two kinds of society – the Ethical Society and ours – and that a dialectical relationship between the two is impossible to establish. To summarize then, we have used "our" definition of society to establish that the Ethical Society should be our logical, primordial starting point. But we will be careful not to use this definition of society as a premise in any kind of argument against this society. If the Ethical Society is to be criticized at all, it must come to criticize itself.

I will work with Hegel's study of "ethicality" in the "Spirit" chapter of the *Phenomenology of Spirit*, but will also turn to his work of empirical dialectic, *The Lectures on the Philosophy of History*, for help. We should thus think of the *Phenomenology* as providing the *concept*, and the *Philosophy of History* as its *existence* – together they form the *Idea*. In the *Phenomenology* Hegel readily employs the Greek world as his working example, so it will be the Greek political structure and Greek cultural life that will form the juridical-imaginary example of the Ethical Society. Hegel's actual observations about the character of Greek society are, of course, debatable, but they are also not necessary to the argument. It is quite possible that a historian or classicist might raise valid objections showing that the Greek world is not in truth a good example of the Ethical Society, but I will, to forward the argument, provisionally agree with Hegel that it is.

Before turning to the beginning of our conceptual dialectic, it is important to clarify one further matter. I will successively study three societies in the following three chapters: the Ethical Society (*Sittlichket*), the Condition of Right (*Rechtszustand*), and Absolute Freedom (*absolut Freiheit*). Hegel picks historical examples for all three forms – for the Ethical Society, as I have just said, the ancient Greek world; for the Condition of Right, imperial Rome; and for Absolute Freedom, France in the era of the Revolution. It is important to emphasize still further, however, that these three historical societies are examples and nothing more.[30] As conceptual dialectic, the *Phenomenology of Spirit* has as its goal not to tell the empirical history of Western civilization but its *conceptual history*. Thus the studies in the *Phenomenology* are only roughly modeled on the example societies and are not in the last analysis dependent upon the claims that historians may well want to make.

With this in mind, I turn to the first of our concepts of social and political life – the Ethical Society.

4

The Dialectic of the Ethical Society

The Ethical Society is the society that is not aware that it is a society. This is to say, the Ethical Society does not recognize about itself that it is self-determining. Its explicit view of itself is that human life is determined by other forces – natural or divine forces. Or again, it is a society that thinks of itself in heteronomous terms – it laws come from "elsewhere." The Ethical Society is unaware that it is a result of a history in which its members have, over time, created its juridical structures and its cultural images by interpreting its existential situation.

It is important to recall here that Hegel's purpose in writing the *Phenomenology of Spirit* was not to carry out the dialectic of sociopolitical life and, therefore, he arrives at a study of ethical life in the course of a different train of argument. Instead of beginning with ethical life as the most primitive possible society, qua society, Hegel makes the transition to the study of the Ethical Society, which begins chapter 6, "Spirit," by virtue of a dialectical criticism of reason as "lawgiving" and "law testing" at the end of chapter 5, "Reason."[1] His goal is to show that abstract rationality (based on universals abstracted from particulars) is incapable of testing laws because it will show both the law and its contrary to be rational (once again, in this abstract sense of reason). Typically, Kant's categorical imperative, *that one should act in such a way that the maxim of one's action could be a universal law*, shows why one should always tell the truth. After all, the maxim of the action of telling the truth is that "I should always tell the truth," and this maxim can be a universal law without contradiction – "one should always tell the truth." The maxim of the liar, on the other hand, is that *everyone should tell the truth except me*, which is plainly self-contradictory. But if the maxim of the liar is construed as *one should always lie when it is in one's interest to do so* it is every bit as universalizable as is the maxim to always tell the truth.[2] Thus, if this form of abstract rationality (a political version of which I examine in depth below) is incapable of generating any kind of binding imperative, then we should look instead to the concrete human experience of imperative, of duty, to a society whose members purely and simply experience its laws as immediately binding – precisely the society of ethical life which lives out the imperatives of the gods – *Sittlichkeit*.[3] The abstract and mediated rationality of chapter 5, "Reason," thus gives way to the concrete and immediate rationality of the Ethical Society, the starting point of chapter 6, "Spirit." In short, even though Hegel's project in the *Phenomenology* leads him to study the Ethical Society as an answer to the *reductio ad absurdum* of the abstract rationality of the understanding (*Verstand*), there is not thereby any problem with taking up the dialectic of sociopolitical life with his study of *Sittlichkeit* as our guide. The study of Ethical Society will be valid both in terms of its role in the "education of self-consciousness" (Hegel's project in the *Phenomenology*) and as the first step in the conceptual dialectic of sociopolitical life (my project here).

I THE JURIDICAL-IMAGINATIVE STRUCTURE OF THE ETHICAL SOCIETY

I now want to clarify the juridical-imaginative structure of mutual recognition in the Ethical Society. This will be, once again, a study of how this society formally organizes itself (juridical recognition) and how it understands itself (imaginative recognition). Hegel's working example of the Ethical Society is, as I have said, the ancient Greek world.[4] Hegel's analysis here can be helpfully understood as taking place in two parts. In the *Phenomenology of Spirit* Hegel focuses on establishing the structure of the Ethical Society and the origin of contradiction within it. In order to do this, he works very closely with Sophocles' great tragedy *Antigone*. In the *Philosophy of History*, however, Hegel places far more emphasis on the later development of this contradiction, especially in the Sophists and the figure of Socrates. Together, these two accounts of the Greek world give a clear sense of why Hegel thinks it fails, and I will, therefore, attend to both.

Hegel begins with the *Antigone*. Creon, the Theban king, has, on pain of death, banned the burial of Antigone's brother, Polyneices, who has been killed in a battle for political control of Thebes and hence branded as a traitor. Antigone, assiduously following her duty as a family member to bury her brother, defies the king and buries her brother. Antigone gives the following argument in defiance of Creon and in so doing articulates the essence of duty in the ethical world.

> And I never thought your announcements
> Could give you – a mere human being –
> Power to trample the gods' unfailing,
> Unwritten laws. These laws weren't made now
> Or yesterday. They live for all time,
> And no one knows when they came into the light.
> No man could frighten me into taking on
> The gods' penalty for breaking such a law.[5]

We see here quite plainly that in Antigone's view the truly authoritative law has its origin not in the interpretive, negotiated activity of the ancient Greeks themselves but in the will of the gods that has been handed down from time immemorial. Antigone feels a visceral, immediate imperative to bury her brother, a responsibility to a divine law whose authority cannot be overridden by the mere human authority of even a king. Indeed, these divine laws exist beyond time, for "no one knows when they came to light" and they will exist forever – "They live for all time."[6] Thus one might well read Sophocles' intention in the *Antigone* as a conservative warning against those who might have begun to cast doubt on the laws – something his younger contemporary, Socrates, would do wholeheartedly. I return to that issue below. But at the very least, it should be clear that we have before us the primitive starting point of our dialectic of the concept "society." The Ethical Society is heteronomous precisely because its juridical-imaginative structures are predicated on divine imperatives whose authority is completely prior to and independent of human interpretive, creative action.

Of course, the argument here will be circular and non-dialectical if, as I discussed just above, I criticize the Greeks in general and Antigone in particular for not knowing the history of her own people and for artificially projecting onto her gods what was the work of her very human ancestors. I must instead take the Ethical Society on its own terms, identifying its juridical-imaginative and its concrete-lived structures in order to understand if and how it will generate its own immanent criteria of self-criticism. Should no such self-criticism emerge, the dialectical engagement stops in its tracks, and I claim the knowledge that the Ethical Society can subsist in harmony with itself. In other words, I may accuse the Ethical Society, from my exterior vantage point, of naively obeying divine laws which I know perfectly well to have been the creation not of gods but of the Ethical Society's own ancestors, but this form of external criticism is of no value whatever in dialectical philosophy. Faced with such a criticism, Antigone herself would simply deny that humans had created the laws and, indeed, find any such suggestion absurd and impious. The Ethical Society must *find itself* in contradiction, and must learn, strictly on its own terms, why its own juridical-imaginative structure of mutual recognition is inadequate.

The laws of the gods are understood to exist prior to any human engagement with them, and these laws are taken to determine the eternally valid duties of the individual and citizen. This could not possibly be a society in which individuals cast doubt on these laws, for even doubting them is already to relocate authority in the *mediating* mind of the doubter rather than in the *immediate* authority of the laws themselves. The member of the Ethical Society thus experiences this system of law not as a repressive force acting as an agent of domination, but as one's own innermost truth and duty. Of course, the origin of this inner truth is the external power of the gods, but Antigone and the Greek consciousness in general experience an immediate union between themselves, the laws, and their divine authors. That is, Antigone's most immediate ethical impulses are one and the same as these very duties. If indeed her relationship to these laws was mediated by her own reflective consent, then the laws would lose their eternal and absolute authority, for that authority would then depend on her as the mediating agent. "As *ethical* consciousness, self-consciousness is the *simple, pure orientation* to the ethical essentiality, or *duty*. Neither arbitrariness, nor even struggle, nor indecisiveness is present in it ... Instead, the ethical essentiality is for it what is immediate, unwavering, and without contradiction."[7] Thus the first characteristic of the Ethical Society is that its laws are the *immediate* truth of its members. The Greek world of "custom" and "habit," Hegel says in his *Lectures on the Philosophy of History*, does not contain the reflective doubt of the singular ego. "While Custom and Wont is the form in which the Right is willed and done, that form is a stable one, and has not yet admitted into it the foe of [unreflected] immediacy – reflection and subjectivity of the Will."[8]

The Ethical Society not only has the structure of the immediacy of duty; it is also what I called above a "good infinite." The members of this society are not isolated units each of which pursues its own interests ad infinitum. This is the so called "bad infinite" found in, for example, the set of all whole numbers and in atomistic liberalism. Rather, the identity of each individual is established on the basis of his or her internal relationship to the unified purposiveness of the society as a totality. The individual in this society does not, therefore, perceive his or her fellow Greeks as limitations on freedom but as the very condition for its fulfillment. The community is that in and through which one cultivates the capacity to thrive as an individual, and one's thriving as an individual is, generally speaking at least, a direct and unproblematic contribution to the good of the society as a whole. To put this in the terms of contemporary political thought, there is no gap or even tension between the good of the individual and the common good. Like an artwork, the society is a harmonious and thus *beautiful* unity of diversity. Of course there might be cases where the good or well-being of individuals and the society do not happen to harmonize, but this is not a systematic issue.

Hegel's choice of the Greek polis to exemplify the Ethical Society might seem odd given what Hegel explicitly says about it. He describes the polis as divided into two mutually supporting spheres. The family, which is overseen by women, is the realm of unconscious immediacy in which the Penates, the family gods, determine the imperatives of the "divine law." These are the laws that Antigone follows. The divine law, however, operates in harmony with the "human law."[9] By the human law Hegel is certainly not referring to some kind of secular realm, but to a human-governed institution, the state, which takes responsibility for making the decisions that allow the gods' will to be actualized in that sphere. If the divine law of the family typically operates in the form of immediate imperatives, "You must bury your deceased family members," the human law of the state typically operates as an answer to a type of question, "How are we, citizens of Athens and children of Athena, best to carry out the law of the goddess? Should we go to war against Sparta or create the conditions for peace? Should we tax this commodity from Corinth or allow free trade? Should we build this altar to Athena and if so, how elaborate should it be and how much should we spend on it?" Thus, the choice of this society as emblematic of ethical immediacy is perhaps odd precisely because the state already seems to be engaged in the kind of mediation-interpretation that we have just said is excluded from the Ethical Society. Indeed, while the divine law of the family is "immediate essence," the human law of the state is "self-conscious doing" that "cultivates and preserves itself by labouring"; if the divine, familial law is an "unconscious, still inward concept," the human law of the state is "open" and "self-conscious," and "higher" and "valid in the light of day." It is "reflected into itself."[10] In short, if the divine law names the ethical *immediacy* of duty, the human law, even if only implicitly, is the self-cultivating, labouring, reflective realm of *mediation*. Yet this implicit character of mediation in the human law is precisely what is at issue. Political leaders, while grappling with difficult choices, still understand themselves as answering to divine imperatives. More generally, and as we will see in more detail shortly, the divine and human laws are both products of self-determination, even if primitively. But the agents of this creativity, the Greeks themselves, are unaware of this. Indeed, Hegel points out that their own experience of ethical imperatives functions much like natural causation rather than human self-determination. "In this customary morality," Hegel says, "laws assume the form of a necessity of Nature."[11]

Indeed, Hegel chooses the Greek world as his example because it was, in his opinion, the apogee of the Ethical Society and, as apogee, it was the society that ultimately destroyed (carried out the empirical self-destruction of) the form of Ethical Society. A more obvious example of the Ethical Society might be, as I intimated earlier, a hunting and gathering society or a society of primitive agriculture made up of small villages where there is little or no sign of deliberative political institutions like the state or auto-reflective cultural practices like Greek drama and philosophy. There is nothing wrong with taking such an example, but its dialectic would show a tendency to gradually create precisely the differentiated spheres Hegel finds in the Greek world: the divine law of the family versus the human law of the state. That is, the dynamic of family life generates the need for what will gradually become a state.

In the last paragraphs of the *Philosophy of Right* and in the *Philosophy of History* Hegel begins his dialectic with a society of "pure immediacy," a society with no self-reflective human law. Since his discussion in these cases is of "World History," it is an example of empirical dialectic and, as such, he differentiates what he calls the "The Oriental Realm" from the "Greek Realm." He defines the Oriental Realm in much the same terms that he uses for *Sittlichkeit* in general, and especially the family, in the *Phenomenology of Spirit*. "The world-view of this first realm is inwardly undivided and substantial, and it originates in the natural whole of patriarchal society ... Within this magnificent whole, the individual personality has no rights and disappears altogether, external nature is immediately divine or an adornment of the god."[12] In the Greek Realm, however, the "substantial unity of the infinite and the finite is present ... [and] ... the principle of personal individuality accordingly emerges, though it is not yet engrossed in itself but still retains its ideal unity."[13] Hegel repeatedly insists that the Greek world is *not merely natural* and is, then, already a mediated result. "The submersion in Nature no longer exists" in the Greek world, and individuals are not "patriarchally united by a bond of *Nature*, but realize a union through some other medium – through Law and Custom having the sanction of Spirit."[14] That is, Hegel selects the Greek world as his example in the *Phenomenology*'s conceptual dialectic because it has already started to manifest the contradiction that is the potential downfall of all ethical societies: beauty, wisdom, the study of nature, and the human law of the state. Hegel allows the Greek world to stand in for both realms in the *Phenomenology of Spirit* and he had good reason to do so. In the terms of the conceptual dialectic, the Oriental and Greek worlds are the same species, for the latter comes face to face with the contradictions that are barely developed within the former.[15]

Indeed, an exploration of the numerous references in Hegel's text to two trilogies of Greek tragic drama, Sophocles' Theban plays (*Oedipus Rex*, *Oedipus at Colonnus*, and *Antigone*) and Aeschylus's *Oresteia* (*Agamemnon*, *The Libation Bearers*, and *Eumenides*) helps clarify precisely why the Greek world is such an effective example of the Ethical Society and its emergent contradiction. In the *Eumenides*, for example, the responsibilities of what we might call the divine law require Orestes both to fulfill the imperatives of the family, by revenging the murder of his father, Agamemnon, but simultaneously transgress the divine law, precisely because he must kill his own mother, who betrayed and then murdered her husband. That is, the very fulfillment of the imperative of the divine law, to respect and avenge one's father, simultaneously requires its transgression, for matricide is an almost unimaginably heinous crime against the Penates. As a result, a supra-familial council which is held at the Areopagus must be set up in order that Athena and the others gods can adjudicate the matter.[16] That is, the inability of the familial law to resolve its own problems generates the need for an interpretive body, the prototype of the state or "human law," the mandate of which is to work out precisely what the gods require in complex or even contradictory situations.

We see similar structures in ancient Greece's first great author, Homer, and its last great philosopher, Aristotle. While Odysseus is undisputed King of Ithaca in Homer's *Odyssey*, he must defer at least in part to the council made up of the heads of subordinate families in the city.[17] The power of this type of council, while at first expedient as a means of settling disputes between families and organizing their co-operative ventures, gradually becomes more powerful and, ultimately, transforms itself into the clear and distinct crown of Hellenic life in the polis. Aristotle makes a similar point in the *Politics*. "The state [polis] comes into existence, originating in the bare needs of life, and continuing in existence for the sake of a good life." The polis gathers together a plurality of "villages," which are effectively extended families, "because they were of the same blood." It is the polis, moreover, that is final cause or end to which individuals, families, and villages are subordinated. "Further, the state is by nature clearly prior to the family and to the individual, since the whole is of necessity prior to the part."[18]

We see in all these examples that *justice* is a decisive feature of the human law. The human law adjudicates conflicts that arise within and between families and villages, and indeed within the Ethical Society as a whole. Justice, *Dike*, in the ethical world is precisely this beautiful harmony between its necessary parts. As we have seen, the divine and human law are the most important constituents within each city, but the particularity of each polis in relation to the others within Hellas is also of great significance. For a variety of reasons, the beautiful harmony can be threatened or lost, such that the state intervenes to re-establish it. Hegel says, "It is the government of the people" that establishes "justice," insofar as it "restores the universal to equilibrium."[19] War is but its most dramatic way of doing so. In order to ensure that private interest, economic and otherwise, does not "take root and become fixed in isolation, with a result [that] the whole is allowed to fall apart and the spirit to flee, government has to shake them to the core from time to time by means of wars."[20] Hegel should also be taken to mean that less dramatic measures to ensure harmonic justice are also the prerogative of the state. Moreover, while this notion of justice might well be understood as merely re-establishing the lost harmony of ethical immediacy, it is already implicitly mediated and will play no small role in the emergence of contradiction within the Ethical Society.

The same trend that creates the polis from villages and gradually generates an autonomous state also tends toward democracy. The principle of deliberation is hereby gradually made universal.[21] The tragedy of the *Antigone* is partly premised on the relative unsophistication of the Greek state in the pre-democratic era in which the play is set. While Creon's state is far more elaborate than the councils of Odysseus's Ithaca, it is still a monarchy and thus still a prisoner to natural contingency of familial inheritance. The fact that it is not clear which of the two biological brothers, Polyneices or Eteocles, should inherit the throne from their father is precisely what leads to Polyneices' supposedly "traitorous" attack on Thebes. If the monarchical state is still very much trapped within the demands of nature, family, and its patriarchal authority, the democratic state, on the other hand, has introduced an important degree of mediation with nature.[22]

We might be tempted, as we try to better understand the Greek exemplar of the Ethical Society, simply to reduce the divine law to the family and the human law to the state. Hegel's analysis, however, is more subtle. There are certain aspects of the family that are merely natural and thus actually fall below the divine law. He states that "The family is ethical *insofar* as it does not have the relationship of *nature* among its members." We find out, in due course, that the natural includes not only sexual desire and other feelings, but even familial love. "Because the ethical is inherently universal, the ethical connection of the family members is not the connection of feeling or the relationship of love."[23] Hegel points out that the relationship of brother and sister, which is not tainted by the naturalness of sexual desire or parental instinct, is thus more ethical – a point of some importance, as we will see shortly, given Antigone's duty as family member, by the divine law, to bury her brother Polyneices.[24] Second, the family is also ethical, rather than merely natural, insofar as it sublates itself, raising the family member, who is but a "*nonactual*, pithless shade," into a citizen. "The *positive* purpose, which is peculiar to the family, is the single member as such," and "consists precisely in the removal of the single member from the family, the subjugation of the member's naturalness and singularity; it draws the family member toward *virtue*, toward life in and for the universal."[25] Third, since death is merely the "*natural state of having been, not the deed of a consciousness*," the burial rites performed in obedience to the divine law ensure the "imperishable individuality" of each person.[26] Hegel even goes so far as to say that the divine duty to bury the dead is the only ethical action of the family. "Every other relationship toward him that does not abide in love, but is ethical, belongs to human law and has the negative significance of raising the single member above his confinement within the natural community, to which as an *actual being* he belongs."[27] We have seen that human law is already a mediated activity beyond the natural, even if its promulgators do not consider it as such. However, we now see how the duties to bury the dead and to transform people from nonactual "shades" to actual citizens arise from the divine law and thus cannot be considered to be merely natural and immediate. Thus the vital contradiction between immediacy and mediation that will destroy the Ethical Society exists not only in the conflict between family and state, woman and man, but within the family itself and within the virtue of women.

Prior to the emergence of this contradiction as conflict, the Ethical Society subsists as a harmonious totality in which a division of labour gives determinate spheres of the society their specific organic vocations within the society as a (universal and infinite) whole. Women are caretakers of the home and children while men carry out the tasks of public life. The divine and human law, then, are gendered, respectively, as female and male and each actively supports the other. "Its movement is a tranquil passage from one of its powers to the other, so that each of them contains the other and brings it forth."[28] We have just seen how, through the education of children into citizenship, the divine law of the family supports the human law. Hegel points out the inverse as well. Since the human law ultimately imposes its unity on the society through war, individual citizens must face death. Yet they are comforted by the funeral rites they will be provided because of the divine law. "Thus the truth and confirmation of the power of the community is in the essence of the divine law and in the *nether kingdom.*"[29] In sum, the society functions organically, a good infinite, such that each sphere in the division of labour works much like an organ in a body.

Hegel greatly admires this kind of society and especially its Greek exemplar. Indeed, for reasons he makes clear in his *Aesthetics*, he claims in the *Philosophy of History* that the Greek world was like a beautiful youth.[30] "Greece presents to us the cheerful aspect of youthful freshness, of Spiritual vitality."[31] This beauty will be destroyed by its own dialectical development, leading to the Condition of Right and then to the "self-alienation" of spirit, and will never return to Western civilization. Yet the death of the youthful and vital Greek world allows for the adulthood of spirit. How, then, does this beautiful Ethical Society destroy itself?

2 THE DEED AND CONTRADICTION IN THE ETHICAL SOCIETY

In the study of dialectic in chapter 1, I identified four criteria for a dialectical critique (which I later augmented such as to establish a primordial starting point for conceptual rather than empirical dialectic). I said there that 1) the original stance is one of self-determination; 2) a contradiction develops within it; 3) this contradiction generates a conflict that invites a solution, and 4) this solution is then incorporated into a new and more sophisticated stance.

The Ethical Society fulfills the first criterion, for as we have seen, it is self-determining. It just does not realize that about itself. Notice, further, the logical symmetry thus established between the definition of primitive self-determination and primitive society – they are forms of freedom that by definition do not recognize themselves for what they are. The Ethical Society is "the society that does not know that it is a society" and the primitive form of self-determination is a form of self-determination that merely lives out its self-determination rather than knows itself as self-determining. The key, however, is that the Ethical Society, in its concrete-lived sphere of recognition, can give rise to precisely the kinds of contradictions that will provoke its own self-consciousness.

The second criterion of dialectic is the development of a contradiction and, moreover, a contradiction that is not fully present at the outset. If there is to be a contradiction in the Ethical Society, it must emerge in time and call attention to itself *within the experience of the Ethical Society itself*. Such a contradiction emerges in the realm of concrete-lived recognition and gradually comes to undermine and collapse the juridical-imaginative structure from within. In the case of the beautiful Ethical Society, we have noted that the very emergence of the human law of the state is already the manifestation of what will turn into its fatal contradiction.

I have referred briefly to a key passage in the *Phenomenology* in which Hegel identifies the form of self-consciousness that will emerge from within the Ethical Society and destroy it. The Ethical Society is determined by the "infallible law of the gods," and the "disposition" of the member of this society "consists just in sticking steadfastly to what is right, and abstaining from all attempts to move or shake it, or derive it." Indeed, it normally does not even occur to this person to question these laws. However, "If I inquire after their origin and confine them to the point whence they arose, then I have transcended them; for now it is I who am the universal, and they are the conditioned and limited. If they are supposed to be validated by *my* insight, then I have already denied their unshakeable, intrinsic being and regard them as something which, for me, is perhaps true, but also perhaps not true."[32] This form of self-consciousness will emerge in the concrete-lived world of Greek society, especially in the person of Socrates, and it will later demand an entire juridical-imaginative structure based on itself – an altogether new form of society.

We have already seen that even the divine law requires mediative activity to raise it above mere nature. This is all the more true of the human law. Even if the individuals upholding these laws do not recognize their emerging powers of mediation – deliberation, interpretation, and choice – these powers are slowly developing, especially in the realm of the state. Sophocles is anything but blind to these powers, and his *Antigone* is at least in part a warning against them. He is aware that we come to amaze and delight ourselves with our creative powers. In the very text that will condemn the actions of Creon and with him the human law, Sophocles has the chorus sing one of the great panegyrics to human creative power.

> Many wonders, many terrors,
> But none more wonderful than the human race
> Or more dangerous ...
> For he is Man, and he is cunning.
> He has invented ways to take control
> Of beasts that range mountain meadows ...
> And put them under yoke ...
> Language and a mind swift as the wind
> For making plans –
> These he has taught himself –
> And the character to live in cities under law.[33]

That is, by our *action* we come to mediate our relationship with nature. If the divine law represents an unmediated obedience to the laws of the gods, then our work proves to us that we are not simply subject to this necessity. When we cannot scoop fish from the sea with our hands, we create fishing rods and nets. When we find it too tedious and difficult to travel long distances, we domesticate horses and let them carry us and our burdens. We could go on, of course, but each of these examples of human creative action shows that we do not have a merely immediate relationship to the world in which we live. Our own powers of interpretation, deliberation, and choice are readily and frequently employed to radically change our relationship to the world.

And, as Sophocles so beautifully puts it, our incredible creative power is not lost on us: "These he has taught himself." Indeed, the chorus sings that as a result of this cunning, "he slithers into wickedness sometimes," and yet "If he honors the law of the land / And the oath-bound justice of the gods, / Then his city shall stand high."[34] We learn so much that we become tempted to disobey the gods and to throw the city out of its beautiful and just harmony, for to have to swear an oath to something is to no longer be in a pure state of immediacy in relation to it. An oath is sworn when an individual resolves to choose to commit him or herself to something. It is already a kind of conversion and thus a kind of mediation. This means that one need not be rashly sinning against the divine law to see here how a "human law" distinct from the "divine law" not only emerges in the form of the public life of the Greek polis but gradually enters into contradiction with the divine law. This is the law that is known to have been made by Solon, and to have been developed, altered, and added to by others like Cleisthenes and Pericles.

The divine law, however, in its normal condition, is experienced in a manner not at all unlike natural causation. Just as cold causes water to freeze, the death of Polyneices immediately and unquestioningly compels his sister Antigone to invoke the rites of burial. But when we domesticate the horse and learn to float on the sea in boats, we no longer respond to nature with the immediacy appropriate to divine law; we mediate our relationship to nature through the crucible of own creative deliberation. That is, as we understand natural causation, we become its masters, and we start to use nature against itself.[35] The person who creates a ship has already implicitly taken it upon *himself* to be the determining force in the situation. Moreover, because it is creative, this form of "self-determination" is new and different – it gives new form, the human form, to the world. Indeed, as the human being transforms the world, she effectively steals it from the gods – just as the slave's work gradually leads him to steal the product of labour from the master. The tree becomes a reflection of human creativity when it is transformed by work into the wood planking for a ship. The human law, therefore, is implicitly and, later, explicitly, in conflict with the divine law. The divine law takes things "as they already are and have always been," but the human law takes things "as they might be, should we learn to so transform them." Human creative action, in other words, slowly but surely undermines the immediate authority of the divine law and augments the human being's sense that she can be the interpreting, deliberating author of her own being. No wonder, then, that ancient mythological and religious texts are full of conflict between gods and mortals – from the divine punishment meted to Prometheus for stealing fire to the jealous preservation of the knowledge of good and evil which the Hebrew god was so incapable of enforcing in the opening pages of the Book of Genesis.

Of course, this process can take a very long time to come to the surface. Even in the face of the fact that the law was given by Solon, it is still possible to see the law as conservative – as *conserving*, strengthening, adjusting, or re-establishing the divine harmony. The importance of mediation, of creativity, is especially difficult to see in the realm of family, where work is repetitive and offers little possibility of transcendence, as Simone de Beauvoir pointed out in *The Second Sex*.[36] Human interpretive power is called for much more often in the realm of the state. It is not an accident that the human law is most fully embodied in the king since the institution of the *state* rises in the Greek polis as the unifying soul of the whole. But as the human law develops its autonomy from the divine law, so too does the state become the most explicit embodiment of the human law. After all, it is in the state and, a fortiori the Greek democratic state, that citizens interpret, deliberate, and choose courses of action. While it may be immediately obvious that the bodies of our fallen loved ones must be buried with all the rites prescribed by the divine law, the decisions of the state are far from obvious. It is not plain whether Athens should extend its city walls down to the Piraeus, if she should declare war on Sparta, or launch a massive attack in Sicily. Human beings must decide these courses of action, and although one might look to the oracle for help, her puzzling riddles leave almost all the interpretation and decision-making in the hands of human beings, as Plato's *Apology* makes so plain. But if the human law becomes more and more expressed in the institution of the state, and the divine law is shown to be rather impotent there, then what becomes of the divine law? It retreats, Hegel shows, into the Penates, the gods of the family.

If the creative power of our interpretive work is the first cause for the emergence of contradiction, the second is that the supposedly harmonious spheres of family and state are very likely to enter into open conflict with each other. This conflict between the human and divine law is precisely what emerges in Sophocles' play. Antigone and her sister, Ismene, face a serious problem when the divine law unequivocally says to them that *they must bury Polyneices* while at the same time the human law, embodied in Creon's official edict as king, says, *they must not bury Polyneices*. Antigone embodies the divine law with perfect immediacy, for she never doubts, never wavers, and heroically does her duty despite Creon's edict, threats, and punishment. Ismene, on the other hand, is conflicted, and ultimately decides to follow the orders of the human law: she obeys Creon. It is vital to note, however, that Creon, for his part, acts with the same kind of ethical immediacy as does Antigone. That is, neither Creon nor Antigone acts with reflective deliberation, but from an inner and total confidence that their dutiful impulse is one with the ethical custom and their station within it.

In another sense, Ismene is a truer representative of the divine law than even Antigone, for Ismene claims that a woman has no right to act in matters of the state. In this light Antigone's action emerges as a transgressive incursion into the public realm and its human law. She may think of herself as purely and simply following the divine law, but her deed is a political one and thus one unfitting for a woman. The actions of Athenian and Spartan women in Aristophanes' play *Lysistrata* can also be interpreted as strategically embracing the human law rather than the divine. They interpret the war between Athens and Sparta to be harmful to everyone, then deliberate about what to do about it, and finally resolve to call a universal sex strike. That women are "naturally" bound to the immediacy of the family and the divine law is, then, itself a belief that only makes sense according to the strictures of the divine law itself. Feminism is conceptually inevitable, and is foreshadowed by Antigone's actions and even more boldly and playfully in the *Lysistrata*.[37]

Either way, a contradiction has emerged in the Ethical Society, and it generates as much or even more conflict than we might expect – a conflict wondrously displayed in both the *Antigone* and the *Lysistrata*. The contradiction is between a society whose explicit juridical norm is that the ethical custom must be immediately obeyed, and its concrete-lived practice that makes this impossible. This contradiction becomes most obvious when the supposedly immediate ethical imperative demands two opposite and mutually exclusive duties:

a Obey the Penates, and bury Polyneices, versus
b Obey the King, and leave Polyneices in the street.

The key to the contradiction, in its nascent form, is that Creon and Antigone are forced to act as singular individuals in a context in which singular action is, by definition, transgressive. Of course, individuals are doing things all the time, but this does not mean that they have acted *qua singular*. The universal ethical customs are to be followed according to the *particular* stations, family and state, into which it is divided. Even if "I" act, I do not act "for myself," but for the universal law of Athens, as per my duty as man or woman, family member or citizen. This is to say, the "self-consciousness" of the ethical world is the universal recognition of *particular roles* but *not of singular judgment*. As Hegel puts it, "Self-consciousness descends within the people from the universal only as far as particularity, not as far as singular individuality that posits in its conduct an excluding self, an actuality that is negative toward itself."[38]

Creon thus believes himself to be correct when he condemns the body of Polyneices to the dogs and birds because Polyneices *is* a traitor to the human law. Antigone, moreover, is certain that she is doing the right thing by burying her brother by virtue of the divine law. Of course, in both cases each is demonstrably right – the state must deal harshly with traitors and the Penates require burial rights for family members. Moreover, Antigone and Creon could each, in principle, recognize the ethicality of the other's action, but since they see this event only from their own point of view, each condemns the other as lacking virtue. Virtue, in the context of the Ethical Society, is the excellence by which singular selfhood is invisible within the context of particular duties fulfilling universal ends. The act, the "deed" of a singular is an aberration, a transgression, and a sin. By breaking the law, each one stands forth as a singular agent, even though that was the last thing they intended and even though neither fully recognizes the enormous implications of this contradiction. "For the deed is its own *doing*," Hegel says, "and the doing is its own most essence; and *guilt* obtains the significance of *crime*, too, for as simple ethical consciousness, self-consciousness has appealed to the one law but has renounced the other and violated it through its deed."[39]

Creon recognizes his crime when he has lost his wife and son, and Sophocles' play might thus be read as a conservative warning against those singular selves whose hubris might tempt them, so to speak, to take the law into their own hands.[40] However, according to Hegel's reading, Creon misrecognizes his crime. The Ethical Society cannot survive by simply attempting to renew its obedience and piety to the divine law since the real criminal act was not this or that contingent impiety, but the deed of the singular self *as such*. Or again, Creon and Antigone accuse each other of a failure qua singular self. Antigone says to Creon, "You think / I've been a fool? It takes a fool to think that."[41] Creon, meanwhile, calls Antigone an "expert in arrogance."[42] As Hegel puts it, "Since each ethical consciousness sees right only on its own side and injustice on the other, the one that belongs to the divine law perceives on the other side the capricious *violence* of men, but the one that is allotted to the human perceives in the other the obstinacy and the *disobedience* of being-for-self."[43] Neither understands that both are right: the singular self has no choice but to transgress particularity and universality and thus announce itself, qua singular, as that which is forced, as it were, to stand out.

Hegel uses the terms "deed" and "action" (*Tat* and *Handlung*)[44] to refer to this form of singular action that stands out as divisive and transgressive. Indeed, prior to this transgression "No *deed* has *yet* been done," and the deed "disturbs the peaceful organization and movement of the ethical world."[45] Moreover, speaking of the Ethical Society, Hegel says, "*Action* separates it into substance and the consciousness of substance."[46] For Hegel the deed is always guilty and criminal in the terms of the Ethical Society: the concrete-lived dynamics of mediated singular action always transgress official juridical-imaginative notions of universal immediacy. The "antithesis" of "ethical immediacy," according to Hegel, is the "*deed* of self-consciousness." The singular, self-conscious self "raises itself out of *simple immediacy* and posits the *division* (between it qua singular self and the universal and immediate imperatives of the Ethical Society) itself." It thus "posits the separation of its own self into itself (as agent) and into what stands opposite to it as actuality that is negative for it." Its action, indeed all of its actions, is thus transgressive of the Ethical Society. "Hence by virtue of this deed it comes to *guilt*."[47]

The contradiction emerges, according to Hegel, in two steps. First, family and state enter into open conflict with each other. The state must subordinate the family, but in so doing "It creates its own inner enemy in what it suppresses and what is at the same time essential to it." We will see in coming chapters that the "eternal irony" of the family, here called in a sexist manner the "female principle," will always be in a vital contradiction with the state.[48] Funeral rites, recall, preserve the singular self from the anonymity and contingency of natural death, and thus, second, singularity also becomes an enemy of the state. "The community can maintain itself," Hegel says, "only through the oppression of this spirit of singularity, and, because that spirit is an essential moment, the community really engenders it as well." In so doing the community "engenders" singularity "as a hostile principle."[49]

The powers of this singular self, which heretofore has been but a "nonactual shade," are only now coming into themselves. Once ethical immediacy has been undermined, the state and the human law become plagued by factional conflict and struggle because it is no longer clear who speaks for the eternal laws. At this point, Hegel's account of the Greek world in the *Philosophy of History* develops the implications of the argument presented in the *Phenomenology*. The city oscillates between varying regimes and, when the regime is democratic, is constantly rent by disagreement. The democratic environment, above all, encourages the emergence of the singular self. "The democratic constitution," Hegel says, "excels all others in virtue of the fact that it not only *allows* the display of their powers on the part of individuals, but *summons* them to the use of those powers for the general weal." In such a context "oratorical suasion" becomes of the greatest importance, and "no member of the community can obtain influence unless he has the power of satisfying the intellect and judgment ... of a cultivated people." The sophists thus emerge as teachers of rhetoric. The sophists "First introduced subjective reflection, and the new doctrine that each man should act according to his own conviction."[50] The power of the self to deliberate self-consciously about the divine law undermines that law's authority because it posits the deliberator as the real authority – "man is the measure of all things," as Protagoras purportedly said – and creates a realm of law that is demonstrably created by and for the human community. Hegel says that "The individual finds himself in a position to bring everything to the test of his own conscience, even in defiance of the existing constitution." Indeed, Hegel continues, "As soon as thought arises ... it forms for itself an idea of an improved state of society, and demands that this ideal should take the place of the way things are." It is thus no surprise that this form of questioning, singular self "plunged the Greek world of ethical immediacy into ruin."[51]

Once discursive suasion emerges as a public necessity, so too do the standards of persuasion. The truth ceases to be the self-evident and exclusive property of the gods and becomes that for which the human mind discloses the criteria. Socrates shows in the *Apology* that a universal skepticism is possible by which all immediately authoritative laws, institutions, and individuals can be undermined. Socrates, for Hegel, seems to make his own mind into the oracle. "Socrates – in assigning to insight, to conviction, the determination of men's actions – posited the Individual as capable of a final moral decision, in contraposition to Country and to Customary Morality [*Sittlichkeit*], and thus made himself an Oracle, in the Greek sense."[52] We have moved a great distance in a short time, between 442 BCE, when Sophocles describes the calm certitude of Antigone, who knows without hesitation that she is doing the right thing, and Plato's *Apology* some fifty years later, when Socrates claims that he is wisest because he knows that he knows nothing. The "*corruption* of the Greek world," Hegel says in the *Philosophy of History*, "is *subjectivity obtaining emancipation for itself*."[53] The agent of contradiction in the Ethical Society is the singular deliberating and choosing self that emerges from within the heart of ethical immediacy.

The divine laws of the Ethical Society may be the eternal, universal truths, but, as Hegel puts it (once again), "If I inquire after their origin and confine them to the point whence they arose, then I have transcended them; for now it is I who am the universal, and *they* are the conditioned and limited."[54] That is, even if Antigone says the divine law is eternal and thus infinite, without beginning or end, when I inquire as to the "origin" of the laws, I posit that they had a beginning and that they could also thus have an end. The status of the law moves from infinite to finite. It is the mind of the singular self, and not the law, that is therefore infinite and universal. Thus, if the divine law used to be the universal truth of all being, it has now become merely a *particular* truth – a truth at *this* time and *this* place. But now the thinking mind of the singular self has posited itself as the universal truth, since from now on the modes of interpretation, understanding, and choice of the singular self will universally determine how that self will comport itself. The self-evident and immediately authoritative laws of the gods which animated Antigone and Creon are left far behind.

We have seen a very similar story told earlier in the *Phenomenology of Spirit*. The obedience of members of the Ethical Society is similar in logical form to the authority of the master over the slave, and so too is the liberation of the citizen as free person similar to the emergent self-consciousness of the slave. Indeed, Hegel explicitly links his analysis of mastery and slavery with his study of the Ethical Society. Just as the slave identifies his own will with that of the master, so the obedient member of the Ethical Society identifies his or her will with the law of the gods. The Ethical Society is the "Immediate *spirit*," Hegel says, "which is the universally sovereign will of all, and equally their subservient obedience."[55] Just as the slave fears the master, so the Greek fears the thunderbolt of Zeus, and any temptation to drift into self-interest is precluded by war and the threat of death. Indeed, as we have seen already, in the Ethical Society "Government has to shake them to the core from time to time by means of wars."[56] If the slave "has experienced the fear of death, the absolute Lord," the members of the Ethical Society are given "a feeling for their lord, Death."[57] Moreover, just as the work of the slave gradually leads her to see in the transformed objects of her labour her own creative power, the same dynamic is present in the work of the members of the ethical order. The "diligence and activity" of the Greeks is creative, such that "Material things are changed, worked up and used for other than their original purposes … it is made an object about which the mind can employ itself, and this occupation becomes an interest in and for itself."[58]

Correspondingly, in chapter 4 of the *Phenomenology*, when Hegel is discussing the development of individual self-consciousness out of slavery, he calls this new stance of universal mind "stoicism," and since the thinking mind is free to interpret how it will respond to its given situations, it is equally free "whether on the throne or in chains."[59] In this political sphere, and thus in chapter 6 of the *Phenomenology* and in the *Philosophy of Right,* Hegel calls this universally free, singular self the "person." By the power of its own interpretation, deliberation, and choice, the reflective, singular person emerges as a destructive force from within the life of the Ethical Society itself. This "person" is the solution to the contradiction of ethical immediacy, and the society that recognizes the person, the "Condition of Right," is the solution to the contradiction of the Ethical Society.

There is no necessity in any empirically existing Ethical Society that its activity lead to the formation of stoic persons, but the capacity of the creative, thoughtful human mind can always be unleashed in this direction. When this happens the traditional authorities start to lose their power. We recognize the stoic person in our capacities as choosing agents. As John Russon puts it, "By saying 'I' one is already committed to all the premises of stoicism."[60] It is a stance with which we can all identify. Indeed, to doubt personhood is to invoke it. Thus, once the potential for personhood emerges within the conceptual dialectic, we are compelled to follow its lead. The person then becomes the foundation for a new form of society, and the Ethical Society has been destroyed from within. The juridical-imaginative structure of the Ethical Society has been dialectically criticized by its own practices of concrete-lived recognition. Moreover, the stoic person and the political institutions adequate to this personhood emerge dialectically from the fatal contradiction of the Ethical Society.

Stoic personhood is plainly a more sophisticated response to the world than the immediacy of the Ethical Society since this form of person literally taught herself her own freedom through her activities of interpretation and deliberation. In the conceptual dialectic, a new attitude is incorporated into the self, but it is important to note that the old, traditional attitude still remains, even if in a transformed way. The realm of nature is still governed by much the same immediate necessity that we identified with the Ethical Society. But more importantly, the Ethical Society is carried forward in human society as the institution of the *family*. I discuss this in much more detail below, but I note now that when a child comes into the world she will have much the same experience of that world as does a citizen of the Ethical Society. She finds herself in a world governed by laws that preceded her, over which she has little or no power, and which she takes to be the natural and eternal state of things. That is, a child experiences the norms of her own world in much the same way that Antigone articulates the eternal character of the divine law. But it is precisely the education of this child that gives her, as the centre of interpretation, deliberation, and choice, more and more power to transform the world and herself. Much as in the work of Hegel's slave or the development of the human law in the Ethical Society, she slowly but surely comes to render the world finite, just as the historical stoic did, and comes to recognize her own creative, transformative power. But this is only a developed or cultivated state: the family remains the site of a kind of temporary immediacy for very young children. The Ethical Society, then, is resurrected or, more accurately, preserved, in the newly forming world of persons in the institution of the family. Moreover, as will be seen below, the family is one of the three essential institutions of a free society, along with civil society and the state.

In sum, the new, more sophisticated stance that emerges in the ruins of the Ethical Society is the triumph of the freedom of the singular "person." While the Ethical Society survives in the form the family, the hallmark of the human law, the state, will emerge triumphant as the governing institution of stoic persons. Our study of the Ethical Society has shown that it develops a contradiction within it and that this contradiction leads to its downfall. But this result, conceptually speaking at least, is not an anarchy of violence because the force of destruction unleashed in the contradictory state of affairs is none other than the free, thinking person, which now emerges as the new universal standard upon which a new form of society can be built.

We have here our first political example of "vital contradiction." Freedom is not realized in the mere fact of choice or the capacity of skeptical doubt. Freedom develops, it is *cultivated*, and this development happens only in and through *contradiction*. Contradiction, then, is the very vitality, the very life, of the self-emergence and elaboration of freedom. A vital contradiction has felled the Ethical Society and invited us into the new political realm of the free, stoic self. The recognition of the free singular person as the truth of political life first emerges in what Hegel calls "The Condition of Right" (*Rechtszustand*) in the *Phenomenology of Spirit*, and I now turn to a study this new and second form in the conceptual dialectic of society.

5

The Condition of Right: Individual Freedom and Tyranny

I THE FREE PERSON AND ARBITRARY WILL

In the Ethical Society, Hegel says, "Self-consciousness has not yet come forth in its right as *singular individuality*." "The singular individual" [*dieser Einzelne*],[1] which counts in the Ethical Society "only as the *inactual shade*," is precisely the kind of self-consciousness that had to emerge and assert itself when the contradiction between human and divine law began clearly to emerge. In its fully developed form, the freedom of the singular, abstract self, which Hegel calls the "person," adopts a skeptical attitude toward custom and severs itself from the ethical "substance." It locates the authority to judge, for the first time, in itself. Since human action in the world always presupposes creative acts of interpretation and choice (varying widely in degree and kind), the achievement of self-consciousness of necessity is an advance in the sophistication of human self-determination. The person, indeed, is no longer the slave of the gods or nature. This singular self then comes to be explicitly recognized in the juridical realm in what Hegel calls *Rechtszustand*, or the Condition of Right,[2] the historical model for which is ancient Rome.[3] "From now on," Hegel says in his introduction to the Condition of Right, "this *I* counts as an essence that subsists *in and for itself*; this *being recognized* in its substantiality."[4]

This "I," the *person*, is no longer immediately integrated into the life of the society as a living, body-politic, and thus takes the fulfillment of its own desires as its foremost end. For this reason, even if the person is an advance on the self of the ethical society, it remains the least sophisticated form of *self-conscious* freedom. That is, it effectively considers its freedom to consist in the liberty to do what it wants, while respecting others' right to do the same. Hegel calls the self of the Condition of Right an "arbitrary will" (*Willkür*) – the stance that understands freedom as the capacity of the singular self to fulfill its own desires, especially indulgence in sensual pleasure and the accumulation of property. This society has no institutions that would cultivate or educate the will to have purportedly higher goals or more sophisticated forms of freedom. To presuppose any such institutions is to invoke a more sophisticated form of freedom than is appropriate at this step of the conceptual dialectic. Once more, conceptual dialectic must always move logically from least to most sophisticated stance, without skipping any necessary steps.

In the Condition of Right, the freedom of singular individuals is universally recognized at the level of juridical-imaginative recognition. If the Ethical Society immediately identified particular stations (family, state) with the body politic itself (to the exclusion of the freedom of the abstract, singular person), the Condition of Right immediately identifies the infinitely free choice of persons with the universal good of the society as a whole. We are, as persons, perfectly equal to each other in our capacity to exercise what has been called negative freedom – the freedom to *not be* compelled by certain determinations of society, law, religion, and so on. And since this kind of negation is an act that we each carry out within our separate singular minds, we are equal to each other as separate, individual persons, "atoms." In Hegel's terms, the Condition of Right is "the universal split up into the atoms of absolutely many individuals." It is an "*equality* in which *everyone* counts as *each* one, that is, as *persons*."[5]

While the Condition of Right institutionally recognizes the "absolutely discrete unit," the singular individual and its choice, as the essential truth of human selfhood and society, it simultaneously regards the concrete, particular realities created by these choices to be inessential with respect to freedom. This is thus an "*abstract universal*," Hegel says, in which "the actual content or *determinacy* of being mine is not contained in this empty form and does not concern it – be it the determinacy of some external possession or again, of an inner richness or poverty of character."[6] That is, the juridical-imaginative truth of the society is found in the abstract universality of the choosing, singular self such that what it does as a free will, including what it owns as property, is, for better or for worse, juridically immaterial. "The actuality" of each of these individuals, Hegel explains, is to be a "*negative* universal self"[7] the content of which is "*this rigid self*, and not the self that is dissolved substance."[8] It is negative because it can negate any particular way it might determine itself and because it thinks of itself as ontologically separate from and prior to any of the institutions in which it participates or commitments that it makes.[9] This person "is neither tied to a richer or more powerful determinate being of the individual as such, nor even to a universal living Spirit, but rather to the pure one of abstract actuality."[10]

The Condition of Right thus takes an abstract part of the individual will, its power of negation, as the essence of freedom. Or again, the Condition of Right is that juridical-imaginative form of recognition that a) identifies singular choice as the principle it is pursuing, and b) proclaims this freedom to reside essentially in the pure capacity of negation. But c), the Condition of Right considers the content of the particular things those individuals actually do choose (particularity) to be accidental with respect to freedom.

This also means that the Condition of Right is the political institutionalization of what I have called, with Hegel, the "bad infinite." The Ethical Society was a "good infinite" in which the internal character of each self and each station made sense only in terms of the whole. This meant that the fulfillment of each individual arose only and in through the support of others in the society and, moreover, the fulfillment of the individual was simultaneously the fulfillment of the society as a totality. If in the Ethical Society there is no difference between the good of individuals, the good of particular spheres, and the common good, in the Condition of Right there is no real common good at all beyond the juridical recognition of the arbitrary will of each citizen. Each citizen is thus a numerical unit. There is no logic of the whole which determines particular duties and no intrinsic limit on the number or behaviour of citizens. The Condition of Right is an aggregate of individual units. In this logic of society, other selves are not conditions of one's own freedom, as in the Ethical Society, but limitations to it.

As I briefly suggested above, the Condition of Right thus lays the groundwork for an institution of freedom that will become essential to the fully developed concept of a just society – *civil society*. If the Ethical Society was characterized by the conflict between the divine law of the family and the human law of the state, the Condition of Right must recognize personhood and its capacity to pursue its own ends independently from any obligation to care for the greater or common good. It is in what Hegel calls civil society that the modern free person is institutionally recognized as empowered to pursue a life that he or she perceives to be best on his or her own terms.[11]

Since this form of self aspires to no higher form of freedom than abstract choice, it has no standard by which to evaluate the relative quality of the determinate things that individuals actually do.[12] Given that it is the second least sophisticated form of self-determination, there are no institutions in which the individual necessarily participates that cultivate desire toward more sophisticated forms of social life. Indeed, it rejects the notion that the institutions of society as a whole could even acknowledge any claim to greater or lesser sophistication, with the only exception being its freedom from divine and natural necessity. Thus Hegel says that the "*fulfillment* and ... *content*" of the ethical order is lost and "this content is now set free completely in disorder; for the Spirit that subjugated it and held it together in its unity is no longer present. Hence the empty one[ness] of the person is in its *reality* an accidental determinate being, an essenceless moving and doing that comes to no enduring state."[13] By juridically recognizing only abstract freedom, the Condition of Right makes itself bereft of the institutions that could provide this "fulfillment and content" – the education of the self.

2 TYRANNY AND THE CONCENTRATION OF WEALTH AND POWER

Even though it is a necessary stage in the development of freedom and is in principle superior to the beautiful, infinite harmony of the Ethical Society, Hegel expresses open hostility toward the Condition of Right. He declares that "to designate an individual as a *person* is an expression of contempt."[14] Indeed, in the *Philosophy of History* he portrays the Condition of Right in terms of death, and the life of the person as feeding on the rotting flesh of the beautiful Ethical Society. "As, when the physical body suffers dissolution, each point gains a life of its own, but which is only the miserable life of worms; so the political organism is here dissolved into atoms – viz., private persons."[15]

Failing institutions that will educate the desire of the self, the practice of the Condition of Right tends, as I said above, toward what Hegel calls "arbitrary will" (*Willkür*).[16] Arbitrariness is defined by Hegel in the *Philosophy of Right* as follows: "The commonest idea we have of freedom is that of *arbitrariness* – the mean position of reflection between the will as determined solely by natural drives and the will which is free in and for itself. When we hear it said that freedom in general consists in *being able to do as one pleases*, such an idea can only be taken to indicate a complete lack of intellectual culture ... because [the will] does not yet have itself as its content and end, so that the subjective side is still something other than the objective."[17] The predominance of arbitrary will and the fact that it is condoned by juridical recognition leads to the development of a fatal contradiction at the level of concrete-lived recognition.

This analysis depends primarily on the last sentence quoted here, that the arbitrary will "does not yet have itself as its content and end." Recall that in our study of the conceptual dialectic of human relations in chapter 1, the human being achieves the satisfaction of its desire only when it mutually recognizes other human beings. That is, the key to our freedom is co-operative and mutually supportive relationships with other people. This is because the only objective reality that can reflect back to desire that it is indeed the determining centre of reality is another co-operating human being, and it does so reciprocally only in co-operative activity. Only another human will can say, "You are determining centre." When this is unilateral we have mastery and slavery, but when it is reciprocal, we have mutual recognition. For freedom to choose itself, it must choose to engage in relationships of mutual recognition. The arbitrary will, however, is not concerned with the recognition of other people except as abstract choosers. It is thus preoccupied not with people, but with things, with the accumulation of property and the treatment of itself as a thing in the procurement of satisfaction for its desires.

Property is a key issue for Hegel and, like many others, he is concerned about the implications of its unlimited accumulation. What is decisive about the right to property for Hegel is not the possession of a thing itself but the *right* to that thing which is respected (recognized) by other selves. When we affirm that "this is mine," what is most important is what is implied – that the human community affirms, "Yes, this is yours." Or, more generally, in private property the community recognizes the right of all of its members to a sphere of privacy, a sphere which excludes others. Private property, then, is not most essentially the possession of a thing, but a system of co-operation, of mutual recognition. It is thus not paradoxical to state that the ability to be private and exclude others is something possible only in and through active co-operation, in mutual recognition, with other people. Without this mutual recognition we return to the contradictions of the struggle to the death.

It is precisely this dual universal/particular bifurcation of private property that the arbitrary will in the Condition of Right does not take into account. It is focused on its property not as a reflection of the collective will of a community of recognizers but as a means to its own private satisfaction. The co-operative moment of private property is ignored in favour of its exclusive moment. The person in the Condition of Right, then, does not recognize "freedom in and for itself" – mutual recognition – but only the arbitrary freedom it has to accumulate pleasures that exclude others. Thus, the Condition of Right is characterized by the accumulation of private property and of the wealth and power that follow from it. Accordingly, the will of the Condition of Right "finds a manifold subsistence, a possession, and ... impresses upon it the same abstract universality by which it is called *property*."[18] The juridical-imaginative system of mutual recognition in the Condition of Right aspires to nothing more than the recognition of the rights of the property-owning free will.

Hegel describes the emergence of contradiction within the Condition of Right as follows: "The content belongs to a *power of its own*, that is other than the formal universal (which is the power that is chance and is arbitrary)."[19] The "formal universal" is the merely abstract yet universal recognition afforded to all singular persons to pursue their private accumulation of pleasures. The "content" here refers to the sum and dynamic of all the ways these free persons actually particularize their freedom. Recall that the specific character of individual action is accidental with respect to freedom in the Condition of Right and thus answers to no standard of the good apart from the arbitrary character of each person's desires. It has no institutions that could educate (cultivate) its desire to do anything other than accumulate pleasures and property. To say otherwise presupposes higher forms of freedom and thus skips steps of the conceptual dialectic.

But this form of pleasure and property seeking really just invigorates a particular form of the appetitive desire, the one described in chapter 1. The logic of that relationship, we recall, is a "struggle to the death." It has the character of what Hegel calls, once more, the bad infinite – an infinite that repeats a determinate cycle without ever, in the case of desire, arriving at a point of real satisfaction. This happens because what the self in the struggle to the death most truly wants is not to defeat this or that opponent, but to be recognized *as determining centre*. This recognition, as we have seen, can take place only in a system of mutual recognition – in co-operation. The person of the Condition of Right does not understand this, and is thus focused on the bad infinite of appetitive desire. The logical structure of desire as temporary and constantly repeated satisfaction is the logic of many forms of human activity. This structure of desire is present not only in hunger and sexual desire but also in the accumulation of wealth and power. Each new achievement of wealth and power only creates the possibility of yet more wealth or yet more power. The respect accorded to each individual qua singular will is meaningful and is a necessary condition of a fully free society, but it is grossly insufficient to hold in check the temptation to pursue the bad infinites that beguile the arbitrary will, epitomized by the exclusive pleasures of private property. Individuals in the Condition of Right thus tend to stake their freedom on the infinite unsatisfiability of these specific forms of appetitive desire embodied in endlessly different forms of material acquisition and the accumulation of power.[20] The Condition of Right comes to be dominated by "the assertion of cold, acquisitive power."[21]

We noted above how the contradiction between juridical-imaginative recognition and concrete-lived recognition motivates a series of conflicts in the ethical order. In the present case, Hegel argues that the concrete-lived world of recognition is characterized by an unregulated competition for power among arbitrary wills. As in any situation of competition over limited material resources and even more restricted avenues of political power, there will be those who are relatively successful and those who are not. Moreover, it is precisely by means of moderate successes in accumulating wealth and power that one is in a better position to accumulate yet more. In short, the competitive structure of arbitrary will pursued in the Condition of Right motivates a concentration of power in fewer and fewer hands, and this concentration is exacerbated further as those who obtain control of the means of coercion, ideological or physical, learn how to better exercise it.

Moreover, this struggle can intensify, and wealth and power can become increasingly concentrated without seeming, at first, to contradict the principles of the society. Since the Condition of Right is made up of free atoms, its logical form of governance is democratic. However, as power and wealth concentrate in fewer and fewer hands, the form of governance changes. Even if it is the intention of the Condition of Right to organize itself on "the principle of free personality in democratic form," the increasing centralization of power leads, correspondingly, to the relative powerlessness of all but a small number of individuals. This leads to "a collision," first between the "democratic" principle and "the substantial intuition of an aristocracy," and from there even further into the tyranny of "an abstract and arbitrary will of increasingly monstrous proportions."[22] That is, since there is nothing to check the concentration of power, this process, if it carries on to its logical conclusion, will pass from democracy to aristocracy and ultimately generate a situation in which there is one singular will that controls everyone else: the tyrant (in Rome, the Emperor).[23]

The self of the Condition of Right, however free in its abstract ability to choose, becomes "the play of these raging elements" that are unleashed in the competitive fray of this kind of society.[24] These "elements" are allowed to rage precisely because they have been understood all along as inessential to freedom. The content of the Condition of Right is nothing other than the accumulated expression of its singular members, but this very externalization turns on its own agents and destroys them as if from the outside.[25] This is what Hegel means when he says, "The actuality preserves its determinate being through self-consciousnesses' own externalization [*Entäusserung*] and abandonment of essence, which, in the devastation which rules in the world of Right, appears to self-consciousness to be brought about from the external violence of the elements let loose."[26] The stability of the Condition of Right can eventually be maintained only by coercion.[27] The extremes of wealth and power turn the formerly equal and free persons into a "corrupt rabble."[28]

In Rome this tyranny is the power of the Emperor and his army, but in other instantiations of the Condition of Right the centralization of power could take other forms. Indeed, Alexis de Tocqueville's notion of "soft despotism," applicable to liberal societies, is very similar in logical structure to the Condition of Right, even if its form of tyranny turns out to be quite different from the excesses of the Roman emperors. "The first thing that strikes the observation is an innumerable multitude of men, all equal and alike, incessantly endeavoring to procure the petty and paltry pleasures with which they glut their lives. Each of them, living apart, is a stranger to the fate of the rest ... Above this race of men stands an immense and tutelary power, which takes upon itself alone to secure their gratifications and to watch over their fate. That power is absolute, minute, regular, provident, and mild."[29] We will see later that contemporary liberal-capitalism, with its powerful forces of capital accumulation, concentration, and the concomitant centralization of political power, also has striking similarities to the Condition of Right.

Thus, if it is the case that the Ethical Society creates the destructive force that undermines it (the singular person), so too does the Condition of Right. This form of society creates a concentration of wealth and power that ultimately destroys the liberty upon which this very development was predicated. The destructive force created in the Condition of Right is not the singular person as such (which was precisely what needed to be recognized as we emerged from the contradictions of the Ethical Society), but the accumulated impact of all the particular actions that these selves arbitrarily choose. The immediate unity of *singular* person and *universal* state is transgressed by the domination of a *particular* individual or class as it accumulates an eventually oligarchical or tyrannical power. Once again, it is not *necessary* that the conflicts engendered by this contradiction will lead to the downfall of actual empirical societies, but in conceptual dialectic, we proceed to the logical conclusion: abstract universal recognition of singular choice leads from a democratic starting point to aristocracy and then to tyranny.

We have thus seen that no *immediate identity*[30] of the self with the universal produces a harmonious society.[31] This was true first of the Ethical Society in which the self is determined by its *particular* role and again in the Condition of Right in terms of the self as a universally recognized *singular* chooser. In the former, the substance of the whole, the universal, is immediately unified with particular roles, which function as organs within a body-politic. The Condition of Right, meanwhile, is the immediate identity between the universal, the society as a whole, and the singular, arbitrary person. It fails as it collapses into tyranny. We have, therefore, observed the dialectical failure of both forms of immediacy. The "shade" of singular freedom haunted and destroyed the Ethical Society, just as the monstrous tyranny of particularity turns against the Condition of Right. But if the self, whether conceived as particular or singular, cannot immediately unite to form a universal harmony, then a whole new and frightening form of life emerges. By virtue of the fact that it creates alien forces that turn on their creators in a fury of destruction, freedom seems to be its own worst enemy.[32] Freedom becomes "monstrous" and humanity becomes alienated from itself. If all attempts at immediate relations of the self and the universal have failed, then these relations must fall apart. A new and more sophisticated society must emerge to cope with this *self-alienation* of human freedom. The vital contradiction that moved the Ethical Society to collapse in the face of the singular person emerged once more in the Condition of Right with the collapse of democracy into aristocracy and aristocracy into tyranny. The danger of an alienated freedom, however, would seem to threaten to destroy the vitality of contradiction and leave only a dead end, a mere *aporia*. We turn, then, to "self-alienated spirit," or "culture."

6

Alienation and the Society of Absolute Freedom

We seem to have arrived at a dilemma. If societies recognize singular, arbitrary freedom, they are destroyed by the concentration of wealth and power created thereby. Yet, if they restrain singular freedom in an organic body-politic, they become repressive, generating the rebellious and subversive powers of singular freedom. Indeed, once the genie of human liberty has been let out of the bottle, it is impossible to put it back in. The predicament which we now confront in conceptual dialectic is, in reality, one with which all societies must cope. The failure to resolve this predicament condemns humanity, it would seem, to a ceaseless oscillation between a repressive, organic logic and reckless, individualistic competition. We have, in effect, become "alienated" from our own freedom since, no matter how we organize our political community, our freedom becomes its own worst enemy. Freedom, Hegel says, is now "Self-alienated Spirit" (*Der sich entfremdete Geist*).

We have, in effect, lost our freedom and must strive to re-attain it. To do so we must change ourselves, we must "develop" or "cultivate" our powers in order to achieve our freedom. Freedom is not something discovered in any kind of immediate identity, but is the product of a deliberate act of self-development, self-creation, and self-cultivation (*Bildung*). Hegel analyses the self-transcending of freedom that seeks a solution to the predicament of the Condition of Right in section B of chapter 6 of the *Phenomenology*, "Self-Estranged Spirit; Culture" (*Der sich entfremdete Geist; Bildung*). The most sophisticated form of Culture, Hegel argues, can be found in the logic of freedom that animated the French Revolution. He calls this "Absolute Freedom." We will see, however, that it also fails by collapsing into its own kind of terrorism. The society of Culture thus culminates in "Absolute Freedom and Terror" (*absolut Freiheit und der Schrecken*).[1]

1 THE CULTIVATION OF RATIONAL FREEDOM

In order to show how we can cultivate our freedom, I dwell on the predicament of self-alienated spirit with some care. As soon as free persons in the Condition of Right *particularize* their freedom, as soon as they choose to do *this rather than that*, they create a mounting momentum that moves the society from its democratic principles to aristocracy or even tyranny. This chaotic content is then no longer reflective of freedom and appears as a "monstrous" alien. Freedom, therefore, when it is defined in terms of the *person* and the *arbitrary will*, which does whatever particular thing it wants, becomes "self-alienated." It is the chaotic particularity of freedom that runs amok and becomes a force of destruction.

However, this is to say that if the free person truly wants freedom, she must choose something *other than* the arbitrary will. However, if she, qua singular chooser, rejects the arbitrary will for *something else*, this something else, whatever else it might be, will nonetheless still be a *particular*. But to be *mandated* to choose one particular over another is to no longer be the person of the Condition of Right, for this person was defined as choosing whatever particular she wanted. To be mandated to choose one particular renounces free personality. If there is a route out of this predicament, the free will must be able to *choose* and yet, paradoxically, cannot be free to choose to do simply what he or she wants. Of course, the fact that this choice of the particular is necessarily the *choice of a singular will* rules out a return to the Ethical Society (although reactionary fantasies of returning to this Garden of Eden plague free human beings). So, this free will now knows what it does not want, the arbitrary will, but it seems that it does not yet know what it *does* want. Or does it?

The arbitrary will created particular factions that pitted themselves against each other, leading the strongest to win aristocratic and then even tyrannical rule. That is, if the arbitrary will of the free person creates a monstrous alien force, then the monster must be prevented from being born in the first place. The free self must choose to follow the imperative to prevent precisely the emergence of the particular factions of wealth and power that destroyed the Condition of Right – or, should they arise, to eliminate them. Indeed, any particular group within the society is potentially a faction that could lead to aristocracy. The free will must cultivate itself to the point where it knows to choose *against particularity as such*. But to choose neither this nor that – to choose no determinate thing in particular – is either to choose all (the universal) or nothing. It is impossible to choose nothing, for such a choice is a disengagement that itself has *particular* impacts on the world. Thus, if one cannot choose "none" surely one must then choose "all" – one must choose the *universal*. The determinate negation of the failure of the societies of immediacy is the self that has learned that it must choose the universal. The citizen must choose the "common good."

More concretely, if we are to choose the universal, common good, we must fight against what we have already learned will destroy it: particular factions. That is, the universal adequate to freedom must be a "mediated" universal – a *created* community whose mandate is to ensure that no particular factions emerge within it. In order to instantiate freedom, then, the singular self must choose to cultivate a free universal society and, in the process, cultivate itself into a stance that is adequate to membership in this new society.

Before following this dialectic, I want to focus a bit longer on the key themes of this section of the *Phenomenology* as a whole, which have as much to do with an evolving notion of the "universal" as with a gradual cultivation of the singular self. The self has learned that it cannot simply follow whatever particular path it wants, as in the Condition of Right, because this leads to chaos and tyranny. The will must therefore submit itself to a universal or common good and reject the particularity of this or that faction. If, then, it was the free reign of particularity that led to tyranny, particularity must answer to the demands of the whole, to the *universal*. Freedom has learned that it has some necessities.

Yet what kind of "universal" are we speaking of here? The first form of universality we encountered in the conceptual dialectic of social freedom was that of a primitive or immediate *totality* in the Ethical Society. It is a concrete universal, a good infinite, which determines the particular within it. The second form of universality, in the Condition of Right, was an abstract universal by virtue of which the freedom of each singular will is perfectly identified with every other will in a realm of abstract, pure equality. But since neither of these forms of universality is adequate to human freedom, as we saw, the free self must commit itself to a new and more substantial universality that (a) has the power to determine or limit the particular (and in this sense is like the universal of the Ethical Society), but (b) still recognizes the freedom of the singular will (and in this sense is like the universal of the Condition of Right).

To pose this kind of demand, however, is to pose the demand to be *rational*. Rationality, after all, determines particulars by virtue of their universal concept. Two examples of reason – geometry and Kant's categorical imperative – serve to demonstrate why this is so. Of course, we are still, here, in the realm of the understanding (*Verstand*) rather than reason (*Vernunft*) so we can anticipate that something is going to go awry. When I calculate the area of a circle using the formula πr^2, I am acting autonomously as a singular self. No external force has compelled me, for it is my own thought that carries out the entire operation. And yet the rationality of that formula subordinates all particularity to its universal imperative: as a particular self I come to the same conclusion as all other particular selves and, moreover, each particular circle has its identity only by participating in the universal concept of all circles. That is, our particularity (whether mine versus yours, or this circle versus that one) does not make any difference, and it does not make any difference precisely because it is the universal that, in its very concept, articulates what the particular is. This or that particular circle is a circle only because it has a certain universal definition.

Similarly, when I follow Kant's categorical imperative, I act freely as a singular will. I am acting in a manner that is not compelled by any external force. And yet my particular action is determined by the rational universal: *to act such that the maxim of my action is a universal law*.[2] The singularity of the will is freely exercised, and yet the particularity of action, once again, is subordinated to the universal. When I choose to tell you the truth in this particular moment and in our particular relationship, I, as a singular agent, am freely choosing some particularity, and yet it is "telling the truth," which is a universal maxim, that determines this particularity – some specific instance of telling the truth. The particularity of action does not make any difference (according to this account) since it is entirely determined by the universal. The determinations of the specific situations in which I tell the truth – to you yesterday, to my mother next week – do not matter; they make no difference.

Yet there is a key difference between geometry and the categorical imperative. The identity of a particular circle with its universal definition is not an achievement because they are in *immediate* relationship. The free self in Kant's philosophy, however, must be cultivated to embrace the rational. Kant's book *On Education*, for example, articulates the appropriate steps required to carry out such cultivation.[3] Rational freedom is *mediated* by the process of cultivation. While triangles do not need to be "made" rational, human individuals and human societies do. An intrinsic or potential rationality must be cultivated to be realized.

What, then, would this rational cultivation look like as the form of a society? The singular members of this society must choose, but choose in such a way as to ensure that particularity "makes no difference," and thus choose for the sake of the universal – the common good. Any particularity that does make a difference is a faction – a particularity that defeats the rationality of the society. The third form of society we must consider is, therefore, the *rational* society, epitomized according to Hegel in the French Revolution, which sought to embody the philosophical principles of Rousseau's "General Will"[4] and Kant's "Kingdom of Ends."[5] The particular groupings within the society, which Hegel calls "masses," must have their identity determined by the universal. The "self-certainty" of "absolute freedom" "is the essence of all the spiritual masses of the real world."[6]

For a political illustration I return briefly to the discussion of property. Property right is a system of mutual recognition in which a universal community recognizes my right, as particular, to exclude others from something. The mistake of the Condition of Right was to prioritize the particularity of property over its universality. Property thus accumulates according to the contingencies of particularity itself, instead of being organized by the universal. The "rational" notion of property right to which we must now cultivate ourselves corrects this mistake. Property, even if exclusive, must serve the system of mutual recognition as a whole: it must not stand in the way of the universal community which is its presupposition. For this reason, St Just argued that all citizens in revolutionary France should have equal amounts of property. Thus, he thought, the particular exclusivity of private property would *make no difference*. To generalize this issue and put it in Hegel's terms, in order to be "in and for itself," the free will must choose to commit itself not to a content outside of freedom, such as this or that pleasure of the arbitrary will, but must make its content the form of freedom itself. Thus Hegel says, "The absolute determination or, if one prefers, the absolute drive, of the free spirit is to make its freedom into its object." We have seen in chapter 1, however, that when the "free will ... wills the free will,"[7] she is willing the universal system of mutual recognition *as such*, for a will is only free at all insofar as it is recognized.[8]

Hegel's argument in the present chapter continues to echo the dialectic of individual self-consciousness discussed in chapter 4. We have already seen that the self of the Ethical Society is a kind of slave to the law as master, insofar as the interpretation, choice, and deed of the singular self is not recognized by the juridical-imaginative structures of this form of society. Moreover, just as the work of the slave generates a stoic self, the Condition of Right juridically recognizes the stoic self as the foundation of its legal system. The universal right of individuals to pursue their own goals, however, collapses into the chaos of tyranny, which corresponds, in chapter 4, to *skepticism*. The response in Self-Alienated Spirit or Culture is a form of self that now posits a universal truth from which it is alienated yet toward which it is bound to strive, called the "unchangeable" in the section that follows skepticism, the "unhappy consciousness" in chapter 4 of the *Phenomenology*. That is, the self must *mediate* its relationship to the truth precisely by *cultivating* or developing itself in such a way as to fulfill the universal and overcome its alienation.[9]

In this long and multi-faceted middle section of the "Spirit" chapter of the *Phenomenology*, Hegel repeatedly articulates different ways in which a free self strives to overcome its alienation and achieve a cultivated, rational union with the universal. Broadly speaking, the "Culture" section of the *Phenomenology* opens with the diremption, the self-division, of the unhappy consciousness into the utter separation of new, radically opposed versions of what used to be the divine, unchangeable law and the human, changeable law. The divine law, which used to be the animating reality of day-to-day life in the Ethical Society, can be preserved only as a divine realm completely beyond and inaccessible to the earthly mortal. This is the relationship, for example, of the Christian who has *faith* in a God who resides only in a heaven beyond the world of mortals. Thus, part 1 (of three parts) of Self-Alienated Spirit in the *Phenomenology* is called "The World of Self-Estranged Spirit" and comprises part a, "Culture and Its World of Actuality" and part b, "Faith and Pure Insight." If each section consists of a certain kind of commitment, and hence cultivation, of the free self, both will collapse into a commitment or conversion to rationality in part 2, "The Enlightenment," such that the enemy of reason is no longer faith but "The

Struggle of Enlightenment with Superstition," and the realm of actuality becomes "The Truth of Enlightenment." The triumph of Enlightenment reason then takes place in part 3 of this section, which is called "Absolute Freedom and Terror." Here the cultivated self and the cultivated, universal community are created. Thus, this last section outlines the most sophisticated logic of freedom that the world of "Culture" can provide and I turn shortly to a careful examination of its juridical-imaginative and concrete-lived structures of recognition.

First, however, I want to explore the demands of this form of rationality still further, and also get a clear hint as to why it will fail, by briefly considering a form of cultivated self in the opening sections of "Self-Alienated Spirit." Early in this section, Hegel postulates a type of "noble consciousness" which attempts to unite the universal good with his singular will through dutiful council to the king.[10] That is, he tries with selfless service to unite his own singular will with the common or universal good as embodied in the monarch. This selflessness (that is, he wants no *particular* benefit to accrue to him qua *singular*), however well-intentioned, fails because in the process he accumulates wealth and power to which other particular selves do not have access. "Thus although the noble consciousness defined himself as one who might approach the universal power as an *equal*, the truth of the situation is rather that in his service he retained his own being-for-self, and in the very abdication of his personality there was still the actual sublating and rending asunder of the universal substance."[11] This dialectic thus ends in the "wit," a cynical consciousness modelled on Diderot's provocative novel *Rameau's Nephew* who recognizes the necessity of the institutions of wealth and power, and yet still understands that they represent the unjust appropriations of the common wealth by certain people as opposed to others. Here particular advantage always taints an effort of the free person to do the purely good (universal) thing.

This same logic develops in "Absolute Freedom and Terror." The task of Absolute Freedom is to institutionalize a state that attempts simultaneously to recognize the free choice of the singular self while ensuring that no particular factions emerge that could disrupt the universal harmony.[12] In what follows, I describe Hegel's account of Absolute Freedom (and its demise) with reference to Rousseau, whose work is constantly at the front of Hegel's mind in this section.[13]

There are several aspects of Rousseauian participatory democracy that allow it to fulfill this rational mandate. First, the community of citizens is not merely an aggregate of singular, arbitrary wills who do what they want but, as Rousseau puts it, there must a "General Will" beyond the "Will of All."[14] Rousseau's rationalism leads him to realize that the elimination of particular factions requires the rejection of any form of representative democracy since the elected representatives are then a faction with greater power than the citizens who elected them. "The English people believes itself to be free," Rousseau charges, but "it is gravely mistaken; it is free only during the election of Members of Parliament; as soon as the Members are elected, the people is enslaved."[15] The citizen of a representative democracy is alienated from her freedom precisely because others make decisions on her behalf. When this happens, the elected representatives become a faction, the de facto autocrats who run the society. "For wherever the self is only *represented* and not *presented*," Hegel says, "it is not *actual*; wherever it is *delegated*, it is does not exist."[16] It is thus those who have power delegated to them that are the dominant and dominating faction: the elected representatives.

Furthermore, the attempt to achieve perfect unity of the singular self with the state requires that any structure that prevents complete integration be eliminated. This society comes into existence, Hegel says, when "each single consciousness is raised above the sphere to which it had been apportioned, and in such a way that it no longer finds its essence and its work in this particularized mass, but grasps its self as the *concept* of the will, all the masses as the essence of this will, and hence can only be made actual in a labor which is a total labor. In this absolute freedom all the estates that are the spiritual essences, into which the whole is articulated, are abolished."[17] Not surprisingly, then, the French Revolution saw quickly to the abolition of the Estates General, and revolutionary ideologues like St Just, as I mentioned above, recommended the equality of private property, such that each citizen would have his own farm equal in size to all others. Each citizen would thus have a stake in the society, but a stake no greater or lesser than his fellow citizens. For Hegel these "masses" include not only the Estates but also (since the society is supposed to be a perfect participatory democracy) the "legislative, judicial and executive power."[18] These particularities must be eliminated because they represent sites of activity that might have interests contrary to those of the whole and thus fail to allow citizens a non-particularized relationship with the state. After all, these particularities could easily threaten to pursue their own interests rather than that of the universal. In Rousseau's terms, "Thus if the general will is to be clearly expressed, it is imperative that there be no sectional associations in the state, and that every citizen should make up his own mind for himself."[19]

2 TERRORIZING PARTICULARITY

For the general (universal) will of Absolute Freedom to be present without alienation, it must be the case that each and every (particular) act of the society fully embodies the general will without remainder. That is, each and every act in the sphere of concrete-lived recognition must be in perfect harmony with the universal or common good of the system of recognition as a whole. This is impossible for a series of reasons, all of which are intelligible in terms of human finitude – that is, human particularity. I will first discuss some reasons that Hegel did not address, but could have, and then move on to Hegel's own analysis.

First, participatory democracies are impossible in even moderate sized groups. Everyone cannot be an expert at everything, nor can everyone be constantly present and debate every decision that is necessary to the ongoing life of the society. Individuals will find it possible to concentrate on only a handful of the aspects of social reproduction and thus will never develop the kind of knowledge needed to make good political decisions on those matters outside their own expertise. Presidents and prime ministers must consult with numerous experts who advise them on the determinations of particular situations.

Furthermore, in a society of limited material resources any decision to allocate certain finite resources in one place means that they must be taken away from somewhere else. This "opportunity cost" means that, for example, one particular sphere must be neglected relative to another such that the particularity of the former is announced as under-resourced and under-realized.[20] Further, the satisfaction of basic needs invites situations in which goods and services are unequally distributed.

The individual self, moreover, is always subject to suspicion, for even when she intends otherwise, she acts in such a way that she achieves something of her own particular good at the expense of others in the community. Indeed, this is what we saw in our brief consideration of the noble consciousness. What is more, the networks of family, friendship, and institutional and sectoral involvement form particular micro-communities within the whole all of which have goals that involve opportunity costs and the accumulation of power and wealth greater than that of others. Perhaps most importantly, no individual or particular group can be immediately identified with a general good (as Absolute Freedom conceives it) of the system of recognition as a whole because there is no "pure universal" – the community is always perceived from this or that particular station.

No matter how we express ourselves, Hegel is ultimately arguing, it is a particular expression. We can never leave behind or purify ourselves of our exclusive particularity and completely harmonize ourselves with the inclusive universality of the *community*. The universal, the realm of ethical and political life, can never determine the particulars as it can in the case of circles or triangles. Individuals and communities always benefit or suffer in exclusive and unique ways in relation to each other and to the community as a whole. Our utterances and deeds, however well motivated, come from our own unique, and thus *particular*, perspectives. Insofar as I act at all, I uniquely determine myself in a way that differentiates me and to some extent excludes me from others and from the universality of general will.[21] Of course, this does not make all action equally particular and thus arbitrary. It makes a great deal of difference that, say, one devote oneself to the formation of an excellent, universal public school system rather than treat others as merely a means to one's own enrichment. Both actions are particular, and even if (as we will see below) the former is beneficial to the society, it is nonetheless still in certain ways exclusive: certain people will benefit from public education more than others. All the same, the creation of an excellent education system does have authentic universal benefits that greatly outstrip whatever benefits selfishness might have (notwithstanding Adam Smith's famous argument, which Hegel in the last analysis rejects).

The same dynamic takes place if we move from the point of view of the citizen of the participatory democracy to its governance. Herein we consider Hegel's explicit arguments. Since not everyone can be assembled for every decision (much less participate in each decision fully and equally even if they could be so assembled), the society of Absolute Freedom must appoint a government to oversee its activities. Yet in so doing, the goal of Absolute Freedom is betrayed. "The government is itself nothing else than the point that fixes itself, or the individuality of the universal will. A willing and fulfilling that emanates from one point, the government will and, at the same time, fulfills a definite order and policy. It thereby excludes, on the one hand, the rest of the individuals from its action; on the other, by excluding them, it constitutes itself as the kind of government that is a determinate will, and hence it is opposed to the universal will. It cannot possibly present itself, therefore, in any other way than as a *faction* [*Faktion*]. Only the *victorious* faction is called government; and just in its being a faction there lies immediately the necessity of its demise; in its being government – this conversely is what makes it a faction and guilty."[22]

The guilt in question here emerges from the transgression that each particular institutional action makes against the general will. Each action expresses a particular will, a particular perspective, a particular set of power relations, and thus each act in some way does violence to Absolute Freedom. Notice, then, that in the Society of Absolute Freedom, each and every action within the realm of concrete-lived recognition violates the demands of the juridical-imaginative sphere of recognition and thus universal freedom becomes universal guilt.

Hegel goes on to show that this guilt produces an equally universal suspicion, the result of which is a furious attempt at repression – the "Terror."[23] The perfect identity of the singular self with the universal is sought by repressing the forms of particularity that emerge. As Hegel observes, the French Revolution "was a time of trembling and quaking and of intolerance towards everything particular. For fanaticism wills only what is abstract, not what is articulated, so that whenever differences emerge, it finds them incompatible with its own indeterminacy and cancels them. This is why the people, during the French Revolution, destroyed once more the institutions they had themselves created, because all institutions are incompatible with the abstract self-consciousness of equality."[24] That is, it is not only the institutions of the *ancien régime* that must be destroyed. The society of Absolute Freedom finds that it must constitute its own institutions that are nonetheless still necessarily alienated from their own explicit goal, which it must in turn destroy once more. It is institutions *as such* that are the enemy of the universal, and that must therefore be destroyed.

In sum, the goal of a juridical-imaginative system of recognition based on Absolute Freedom is impossible to institutionalize successfully. The concrete world of lived recognition, as we have seen, requires a particularization that eliminates the possibility of the universal community defined in terms of Enlightenment reason.

The society of Absolute Freedom is thus left on the horns of a dilemma. On the one hand, it can continue its project of repressing all particularity and thus engage in a practice of incessantly chasing its own tail. It may, for example, end up like a stereotypical twentieth-century communist regime that maintains the fiction of an abstract equality only by means of the tyrannical power of a fanatical ruling party whose power is in direct contradiction with its own egalitarian mandate. On the other hand, it can drop its contradictory commitment to repressing particularity and then allow particular spheres to flourish on their own terms – that is, revive the Condition of Right. It is in fact this latter course that the great nations of Absolute Freedom have taken. The French and American revolutions have seen the republican, participatory ideal abandoned[25] in such a way as to unleash a mostly unfettered capitalism that, as we shall see in detail below, creates a version of the tyranny of the Condition of Right.

This society is logically contradictory even before the repercussions of its repressions start to fall into place. That is, the attempt of singular persons to eradicate particularity is *itself a particular action* – it is to do *this rather than that*. This logical contradiction arises in the monstrous return of the particular, which haunted French society (according to Hegel) all too literally during the Terror of the Revolution. The third form of society in our conceptual dialectic has failed, just like its two predecessors.

Once more the vitality of contradiction has generated a sophisticated even if failed attempt to cultivate freedom. And indeed, the Society of Absolute Freedom is much closer to the realization of freedom than either the Ethical Society or the Condition of Right. By committing itself to universal and rational freedom, the Society of Absolute Freedom lays claim for the first time to *autonomy*: a freedom that gives itself its own laws. Furthermore, it thus knows much more about freedom than the Condition of Right, for it knows that in an essential way freedom must choose to affirm *itself*, in and through a system of mutual recognition, rather than choose to follow its arbitrary and exclusive desires. It knows, moreover, that freedom has its own necessity – choices it must necessarily make to realize itself. The society of Absolute Freedom knows the dangers of particularity and the threat of a domineering universality, and it knows that freedom is not merely a state of choosing but is a sophisticated form of human interaction that must be carefully cultivated. Yet even this attempt to establish institutions adequate to freedom has foundered on a vital contradiction of its own.

All three forms of society considered so far have failed because of emergent contradictions between their juridical-imaginative and concrete-lived spheres of mutual recognition. In this case, the juridical-imaginative sphere of recognition insisted that the particular be determined by the universal. At the level of concrete-lived recognition, however, particularity always asserted itself. Where does that leave the project of human freedom? In the next section I seek to understand Hegel's solution to this predicament.

PART TWO

FREEDOM AND THE JUST SOCIETY

7

The Fundamental Institutions of a Just Society

The vital contradictions of freedom have propelled us past the Society of Absolute Freedom and its cultivation of abstract, Enlightenment rationality. It may well seem, however, that we have reached an impasse: the rationality of freedom appears to be at odds with itself. The three essential elements in the concept of freedom that we have identified – universality, particularity, and singularity – are persistently in conflict with each other. The Ethical Society was able to maintain the harmony of particular spheres within a concrete universal whole, but the fact that it excluded the third term, singular freedom, led to its downfall. The Condition of Right universally recognized this singular freedom only to have particularity run amok and create tyranny. Finally, Absolute Freedom attempted and failed to discipline the particular choices of singulars in the name of a universal common good, resulting in the Terror. It would seem, in other words, that the singularity, particularity, and universality of freedom are, no matter how they are combined, irrevocably at odds with each other.

However, Hegel's philosophy spurns just this kind of aporia. For Hegel the vitality of contradiction generates *development, movement, growth – life*. An examination of Hegel's critique Kant's antinomies of pure reason serves to show how he moves beyond the apparent impasse.

Hegel argues that Kant, in the *Critique of Pure Reason*, fails to see the vitality of contradiction. A Kantian antinomy juxtaposes two propositions which are both necessarily true and yet contradict each other. Kant concludes that reason "criticizes" itself for its own failure to achieve a unified system: its project to grasp the intelligible unity of reality reaches unsurpassable obstacles.[1] Hegel points out that antinomial terms are typically abstractions which, when held together in a concrete concept, serve as the logical poles of an ontological tension or antagonism that puts something into motion in human experience. If we take Kant's famous Third Antinomy as a working example, it can be shown that humanity is not trapped by the imperative to conceive the world both as governed by necessity and as containing free will. When the understanding (*Verstand*) conceives freedom and necessity in their purity, they are mutually exclusive abstractions. But when considered concretely by reason (*Vernunft*), freedom and necessity are perceived in their appropriate context and mutual mediation. For a human being, an action is *motivated*, as Merleau-Ponty puts it in his great "Freedom" chapter of the *Phenomenology of Perception*. A human action is never utterly conditionless or utterly necessary. Our experience is characterized by something more like degrees of motivation in which the "in-itself" of necessity and the "for-itself" of liberty never exist in a pure state, but are blended in various degrees. The power of the *understanding* is to grasp the abstract conditions of action, freedom, and necessity, but its failure is to hypostasize them and thus to completely lose sight of their dynamic tension with each other. This is the contribution of *reason*, which conceives what we have called the transcendental antagonisms of vital contradiction.

At the same time, Hegelian philosophy is strictly opposed to a priori rule-making. If an unfolding process of becoming reaches an impasse, then we are compelled to recognize the truth of that impasse. Indeed, we seem to have found ourselves at such an impasse now. The conceptual dialectic of societies plainly rules out a return to previous forms, yet simultaneously offers no obvious route forward. We cannot entertain the reactionary option of returning to the Ethical Society because this is a renunciation of our freedom as singular agents: it is to abandon the for-itself for the comforting security of the in-itself. Attempts to return to ethical life are always failures since to choose to give up one's freedom is still to choose, and to choose is to be self-determining rather than pre-determined. Fascist and other reactionary regimes can thus go through the motions of renouncing the manifestations of freedom – "Gesellschaft," "liberalism," or "capitalism" – and do so in the name of *Volk*, traditional and family values, or what have you, but the mystique of these obsolete institutions is a deceptive trick and the longing for them a manifestation of a truly conservative and self-destructive, even masochistic, element of the human psyche.[2] If liberalism institutionalizes the juridical recognition of persons as free, then any future society will have to be at least in some sense liberal. In recognizing our freedom, humanity achieved a more sophisticated way of being, and there is no (successful) turning back.

A kind of three-way antinomy has formed in the concept of freedom. The singular choice of the free person, the masses and organizations of social particularity, and the common or universal good are all necessary and yet each is systematically incompatible with the others. We could neither exclude one term nor find a way to harmonize all three. If the dialectic truly ends at this point, human political history will consist of an endless oscillation between the three basic types of society we have identified, with no stable resolution possible.

Indeed, Hegel himself seems to suggest that the dialectic of the free society ends by going around in circles, ceaselessly rotating through the Ethical Society, the Condition of Right, and the Society of Absolute Freedom. This happens because the Terror of the Society of Absolute Freedom may frighten individuals into the slavish attitude that dominated the Ethical Society. Speaking of the chaotic and paranoid violence of the Terror, he states, "Out of this tumult, spirit would be hurled back to its starting point to the ethical and real world of culture that has merely been restored and rejuvenated by the fear of the Lord that has returned to men's minds. If the result were only the complete interpenetration of self-consciousness and substance, spirit would have to run through this cycle of necessity once more, and repeat it over and over again."[3] And yet even if this return is possible (and human beings will often be tempted to make reactionary decisions), Hegel does not see it as the final position. He argues that there is indeed a fourth stair on the dialectical ladder of society.

The key insight of the Society of Absolute Freedom was that freedom requires *Bildung – culture*, or better yet the *cultivation* of universality.[4] We have seen where that led, however. So I instead ask a more general question about cultivation: How, if at all, has the conceptual dialectic of the free society, which we have so far traced through three different failed societies, *cultivated our own wills*? What has it taught us, if anything, and has it perhaps given us a clue as to how we could determine the institutions of the just society?

In a way, each of the failed societies fails because it absolutizes a necessary and insufficient feature of freedom. That is, each society articulates the correct logic of *one essential part* of the free society as a whole and yet each fails by virtue of its identification of that logic with the whole society. A consideration of the dialectical path traversed so far from this perspective will bring us to the fourth and final stair on the conceptual dialectic of society. First, I identify the three necessary institutions of any free society: family (the logic of the Ethical Society), civil society (the logic of the Condition of Right), and state (the logic of Absolute Freedom). Second, I show that each of these three institutions is in an ongoing, vital contradiction with the others. Third, I conclude that even if this vital contradiction is never effaced, it is the universal life of the state (understood in Hegel's complex way) that most fulfills human freedom.

In the *Philosophy of Right* Hegel argues that there are three necessary institutions in any society that has cultivated itself to be truly free: *family*, *civil society*, and *state*. The dialectic of societies in the "Spirit" chapter of the *Phenomenology of Spirit* gives us the logic of the family as articulated in the Ethical Society, the logic of civil society as articulated in the Condition of Right, and the logic of state as articulated in the Society of Absolute Freedom. The fourth form of society, then, is the society that has learned how to synthesize what each of the previous three forms has taught about the character of freedom. That is, the vital contradictions of freedom have not left us empty-handed or at an antinomial impasse, but have been articulating all along the necessary and sufficient conditions for a free society.

I THE ETHICAL SOCIETY AND THE FAMILY

The Ethical Society is characterized by the principle that its customs, as epitomized by the divine law, are purely and simply the immediate truth. The will of the gods here is logically the same as the will of the master over the slave. We saw how the "deed" gradually educates the member of this society in the direction of recognizing the deliberative and choosing power of his or her singular will – as was also the case with the slave's work. Once singular selves recognize their power to alter and change law, indeed to cast the authority of human and divine law into doubt, they have in fact relocated authority from those laws to the judging mind.

Yet this is the character not just of a "primitive" society, the beginning of our dialectic, but is the primitive stance of all human self-determination, for this is essentially what it is like to be in a family. While the reality of the child – the norms of her family life and the laws and customs in which she grows up – is the result of a history of human interpretive action, the child does not experience it in this way. For the child, as for the member of the Ethical Society, the reality determined by her family is purely and simply identified with reality as such. She has no experience of any reality beyond that which is "familiar" to her. Just as the member of the Ethical Society must obey the laws of the gods, which come from "elsewhere" and yet determine all reality, the child finds herself in a world of customs which she had no part in creating and which present themselves to her as the terms of being itself.[5] In both cases, self-determination is in its infancy. To become self-conscious both the child and the member of the Ethical Society must elaborate their powers of self-determination.

While this experience of immediacy is most clearly the reality of a young child, something very similar is true of the other roles in family life – parents, grandparents, aunts, uncles, and so on. Indeed, just as Antigone knew that her duty was to bury her brother, so too do fathers, sisters, brothers, uncle, aunts, and grandparents generally know, with unreflective immediacy, what their responsibilities are. Of course, this does not preclude the common and dramatic failure of family members to fulfill these roles. However, the failures of adult family members are often echoes of the failures of previous generations and thus they themselves retain something of this immediacy. As Aristotle made clear in the *Ethics*, habituation (cultivation) is as persistent in harmful behaviours as in facilitative and enabling behaviours.

Familial immediacy, moreover, has another essential feature in common with the Ethical Society. Both are organic unities, totalities, such that ethical immediacy is differentiated into particular roles like the organs of a body. Parents, children, sisters, and brothers have different and yet immediately complementary functions. In sum, if the conceptual dialectic of society starts in the immediacy of ethical life, our first empirical "society" is the immediacy of our own family.

I have moved beyond Hegel's own explicit statements about the family to make this analysis. But the essence of familial life, for Hegel, is the immediacy of self-determination, which is the decisive characteristic that the family and the Ethical Society have in common. Hegel says of the Ethical Society, "In so far as it is the *immediate truth*, spirit is the *ethical life of a people*. It must advance beyond what it immediately is for consciousness, it must sublate the beautiful ethical life."[6] Hegel also describes the family in terms of its immediacy. "The family, as the *immediate substantiality* of spirit, has as its determination the spirit's *feeling* of its own unity, which is *love*. Thus the disposition [appropriate to the family] is to have self-consciousness of one's individuality *within this unity* as essentiality which has being in and for itself, so that one is present in it not as an independent person [*eine Person für sich*] but as a *member*."[7] That is, one is emphatically not in the family as a *legal person*, for that is the individual's status in civil society, but as a *member* – a member of an organic totality. One's identity in the family, then, is established not on the basis of one's free and universal personhood, which is in principle equal to all others and presupposes the (stoic) reflection of the free "I," but on the basis of the particular role in the family which is conferred by membership – son, daughter, father, mother, aunt, grandparent. In the family, as in the Ethical Society, the singularity of personhood is but a "shade" (to use Hegel's term for singularity in the Ethical Society).

As we saw briefly above, the child at first experiences familial norms as co-extensive with reality itself. Familial imperatives are, for her, reality's imperatives. However, as the child grows up, she plays at the interpretive, choosing, and acting life of the adult and gradually comes to recognize not only the powers of her own autonomy but the particularity of her family – her familial reality is one among many. The task of the family, Hegel says, "has the *negative* determination of raising the children out of the natural immediacy in which they originally exist to self-sufficiency and freedom of personality, thereby enabling them to leave the natural unit of the family."[8] That is, the kind of free "personhood" appropriate to adult life in civil society is an achievement of the family. The "discipline" of parents has a "deterrent effect on a freedom which is still entrammelled in nature" and seeks to "raise the universal into the children's consciousness and will."[9] From the point of view of the child, this discipline and cultivation literally "creates a longing to grow up."[10] The key to the family is to transcend the natural immediacy of the child, giving the children "their own feeling of dissatisfaction with themselves at the way they are – as the drive to belong to the adult world whose superiority they sense, or as the desire to grow up." As such, "The children are increasingly independent and gain in strength, thereby leaving their parents behind them."[11]

Hegel defends what is sometimes called the "bourgeois family" rather than any kind of extended family or other familial arrangement. But the precise form of his notion of the family is not essential to dialectical philosophy. If the family is an organic unity of ethical immediacy, there is no reason to assume that this family must consist of a heterosexual, monogamous, and life-long marriage commitment in which couples raise their children. It need consist only of at least one committed and loving adult who is willing to provide for the material and emotional well-being of his or her child. We might speculate that a family is better off with more than one adult, or debate other important themes in the constitution of families, but that is not a debate I will enter into here nor is it one that needs to be resolved for Hegel's fundamental point to be valid.[12]

The key is that the primitive stance of all human freedom is a kind of dependency on a natural immediacy not unlike the "divine law." That is, the child perceives these norms much like Antigone perceived the laws of the gods – as eternal, immutable, and "to be obeyed." I speak here not of this or that imperative imposed by a parent and resisted by an unwilling child, but about the broader axes of norms that a child identifies with reality as such. This is to say, the Ethical Society is the society for which the logic of the family, ethical immediacy, is the logic of society itself.

In the just society, however, the family knows that its own essence is to surpass itself. If the logic of the Ethical Society was an implicit self-surpassing, the family is the self-conscious recognition of the need for the self-surpassing of immediacy. The Ethical Society is quite literally the childhood of freedom. The vital contradiction that destroyed it is rendered self-conscious in the family that knows its own purpose to be its "dissolution" and "disintegration."[13] Just as the Ethical Society harbours within it the dialectic of its own self-transformation into the Condition of Right, so too does the family nurture *its own* transcendence toward civil society. The child, of course, sometimes rebels against the rules imposed on her, and she is constantly in a process of learning how to deal with her world in more and more sophisticated ways. Not unlike the slave in the "Self-Consciousness" chapter, or the singular agent in the Ethical Society, the child labours in the creation of her own freedom, albeit this time with the strong encouragement (hopefully) of her parents. Through her ever-increasing ability to transform her world, she simultaneously transforms the sense in which that familial world is co-extensive with reality itself. As she encounters other families and other realities and, indeed, as she learns to transform her world through her own creative activity, the ethical immediacy of the family starts to lose its power for her. The stages of childhood development mapped out by theorists like Freud, Lacan, Piaget, Kohlberg,

Gilligan, and others can all be constructively read as moments in the transformation of the child's world from a dependence on a familiar reality toward a creative, self-transforming, autonomy.

Ideally, and, indeed, to some degree at least, *usually*, the child becomes a "person" in the sense we have been using the term – independent and self-determining, someone who lays a claim that she should be able to do what she wants within the context of the mutual recognition of her own rights and those of others. At this point she leaves her family of origin and enters the world of *civil society* as a free, singular person. In civil society, as we shall see in more detail, everyone is a free and equal person, equipped to the greatest extent possible to particularize that freedom in any way each sees fit. Suffice it to say, however, that all human freedom begins in childhood and with the logic of family life and that the family, in some form, is the absolutely necessary starting point for the cultivation of human freedom.

However, even as she comes to perceive the mere particularity of her family and even as she comes to uphold a notion of the free and equal dignity of all persons, she does not thereby start to treat her family members according to the logic of civil society. My mother or my father is never reduced to a status of free and equal: by virtue of my love for and intimacy with them I *prefer* them over others. The bonds we have with our own family members are strong and very explicitly exclusive: these feelings are not shared with other people and never will be. The bonds of the family are powerfully and stubbornly particular. That is, to be in a family is to be committed to a logic of particularity: *my* family rather than *yours*. The family, moreover, is an odd institution in the sense that it uses this logic of *exclusive particularity*, *organic totality*, and *ethical immediacy* to prepare its children to enter a sphere, civil society, in which all these forms of human relation are repudiated. In civil society we reject exclusive particularity in the name of inclusive universality; we reject organic totality, the concrete universal, for the sake of abstract universal equality of a multiplicity of singular, free selves; and we transcend ethical immediacy for the sake of reflective freedom – the self-consciously free, choosing agent that bears rights and takes up his or her own sense of moral responsibility. We will need to return to this odd, self-repudiating character of the family shortly.

2 THE CONDITION OF RIGHT AND CIVIL SOCIETY

With the advent of self-conscious freedom, as we have seen, there is no turning back. Once human beings begin to cast skeptical doubt on "the will of the gods" or supposedly "natural laws," the human mind becomes an overwhelmingly subversive force. These natural laws and divine wills lose their power to command. The only form of law and custom that can survive skeptical doubt is one that institutionally and culturally recognizes the definitive importance of skeptical doubt itself. This is precisely what the Condition of Right sought to do: institutionalize a form of society in which the skeptical individual, the free person, could act in a self-determining manner. Clearly, then, if there is to be a way of organizing a society adequate to freedom, it must recognize this characteristic of free personhood. Hegel calls the institution that creates this space of personal freedom in a fully free world "civil society" (*bürgerliche Gesellschaft*). Moreover, he is the first philosopher to have identified the necessity of civil society for freedom and to have examined its consequences. Civil society becomes the institution of personal freedom that arises between the family and the state. Moreover, just as the Ethical Society is in a sense the logic of the family writ large, the institutionalization of free personhood in the Condition of Right is carried forward as the logic of civil society.

Hegel says that there are two essential features of civil society. First, civil society recognizes the singular person in his or her capacity to particularize herself *as she sees fit*. Hegel thus holds that "The concrete person, as a *particular* person, as a totality of needs and a mixture of natural necessity and arbitrariness, is his own end, is *one principle* of civil society."[14] Even to the point of reproducing the arbitrary will of the Condition of Right, it is emphatically important that freedom means that we can each choose our own course, our own way of life.

Of course, when we all do this, a richly complex web of interdependence develops and elaborates itself. This web is the second principle of civil society. "But this particular person stands essentially in relation to other similar particulars, and their *relation* is such that each asserts himself and gains satisfaction through the others, and thus at the same time through the exclusive *mediation* of the form of *universality*, which is the *second principle*."[15] This web is a complex "system of needs"[16] – an economy as well as particular institutions, bodies, and organizations. Even if civil society is constituted by the freedom of persons to do as they please, the actions they undertake to satisfy themselves will create interdependence, and this system of needs elaborates itself into a web of mutual interaction organized by law. Hegel summarizes this succinctly, saying that civil society is "an association of members as *self-sufficient individuals* [Einzelner] in what is therefore a *formal universality*, occasioned by their *needs* and by the *legal constitution* as a means of security for persons and property, and by an external order for their particular and common interests."[17]

Hegel believes that a society as a whole must create institutions that protect and enable civil society to embody its two essential functions, and in our time we generally ascribe these institutions – the police, judiciary, public services, and so on – to the state. However, according to Hegel, a state that carries functions like these in the name of civil society is not (yet) in any sense a separate institution from civil society since it is really a creature that answers to the logic of civil society itself. Its whole purpose is nothing other than to protect and regulate the activities *of* civil society. Hegel rather disparagingly calls this notion "the *external state*, the *state of necessity*"[18]

The universal equality of civil society exists only when we abstract from all the particular actions in which individuals engage. This universality is thus abstract or, as Hegel often calls it, merely "formal." This formal universality unites a multitude of individual atomistic persons each and every one of which is identical to all the others in his or her freedom. By virtue of this self-identity, it is also axiomatic that formal freedom is a freedom of universal equality.

It is not difficult to see how the logic of civil society corresponds to the Condition of Right: free persons in a relationship of universal equality particularize themselves as they see fit. Nor is it difficult to clarify the contrast between this, the logic of civil society, and that of the family. While the family is stubbornly particular and exclusive (my family rather than yours), civil society is universal and inclusive. That is, the categories of freedom and equality apply to everyone – no one is excluded. Moreover, while the family is an organic whole, a concrete universality in which members have different roles, civil society is defined by its abstract universal identity of an infinite number of equal and free citizens. Persons are considered not from the point of view of their particular differences but in their complete sameness to each other as rights-bearing, singular agents. Finally, while familial imperatives are by and large immediate, the person of civil society reflects on and chooses what she will do with her life. Furthermore, each person has the right to sift through on her own the moral principles that will guide her action and animate her conscience. The fact that many people may well act in civil society with the kind of unreflected immediacy that one finds in the family does not undermine Hegel's claim here. Civil society guarantees the right to such reflection and choice and even encourages individual persons to lay hold of these powers as part of the essence of a fully realized free person. In sum, civil society is the sphere of the abstract and inclusive universal recognition of free persons to mediate their engagement to the world through their own judgment.

Noble principles of universality, equality, and community may animate civil society just as they did the Condition of Right, but we have already seen in the latter case the kind dynamics that emerge when formal universality is put into practice. In the Condition of Right, the realm of particularity that emerges from formal universality is characterized by inequality and indeed, *escalating inequality*. Since civil society institutionalizes the same logic as the Condition of Right, we should not be surprised to find, as we shall see in some detail in the next chapter, that it easily lends itself to the same fate: forces that concentrate wealth and power in aristocratic and even tyrannical forms. Indeed, in the context of a capitalist society, we shall explore the almost ineluctable tendency toward plutocracy.

Those rather serious problems aside (for the moment), a free society nonetheless demands the existence of civil society. Since singular freedom is a necessary condition of freedom, as the Condition of Right discovered, any free society must have a civil society. The logic of the Condition of Right is sublated such as to become the logic of civil society.

3 THE VITAL CONTRADICTION OF FAMILY AND CIVIL SOCIETY

A free society is characterized by the institutions of the family and civil society and, as we shall see shortly, the state as well. It is tempting to conclude here, and Hegel's text in the *Philosophy of Right* is not much help on this point, that there is a tidy relationship between the family and civil society. Families, after all, quite naturally raise their children in such a way that, when the time comes, they fluidly enter civil society as free persons. This is not the whole story, and the first clue is that familial logic, when it is embodied in the Ethical Society, destroys itself. A clear-minded phenomenology of the relationship of family and civil society shows that they are not only necessary to each other but that they are also in ineluctable conflict. There is an abiding vital contradiction between them.

The ground of this conflict rests, first, in their contradictory logics. Whereas the family is based on ethical immediacy, concrete universality, and exclusive particularity, civil society is based on inclusive and abstract universality coupled with reflective (mediated) choice. Second, these contradictory logics cannot rest harmoniously one beside the other, for every person is animated by both logics simultaneously. That is, it is inevitable that our duties as family members and our freedom as members of civil society will conflict and we may even be tempted to impose the logic of one on the other. Moreover, given that the vocation of the family is to transform its own children from the logic of the family to that of civil society, the boundaries between these institutions can never be characterized by a clear or determinate distinction.

Since the family is typically based on extremely strong bonds of love, loyalty, and attachment, the emotional character of families does not harmonize perfectly with the supposed universal principles of civil society or the state. If, for example, everyone is universally "equal under the law" in civil society, there is not even the slightest pretence to this in the family. One typically favours the members of one's family over others. Parents can spend hundreds of hours stressed about the grades of their children and barely bat an eye at the recent death of thousands of foreigners in a distant earthquake. And there is nothing callous or insensitive about this attitude since family membership nurtures this highly committed, personal involvement, one that generates enormous love, devotion, and concern for one's own family members (or, indeed, anger, frustration, and anxiety). Moreover, it is not simply narrowness or base loyalty that is at play here, for each child requires for her cultivation the enormous dedication of love, time, energy, and teaching that parents, hopefully, provide. With respect to each other, family members do not follow the principle of civil society to treat everyone as equal, and to do so would be to fail to live up to one's responsibility as a family member. Rather, they treat their *particular* family members with the logic of "feeling" and "love" and, moreover, express this love differently on the basis of their particular role – father, mother, grandparent, daughter, aunt, and so on (depending, of course, on various cultural differences).

The strength of these bonds interferes directly in the workings of civil society, as one finds in various forms of corruption, such as nepotism. The fact that the family and civil society function with *different constitutive logics* animates their vital contradiction. Nepotism refers to the misplaced yet perfectly normal logic of familial favouritism when it takes place within the very different logic of civil society.

If civil society must protect itself from the tendency of familial logic to corrupt its proper governing principles by, for example, legally prohibiting nepotism, the family must protect itself from the corrupting influence of civil society. Hegel points out an obvious example. Since partners in marriage (or for us, in committed, long-term relationships) freely choose to commit to each other, it is tempting to conclude that marriage is governed by the logic of contract. We should not be surprised, in our day, that people draft and sign "marriage contracts" such that the terms of entering and leaving the contract are clearly delineated and subject to mutual agreement. That is, there is a tendency to organize the family according to the terms of civil society.[19] Hegel is at pains, however, to show that this moment of choice is surpassed by the love relationship and that treating a love relationship in the terms of contract is to fail to notice what love is. Yet the tendency to reduce marriage to contract is just as inevitable as nepotism. Francis Ford Coppola's film *The Godfather* is a more dramatic case still, for here there is a refusal on the part of the Corleone family and its competitors to recognize anything other than the logic of the family. And yet it is impossible for them to shut out the logic of civil society. "It is not personal, Sonny," Michael Corleone says to this brother, "it's just business." In the logic of the family, everything is personal and nothing impersonal.

But, of course, the necessary conflict, the vital contradiction, of family and civil society is hardly an absolute barrier to their co-existence and mutually interdependent functioning: it is indeed the very condition for the possibility of that functioning itself. The logic of civil society has as its intrinsic necessary condition the logic of family. One becomes a member of civil society only if one has been properly raised by one's family. Indeed, failures on the part of the family that create depression, anxiety, and other neuroses and psychoses often directly inhibit people from functioning well in civil society.

It is, therefore, the "particular" love of parents for their children that cultivates the "universal" person of civil society. Universality can thus never exclude particularity since the latter is the precondition for the former. This insight sheds new light on the failure of the Society of Absolute Freedom, which claimed that particularity is a menace to the universal. We see here, at least with respect to the family, that *the universal equality of civil society* is only ever achieved as originating in the particular exclusivity of the family. Indeed, the particular exclusivity of the family is a *necessary condition* for the development of the universality of civil society since it is the logic of particularity of the family to transcend itself in the creation of the new, abstractly universal logic of civil society.

As we have now seen, the "universality" of civil society is "inclusive" only by virtue of being abstract or formal, in contrast to that of the family, which is exclusive only by virtue of being concrete and organic. And yet the inclusiveness of the universality of civil society excludes almost everything because it makes no reference to the myriad ways that free, singular, and equal wills particularize themselves. We should thus anticipate that the universality of the state will have to respond by being inclusive, like civil society, but also by being concrete, like the family. That is, the state will have to include its own others – family and civil society – since it is only in and through these others that it arises.

This dynamic provides a hint of the key issue in our fourth species of society. At the level of concrete-lived recognition, the contradiction of familial particularity and the (abstract) universality of civil society is not a radical barrier to their co-existence, but is the very dynamic of their mutual interdependence. Let me state this more baldly still: the contradiction between family and civil society is not what impairs the functioning of either institution (even if it constantly creates problems), but is one of the essential elements of the vitality of human life. Indeed, the family is charged with its own supersession – the creation of citizens ready for an autonomous life in civil society. The contradiction between family and society is both necessary and vital.

More generally, we have learned three things about the logic of the fourth form of society, the just society:

1 It is precisely in and through particularity that the universal is realized.
2 It is precisely in and through a *vital contradiction* between particularity and universality that family and civil society relate to each other.
3 The vital contradiction of family and civil society means that though

> they are necessarily in tension with each other, this tension is that in and through which freedom is cultivated.

We have begun to see here that vital contradiction not only propels change through the failure of forms of self-determination, but that it is also abides as an animating tension at the heart of fully developed freedom. We have seen how vital contradiction propelled societies beyond themselves in chapters 4 through 6. Now we have a glimpse of how vital contradiction abides as the ongoing and unavoidable tension between family, civil society, and state. This tension is the necessary condition for the vitality of freedom. I will explore this second notion of vital contradiction in more detail in the next chapter, but I turn now to consider an outline of the third necessary institution of a free society – the state.

4 THE SOCIETY OF ABSOLUTE FREEDOM AND THE STATE

If the logic of civil society determines the character of society at large, the result is the Condition of Right, and Hegel argues that this society will tend to toward aristocracy and tyranny. The decisive insight of the Society of Absolute Freedom, in response, is that the free self cannot be left to run amok in pursuit of the ends of its arbitrary will, but must be cultivated or educated toward the universal as embodied in the state. There must be a pedagogical commitment to the state, to the common good. The error of the Society of Absolute Freedom, as is now clear, was to insist that this pedagogical commitment take the form of a purging of particularity. This society terrorized the particular only to discover that this terror was itself particular. If we are to retain the decisive insight of the Society of Absolute Freedom (that the universality of the state be cultivated), but transcend its error (that cultivation means eliminating the particular), then cultivation must happen in and through the particular. Indeed, this is precisely what we have said above regarding the family. The inclusive, abstract universality of civil society must be cultivated in and through the concrete and exclusive particularity of the family.

Yet civil society too has its particularity: the ways that free wills particularize themselves as they pursue their own ends and create therein a web of interdependence. The state, then, must cultivate the universal in and through not just the particularity of the family but in and through all the particular associations that emerge in civil society – surely not an easy task. And the state will have to be a concrete universal composed of families and the potential anarchic particularities of civil society.

According to Hegel, if "particularity [has] the right to develop and express itself in all directions" in civil society, the universality of the state must "prove itself both as the ground and necessary form of particularity, and as the power behind it and its ultimate end."[20] The state, then, refers to that truth which is both the *ground* of civil society and its proper *end*. It is not obvious how it is that the state can be either ground or end, much less both, especially when one of the two essential features of civil society is that people choose themselves as their own proper end.

Hegel's theory of the state is not as easy to grasp as is his theory of the family and civil society. I begin by considering the insights of the Society of Absolute Freedom in more detail since, just as the family is the sublated form of Ethical Society and civil society the sublated form of the Condition of Right, so too will the sublated form of the Society of Absolute Freedom yield what is essential to the nature of the state.

On its own terms, the Society of Absolute Freedom claimed that the education or cultivation of the citizen must consist in a conversion to the canons to Enlightenment rationality, such that the self knows how the particular should be disciplined or determined by the universal. We saw, however, that this led to a new form of tyranny: the tyranny of one particularity (the ruling faction) over other particularities.

Yet the claims of Absolute Freedom remain intriguing and important. Its insight is that if there is to be a route out of the concentration of wealth and power, then it lies in the notion of the *cultivation of universality*. Is there, then, another notion of cultivation, answering to a more sophisticated notion of rationality, that can provide a solution to this problem? It is helpful here to recall what we have just learned about the relationship of the family to civil society: the universality of rights in civil society is in vital contradiction (is dependent upon yet in conflict with) the exclusive particularity of family as its necessary condition. If the relation of civil society to state is analogous, then the exclusive particularity of the content of civil society will be in vital contradiction with the inclusive universality of the state.

Yet, if the particular associations of civil society (and the family) are not to be suppressed but respected, then it seems we are doomed to the aristocracy or tyranny of the Condition of Right. This would be so only if these particular associations remained completely self-oriented, like sounds that have not been composed into a melody. Cultivation, then, must be some kind of harmonization. As Hegel puts it in the *Philosophy of Right*, "Particular interests should certainly not be set aside, let alone suppressed; on the contrary, they should be harmonized with the universal."[21] But it is not clear how such a harmonization would take place without reproducing the coercion of Absolute Freedom. Indeed, it is not even clear in what this universal would consist, beyond the protection of the right of individuals to choose. Surely, if that were the case, we would simply return to the familiar problem of the taint of particularity, no matter whose (particular) notion of "universal" we pick. The victorious faction will decide in its own interest to enforce what it considers to be the good, but this good will be a particular rather than a universal good.

Perhaps then, since the logic of civil society is predicated on the self-determination of its members, the members of civil society must learn to limit *themselves* rather than be repressed in the name of the common good. Indeed, self-limitation seems to be consistent with the demands of civil society, since surely it is in the interest of the great majority to prevent tyranny. This self-cultivation is plainly not the founding logic of civil society nor of the Condition of Right – which is that everyone do what they want within the limits of respecting the rights of others to do the same. They must choose to cultivate themselves in a manner that respects the universal. And yet this is not the logic of the Society of Absolute Freedom either, for this cultivation will harmonize rather than repress the particular associations of civil society and families. Anti-combines legislation, progressive income tax, and various forms of the welfare state seem like good and familiar candidates for this kind of harmonization. Universal health care, for example, reduces the resources of the wealthiest, redistributes it by way of social programs, and benefits all of the society equally, yet it never attempts to eliminate the particular associations that generate wealth in the first place.

There is something to this claim, and measures like universal health care are absolutely necessary to Hegel's political philosophy, but his argument for the existence and character of the state is far stronger. Indeed, Hegel would say that such policies and the institutions that enforce them, however logical, would not describe a state in the true sense of the word. As we saw above, in the *Philosophy of Right* Hegel places such functions within the sphere of civil society rather than the state.[22] Hegel maintains that "If the state is confused with civil society and its determination is equated with the security and protection of property and personal freedom, *the interests of singular selves* [*der Einzelnen*] *as such* becomes the ultimate end for which they are united."[23] All the measures I have just outlined, progressive income tax, welfare structures, and anti-combines legislation, are precisely designed to limit property right and other features of civil society if only to better ensure their survival as the determining logic of (civil) society. They are the means to the most effective possible individualism. As such they are really just the self-modifications of civil society itself, and not a new and different logic. That is, they answer to the particularity of civil society and not the universality of the state (whatever that might be). Hegel, accordingly, includes all such measures *within* his discussion of civil society and he is right to do so, for these measures really amount to a strategy to preserve the logic of the Condition of Right, as embodied in civil society, as the determining logos of the society as a whole (with the exception, of course, of the family).

This is the terrain of the liberal contract thinkers – especially Hobbes, Locke, and Rousseau. The state of nature is the sphere of maximum liberty, but since this state turns out to be insecure or even warlike, human beings agree to observe the limitations of law and morality in a state. Indeed, one might even draw interesting comparisons between Hobbes's state of nature, which is the "war of all against all," and Hegel's study of the violence of the Condition of Right. Regarding social contract theories of the state, Hegel acknowledges the importance of basing the state on freedom and the will, but argues that this kind of thinking "regarded the universal will not as the will's rationality in and for itself, but only *as* the *common element* arising out of this singular [*einzelnen*] will *as a conscious will.*" This, Hegel thinks, reduces the state to a mere "contract" which is based on nothing more than the "arbitrary will and opinions" of the citizens. This understanding destroys "the divine" truth of the state, which Hegel says is "*supposed* to be a purely rational basis."[24] The logic of the Condition of Right and civil society, note, might be "rational," but it is not "rationality in and for itself." Only the latter notion of "rationality," absent in civil society and in contract theory, merits the term "divine."

Marx reminds us that even when civil society attempts to limit itself, powerful particularities seem to gradually work out the means to subvert these limitations. I return to this study in more detail below, but here I offer two examples. First, the Founding Fathers of the United States envisioned a self-limiting form of governance in their constitution, framed as it was with its myriad "checks and balances" between and among its legislative, executive, and judicial offices. There is nothing, however, within these structures preventing a dominant class from gaining effective control of all three institutions and thus of the whole state. Second, although the welfare state, union legislation, environmental controls, and so on proliferated in Europe and North America in the mid-twentieth century, they came under relentless assault in the last quarter of the century and are being constantly undermined in most Western nations. While the problems of civil society will continually motivate their re-emergence, the increased power of a dominant elite could prevent their reinstitutionalization. Two tentative conclusions follow. First, the notion of self-limitation subsists within the logic of civil society/Condition of Right and is thus not a third, qualitatively new logic – not a "state" in Hegel's sense. Second, a tentative and preliminary study of empirical evidence suggests the hypothesis that self-limitation is precarious at best. In sum, it is still not clear what Hegel means by the *state*, and civil society seems incapable of countering the forces of tyranny that lurk within it.

So what is the "divinity" of the state, and what does it mean that it is "rationality in and for itself"? Hegel says, "The state in and for itself is the ethical whole, the actualization of freedom, and it is the absolute end of reason that freedom should be actual … Any discussion of freedom must begin not with singularity [*Einzelheit*] or the individual self-consciousness, but only with the essence of self-consciousness; for whether human beings know it or not, this essence realizes itself as a self-sufficient power in which singular individuals [*die einzelnen Individuen*] are only moments. The state consists in the march of God in the world, and its basis is the power of reason actualizing itself as will."[25] Of course, the "reduction" of individuals to mere "moments" in the "march of God" has struck many people as giving the lie to Hegel's commitment to freedom, such that freedom can only mean the power of states to override individual human beings. This is an odd and indeed impossible interpretation for anyone who has read Hegel with any care. We have already seen that each and every one of the three forms of society we have considered has failed precisely because, in each of three ways, it has created a tyrannical state that enslaves its citizens. And yet we must understand what Hegel means by "moment," "reason," "essence of self-consciousness," and "God" in order to understand what it means to be a state.

I could turn to Hegel's *Science of Logic* for help in this task and, indeed, a completely thorough study of this topic would require that I do so.[26] However, we have already seen "reason" at work throughout the dialectic so far. Each step of the dialectic required that we discuss issues of the *concept*: how *singular* individuals, *particular* roles, and *universal* state or community related to each other. Indeed, the abstract *universal*, "self-consciousness" (which is, equally, "desire"), examined in chapter 1, turned out, as its conceptual dialectic unfolded, to have five *particular* steps (the struggle to the death, mastery and slavery, stoicism, skepticism, and the unhappy consciousness), which were then united into the singular or unique whole that is the fully unfolded dialectic of desire. We are in the midst of the same kind of project with "society," the abstract universal of which (a system of mutual recognition) has particularized itself as the Ethical Society, the Condition of Right, Absolute Freedom, and, now, the preliminary notions of the just society. Together these four species of the genus society form a unique, singular whole – the unfolded concept of society. Similarly, each singular self is singular because he or she is the abstract universal person particularized into the multiplicity of desires and projects which are united together as this unique person's quest for happiness.[27]

Moreover, we have also explicated some of the *qualities* (*qua* or *as* – how something is *qualified*) of freedom: how each singular, particular, and universal developed itself in certain ways. For example, in the Ethical Society there were plainly "singular" beings – unique and distinct selves like Antigone and Creon, Socrates and Aristophanes. But, as Hegel observes, these singulars had the *quality* of being only "shadows" because their free, infinite singularity was not recognized in this society. The moment of singularity, then, must be recognized *as free*, and moreover, it must be cultivated in its capacity to deliberate, choose, and act *well*. That is, it must be recognized *qua* free – as embodying the fully cultivated *quality* of freedom. Similarly, the ways in which these singulars particularized their freedom made all the difference to each society. The *qualified* particularity of "man" or "woman" also made all the difference in the lives of Creon and Antigone respectively, for in the Ethical Society one's particular role in the divine or human law determines how one acts. Indeed, each step of the dialectic has involved a complex unfolding of quantitative and qualitative distinctions. The particularity of singulars in the Condition of Right was freely chosen, and thus gradually ran amok as the accumulating power of particulars over other particulars. Finally, in the Society of Absolute Freedom, the singular self cultivated itself to choose the rational particular over the arbitrary particular. It took this rational particular to be a universal, but we saw that it was really a "victorious faction," a particularity that falsely acted in the name of the universal. I could also, to be much more thorough, elaborate all these terms within the key categories of Hegel's logic – being, essence, the concept, and the Idea.

The "reason" we have been observing, then, is nothing other than the play of unities and differences that both animates (insofar as it is alive and self-moving) and structures (insofar as it is alive and self-moving in a characteristic, self-determined way) the ongoing cultivation of societies in both empirical history (if we had been studying an empirical dialectic) and conceptual history (which we have been employing here), and in the relation between the two (the Idea, as unity of concept and existence). With respect to the rationality of singularity, particularity, and universality, we have come to recognize that (a) all these *moments* must be simultaneously present, recognized, and cultivated despite being in vital contradiction with each other; that (b) each must be cultivated from some primordial condition into its most developed (qualified) conditioned, such as to be "in and for itself," and that (c) the dialectical development of societies is precisely the history of that cultivation.

The foregoing provides a very brief sketch of what Hegel means by "reason." When Hegel refers to the "rationality" of the state, he means not the canons of abstract synthesis, as in Kant's pure concepts of the understanding or the Society of Absolute Freedom, but the logical structure of self-determination *as such*. Of course, this notion of rationality is dialectically developed by Hegel and passes through the stages of abstraction in the course of its self-elaboration, as in chapter 5, "Reason," of the *Phenomenology of Spirit* and, in the same volume, as the Society of Absolute Freedom in chapter 6, "Spirit." These abstract notions of reason find their true place only when they reveal themselves dialectically to be part of a concrete whole. Abstract rationality sublates itself into self-determining, concrete rationality. Thus, when Hegel speaks of the rationality of the state, he means that the state embodies the concrete universality of human freedom as determined by human beings in community. He calls the emergence of the state, recall (from the key passage quoted above), "the power of reason actualizing itself as will."

Now, if it is concrete reason that animates the state, this very concreteness means that the particulars that form the universal must be constitutive of that universal. Moreover, we have also begun to see in our study of the family and civil society that particularity and universality will always be in vital contradiction. That is, the exclusive particularity of the family generates from within itself the inclusive, formal universality of civil society. Now we see that the exclusive particularity of the family and civil society (qua the particularity of its myriad contents) are that in terms of which the concrete universality of the state must emerge. Thus the state, which is concrete reason, emerges when it allows these vital contradictions to animate the universal. We might thus say that this universality is always "tainted" by this particularity, but this is not Hegel's strategy. Such an attitude still privileges and is nostalgic for a pure universality and, consequently, it laments its impossibility. Hegel holds that universality arises only in and through particularity, and that their relationship in vital contradiction makes freedom (and rationality) what they are. I return to this issue in the next chapter.

Perhaps the foregoing analysis provides a better idea of what Hegel means by reason, but what does he mean by "state"?

In the key passage quoted above, Hegel refers to the "essence of self-consciousness" and then says that this essence "realizes itself as a self-sufficient power." So, what is the "essence of self-consciousness"? In fact, we have already discovered in chapter 1, in which we studied "self-consciousness" as "desire in general," that the "essence of self-consciousness" is *mutual recognition*. Appetitive desire, the most primitive form of self-consciousness (recalling that "self-consciousness is desire in general"), finds its only satisfaction in mutual recognition.

So what, then, is this "self-sufficient power"? As an empirical dialectic, the development of systems of mutual recognition, societies, has been painstakingly underway for millennia, and we inherit the achievements and failures in our own singular lives. That is, to be born a living, singular self is not to be that which confers reality on things (despite what appetitive desire might think) or that which builds things from the ground up (despite what Absolute Freedom posits); it is to find oneself to be, in a way that is radically beyond one's own power to determine, always already along for a ride on the back of a collective project (a "substance") of mutual recognition which has a long history of self-development. One's starting point is determined by the contingency of the place and time into which one is born. In a specific sense, this vindicates Antigone, for we ourselves are not the authors of our laws and customs. They were created by powers far beyond our own, which stretch back in history. As individuals we can show initiative, of course, in the way we take up and transform this inheritance and, moreover, we can recollect in both empirical and conceptual form the course of that journey, but it is the history of societies, and not the personal story of individuals, that determines the enormous weight and character of that which individuals may, or may not, develop or recollect. This is what Hegel means by the "self-sufficient power."

You and I, then, are "moments" in the development of this self-unfolding "rationality," this "substance." But this rationality is precisely the rationality not of rocks or plants but *of human self-determination*. Thus, my own capacity to influence and cultivate myself is most fully developed if I understand all the parameters within which my freedom subsists. I am most free, in other words, not when I arbitrarily choose but when I choose in a way that fully recognizes that I have inherited all the privileges of, for example, a democratic regime that took millennia of conflict and war, negotiation and discussion on the part of everyone in the history of my civilization, to develop. Indeed, if I and others do not cultivate, maintain, or develop this civilization, it will enter into decline and perhaps collapse. Or, again, I am free not simply when I do what I want, but when I recognize and respond according to the fact that, for example, the productive economy allows me to fulfill my goals and earn a high standard of living. Moreover, this is so only because my own personal condition depends squarely on the millions of people who for dozens of centuries have toiled to generate all these wealth-producing structures (and indeed have been exploited in so doing, as we shall soon see). Once more, the laws that protect me and the customs that enable me were not created by me, yet I inherit all the opportunities and limitations they confer.

But what does all this have to do with the state? The state is the institution that *explicitly* embodies this universal substance which we all inherit and upon which we all rely. Family and civil society *implicitly* embody this same universal substance, for they too have it as their "ground," their necessary condition. The state institutionalizes the self-consciousness of the self-determining substance of freedom in history.

It is very easy, as I earnestly pursue my own goals in civil society, to think that I alone am responsible for the benefits I gain or, indeed, for the failures I encounter. Indeed, it is easy to think this precisely because to some degree this is always true and, indeed, everything created in the history of societies has been created by singular persons like you and me. However, in a far broader and deeper sense, it is the enormously sophisticated and indeed ancient web of mutual recognition that carries us upon its back and determines for us what kind of world it is upon which we will deliberate, choose, and act as free singular selves. "God," for Hegel, is precisely this unfolding of rationality in its broadest possible sense, such that the "state" is one (albeit important) moment in the unfolding life of rationality thus understood (along with nature, our personal relationships, art, religion, philosophy, and so on).

Yet, if this web of mutual recognition is not cultivated, and if you and I take as our ends only our arbitrary interests, then the civilization will rot from within (the fate of the Condition of Right). This universal web of mutual recognition, in other words, is not only ground; it must also be end. That is, the state refers to the comprehensive web of mutual recognition that is a project of cultivation that has been underway throughout history and which has created family, civil society, and everything else (the state as *ground*). Yet, for the universal network of mutual recognition to flourish in and through our own lives, the cultivation of this system of mutual recognition itself must be taken up as a collective project. This project is embodied in family and civil society, but it is embodied most fully and most self-consciously in the state as our *end*.

The purposeful cultivation of the universal is something we have already seen in the Society of Absolute Freedom. We can now see that it was absolutely right about the mandate to cultivate rationality, but wrong about the nature of "reason." The truly rational universal is not an abstract and unattainable "kingdom of ends" or "General Will" that regulates and determines the particular, nor is it an ad hoc revolutionary creation. Rather, it is the concrete rationality of the universal, historical community of mutual recognition of which all of us are always already members. But this universal has shown itself to us to be nothing other than the cultivation of freedom itself through a series of mutually inter-related particularities that together make it the unique, singular experience we are now having – the process by which we as free beings have learned what it would mean for us to be free and engage in that project as best we can, here and now. This is Spirit – "The 'I' that is 'We' and the 'We' that is 'I.'"[28] Thus, the mandate of membership in the state is, quite literally, to *cultivate the conditions of shared community, of mutual recognition* – to make the rich, ongoing self-development of freedom as sophisticated as it can possibly be by making this cultivation its own most explicit mandate.

We have already seen that this cultivation will never succeed by harming the family (which embodies the logos of the Ethical Society). Nor will it accomplish its mandate by repressing the particular ways we develop ourselves in civil society (which embodies the logos of the Condition of Right), even if the abstract equality of civil society leads to particular self-expressions and factions that generate conflict. Nor will it accomplish this if it is ignorant of all the other conditions, deriving from the universal history of the human condition, which we have learned are essential to the development of our freedom. It is the institution of the state which has this vocation as its unique task in human history. That is, the task of resolving the inevitable conflicts of civil society is not merely in the name of those compromises that will best allow us to do what we want, but answers to the question, "How can we best cultivate freedom in a system of mutual recognition?" The inevitable conflicts in civil society should be resolved in a manner that best cultivates the sophistication of the freedom of the society as a whole, and that involves making it explicit that the goal of this process is sophisticated forms of mutual recognition, of being "at home" with those, as we shall see, who are different, dominated, excluded, or exploited.

We have come to understand the state as embodying the "cultivation of concrete freedom," a vocation that builds on the specific forms of cultivation already developed in the other two essential institutions of a free society – family and civil society. But this notion of the "cultivation of concrete freedom" is an odd and abstract bit of philosophical jargon if we do not study what it might mean in concrete terms. We see an example of this concreteness in the way a loving parent naturally embodies cultivation in raising a child. That is, ideally, we do not just teach our children how to cope with specific situations –meeting new people, getting along well in school, developing friendships. We do not just *cultivate* them to deal with specific situations. On top of this, we also teach them to embrace the attitude that they should welcome difference and challenge *in general*. Or again, we encourage not just learning about determinate situations, but we encourage children to embrace learning itself, so that they see their own vocation as human beings to always engage in life in ways that will make them more sophisticated, more free, in their engagements. That is, as parents we do not just *cultivate*: in a way, we *cultivate cultivation*. Of course, this process has no determinate end. It is the ongoing, always self-elaborating life of freedom itself. This is the task of the state for society as a whole.

We have yet to see how the logic of this can and must be embodied in the juridical institutions of the state. This task needs to be put off for two reasons. First, it is necessary to pause to take stock of the new sense of vital contradiction that has emerged in our study. I do that in the next section of this chapter. And second, if the task of the state is to cultivate the universal in and through the particular formations of civil society, then we cannot grasp the juridical structure of the state without understanding much better the predicaments of civil society. This will be the task of the next chapter.

5 ABIDING VITAL CONTRADICTION

The fully free society may result from the vital development of contradiction, but it is not the complete abolition of contradiction. Quite the contrary, for Hegel "being at home in the other" demands a sophisticated attitude toward the constitutive contradictions of life itself. Indeed, this very sophistication is itself a result of engagement with this contradiction. Thus, when Hegel speaks of contradiction in his general studies of the logic of freedom, he identifies the sense in which it is the very vitality, the very life, of freedom. In the *Science of Logic*, he says that "contradiction is the root of all movement and vitality; it is only insofar as something has a contradiction within it that it moves, has an urge and activity."[29]

We have now seen this vitality of contradiction in its two forms.[30] The first propels a free being or society to cultivate itself into more and more sophisticated forms of freedom. This form moved the conceptual dialectic from the Ethical Society, through the Condition of Right and the Society of Absolute Freedom, into the mature institutions of juridical-imaginative recognition now under consideration. This form of contradiction calls for sublation – transcendence. The second form of vital contradiction became visible as the dynamic tension between the differing constitutive logics of the institutions that make up the just society, which are themselves sublated versions of each particular failed society. Once again, family is sublated *ethicality*, civil society is sublated *right*, and the state is the sublated *absolute*. The second form of vital contradiction, in other words, is the sublated result of the first. It points to a permanent sustaining tension that "animates" or "moves" being but that does not call for transcendence toward a higher or more sophisticated form of being.

This dynamism provides the very structure by which something is *at stake* in human freedom. It is not clear, for example, that the transition from family to civil society will happen properly or that any given individual will successfully negotiate the minefields and opportunities of civil society. Human social life is full of successes and failures. Indeed, there are both vital contradictions *between* these institutions and vital contradictions *within* them. Hegel's concept of freedom, once more, is a sophisticated elaboration of the Heraclitean aphorism, "They do not apprehend how being at variance, it agrees with itself: there is a back-stretched connexion, as in the bow and the lyre."[31] Moreover, contradiction is not "irrational" but the structure of reason itself.

To be a "vital" contradiction means precisely that there are irresolvable tensions in human experience that will be the terms of our failures and our successes on the road to more sophisticated forms of freedom. Moreover, these successes and failures will never be *pure*. As we saw in the dialectic of the Society of Absolute Freedom, it is impossible to engage with the universals of civil society, for example, in a way that is not mediated by our particular families. Each individual will always carry with him or her (constantly transforming) formations of his or her familial cultivation.[32] But this does not mean that we fail to be free. The concept of a *full* or *perfect* freedom is precisely what has been refuted in the three societies that attempted to create differing versions of such freedom. Thus we have learned, in our process of cultivation, that no form of freedom is uncontradictory and that the search for this kind of perfection is itself a failed form of freedom. Freedom does not fall short of some abstractly posited ideal (this was a mistake of the Society of Absolute Freedom), but freedom is realized precisely in the way we negotiate the vital contradictions of our lives. Moreover, because we can negotiate these vital contradictions in better and worse ways, to be more rather than less free means to negotiate them well rather than poorly. We all must, as Simone de Beauvoir puts it in her (very aptly named) work, *The Ethics of Ambiguity,* undergo "an apprenticeship of freedom."[33]

We have studied this dynamic with respect to the contradictory logics of family and civil society. I now turn to a study of civil society and the state. Indeed, the dynamics of the vital contradiction that involve civil society and the state will preoccupy us for the remainder of this book.

8

The Vital Contradiction of Civil Society and the State

Hegel anticipates Marx in showing that unemployment, serious poverty, and alienated labour are caused by the *successful* functioning of civil society.[1] For Marxists, Hegel's political philosophy falls short not because he fails to recognize some of the contradictions of emerging capitalism but because he has no theory of class and exploitation and because, in their view, he naively tries to protect society from the worst effects of capitalism by means of a very strong state – a state, Marxists argue, that would disappear with the inauguration of socialism. Stephen Houlgate is a good representative of the moderate, roughly social democratic Hegel that Marxists criticize: Houlgate thinks that Hegel is realistic about the predicament civil society. Since it is the case that the free market systematically causes poverty, alienation, unemployment, and so on, the state must have an equally systematic function to mitigate these problems as much as possible.[2] Hegel may well be a realist, I argue instead, but his realism is grounded not just in the beguiling complexity of contemporary socioeconomic life but in the view that there is an abiding, vital contradiction between civil society and the state that creates these difficulties and indeed the dynamism of political freedom.

Accordingly, the interpretation of Hegel originally developed by Georg Lukacs and defended by Shlomo Avineri and H.S. Harris is closer to the truth (and is the predecessor to the interpretations of Žižek and Judith Butler mentioned briefly above). Lukacs claims that there is what could be called a kind of necessary alienation in Hegel. "In the term alienation," Lukacs says, Hegel "includes every type of objectification."[3] Citing Lukacs, Avineri says, "While Hegel sees alienation as a necessary aspect of objectification, Marx maintains that alienation does not reside immanently in the process of production itself, but only in its concrete historical conditions.

For Marx, therefore, there exists the possibility of ultimate salvation, whereas for Hegel one will never be able to dissociate the cross from the rose of the present."[4] H.S. Harris, for his part, says that "No one rationally can dissent" from this interpretation.[5]

When Hegel uses the term "alienation" (*Entfrendung* or *Entäusserung*), he generally refers to states which are dominated by the understanding and have not yet lived up to reason – the alienation of property in contract, the externalization of various forms of expression,[6] or, especially, the task of rediscovering the lost universal in the self-alienated spirit of Culture (*Bildung*). We reach the same conclusion here as we did in our discussion of Žižek's "radical loss" and Butler's "shadow." Externalization and objectification are only alienating losses for the self conceived by the understanding. Reason's (*Vernunft*) task is to show that at least some of the struggles and tensions in civil society are, to varying degrees, inevitable elements of a dynamic system of relations.

This chapter has four goals, all pursuant to coming to terms with this system of relations. First, the key features of civil society are explored by means of a close reading of relevant sections of the *Philosophy of Right*. Second, in the process, the decisive problem of civil society, the crux of vital contradiction, will emerge as the transformation of citizens' arbitrary and contingent points of view toward the "universal opinion." Third, Hegel thinks that work in professional associations called "corporations" enables this transformation to take place. That is, Hegel's political philosophy demands that citizens become self-conscious of the full demands of their freedom by participating in what I will call, drawing on Hegel, the "universal conversation." Fourth, employing this notion of the universal conversation, the initial terms for a dialectical criticism of Hegel's philosophy of civil society can be set. This criticism, which will be fully developed in chapters 9 through 11, amounts to showing that the goals of the universal conversation cannot be met by means of private property and the kind of constitutional monarchy that Hegel proposes.

In Hegel's political philosophy, the essential feature of a just society is that its institutions follow directly from the character of freedom itself. But precisely because freedom is animated by vital contradiction, there is always something at stake, something at risk. This means that freedom is not an invulnerable and permanent faculty, but a condition that can flourish, stagnate, or wither. Indeed, if the mandate of the state is to cultivate concrete freedom, it will be incapable of doing so if the character of civil society is to radically oppose that cultivation: if this were to be the case, then the actions of the state would appear as repressive. Thus, even if civil society and state are in vital contradiction with each other, freedom is best cultivated when civil society is instituted in such a way that citizens learn on their own terms that they must care for the common good. Even if it is the mandate of civil society to permit and indeed encourage particularity to thrive, it must do so in a way that encourages particular individuals, organizations, and associations, economic and otherwise, to recognize the universality that is the condition for its own possibility and its proper end. However, if society is unable within its own projects to find any interest in the universal life of the community, then it is liable to show no support for the actions of the state. Worse yet, if forces in civil society come to find that the state is an impediment to their projects, they are likely to seek to control it by limiting its powers and influence and indeed by coercing it toward a structure that supports the particular interests of powerful classes or sectors. In short, universal interests must not be the private domain of the state and its institutions, but must be cultivated within civil society.

In other words, Hegel warns that though civil society is necessary for freedom, it also poses a grave danger, under certain conditions, to the flourishing of freedom. The forces unleashed in civil society are potentially so destructive that radical egoism and tyranny necessarily lurk on the horizon of possibility – precisely the lesson of the Condition of Right. That is, despite the fact that civil society is an absolutely necessary sphere of human freedom, its own structures motivate the kind of atomism and extremes of wealth and poverty that permit a tiny and extremely powerful elite to gradually attain power to dominate the system of mutual recognition and in so doing destroy the freedom that was the condition for the emergence of this elite in the first place. Even more fundamentally preoccupying, Hegel claims that the contradiction that gives rise to this possibility can never be eliminated. This is the character of vital contradiction.

1 PARTICULARITY AND UNIVERSALITY IN CIVIL SOCIETY

For Hegel, then, civil society itself is the institution of political life whose character is to recognize the self-determining character of singular individuals to particularize themselves in their own distinct ways. "In civil society," Hegel says, "each individual is his own end, and all else means nothing to him."[7] Civil society, Hegel continues, is the sphere in which "all singular characteristics [*Einzelheiten*], all aptitudes, and all accidents of birth and fortune are liberated, and where the waves of passions surge forth, governed only by the reason that shines through them."[8] I have already considered the theme of the "reason that shines forth" through these mostly egoist and contingent actions, and I will return to that theme again, but for the moment the key issues for Hegel are that (a) the freedom of the singular individual is a condition for the possibility of freedom in modern society; (b) this freedom exists only if the singular will is self-determining with respect to the particular actions that he or she pursues, and (c) this freedom is institutionally recognized in the sphere of civil society. It is therefore essential that the member of civil society neither be simply preoccupied with the particular good of her family nor be coerced toward a concern for the common good of the state. Rather, she must pursue her own interests and learn therefrom how that interest presupposes a concern for the common good, the universal. The common good should be that particular principle of action that she herself chooses. The freedom of the singular self must be respected both juridically, in terms of her individual rights, and economically, in terms of the capacity to exercise these rights as she sees fit in her work and accumulation of private property in a free market economy (according to Hegel).

When the forces of singular freedom are liberated in civil society, especially when its powers combine with the technological advances of modern industrial capitalism, a turbulent and fabulously productive economic and social life emerges. Civil society, Hegel says, is "infinitely agitated" and "a spectacle of extravagance."[9] Our capacity to create new pleasures has no logical resting point, "for every comfort ... [soon] reveals its less comfortable side, and the resulting inventions are endless." Indeed, the generation of human needs becomes abstracted from the needs themselves such that the desire for profit induces individuals to create needs in others. "A need," Hegel continues, "is therefore created not so much by those who experience it directly as by those who seek to profit from its emergence."[10] Indeed, we have already seen this logical structure in appetitive desire and the arbitrary will, both of which are constituted by the bad infinite that restlessly seeks yet more satisfaction, more pleasure, more wealth, more status, more power.

Yet the more civil society elaborates needs, the more the satisfaction of any particular need presupposes ever more complex webs of production, transportation, marketing, finance, legal services, policing, governance, and so on. The infrastructure of mutual recognition becomes increasingly elaborate and interdependent. The universality of this web of interdependence is thus a condition for the possibility of any particular action on the part of each and every singular self in civil society. Yet despite the fact that this universal web of co-operation is a necessary condition for all action, individuals in civil society are frequently egoistic and, to the degree they perceive this universal web at all, they tend to perceive it as a means to their own private ends.

This situation is not fatal to freedom if the standard caricature of Adam Smith's theory of the "invisible hand" is purely and simply true – that the particular action of selfish and utterly egoistical agents in capitalism functions in the interest of the universal, the common good, insofar as it generates wealth and employment for others and for the society as a whole.[11] While Hegel is fascinated by Smith's argument, he systematically shows why it is not valid. Hegel much prefers the interventionist political economy of Sir James Steuart.[12]

Indeed, Hegel shows that civil society introduces poverty and alienation by the *normal* and *successful* functioning of *its own mechanisms*. "The emergence of poverty," Hegel says in the 1819–1820 *Lectures*, "is in general a consequence of civil society, and on the whole it arises necessarily out of it."[13] The cycles of productivity and demand constantly create unemployment and artificial shortages. Improved technology increases productivity and often decreases employment, sometimes creating situations of over-production, layoffs, and rapid price deflation. In a memorable formulation Hegel says that "despite *an excess of wealth*, civil society is *not wealthy enough*."[14] Particularization in all social orders is inevitable and thus it is equally inevitable that some social spheres have more wealth and power than do others.

Hegel is plainly aware of the precariousness of this vital contradiction, and he thus takes care to outline the worst-case scenario – the formation of an utterly alienated "rabble" (*Pöbel*).[15] Civil society's "own distinct resources are not sufficient," Hegel says, "to prevent an excess of poverty and the formation of a rabble."[16] For Hegel, the rabble is defined not only in economic but more importantly in political and psychological terms. A rabble is a class of people whose situation encourages them to feel that they have no ethical bond or responsibility to the society as a whole. A rabble thus behaves selfishly and egoistically.

Of course, it is normal to use the word "rabble" in English and *Pöbel* in German to describe only the gravely impoverished. Hegel accordingly observes, "When a large mass of people sinks below the level of a certain standard of living – which automatically regulates itself at the level necessary for the society in question – that feeling of right, integrity, and honour which comes from supporting oneself by one's own activity is lost. This leads to the creation of a *rabble*, which in turn makes it much easier for disproportionate wealth to be concentrated in few hands."[17] With respect to the rabble, Hegel once again uses the language of an alien, arbitrary, and contingent force acting against the free self, just as he did in his discussion of the Condition of Right.[18] "The poor man feels as if he were related to an arbitrary will, to human contingency, and in the last analysis what makes him indignant is that he is put into this state of division through an arbitrary will." He thus feels driven to feel he "no longer has any rights, where freedom has no existence." As a result, "the recognition of universal freedom disappears" and thus arises "that shamelessness that we find in the rabble."[19]

In this situation, not only is it the case that the worker loses a sense of pride and honour in his own freedom, but the society as a whole becomes alien to him because it is no longer a reflection of his own activity: he makes no contribution to it and thus does not experience it as "his own." As Hegel puts it, "The individual is not at home even in his immediate environment, because it does not appear as his own work."[20] Recall that for Hegel, one is free only when one is "*at home* and *with [one]self* in ... *externality* as such."[21] Thus when he says that the poor person is not "at home in his immediate environment," he means that such a person is not free except in the arbitrary and meaningless juridical sense of abstract or formal right. One is at home in the structure of civil society and state when one understands them and indeed experiences them to be necessary conditions for the possibility of freedom and structures to which one has made a contribution, even if, in certain ways, they transgress the particular freedom of certain individuals and groups. In the rabble mentality, as in the chaos of the Condition of Right, one is not at home in the institutions of social life because one sees little sense in which one depends upon or contributes to them and, indeed, they more and more take the form of utterly alien forces of coercion toward which one is indifferent or hostile. In this case, society as whole inhibits rather than contributes to the flourishing of the individual and thus there is no "common good." The universal is merely the totality of competing factions in its gradual trajectory toward tyranny.

Just as the very poor lose a sense of responsibility and satisfaction and become a rabble, so too do the very rich cease to feel that they depend on the rest of the society. As the ties of interdependence weaken, the very rich themselves become a rabble. Hegel says, "In these opposites [of wealth and poverty] and their complexity, civil society affords a spectacle of extravagance and misery as well as of the physical and ethical corruption common to both."[22] In the *Aesthetics* Hegel goes into more detail still. The wealthy "are freed from working to satisfy their needs." He continues, in a passage that includes the citation above regarding the importance of freedom as "being at home," "In that event of course, in this superfluity, the constant reflection of endless dependence is removed, and man is all the more withdrawn from all the accidents of business as he is no longer stuck in the sordidness of gain. But for this reason the individual is *not at home even in his immediate environment* [italics mine], because it does not appear as his own work. What he surrounds himself with here has not been brought about by himself; it has been taken from the supply of what was already available, produced by others, and indeed in a most mechanical and therefore formal way, and acquired by him only through a long chain of efforts and needs foreign to himself."[23] Hegel observes that the wealthy person may be able to devote himself to "higher interests," but "physical and ethical corruption" is just as much a possibility. In the 1819–1820 *Lectures* Hegel is even more emphatic about a rabble of the rich. "On the one hand, poverty is the ground of the rabble-mentality, the non-recognition of right; on the other hand, the rabble disposition also appears where there is wealth. The rich man thinks he can buy anything, because he knows himself as the power of the particularity of self-consciousness. Thus wealth can lead to the same mockery and shamelessness that we find in the poor rabble ... These two sides, poverty and wealth, thus constitute the corruption of civil society."[24]

Just as the pauper is not "at home even in his immediate environment," neither is the very wealthy person. Extremes of wealth and poverty threaten, therefore, to rob citizens of their freedom, for they cease to see themselves reflected in the institutions of social life. To return to the terms of the "cultivation of concrete freedom," one can readily see how the very structure of civil society can easily cultivate tyranny and alienation rather than the flourishing of freedom.

With the creation of an alienated class of wealthy and poor citizens, the society is in danger of becoming an oligarchy or tyranny. Like Marx's notion of the *lumpenproletariat*, the poor rabble is unlikely to work to achieve its own self-determination. Their condition is too degraded and hopeless, and they have, as we shall see shortly, few opportunities to cultivate their self-determination through work. We have here, then, the same kind of conditions that produce the tyranny described by Hegel in the Condition of Right. A society which began by recognizing the abstract freedom of the singular self to do any (particular) thing she wants always faces the danger of becoming tyrannical and of thus obliterating the very freedom that was its initial premise. In the worst-case scenario, the "vitality" of the contradiction of civil society is virtually killed such that its conflict becomes expressed by the wealthy as a decadent irresponsibility or a tyrannical authoritarianism and by the poor as hopeless indifference or reckless and destructive rebelliousness.

We can thus see that the vital contradiction of civil society can lead to degrees of inequality that break a society into disconnected and antagonistic parts. This is the *worst-case scenario* for the vital contradiction of civil society, but from it we can deduce three key conditions for the *best-case scenario*. The maximally free society would be one in which, despite having unavoidable differences in wealth and power, all or nearly all citizens experience their society as co-operating with them in the achievement of their goals – they are at home. Second, they are thus much more willing to participate in the pursuit of the common good – that is, in supporting the universal structures that embody freedom in its most sophisticated forms. Evidently, this is impossible if the gap between rich and poor is too great, or if the relatively poor do not have meaningful work. Third, such a society is possible only if individuals are cultivated toward a sophisticated form of citizenship in their education and their work, *within civil society*. Hegel thus devotes much of his discussion of civil society to the solution of the predicament it poses. This task requires above all a discussion of *work*.

2 WORK AND THE UNIVERSAL CONVERSATION

The key to achieving community for Hegel is the cultivation of the individual which takes place in her community of *work*. As discussed above, the work of the slave is precisely what allows her to develop a sense of her own freedom. Work creates an object that reflects back to its producer that person's deliberative creativity. Work in civil society is similar, and Hegel carefully constructs the institutions of civil society to cultivate a commitment to the universal through each citizen's professional activity.

The individual person, Hegel argues, is characterized by two different forms of need. First, each of us has what he calls "natural need" for things like food, housing, and indeed many other products that extend, as we have seen, into an infinitely expanding material abundance. Second, we have what Hegel calls "spiritual needs"[25] for what ultimately amounts to *mutual recognition*. Hegel discusses mutual recognition in the context of civil society most often under the rubric of the term *honour* (*Ehre*).

Through work natural needs and spiritual needs are synthesized into what Hegel calls "social needs"[26] and, therefore, both can also largely be satisfied in a single activity: *co-operative work with others*. Work creates the products that satisfy natural needs, while simultaneously establishing the autonomy of the worker. This form of autonomy is not, of course, any kind of self-reliance that we might find in the philosophies of possessive individualism, for workers in civil society are arguably more dependent on each other than are individuals at any prior time in history – and increasingly so. The autonomy we speak of here is the capacity to provide an income for oneself through one's own work in community and in a manner that cultivates what Hegel refers to as *theoretical* and *practical* sophistication.

In the *Philosophy of Right* Hegel says, first, that work of a certain quality creates the possibility of a *theoretical education*, which he defines as the ability to generate knowledge, to grasp complex and general relationships, and to move with versatility and agility to and from that which one knows. It is therefore an "education of the understanding" that includes, especially, *language*.[27] Second, work creates the possibility of a *practical education* which develops by working not merely with a given material, but more importantly by working in co-operation with the will of others. It also creates the discipline of objective activity and generates universally applicable skills.[28] One feels satisfaction and pride in one's ability to provide an income for oneself and in making a contribution to the common wealth of the society. Since, for Hegel, we are always already embedded in relations of mutual recognition, pride in ourselves and feeling honoured in the eyes of others is frequently one and the same experience. For Hegel, these psychological benefits of work – self-respect and honour – reflect the way in which spiritual needs predominate over material needs.

Indeed, when natural needs become social needs, a liberating sense of autonomy emerges. "Within social needs, as a combination of ... natural needs and spiritual needs ... the spiritual needs, as the universal, predominate. This social moment, accordingly, contains the aspect of *liberation*, because the strict natural necessity of need is concealed and man's relation is to *his own opinion*, which is universal, and to a necessity imposed on himself alone, instead of simply an external necessity, to inner contingency, and to *arbitrariness*."[29] Each person, in other words, feels the satisfaction of being autonomous, of being subject no longer to an "external," "strict, natural necessity" but to "a necessity imposed on himself alone." The worker thus has an "opinion," a point of view, a take on the world which is not merely contingent or deriving from the arbitrary will, but is "universal." How, according to Hegel, does the universality of this opinion emerge such as to transcend its arbitrariness? A clear answer to this question is decisive, for this is the issue upon which the vital contradiction of civil society turns. How can an institution that sets the arbitrary singular will free at the same time cultivate that will to take up the universality of the common good? Hegel's answer is nuanced, and begins with the character of work considered in the abstract and extends to consider work considered more concretely. It is a crucially important issue.

The key is that work is co-operative. Hegel says, "Needs and means, as existing in reality, become a *being* for *others* by whose needs and work their satisfaction is mutually conditioned." "Isolated and abstract needs, means, and modes of satisfaction," which are merely particular, take on in the context of co-operative work, "the *quality of being recognized*" such that needs, means, and modes of satisfaction become "*concrete*, i.e., *social* ones."[30] That is, the abstract and particular become concrete and universal in the context of co-operative work.

It is decisive to emphasize that the citizen herein becomes self-conscious of the universal, which becomes his or her explicit opinion. It is not enough that the co-operative character of human social life lurk in the shadows, but that it become explicit in the mind of the worker such that he or she is self-consciously committed to the universal. That is, the mixing of "opinions" in co-operative social life places workers in a kind of conversation that tends toward the universal. The fact that people work together means that "I have to fit in with other people," and this "brings the form of universality into play." Since, "I acquire my means of satisfaction from others," I must "accordingly accept their opinions." The same is true in reverse, so that "everything particular takes on a social character," and there "are certain conventions one must accept," and it is "wisest to act as others do."[31] Hegel's remarks here might seem to refer to the formation of merely conventional opinion, but co-operative work is an extraordinarily important phenomenon for Hegel, especially in the context of civil society. Indeed, in the *Phenomenology of Spirit* Hegel says that when the particular opinion of individuals encounters those of other people, a dialectical movement is created which generates a universal, a "community of minds." He claims, "Since the man of common sense makes his appeal to feeling, to an oracle within his breast, he is finished and done with anyone who does not agree; he only has to explain that he has nothing more to say to anyone who does not find and feel the same as himself. In other words, he tramples underfoot the roots of humanity. For it is the nature of humanity to press onward to agreement with others; human nature only really exists in an achieved community of minds."[32] Once again, for Hegel freedom is realized only in communion with others – "The 'I' is a 'We' and the 'We' is an 'I.'"[33] The dialogue of opinions that emerges from work does not efface the particularity of the individual, but coaxes her into opinions that reflect the universal and co-operative nature of work itself. This "universal conversation" facilitated by work makes the interdependent nature of civil society explicit to its members. In the next chapter, I argue that such conversation is essential to a fully just society, that it is the foundation of democracy, and that Hegel himself may have understated its importance.

As we have seen, work satisfies the material needs of livelihood and the spiritual need of honour and self-respect, cultivates theoretical and practical abilities, and initiates the worker into the universal conversation of public life. This is a fine story in the abstract, but it makes a great deal of difference to Hegel what kind of work one does and in what conditions. For Hegel, in other words, the universal conversation facilitated by co-operative work is possible only under specific conditions. It is already plain that members of the rich and poor rabbles would typically form opinions that remain stubbornly particular and arbitrary. Even outside of the rabbles, specific forms of work mitigate or even destroy the otherwise positive outcomes of co-operative activity. Hegel's theory of alienated labour is thus complicated, and arises first in his discussion of the three estates – the agricultural, formal (trade and industry), and universal (bureaucratic) estates.

According to Hegel, the work of those in the agricultural or "substantial" estate requires less reflection and provides few opportunities for creative use of the will. It thus remains closely tied to dependence on the traditional family and its patriarchal ethos.[34] Hegel thinks that the farmer, while increasingly like the urban worker, is still ultimately submissive to authority primarily because the form of work he does fails to cultivate his free individuality. Of course, Hegel speaks here of agriculture in the early nineteenth century, rather than of the farmers in our day who in many respects must cope with the world in much the same manner as urban business people. This point is even more tellingly true if we take, for example, members of Brazil's Movement of Landless Rural Workers, who seize land from wealthy landowners, build co-operative farming communities, and engage in political activism on issues poverty, agrarian reform, and human rights at national and international levels.[35] Given the massive technological, social, cultural, and political changes in the agricultural sector, there is no longer good reason to hold Hegel's view. We can instead extrapolate on what we have said so far to clarify his criteria – work that is solitary, isolates the worker from society, involves him in repetitive and unchallenging tasks, embeds him in communities where traditional authority holds sway, and rarely involves him in contact with people who think differently from him is unlikely to cultivate autonomy and a sophisticated attitude toward the world. Indeed, another way to put this is that in a sense the agricultural estate never leaves behind the social logic of the Ethical Society. It seems to be Hegel's view that, despite the stultifying work of the agricultural estate, farm workers' alienation does not pose a threat to the society as a whole precisely because their work tends to habituate them to obedience and passivity. Suffice it to say that Hegel's analysis of agricultural work is not of great value to understanding contemporary agricultural work.

The third estate, meanwhile, the *universal* estate, consists essentially of what we would call bureaucrats and public service workers, in the broadest sense – those who are employed to take care of the society as a whole.[36] The personal and professional goals of members of this state tend to dovetail with the universal good of the society. They have a much better chance of grasping the demands of the common good because it is, after all, the object of their labour. There is thus less contradiction between the particularity and universality of work in this estate and much less likelihood of the atomism that would destroy the society. Each worker's desire to satisfy his or her own natural and spiritual needs is satisfied by tasks that, in principle at least, have the common good as their end. We might find Hegel's study of bureaucratic work overly sanguine, but (at least in a just state) public workers do indeed pursue their own particular goals in a manner that immediately orients them to the good of a society as a whole (within the limits of how that is understood). A public school teacher, for example, can hardly fail to notice (no matter how personally ambitious she might be) that she is participating in an institution whose goal is the universal education of every citizen. In the process by which she achieves her own self-respect and honour she is simultaneously and directly strengthening the autonomy of all citizens. Even her own very personal ambitiousness (to achieve promotion and so on) can, under the right circumstances, strengthen the public education system since her personal success requires that she contribute to the realization of public education. Moreover, she is intellectually challenged and participates through her place of work and her union in debates that are truly of national and international significance.

Hegel's account of government work, however, still must meet the challenge of Marx (and many others). If the state becomes purely and simply the tool of a dominant class, then bureaucrats and public service workers tend to do a merely particular rather than a predominantly universal work. Hegel would, of course, argue that this is inevitable to some extent, but that a state dominated by one class is one that has already fallen a good distance from the best-case scenario of human freedom. Indeed, in order to discourage this kind of eventuality, he designs the constitution of the state so that all three estates are guaranteed representatives in the legislative body.[37] All the same, this is a decisive issue to which I will return in chapters 10 and 11. I will argue that on this and other key matters, Hegel seriously underestimates the power of capitalists to forge a notion of the "common good" that is significantly slanted in favour of their particular class interests.

The second or "formal" estate of "trade and industry," however, is the key issue for Hegel insofar as this estate dominates civil society and poses the key problem to modern society.[38] The members of this estate epitomize the new spirit of liberty and it is they who pursue their own selfish and sometimes extravagant goals, often at the expense of the rest of the society. Thus, these individuals are also most vulnerable to the excesses of civil society and to the dangerous atomism that we have already considered. People fall into destitution and collapse into rabbles of both the wealthy and the poor as the result of this activity. Therefore, the labour of members of the second estate is typically on Hegel's mind when he discusses problematic issues of work.

Of course, workers in civil society perform a bewildering variety of tasks which differ enormously in their capacity to educate workers in the ways I have discussed above. Most of the time Hegel approaches this issue quite broadly, arguing that there are three general requirements that a society must institutionalize if it is to cultivate the workers of civil society in the direction of fulfilling their freedom:

a The provision of public utilities, social welfare, and education
b The capacity of specific forms of labour to educate workers in the direction of a sophisticated engagement with the world
c The emergence of respect and honour arising from membership in what Hegel calls "corporations."

2a The Provision of Public Utilities, Social Welfare, and Education

Given that civil society has torn the urban worker from his more secure agricultural past, weakened the capacity of his family to support him, and introduced numerous forces of contingency that increase anxiety and threaten abject poverty, the society as a whole has a duty to take care of the welfare of its members. Indeed, if the family is the original institution that protects individuals from these kinds of contingencies, and the individual has now become, as Hegel puts it, "a *son of civil society*"[39] rather than of the family, then civil society must itself become the individual's "*universal* family"[40] and protect him from the numerous problems that civil society itself creates. Indeed, "I have a right to demand," Hegel says, "that ... my particular welfare also be promoted."[41]

The provision for utilities, welfare, and education is thus a right of citizenship, and these structures are essential features of justice. The provision of utilities not only ensures the smooth functioning of social life but also publically demonstrates the importance of the universal infrastructure of the state.

One also sees in the *Philosophy of Right* the emergence of a prototype of a universal system of public education. Because of the widely varying standards of education the family provides and because of a lack of consistent commitment to the goals of a universal education for responsible citizenship, the family is not qualified to educate children. Only the state can provide the appropriate level of education.[42] It is essential, Hegel points out, that education be understood not merely as a means to material advancement but as the cultivation of all the abilities already outlined in our discussion of work above.

Regarding welfare, Hegel is famous for his comments on the problem of poverty – especially for his frankness about the impossibility of its elimination.[43] The rabble, of course, expresses the worst-case scenario, but Hegel is convinced that in certain ways civil society creates poverty through the *successful* operation of its own structures. In a situation of poverty, Hegel claims, "members of civil society, who depend for their livelihood on *their activity, their own knowledge and volition*, remain *alienated* not only from their own most personal interests but also from the substantial and rational basis of these, namely *right*, and they are reduced to a condition of *tutelage*, or even a kind of serfdom."[44] In these circumstances neither natural nor spiritual needs are met, and thus little or no participation in the universal consensus is likely to result. Hegel states, "The feeling of right, integrity and honour which comes from supporting oneself by one's own activity and work is lost."[45] The poor person is likely to feel "mocked" and "excluded"; she likely senses an "inner indignation"; she feels that she "no longer has any rights" and that her "freedom has no existence." The "recognition of universal freedom disappears" and "shamelessness develops."[46] Handouts to the poor fail to address this problem, Hegel thinks, because they eliminate the individual's autonomy and thus also the sense of pride and honour that follows from it. Putting the poor to work creates surplus production and thus exacerbates the very market forces that caused unemployment in the first place. Hegel's views on colonization are a complex matter, especially given his racism and his ignorance of non-European cultures,[47] but from the point of view of the issue at hand here, he believed that emigration to colonies would relieve but not eliminate some of the constitutive tensions of civil society.

Since Hegel's time, Western nations have experimented with a number of measures to address poverty, most of which have had some degree of success – universal public education, universal public health care, provisions for employment insurance and pensions, welfare, progressive income tax, and so on. While there is no "solution" to poverty – Hegel's point once again is that it is to some degree inevitable – there is a combination of measures that alleviates its worst effects and that prevents the rabble mentality from developing. I will have to return to this issue again below when I consider the ways in which Hegel seriously underestimated the degree to which capitalism could undermine his notion of justice.

In general, Hegel argues that none of the measures of public utility, education, or welfare should be placed in private hands. He says, "Public conditions should be regarded as all the more perfect the less there is left for the individual to do by himself in the light of his own particular opinion (as compared to what is arranged in the universal manner)."[48] Thus, "it is better if the state cares for the needs of the individual."[49] If the provision of these measures is a right of citizenship, the success of the state in providing them might be said to meet both natural and spiritual needs, and thus encourage a sense of concern and responsibility for the community as a whole.

2b Work and Sophisticated Engagement with the World

We saw above that work should develop the theoretical and practical capacities of the worker. This plainly presupposes that labour must involve various kinds of intellectual challenge. A craft-worker who makes violins, for example, must not only be intimate with music, wood, and string, but must also develop skills in working with other people, become cognizant of various aspects of marketing and government legislation that impacts upon her trade, and so on.

But there are many forms of work that fail to cultivate a sophisticated engagement with the world. Indeed, in Hegel's view traditional agricultural labour fails to develop the capacities of workers. Hegel notes a similar, but far more serious problem emerging in modern industrial capitalism. He describes how both machine labour and the excessive division of labour make the typical work of capitalism increasingly incapable of educating workers. Machines and excessive specialization make certain kinds of labour so simple and abstract that little of any theoretical or practical value is learned.[50] The trend toward these forms of alienation was increasing in Hegel's time – a point he notes. Work thus becomes increasingly "dull" and "spiritless."[51] Both these trends increase the chance that members of civil society will remain relatively egoistic and unsophisticated. On this point, we should be concerned that factors that increase the likelihood of rabbles reside in the character of modern capitalist labour.

Of course, even workers engaged in this "dull" and "spiritless" work have other avenues through which they might develop their capacities and generate self-respect, honour, and an ability to participate in the common good. Membership in "corporations" is the most important of these, but institutions of education, the church, and other community and social organizations provide a similar value that may (or may not) compensate for the stultifying character of many forms of work. Suffice it to say that in an economy dominated by this form of labour, these alternative institutions would have to be particularly strong and sophisticated. We have come to see, thanks to the union movement, that even dull and repetitive work can nonetheless be the occasion for sophisticated and elaborate gestures of self-determination. The "vitality" of the contradiction in civil society fails completely to motivate workers to take action on their own behalf only when they have truly entered into the rabble mentality.

2c Honour and Membership in Corporations

Hegel gives a decisive place to "corporations" – collective organizations of workers within a given trade or sphere of the economy. A corporation includes both employers and employees and provides education, support, and community for its members. Corporations were gradually eliminated all over Europe in the period in which Hegel lived, but it is nonetheless essential to understand the extremely important role they play in Hegel's political philosophy, and thus also to understand the implications for any civil society that fails to institutionalize corporations or something very like them.

What happens in the corporations can best be understood by considering a passage in which Hegel foretells the fate of those who *do not* belong to them. "If the individual is not a member of a … corporation … he is without the *honour of belonging to an estate*, his isolation reduces him to the selfish aspect of his trade … He will accordingly try to gain *recognition* through the external manifestations of success in his trade, and these are without limit."[52] Hegel suggests that the "universal conversation" that potentially arises from work reliably takes place only if citizens belong to corporations. First, the individual without a corporation is "isolated." That is, he tends to become individualistic rather than communitarian in his outlook. Hegel observes that the egoistic individual finds honour in his "individuality and not in what is common."[53] This atomistic attitude is the opposite of the sense of community fostered in the corporation: it not only results from the failure to be a member in a corporation but it also undermines the corporation from within. "This spirit of atomicity … is destructive, and has caused the corporations to fall to pieces."[54]

We may work to meet whatever we perceive to be our natural needs, but above all we seek *to be recognized* – we work to meet our spiritual needs – and this recognition takes the form of honour in which the individual learns "the fact that he is *somebody*."[55] If we are not recognized through a corporation, we are most likely to strive to achieve this honour by means that are doomed to fail: we will put ourselves on a treadmill of material success that is an example of the bad infinite of appetitive desire discussed in chapter 2. Each new success, each new promotion, or each new gain in wealth has the character of a temporary satisfaction, but since these successes are not the real goal of one's longing (which is mutual recognition qua honour), the feeling dissipates and simply sets up for itself a new goal which, should it be achieved, will fail for exactly the same reason. Hegel, of course, thinks there is a positive role to this form of desire. "Human beings expand their desires, which do not form a closed circle like animal instinct, and extend them to false infinity."[56] That is, it is this false infinite that makes the society so productive and extravagant. But this form of desire is contingent and impossible to satisfy fully. "Particularity in itself, on the one hand indulging itself in all directions as it satisfies its needs, contingent arbitrariness, and subjective caprice, destroys itself and its substantial concept in the act of enjoyment; on the other hand, as infinitely agitated and continually dependent on external contingency and arbitrariness and at the same time limited by the power of universality, the satisfaction of both necessary and contingent needs is itself contingent."[57] Without corporations, that is, without a community that honours us for our labour and values us in a manner that protects us from the contingencies that would otherwise threaten our dignity, we become like Tantalus.[58]

Thus, market forces that create sudden unemployment, for example, are threatening not merely to the health and welfare of workers and their families but to their capacity to feel respect for themselves and feel the respect of others. The corporation, in other words, provides for the material and, more importantly, psychological dignity of workers vulnerable not only to contingencies in the economy but also to that which tempts workers to seek self-respect and honour through the false infinite of material success.

This means that the corporation is every bit as important for the wealthier and more powerful members of the community as it is for medium- and low-income individuals because, although the former are much less materially vulnerable, they are more likely to associate their honour with material success. As Hegel says, "within the corporation the help which poverty receives loses its contingent and unjustly humiliating character, and wealth, in fulfilling the duty it owes to its association, loses the ability to provoke arrogance in its possessor and envy in others."[59] In the corporation, the wealthy learn that their wealth presupposes the universal community. Thus the corporation is decisive in preventing both the impoverished and the wealthy sectors of civil society from moving toward alienation and the concomitant loss of sense of interdependence and responsibility.

There is one further feature of the corporation that is decisive for its capacity to mediate between civil society and the state. The modern state, Hegel says, is too remote from the day-to-day life of individual citizens and is thus likely to appear as a force of external necessity.[60] The corporations, on the other hand, are represented in the state by delegates that the corporations themselves elect and thus the corporation functions concretely to link individuals to the state authority. This means that the linkage between citizen and state is forged on the basis of one's vocational involvement in society and is thus a more concrete form of representation than the geographical structure of representation that is typical of contemporary liberal democracy.

As we saw above, work on social needs generates the possibility of participation in the collective or universal conversation. The corporation is thus the ideal location for this conversation to develop on a basis of particularity but in a manner that moves toward universality. For all these reasons, the corporation follows the family as, in Hegel terms, the second "*ethical* root of the state."[61]

Corporations were eliminated in France in Hegel's day, and soon after all over Europe. Can similar institutions – labour unions, NGOs, and other community organizations – provide the recognition and cultivation that individuals require? If these organizations are either insufficiently numerous or ineffective in providing the recognition Hegel requires of them, then the conditions for the creation of rabbles and the tyranny of the Condition of Right are created.

As with other issues of pertaining directly to capitalism, Hegel underestimates the power of the capitalist class to forge a society in its own interests. I argue below that the corporations collapsed in Europe for reasons best explained by the insights of Karl Marx. When a society is predicated on private property, as is Hegel's civil society, the forces that lead toward the tyranny of the Condition of Right are least inhibited. That is, the corporations were eliminated by the growing power of capitalist classes that (correctly) perceived them to be antagonistic to the most efficient possible accumulation of capital. If Marx is right, then a society based on private property is very unlikely to be able to successfully institutionalize a "state" – an institution that fulfills the demand of a free society to create the conditions that cultivate freedom.

3 THE PREDICAMENTS OF CIVIL SOCIETY

As we saw above, the family is organized according to a logic of exclusive particularity and yet its task is to prepare for its own transcendence. Children must be cultivated in the family to embrace the inclusive, yet abstract, universality of civil society in which all people are free and equal as persons. Although the family and civil society are animated by contradictory logics, their relationship is a "vital contradiction" because a) it is only in and through the logic of the family that those capable of the logic of civil society are cultivated, and b) this contradictory relationship leaves them in perpetual tension.

A similar vital contradiction animates the relationship of civil society and state. The inclusive universality of civil society is formal insofar as it abstracts from all the particular ways that free and equal persons express themselves. Like the Condition of Right, free persons thus particularize themselves in a plurality of ways that threaten to create an aristocratic or tyrannical logic. If this fate is to be averted, the civil society must cultivate from within itself the concrete universal of the state – a commitment to the common good. Both family and civil society, then, must generate individuals capable of transcending each of these two constitutive logics. This means that there is not only a vital contradiction between family and civil society, but also between civil society and state. This is a vital contradiction because (a) civil society must cultivate in its members an attitude that contradicts its own logic: a commitment to the common or universal good, and yet (b) the two institutions remain in permanent tension.

Individuals pursue their own private or particular good in civil society, especially in and through their work in the economy. Yet this very work creates an increasingly sophisticated and complex web of interdependence. Despite rampant competition, at a deeper level production and the satisfaction of need in civil society are highly co-operative activities. The successful operation of even a very competitive economy requires elaborate structures of co-operation that include contract right and other forms of law, money and monetary policy, systems of transport and communication, and so on. Moreover, persons who begin with very particular, contingent, and arbitrary opinions must work with others, depend on others, and produce for others. Hegel thinks that the implicit co-operation of civil society starts to become explicit in the universal conversation that forges particular opinions toward the universal. This process of cultivation, however, depends squarely on the participation of most people in corporations, for it is only in corporations that individuals receive mutual recognition, honour. The corporation is the key transitional term in the vital contradiction. It is a particular institution and yet it is the site where the cultivation of the universal conversation begins.

But the individualistic logic of civil society can very easily send things in a different direction. Without the corporations and an elaborate set of provisions that prevent the formation of rabbles and maintain the unity of society, a dominant particularity will become increasingly powerful. Hegel warned that members of civil society tend to treat the universal, the community, as a means to its own ends. This happens explicitly in the wealthy rabble, which dominates the rest of society and thus reduces the state to a reflection of its own particular interest. Hegel does not articulate this eventuality explicitly in the *Philosophy of Right*, but we know this to be his concern from his study of the Condition of Right in the *Phenomenology of Spirit*.

More generally, if civil society is animated by particular groups, especially private stock companies that compete with each other in a capitalist economy, then it is inevitable that certain groups and individuals will be much wealthier and more powerful than others. The vital contradiction of civil society turns on this eventuality. Subordinate particulars can become increasingly powerless and, in the worst case, become a rabble. Or they can organize themselves against and resist their subordination. Hegel does not articulate this dynamic, but it is plainly consistent with the account of civil society that he gives. To put this another way, the universal equality of civil society is only abstract and, in its normal functioning, civil society gives rise to inequality and sometimes dramatic inequality. Moreover, there is nothing preventing dominant particulars from seizing the power of the state except other particulars and, indeed, nothing preventing other particularities from forming a resistance.

Hegel envisioned a double strategy. He thought that the chaos of civil society could be controlled by the twin action of the corporations cultivating the universal from below and a very strong state organized around a professional governing class. Because capitalism has made the constitutional structures of the state completely obsolete, they will not be considered in detail here. Instead, I briefly consider these structures as a way to strengthen our sense of the rationality that the state is called upon to maintain.

Hegel certainly did not reject democracy altogether, but he had little respect for the kind of representative democracy which is common in Western liberal nations. He believed that this creates little more than atomism and alienation from the state. In Hegel's view, democracy is successful only under two conditions. The people must be virtuous and the polity must be small.[62] The pursuit of mere "particularity" instead of virtue (which we saw in the Condition of Right) leads the democracy into aristocracy and tyranny. "The principle of particularity," Hegel says, "is not contained in democracy, and if it comes on the scene, it has an annihilating effect on it."[63]

But if Hegel is opposed to modern representative democracy and knows that the ancient democracy of the polis is impossible, he is nonetheless very much a democrat in the deeper and more philosophical sense. Democratic participation is very insubstantial in mere voting but is literally a way of life in the corporations that Hegel thought would cultivate real democratic participation in civil society. Democracy is embodied in the concrete participation of citizens in progressively more general spheres of community life, hinging on the corporation. Corporations nominate representatives to the legislature, which is itself divided into the three estates already considered – agriculture, commerce, and the bureaucracy. Thus democratic participation is tied to real responsibility and efficacy rather than the franchise of representative democracy. Indeed, Hegel says, "For some time now, organization has always been directed from above, and efforts have been devoted for the most part to this kind of organization despite the fact that the lower level of the masses as a whole can easily be left in a more or less disorganized state. Yet it is extremely important that the masses should be organized, because only then do they constitute a power or a force; otherwise they are merely an aggregate, a collection of scattered atoms. Legitimate power is to be found only when the particular spheres are organized."[64] Representative democracy of the kind to which we are accustomed in liberalism leaves citizens as a "collection of scattered atoms." As atoms, it is impossible for them to have any "power or force." Real democratic organizations, in other words, and the real power of the masses, arise only when the people are organized. It is in this far more substantial sense, then, that Hegelian philosophy is democratic.[65]

This does not mean that we should be too sanguine about his view of the "masses." Hegel also thought that only the "universal class," made up of seasoned career bureaucrats, could ensure the universality of the state. Indeed, in his scheme, the democratic structures rooted in the corporations reach only as far as the legislature. The executive is made up entirely of career civil servants. The apex of this pyramid is a monarch who, though he has no power, is responsible for formally ratifying all legislation.

In light of Marx's critique, Hegel appears naive about the universal class. In his constitutional scheme the bureaucratic class and the executive branch of government are even more vulnerable to control by a dominant class than in contemporary representative democracy. If, in typical structures of representative democracy, the people have the power to elect their own representatives not only to the legislature but to the executive as well, then the domination of the state by a capitalist class is to that extent mitigated. There is no such check in Hegel's constitutional proposal. Hegel seriously underestimated the power of capitalist development to undo his vision of a just society. Not only can the threat of atomism arising from civil society not be contained by the quasi-authoritarian nature of Hegel's state executive but such a structure would actually increase this threat once the bureaucracy was firmly controlled by a particular class.

Hegel underestimated and, indeed, did not fully perceive, the class dynamics of capitalism in which the dominant (though not only) particularities of civil society became capitalists, those who own the means of production, and workers, who must therefore sell their labour-power to the capitalists. The particular class interest of capitalists came to dominate the state and thus steered it decidedly in their particular or class interest.

Yet, even in Hegel's failure to perceive the power and structure of capitalism, the state remains a site of "universal conversation" – workers and other marginalized particularities organize themselves in unions and political parties to mitigate the control of the state by capitalists. Thus, Hegel's notion of the state as a place of universal conversation is vindicated, even if in an essentially failed form. The fact that class conflict is played out in public means that to some extent the state retains its universal vocation, although in a distorted form.

Whether Hegel could or should have better perceived the power of capitalism, and thus the dominance of the state by civil society, is not a philosophical question. Philosophy, again, "is *its own time comprehended in thoughts*."[66] A philosophy is un-Hegelian if it fails to articulate the dialectical dynamics of freedom, not if it disagrees with Hegel's texts. Hegel's study of Germany in the 1820s can teach us much about how we should approach political life, but, ultimately, to do Hegelian philosophy is not predominantly to study someone else's historical period but one's own. Suffice it to say that if Hegel's constitutional proposals for the state failed to grasp the dynamics of capitalism in civil society, the concrete rationality of the state identified above must be configured in a different set of institutions. The task of the next chapter is to begin the process of clarifying an essential core of Hegel's philosophy that is carried forward from the *Philosophy of Right*, while the final two chapters will turn that analysis directly to a study of kinds of political institutions rendered necessary by the hegemony of liberal-capitalism.

9

Economy and Governance

The vitality of contradiction in civil society comes down to this: Particular institutions, economic and otherwise, are simultaneously a threat to freedom and its necessary condition. It is only too easy to say that "the concrete universal of the state must be cultivated in and through particularity in civil society," but the forces at work in civil society are formidable. Indeed, the key to finding the requisite balance lies in recognizing on a deeper level what the vitality of contradiction in civil society and the state really means.

The logic of civil society institutionalizes the mutual recognition of singular selves as universally equal and free to determine (particularize) their lives as they see fit. Civil society, then, preserves the claims of the Condition of Right. The logic of the state institutionalizes, as we said, the "cultivation of concrete freedom." This amounts to the claim that the state is responsible for ensuring that its citizens recognize the enormous web of co-operation that is necessary for the society as a whole and, a fortiori, for the family and civil society. The state, as ground of freedom, makes explicit that the society as a whole is a necessary condition for the flourishing of all its potentially fractious particularities. Since this universality is a precondition for particular freedom, the state, as end, must be carefully cultivated by the whole society. This enormous web of co-operation is made up not only of all the different ways in which singular selves particularize themselves in family and civil society but indeed of all the ways that a society has expressed and cultivated itself in its history, gradually accumulating a legacy of economic production, custom, and law which singular selves inherit and develop, whether in their capacity as members of a family or civil society, or in their work on behalf of the state.

That is, individuals, as they pursue their lives as members of families and in the businesses and organizations of civil society, must recognize that their own particular good is ultimately best served, best *cultivated*, if they have a concern for the collective good of the society as a whole as expressed in the institutions of a justly constituted state. If their actions presuppose the web of co-operation that is the concrete and universal condition for the possibility of everything they do as members of families and civil society, they must choose to particularize themselves in such a way as to strengthen and elaborate these bonds of co-operation rather than in ways that weaken and undermine them.

For Hegel, this task is at once necessary and yet, to a significant degree, impossible. The demands of particular lives and institutions within civil society can never be perfectly reconciled with the universal totality of mutual recognition. There is always a sense in which the state is serving certain particular interests better than others. It is therefore essential that the term "common good" not be conceived in the abstract terms of the understanding as signifying an (impossible) unity of the singular, particular, and universal in modern society. The "common good" must instead point to the way in which, despite the inequalities of wealth and power that are inevitable in a free society, everyone must be cultivated to participate in the "universal conversation" by which, to as high a degree as possible, "the freedom of each is a condition for the freedom of all." The very inequalities that structure civil society are also what animate the universal conversation. In this way, the structural inequalities and forms of political marginalization that are the vitality of contradiction are constantly minimized though never utterly negated.

Hegel is opposed to both the right-wing and left-wing forms of argument that would deny this unavoidable tension. On the right, Adam Smith famously claimed that self-interested individuals would unconsciously generate the common good. Libertarianism is based on a fantasy of society with, at most, the "ultra-minimalist state" of Robert Nozick.[1] Hegelian philosophy claims that these happy stories of the Invisible Hand or libertarian freedom are merely the Condition of Right in a primitive, pre-tyrannical stage of its existence. Indeed, the market, if left to its own devices, will create chaos, recession, depression, and oligopoly, if not monopoly. Even the right wing of the contemporary political spectrum concedes at least some version of Hegel's position, such that the debate in Western capitalist nations is not whether the state will intervene in the affairs of civil society, but *how much* and *in what ways*.

The left-wing version of the dream of a seamless freedom, of a society without vital contradiction, was articulated by Karl Marx and by anarchist thinkers like Bakunin and Kropotkin. Traditional Marxists and anarchists do not disagree about the abolition of the state but about the pathway to that abolition. Either way, they hold that the abolition of classes leads inevitably to the abolition of the state. And yet if workers' co-operatives (the soviets) really were autonomous (as many hoped they would be), then they would, according to Hegelian philosophy, inevitably develop differences of power with respect to each other. Some form of state would have become necessary to mediate their relationships to each other. Of course, the Soviet Union took a different route altogether, adopting a system of central planning – a new form of "Absolute Freedom" – in which a centralized government – a powerful faction – continuously and inefficiently repressed and stifled the initiatives of the society while simultaneously benefiting from its own power. Stateless or minimal-state fantasies of the right and the left arise from the fantasy that vital contradiction can be removed, whereas Hegel argues that the state is the forum where the inevitable inequalities and conflicts of society are addressed and, to some degree, resolved.

Civil society is constituted by the logic of abstract universal equality, as form, in the right to particularize oneself as one best sees fit, its content. This content is a universal web of co-operation animated by inequality and conflict. The state must thus consist of a concrete universal built out of all the particularities of the society, but constituting itself as a kind of universal particularity. That is, if civil society is made up of particularities that must be structured in such a way as to lean toward the universal, the state is a universal conversation of these particularities in which their relation to each other is negotiated. The particular exclusivity of civil society in its concrete self-manifestation (i.e., not in its abstract principles) is in vital contradiction with the inclusive universality of the state, such that it is impossible to fully choose or affirm either.

The only solution, then, is to live in the midst of this vital contradiction and thus to engage in those forms of particular action that best cultivate the well-being of freedom in general. On the other hand, this vital contradiction may indeed destroy the society, so that it becomes antagonistic to its own freedom. Whichever way it turns out, this vitality is the possibility and promise of freedom's fulfillment. It sets the terms for what is at stake in the struggle to realize freedom. For example, if groups within civil society always have varying amounts of wealth and power, the attempts to address these difficulties in light of the common good (or not) will be a dominant, animating tension that makes freedom in the socioeconomic and political realms what it is. Human beings will cultivate the best ways they can to pursue their own interests in a world where others are doing the same. Yet that world is also a *shared* world in which the real co-operation necessary to everyone's actions needs to be cultivated – nurtured, preserved, and developed. The task Hegel sets for us in his political philosophy is not just to figure out by means of conceptual dialectic that family, civil society, and state are the essential institutions of freedom, but to understand how to cultivate the best possible life within the vital contradictions that animate the relations of each to the others.

As we saw in the last chapter, Hegel maintained that the cultivation of freedom in these conditions required a bottom-up and a top-down mediation. First, corporations would cultivate universality from within the particular spheres of civil society. Second, the state – led by an executive made up of the trustworthy class of universal bureaucrats – would ensure that the universal vocation of the state was preserved in the face of the less-than-trustworthy particularities that make up civil society.

The next task, then, is to make clear why Hegel's juridical formulation is a failure and to begin to articulate the parameters of a just alternative. I do this by focusing on two important dimensions of the vital contradiction of civil society and state. The first, property right, gives the fundamental terms for the economy, while the second, democratic participation, gives the fundamental terms for participatory self-governance. It should not come as a surprise that they overlap.

I ECONOMY: PRIVATE AND COMMON PROPERTY

Hegel is an emphatic defender of private property, contract, and the market economy. He argues that the freedom of all persons begins in their universally recognized right to acquire private property, and in the *Philosophy of Right* he explicitly rejects the notion that common property could serve as the foundation for a just society. He also recognizes that the universal recognition of the person in the Condition of Right leads to tyranny. Hegel trusts that the moral and political cultivation of the person toward a more comprehensive notion of freedom will protect modern society from the fate of the Condition of Right. He thinks that corporations and the state can ensure this education of the soul. But I have suggested that Hegel underestimates the power of capitalism to override both. Nonetheless, Hegel's theory of property is nuanced, complex and, all the same, in need of revision. In this section I briefly summarize Hegel's key claims regarding property right, and then move directly from there to a Hegelian critique of Hegel himself. This leads to the conclusion that a just society must indeed be founded on common rather than private property, such that each singular person has an inalienable right to exclude others from his or her share of the common wealth.

The first section of the *Philosophy of Right*, "Abstract Right," is very easy to misread. Here, Hegel begins with the most abstract and empty form of the free selfhood – "the person." He considers the person first in abstraction from all other persons and, indeed, from any consideration of temporality or history. Hegel's strategy is to develop a conceptual dialectic on the basis of free singular personhood precisely because the "sunburst" of Hegel's revolutionary age inaugurates the notion that all politics must be premised on freedom. By beginning a conceptual dialectic with self-conscious freedom in its most stark and indeed primitive form, Hegel can prove that the society that follows from it adequately recognizes freedom. The irony is that in a curious way this dialectic turns out to be something of a *reductio ad absurdum*. The stances of abstract freedom (most generally, "abstract right" and "morality") keep proving themselves incapable of grounding themselves. The arguments for freedom of the person and moral freedom prove themselves to be dependent on a fully concrete system of mutual recognition – Ethical Society (*Sittlichkeit*) (just as it does at the end of chapter 5, "Reason," of the *Phenomenology of Spirit*). Of course, the "*Sittlichkeit*" of the *Phenomenology* refers to the Ethical Society we studied above, for which the full forms of freedom, including personality and morality, are not yet developed. Hegel, somewhat confusingly, also calls the fully free society of family, civil society, and state "*Sittlichkeit*" in the *Philosophy of Right*. The latter is plainly different, since it contains all the forms of subjective freedom within it. To generalize, then, the argument for personhood and its private property as developed in the *Philosophy of Right* is shown to presuppose the concrete conditions of human life.

We get a hint of Hegel's strategy when he explicitly identifies the vital contradiction of the person. "The highest achievement of a human being is to be a person," Hegel says, and "yet in spite of this, the simple abstraction, 'person,' has something contemptuous about it, even as an expression." Indeed, he calls personhood the "life of worms" in the *Philosophy of History*. He continues in the same passage of the *Philosophy of Right*, "Personality is thus at the same time the sublime and the wholly ordinary; it implies this unity of the infinite and the utterly finite, of the determinate boundary and the completely unbounded. The supreme achievement of the person is to support this contradiction, which nothing in the natural realm contains or could endure."[2] To understand Hegel's theory of property, it is necessary to delve into this vital contradiction.

"Personality," Hegel says, "begins only at that point where the subject has not merely a consciousness of itself in general as concrete and in the same way determined, but a consciousness of itself as a completely abstract 'I' in which all concrete limitation and validity are negated and invalidated."[3] To be a person one must be able to withdraw from all of one's commitments and find oneself in the pure emptiness of abstract freedom – this is essentially the stoicism of the *Phenomenology*. For that reason, Hegel takes pains to distinguish the person from a mere "subject." "The person is essentially different from the subject for the subject is only the possibility of personality, since any living thing whatever is a subject. A person is therefore a subject which is aware of this subjectivity, for as a person, I am completely for myself: the person is the individuality of freedom in pure being-for-itself. As *this* person, I know myself as free in myself, and I can abstract from everything, since nothing confronts me but pure personality."[4] It is absolutely essential that this stance of singular freedom be asserted by each person and recognized by others.

The person's first externalization, according to the rules of conceptual dialectic, must be the most primitive, and this is to put one's will into one's own body. This is precisely what a slave does not do with his or her own being. "It is only through the *development* of his own body and spirit, *essentially* by means of *his self-consciousness comprehending itself as free*, that he takes possession of himself and becomes his own property as distinct from that of others."[5] The person must assert him or herself as a free, embodied being.

The second step of the conceptual dialectic is that this being must be capable of "placing his will in any thing" such as to make them his property.[6] The person asserts its freedom, then, by laying a claim to its freedom as embodied both in its own body and in external possessions. Yet Hegel insists that neither assertion has any validity, any objectivity, without the mutual recognition of others. "The inner act of will which consists in saying that something is mine must also become recognisable by others." "If I make a thing mine," Hegel says, "I give it this predicate which must appear in it as an external form, and must not simply remain in my inner will. It often happens that children emphasize their prior volition when they oppose the appropriation of something by others; but for adults, this volition is not sufficient, for the form of subjectivity must be removed and must work its way out to objectivity."[7] Hegel makes his point in the subtle way he uses a conceptual dialectic to articulate three progressively more sophisticated forms of private property. Each form of private property consists in one degree less physical control and one degree more simple collective agreement in mutual recognition. Hegel thus starts from "physical seizure," moves to the intermediary stage of "giving form" (transforming), and concludes with mere "marking." "I mark the thing with a sign to indicate that I have placed my will in it." The giving of a mark or a sign is the most sophisticated because it is addressed to nothing other than the status of recognition. "For the concept of a sign," Hegel says, "is that the thing does not count as what it is, but as what it is meant to signify."[8] Thus even if seizure and transformation implicitly make a sign, when I mark something as mine the essence of property as a mutually recognizable, communicative gesture is rendered fully explicit. We see property right qua system of mutual recognition at work in the mere fact that for the vast majority of time, my right to exclude others from things is purely and simply respected by everyone.

With this architecture of personhood and private property Hegel can easily show why common property presupposes private property. "Common property, which may by its nature be owned by separate individuals, takes on the determination of an inherently dissolvable community in which it is in itself a matter for the arbitrary will whether or not I retain my share of it."[9] That is, any instantiation of common property presupposes a free will that can put itself into something to make it private property. That I would choose to do this with other people, such as to have common property, is certainly possible, but it presupposes the more fundamental stance of private property. Common property is essentially a form of contract for Hegel, such that I can agree with others to hold something in common, and yet alienate myself from it again at my discretion. Or again, Hegel is arguing that all common property presupposes private property.[10]

In the *Philosophy of Right* Hegel points out several occasions in which the right to private property is superseded. For example, he poses the problem of an individual who is faced with death if she does not violate the institution of private property by stealing food. Hegel says, "Life, as the totality of ends, has a right in opposition to abstract right. If, for example, it can be preserved by stealing a loaf, this certainly constitutes an infringement of someone's property, but it would be wrong to regard such an action as common theft. If someone whose life is in danger were not allowed to take measures to save himself, he would be destined to forfeit his rights; and since he would be deprived of life, his entire freedom would be negated."[11] This example presupposes a situation of relative poverty – of scarce and unevenly distributed resources. Hegel argues that this very situation is itself a result of the institution of private property since the distribution of private property in a market economy is far from equal.[12] Private property is an institution borne out of the need to recognize the singularity of human experience, yet as is the case with respect to poverty, the institution does so in such a way as to sometimes transgress the singular self. Accordingly, private property must occasionally be superseded when higher forms of freedom are at stake.

This argument reaches its most extreme form in war. Individuals, Hegel says, must go to war "even if their own life and property, as well as their opinions and all that naturally falls within the province of life, are endangered and sacrificed. It is a grave miscalculation if the state, when it requires this sacrifice, is simply equated with civil society, and its ultimate end is seen merely as the *security of the life and property* of individuals. For this security cannot be achieved by the sacrifice of what is supposed to be *secured* – on the contrary."[13]

Even in these passages, the end to be secured is at least in part the protection of the person, his or her private property, and a society predicated on a free market. That is, sometimes the free person must agree to sacrifice himself in war for the sake of protecting free personhood. Moreover, there can be no existence of free personhood at all without food, so stealing bread is justified. In both cases, the argument for the supersession of private property has, as one of its premises, the preservation of personal freedom and private property itself. Indeed, Hegel says, "Even if exceptions may be made by the state, it is nevertheless the state alone which can make them."[14]

Of course, Hegel does not think that personhood and private property, in the terms of abstract right, are adequate to freedom. Such a state of affairs is nothing short of the Condition of Right. Recall what he said there about the person and private property. The Condition of Right is characterized by an "*equality* in which *everyone* counts as *each* one, that is, as *persons*."[15] Just as in the *Philosophy of Right*, the freedom of the person of the Condition of Right discloses itself in private property. The person of the Condition of Right "finds a manifold subsistence, a possession, and ... impresses upon it the same abstract universality by which it is called *property*."[16] And yet, if Hegel then praises the person and his or her private property in the *Philosophy of Right*, his condemnation of it in the *Phenomenology* could hardly be more stark. He asserts that "to designate an individual as a *person* is an expression of contempt."[17] In the *Philosophy of History*, he offers this analogy: "As, when the physical body suffers dissolution, each point gains a life of its own, but which is only the miserable life of worms; so the political organism is here dissolved into atoms – viz., private persons."[18] As we saw in earlier chapters, the person must be cultivated into higher forms of freedom. Hegel argues, in other words, that the person and his or her private property are a necessary but not sufficient condition for freedom. All the same, he clearly argues that common property presupposes the person and private property.

I think that Hegel makes a mistake here, and that he does so on his own terms. I shall gradually build an argument here, on Hegelian terms but against Hegel's texts, that private property presupposes common property.

Hegel is very clear that the stance of personhood is the result of a development, articulating this development in four decisive ways. First, the stance of personhood is essentially the same as the stoic of chapter 4 of the *Phenomenology of Spirit*. As we know, the stoic emerges only after work as a slave in the context of mortal fear. Second, the person is explicitly identified as the citizen of the Condition of Right in chapter 6 of the *Phenomenology* and thus is the developmental result of the conceptual dialectic that begins with the Ethical Society. Third, the Condition of Right is itself the conceptual correlate of ancient Rome, where Hegel first identifies the emergence of the person in empirical history (i.e., in empirical dialectic). Finally, the person is the result of successful parenting by the family in the *Philosophy of Right*. In each case, free personhood emerges only in the context of the encounter with other people, in mutual recognition, and a fortiori, only after a long and sometimes difficult history. The presupposition of personhood, and his or her private property, is a long process of cultivation in mutual recognition.

Since the person is a mediated result of transformation, Hegel rejects state of nature theories: they artificially posit the person outside its historical and developmental context. It follows that he should reject, for the same reason, state of nature arguments for the emergence of property right. For John Locke, for example, property arises when someone in the state of nature has "mixed his labour" with something.[19] A system of right is then established to protect the vulnerable person and his or her private property. Hegel acknowledges that in certain situations outside of systems of mutual recognition one can seize something and hold it for oneself, but this is not "property" but merely "possession." Property emerges only when a community implicitly or explicitly agrees to allow its singular members to exclude others from the use of something. In other words, when private property is considered in its concrete historical context and not in the isolated terms of abstract right, it presupposes a system of universal agreement (that we will all respect each other's property) – a system of mutual recognition.

Already an interesting "in-itself" versus "for-itself" vital contradiction is emerging with property right. In-itself, property right is a kind of universal agreement, a structure of mutual recognition. However, all too often its for-itself is marked by an ignorance of this universal presupposition such that property is reduced to its particular exclusivity, as in Locke and indeed perhaps Hegel as well.[20] Yet, even when we are self-conscious of the nature of property, its vital contradiction does not go away. Private property, after all, is the inclusively universal right to exclude. We can thus see in another sense why Hegel says that personhood is both glorious (in its universal inclusivity) and contemptible (in its expression as the tyrannical accumulation of wealth and power).

I turn now to the task of showing why private property presupposes common property. When I use the term *property* I refer not to particular material things, but to structures of mutual recognition – of co-operation. As C.B. Macpherson puts it, "In current common usage, property is *things*; in law and in the writers, property is not things but *rights*, rights in or to things."[21] A right, of course, is a structure of mutual recognition in Hegel's philosophy – a universal mode of co-operation that recognizes singulars as particular. The general means of enforcement of this right is nothing other than mutual recognition itself. We commonly acknowledge the rights of others simply by respecting them. We call on the police only in those instances when these rights are not respected. Accordingly, Macpherson echoes Hegel's philosophy when he says, "What distinguishes property from mere momentary possession is that property is a claim that will be enforced by society or the state, by custom or convention or law."[22]

Private property, then, is the right accorded to individuals in a system of mutual recognition to exclude all other members of that community from the use of something. Private property is, therefore, the inclusively universal recognition of an exclusive particularity. Private property addresses the need of the singular individual who, in order to live and express him or herself in the world, must have the ability to exclude others from certain things – for example, only I can eat the food I eat, and I need a certain amount of space in which to live. It is worth noting the tight link between private property and capitalism. Liberal notions of private property are, Macpherson observes, "exactly the kind of property right needed to let the capitalist market operate. If the market was to operate fully and freely, if it was to do the whole job of allocating resources and labour among possible uses, then all labour resources had to become, or be convertible into, this kind of property. As the capitalist market found its feet and grew, it was expected to, and did, take on most of this work of allocation. As it did so it was natural that the very concept of property should be reduced to that of *private* property – an exclusive, alienable, 'absolute' individual or corporate right in things."[23] Private property, then, is the system of recognition in which individuals have the right to exclude others from goods and services, and private property is the means by which goods are distributed in a capitalist economy.

Singular individuals, however, are not the only holders of private property. Collections of individuals can also act as owners of private property insofar as they act as "artificial persons." In Western capitalist countries there are two such collectivities worthy of our mention here. First, corporations, from private stock companies to registered charities, can own property. Second, the state can act as an artificial person when it excludes citizens from using what is its property. Not everyone can have access to a government-owned airline in the way they can have access to other forms of state-owned properties such as a public park or a freeway. In this sense the state is acting as a corporation, an "artificial person," and state property is "akin to private property" – even if the state's private, corporate property is in some sense meant to benefit the common good, such as when the profits of a state airline are distributed to schools or hospitals.[24]

In addition to the categories of singular and corporate private property, there is also "common property." Common property, Macpherson says, "is created by the guarantee to each individual that he will not be excluded from the use or benefit of something."[25] A good but also somewhat misleading example of common property is the public park, access to which is guaranteed to every citizen: each has "a right not to be excluded." Moreover, it is imperative to notice with Macpherson that both private and common forms of property, "being guarantees to individual persons, are individual rights."[26] This is why the example of a park could be misleading, for common property still has an essential principle of exclusion. The park may be our common property, but that right is realized only if I can exclude others from, in this case, the space I need to enjoy it. If the park is too crowded, for example, my right to exclusivity in its use is not respected and the raison d'être of the common property is not realized. Thus the right "not to be excluded" contains within it the "the right to exclude" such that my private satisfaction be realized. This point will be decisive when I return to consider Hegel's arguments for the importance of personhood and its privacy.

Moreover, it is worth noting that Hegel never refutes common property understood as "the right not to be excluded from the use or benefit of something." While Hegel condemns "holding goods in common," his three examples of this, the guardians in Plato's *Republic*, Protagoras's rejection of a similar idea among his followers, and the holding of property by monasteries, are all cases of common property where singular freedom is marginalized.[27] The essence of Hegel's concern, then, is that the person be able to exclude others from the use of something. This concern, I will argue below, is preserved by the notion of common property understood as an exclusive right to a share of a common wealth.

Four further features of property follow from these arguments. First, the *internal* structure of a group that holds corporate private property denies its own members singular property rights unless it is internally structured as *common property* in some form of the version given just now. As a slave, I might be a member of a corporate body that mines gold and yet have no rights to anything within that corporate body because its internal organization is in no sense organized on the basis of common property. This is very different if the mining company is a co-operative, for in this case each member has a right to a share of the total profit. A body of corporate private property that respects singular right is, therefore, an ambivalent structure. Internally, it is founded on some form of common property, insofar as each member has a right to a share of community property (however that is organized). Externally, it is founded on the exclusiveness of private property.

Second, the relations of internality and externality just raised with respect to corporate private property must be recognized as extending ultimately to the totality of all persons. For example, from my point view as a Canadian citizen, the funds of the Canada Pension Plan are common property, for I am guaranteed access to them by virtue of my citizenship. Yet from the point of view of a Nigerian, these funds are corporate private property in which the corporate body in question is the nation-state of Canada. Indeed, the issue of internality/externality with respect to nations will become increasingly important as the nation-state is superseded by international jurisdictions of different kinds.

Third, there are numerous forms of hybrid property. For example, the Homestead Act of 1869 in the United States granted land to individuals conditional upon their commitment to live on it and cultivate it. Similarly, the Brazilian constitution of 1988 mandated a land reform such that government is entitled to seize private property if it is not fulfilling its "social function" (which is defined as a contribution to the common wealth of the nation). That is, the hybrid case of property is defined as that which involves a form of exclusivity that is conditional on the fulfillment of some provision established by, in these cases, the government. A distinction between *legal ownership* and *economic benefit,* which was drawn by Yugoslavian Marxist Alexander Bajt, is very helpful here.[28] He makes the following argument that the form of private property in capitalist countries actually approximates, at the end of the day, common property (note that for him socialist common property is called "social ownership"). "As we know, the legal order together with the price structure formed by the economy determines the content of ownership. Today there are public instruments (progressive income tax, property tax, progressive inheritance tax, and so forth) that can bring the distribution of national product in a system of private ownership to approach the principle of distribution according to work, and hence close to that which corresponds to social ownership."[29] In other words, Bajt thinks that taxation and other institutions common in Western states appropriate private property for the common good to a degree potentially close to that of a socialist regime of common property.

Fourth, in a further and deeper sense, *all property* is hybrid and the hybridity of property is its vital contradiction. On the one hand, we have already seen that common property is defined in terms of the right of singulars to an exclusive share. In this sense, the universality of common property presupposes particular exclusivity. On the other hand, if private property is a right given to me by a community of mutual recognition, then privacy and exclusion always presuppose commonality and inclusion. In this sense, particular exclusion presupposes universal inclusion. That is, it is impossible to define private property without making reference to inclusive commonality and impossible to define common property without making reference to exclusive particularity.

Thus, common property and private property are mutually dependent. We have seen this constitutive structure already, for it is the structure of vital contradiction. All issues of property are in truth suspended in the tension between *inclusive* right (common property) and *exclusive* right (private property). That is, there is no such thing as pure common or pure private property, and yet no instance of "hybrid" property is conceivable without these opposed poles of "inclusive commonality" and "exclusive privacy." The concept of property and, indeed, all social conflicts involving property arise within this animating tension – even if the agents in these situations do not recognize that this is the case. It is impossible to live in a world of property or to think the concept of property without a vital contradiction.

The key Hegelian claim, I will argue, is that while all forms of property are legitimate and necessary, they are all predicated on the primordiality of a certain more comprehensive notion of common property. All modes of producing property are essentially ways in which a community of mutual recognition externalizes itself in the world. Property is essentially the common property of the system of recognition. And it is the state that embodies this commonality as both ground and end. Why is this so?

Imagine the division of labour and customs of a hunting and gathering society in which, when one man kills a moose, the whole community, and not just that man, has a right to eat it. This society is effectively employing the notion of common property as we have defined it. It is, moreover, a system of primitive common property in Marx's sense. The moose is the common property of the community as a whole and each member has a right to a share of it. Underlying the observation of these rules by the members of the community is the system of co-operation (in mutual recognition) presupposed by the actions of the hunter. That is, the successful hunting expedition presupposes the labour of other members of the community, who have raised the hunter as a child; gathered, preserved, or cooked the food he eats; made his tools and his shelter; provided him with protection and companionship; and so on. Moreover, the successful hunter also presupposes the whole history of his culture, by which individuals long before his time painstakingly learned how to make hunting weapons; how to cure and cook meat; how to protect themselves against cold, hunger, animals, and other people; how to negotiate differences and establish customs. The success of the hunter, in other words, has as its necessary condition the entire system of mutual recognition of which he is a part, understood both in terms of its current co-operative activities and their long history of co-operative development. Thus, it is not merely the hunter who kills the moose, but the system of recognition as a universal, historical whole.

This can be translated into Hegel's terminology of property right. When Hegel defines property right, he says that it arises when someone puts his "will in [the] thing."[30] However, in the case of the hunter, it is not he alone who puts his will into the thing, but the community of mutual recognition as a whole. "We" put our will in the thing. It is true that the moose has been transformed by human agency, but it is a collective will that is "in it." The moose is, then, the property not just of the hunter but of the community of mutual recognition. Accordingly, the food generated by the hunter is not considered to be his exclusive, private property. Rather, it is considered to be first and foremost the common property of the community of recognition, and shares are thus distributed to the various members of the community. Notice that property in this society is already considered a right rather than mere possession (even if unself-consciously),[31] and the model of property is *common* (such that each member of the community has a right to a share).

This does not mean, of course, that the hunter-gatherer society necessarily decides to distribute shares of its common property *equally*. It might, for example, recognize the singular skill of the hunter who felled the moose by giving him the first choice or a larger quantity. Or it might favour the most powerful, venerable, or the oldest members. Thus, common property does not require that all shares be equal – shares are distributed proportional to the demands and powers of particular groups and singular individuals. Indeed, the most sophisticated regime of common property would be governed by Marx's famous formula of distributive justice in the *Critique of the Gotha Program*: "From each according his ability, to each according to his needs!"[32]

In contrast to the hunting and gathering society, modern liberal-capitalist societies presuppose the development of individual rights, trade, money, legal contract, a high level of technology, a very complex interrelation of producers, consumers and other agents, and a host of other important features not present in the more primitive society. More importantly, the modern liberal-capitalist society is organized not according to the primacy of common property but according to private property. It might be assumed that these differences mean that the argument made above is applicable only to the primitive society and not to liberal-capitalism. Despite these differences, however, the dynamics of property right are the same in the most decisive respect. That is, the essential character of liberal-capitalist production presupposes an even more sophisticated form of *co-operation* and thus of *common property* within its system of mutual recognition than does the hunting and gathering society.

The purchase of a newspaper at the corner store, for example, requires a vast network of mutual recognition. The purchase requires not merely my own agency as purchaser, but also the co-operative agency (in a system of mutual recognition) of the owner of the store and the truck driver who delivered it. It requires the co-operation (once again, in mutual recognition) of the loggers, paper-mill employees, ink-makers, writers, researchers, printers, editors, and other people linked in whatever way to the print-media industry. The road that I use to travel to the store presupposes the co-operation of construction workers, miners, architects, city planners, government regulators, law-makers, and so on. The money I use to purchase the paper must be made by individuals and loaned, distributed, and regulated by the government and the financial industry. Lawyers and other members of the legal profession ensure the contracts by which this whole process takes place, and police officers, judges, and other members of the judiciary and law enforcement agencies are essential to the security of these exchanges. Furthermore, all these people must eat and have shelter, health care, and education, and thus my purchase presupposes the co-operation of farmers, house-builders, health care professionals, and teachers.

Indeed, this network of co-operation extends backward in time as well. It includes all those who over centuries gradually developed printing technologies, who founded and distributed newspapers, who invented the techniques for making paper, who developed the conventions of written language and, indeed, all those who have participated in the ongoing life of the English language, and other languages. In short, the simple purchase of a newspaper requires an enormous and extremely complex system of mutual recognition that includes not only those working in the present but a vast web of co-operation extending into the distant past.

To use Hegel's terminology for property right once again, with respect to the newspaper it is impossible to say purely and simply that "I put my will" into it and thus made it mine. While it is true that the newspaper is legitimately mine after I have made the purchase, it also has "in it" the "will" of the countless people who co-operated with each other (in mutual recognition) in its production within its immediate but also its infinitely distant past.[33] Indeed, we do not exaggerate even when we say that the "will" that is "in it" is that of all, or virtually all, people in the history of civilization. The will that is in the thing is the collective will of the whole system of mutual recognition – *Spirit*.[34] My singular will is but the most recent contribution to that process (and one that will then be supplemented when the recycling person comes). The thing is rightfully, *in itself* (or, in truth), *proper to* the community of recognition as a whole, for the act of the purchase presupposes as a necessary condition this system of recognition. Or again, the thing is the *property of the whole community*: it is, in truth, *common property*. It is the enormous, universal substance of co-operation, including all the singular individuals and particular groups within it, that makes newspapers.

In comparison to this almost timeless and immeasurably vast substance of freedom, my own contribution is very small, and for this reason Hegel sometimes seems to favour the universal substance over the singular individual – the former is disproportionately important. This is also why, in the vital contradiction of private exclusivity and universal inclusivity, the latter has pre-eminence. And yet there is not one single aspect of this entire history and process that was not carried out by singular individuals organized within particular groups. Thus, even if the universal has priority in terms of property – even if property is primordially common – the right of singulars (and particulars) to a share of this property is decisive. Herein lies the vital contradiction of property understood at another level of depth. Its nature is hybrid, but common property is the higher term.

To summarize, when I bring the newspaper home after giving my coins to the shopkeeper I am, with respect to the *in- itself* of the production of the newspaper, taking what is (I now claim) my share of the communally produced good. My society, a Western liberal-capitalist society, recognizes my purchase as the expression of a "right," but it does not recognize that this right derives from the fact that the newspaper is primordially common property. The system of private property is, in truth (though few recognize this explicitly), that mechanism in our society by which shares of essentially common property are distributed to singular individuals (or groups). The market mechanism and system of private property in capitalist economies is really a mechanism by which a common property is distributed to singular individuals and collectivities. Of course, *right* in liberal-capitalism completely hides this fact. In liberal-capitalism property right in-itself contradicts property right for-itself.

Recall that for Hegel it is essential that the person have private property. And yet a system of common property still accords the singular individual the right to exclude others. This might not be true in the form of common property seemingly defended by Socrates in the community of guardians in Plato's *Republic*. In that case the commonality of property obliterates singularity – or at least tries to. In the system of common property I am defending here, however, the singular self must not only have a right to a share of the collective product, but a right to participate in determining with her own interpretation, deliberation, and choice how that product will be distributed in relation to work and so on. In sum, for a society to be *for itself* what it is *in itself*, it must be organized on the basis of common property. Common property must be understood as guaranteeing to singular persons a share of that property as well as rights to participation in determining how it will be produced and distributed.

Indeed, one might grant the priority of common property and yet still claim that the capitalist mode of distributing shares to individuals is the most efficient, the most respectful of singular freedom, and, given appropriate mechanisms to redistribute wealth, the most fair.[35] However, in anticipation of my imminent discussion of exploitation, I can describe in a preliminary sense how Marx's claims emerge against a very similar form of argument.[36] For Marx, the surplus value created in the production of the newspaper is really a collective or "social" surplus value, and the collectivity that created it should, if the society is to be *for itself what it is in itself,* determine how this surplus value should be produced and distributed. Capitalist private property, however (as Marx argues in his account of alienation), allocates the surplus value not to the entire community but only to those who own the means of production (as corporate and singular private property) and who have bought the labour power that produced it. Liberal-capitalist private property is a regime for the allocation of resources that contradicts in its explicit organization (what it is for itself) the necessary structure of its own existence (what it is in itself).[37] *In itself*, capitalism is a system of mutual recognition that, as a whole, creates surplus value. *For itself*, it is an aggregate of individual property owners or propertyless wage-earners such that only the former have rights to the surplus value. This is exploitation. I will delve into this issue more carefully below.

The domain of property right is hotly contested and filled with conflict because of its vital contradiction – and it could not be otherwise. This applies even in socialism since there is some truth to Adam's Smith's famous claim that the aggressive pursuit of self-interest by entrepreneurs creates benefits for everyone. Socialism needs entrepreneurs who will, presumably, expect a greater share of the common property than others. Thus, to try to enforce a standard of equality with respect to property would require the repression of (and the failure to recognize) those determinate individuals who have more to contribute to the common good by virtue of their abilities to generate wealth for themselves. On the other hand, it is impossible to determine just how much wealth an entrepreneur can exclude others from, even in socialism – except through negotiation. There is no complete solution to this predicament: that is, there is no way to eliminate the contradiction of civil society and state with respect to property right. The state will focus on the commonality of property, and it is right and just that it hold this priority, but the focus of civil society on the privacy of property is not thereby effaced. Just as the exclusive particularity of the family is in vital contradiction with the inclusive, abstract universality of civil society (in the system of universal and equal rights), so too is the exclusive particularity of civil society (in the realm of property accumulation) in vital contradiction with the inclusive universality of the state.

Indeed, there is also a vital contradiction between the exclusive particularity of the state (insofar as some states will have or generate more wealth than others) and the inclusive universality of the global system of mutual recognition embodied in those institutions, like the UN, which purport to care for the universal human community as such. Much of the dynamic debate and struggle in contemporary civil society and state and in the international arena is about who should get what part of the common wealth. The fate of civilization, to a very significant degree, hangs on this vital contradiction.

As is always the case with the vital contradictions of the free society, a great deal depends on how well or how poorly this founding tension is negotiated. The negotiation of this vital contradiction is a matter for a self-determining people to decide for itself. I now turn to the issue of governance. I have not finished with the topic of property right, however, and will return to that question in detail in chapter 11. It is one thing, after all, to claim that common property is the "in and for itself" of human freedom, quite another to devise a juridical structure of property right that fulfills the essence of civil society and state.

2 GOVERNANCE: EXCLUSION AND PARTICIPATION

The negotiation of the vital contradiction that animates property right and, indeed, a society in general, is, at least provisionally, addressed in the laws and customs that determine how property is distributed in the society and to whom – who gets what and how much. Moreover, every member of every society, insofar as they take up an attitude toward these laws and customs, participates in their ongoing development – even if their attitude is slavish obedience. This is to say, *every* member of the society participates in the formation, affirmation, and development of property right within the system of mutual recognition in which they live. In short, the realm of property right presupposes the realm of negotiation in the system of mutual recognition. Thus, in order to adequately grasp property right, it is necessary to discuss how communities make decisions. As with property right, I will show that Hegel's theory of governance is in need of Hegelian criticism.

On the face of it, Hegel's philosophy is profoundly democratic in essence and yet wary of democracy as a form of governance. On the one hand, Hegel's philosophy is devoted to the task of helping humanity disclose to itself the conditions of its own freedom. According to Hegel, the in-itself must become for-itself and self-consciousness constantly transcends itself upward on a ladder toward absolute knowing. This odyssey of self-understanding toward absolute knowledge, Hegel says in the preface to the *Phenomenology*, is one that everyone can make. "The individual has the right to demand that Science should at least provide him with the ladder to this standpoint."[38] The universal human longing for self-conscious freedom is eminently democratic. By developing our powers as free beings, we become capable of ruling ourselves.[39]

As I have emphasized earlier, however, this project of human self-determination is historical. Human beings learn about the conditions of their freedom slowly and unevenly. We are capable of regressing and we are capable of making grave errors of judgment about extremely important matters – in our personal and political lives. A people has to be ready to govern itself.

Moreover, Hegel shares Rousseau's suspicion of representative democracy. He holds that it emerges from the atomistic principle that governs the Condition of Right, and that it isolates and disempowers people. Hegel favours more participatory forms of civic engagement, such as active participation in one's corporation. Participation in a corporation cultivates the capacities of its individual members. However, while corporations nominate members to the legislative body, the legislature itself has many appointed members (from the bureaucracy) and lifetime members (from the agricultural estate). Hegel plainly believes, with respect to *his own* historical context, that the legislature (to a considerable extent) and the executive (completely) should be under the control of a professional and democratically unaccountable class. From our own point of view, Hegel's position on the suitability of the German people for various kinds of democracy is of historical rather than properly philosophical importance. In this section, the key is to become clear about the philosophical fundamentals of this issue. In chapter 11, I develop this study of democracy with respect to our own historical period – particularly in light of the development of liberal-capitalism since Hegel's day.

The definitive position on this issue, indeed the definitive Hegelian position, is given by Marx in his *Contribution to the Critique of Hegel's Philosophy of Right*. Marx says, "Democracy is the truth of monarchy, monarchy is not the truth of democracy. Monarchy is necessarily democracy in contradiction with itself, whereas the monarchial moment is no contradiction within democracy. Monarchy cannot, while democracy can, be understood in terms of itself. In democracy none of the moments obtains a significance other than what befits it. Each is really only a moment of the whole *Demos*. In monarchy one part determines the character of the whole; the entire constitution must be modified according to the immutable head. Democracy is the generic constitution; monarchy is a species, and indeed a poor one. Democracy is content and form; monarchy *should* be only form, but it adulterates the content."[40] The context of Marx's observations here is a development of Aristotelian categories of rule in the light of the quantitative concept. That is, political rule must take one of three forms – monarchy (rule of the one), aristocracy (rule of the some), or democracy (rule of the all). There are no other options save the various hybrids of these three primordial possibilities. Marx analyses the three forms of governance as a conceptual dialectic. Drawing on Hegel's dialectic of the master and slave, Marx makes the decisive point that all forms of governance depend on the implicit or explicit consent of everyone in the society. That is, all government is implicitly democratic – including those forms in which consent and participation take the form of obedience, even slavish obedience, to monarchical or aristocratic rulers. The fulfillment of the conceptual dialectic demands that the implicit become explicit and thus that human beings become self-consciously democratic, such that their consent and participation is active, self-aware, and efficacious. In this dialectical logic, the essence of governance is incompletely realized in its two lower species, monarchy and aristocracy, while the definition of the highest form, democracy, is identical with the concept in general.

Hegelian philosophy, in other words, analyses the political realm in the light of a drive toward the democratic. A generous reading of the constitutional proposals of Hegel's *Philosophy of Right* takes his arguments for the corporations, the legislature, and the executive in this light. Hegel's proposals ascribe as much democratic self-governance to early nineteenth-century Germany as he thought, rightly or wrongly, appropriate.

If the human political project is characterized by a drive toward democracy, it is not enough that democracy simply be encouraged as a means of decision-making. A society may well embody a formal democracy and yet fail to cultivate the conditions in which the self-rule of citizens is wise and efficacious. Essentially aristocratic forms of rule are perhaps most effective when they garb themselves in a superficial and merely formal democracy. Walter Lippmann's infamous claim that it is the task of modern (democratic, American) government to "manufacture consent" neatly identifies the political task of an aristocracy that solidifies its power in and through the mere appearance of democracy.[41] The Hegelian democratic imperative, which appears only in muted form in the *Philosophy of Right*, is to cultivate the capacity of citizens to rule themselves to as sophisticated a degree as possible, given determinate historical conditions. Hegel's own commitment to this view is disclosed in his discussion of the "universal conversation" and the importance of education. In his exploration of life in corporations and the demand for a public education, Hegel demonstrates that the cultivation of freedom requires concrete institutions, some of which function in the economic realm. A corporation, in other words, has two tasks. The first is to ensure the well-being of a particular sector of economic production, and the second is to cultivate the conditions of universal engagement with the state. To put this point more generally, the imperative to cultivate the conditions of self-governing democracy must extend beyond merely juridical boundaries and squarely into the economic realm. Indeed, given the importance of economic production not only to the life of the nation but to the concrete day-to-day experience of so many citizens, no democracy can thrive if participation in the economic sphere does not cultivate the conditions of self-governance. As is now evident, Hegel's proposal that this cultivation take place in the corporation failed and, moreover, there is good reason to be suspicious of the efficacy of merely representative democracy. Thus, the imperative to cultivate democracy demands new institutions the nature of which I will discuss in the last two chapters.

If the human political project is animated by a drive toward the democratic, it can equally be said that it is driven by vital contradiction toward democracy. Indeed, the conceptual dialectic that leads from the Ethical Society through Absolute Freedom can now be identified not just as the conceptual dialectic of self-determination but indeed of democracy. Moreover, given that liberal-capitalist society embodies undemocratic structures in the economic sphere and merely representative democracy in the political sphere, the vitality of contradiction will inevitably lead to conflict – of which union organizing is but one example. There are no rational grounds (as I argue in the last two chapters) for preventing the economic realm from becoming democratized.

Finally, Hegelian philosophy should also remind us that the drive toward democracy should not be conceived in the idealistic or utopian terms mandated by the understanding (*Verstand*). The understanding conceives of democracy in a pure and abstract form: the pure, full, and transparent participation of everyone in all collective decisions. This was arguably Rousseau's dream and has already been refuted in the study of the Society of Absolute Freedom. When we conceive democracy in terms of concrete rationality (*Vernunft*), we recognize that it is always characterized by abiding vital contradictions. There are always particular groups who have more power than others in the "universal conversation" of collective life. Even these dominant particularities have incomplete knowledge with respect to their own advantage and to the demands of the common good. The abiding vital contradiction of democratic society is one in which there are always degrees of participation and exclusion. However, the demands of the relatively marginalized are themselves a key to the vitality of democratic life. These particular sectors organize themselves to, as we say, make their voices heard and have their demands recognized. Democratic life is always animated by this kind of strife and struggle and, under the right conditions, this struggle is precisely what allows democracy to thrive. I now turn to a detailed discussion of the forms of institutional life that will allow human democratic vitality to fulfill itself.

PART THREE

LIBERAL-CAPITALISM AND THE CULTIVATION OF FREEDOM

10

The Dialectics of Liberal-Capitalism

It should now be reasonably clear why the communitarian tradition, which includes philosophers like Charles Taylor, Michael Sandel, Michael Walzer, and many others, draws deeply on Hegel's philosophical legacy. The atomistic individual, for both Hegel and the communitarian tradition, is not the first premise of political philosophy but the result of historical development. Ontogenetically, she is the result of a family and educational system whose goal is to cultivate the self-confidence, skills, and self-concept of autonomous life in civil society. Yet the very mode in which the family and the educational system cultivate the individual is itself the product of a long phylogenetic process by which the customs, institutions, and laws of a society that upholds and encourages individual freedom were developed. In the case of Western notions of the free, rights-bearing individual, the phylogenetic heritage of cultivation is typically traced more than two millennia back to the Greeks – during which the sophisticated notions of freedom slowly and painstakingly developed themselves.[1]

There is a strange tendency, however, to take both these ontogenetic and phylogenetic processes for granted in Western civil society. For example, the notion of the "self-made man" could not be a more grave conceptual error, the repercussions of which often tend toward the neglect of and even contempt for the very institutions that were necessary conditions for the possibility freedom. Michael Sandel's work exemplifies the concern on the part of communitarian writers. In *Democracy's Discontent*, for example, Sandel argues that the "neutral state" exemplifies a trend long underway in American political and judicial practice by which the republican notions of public responsibility and the institutions that supported it have been undermined.[2] Sandel's subtitle, *America in Search of a Public Philosophy*, is an expression of both his preoccupation with and his hope that such a search might be successful, and he clearly takes his own philosophical project to be working toward that end. Sandel's philosophy thus implicitly denies the claim made from within the Marxian tradition that the problems of liberal-capitalist societies cannot be undone from within the resources of liberal-capitalism itself. Indeed, if authors influenced by Marx charge Sandel with underestimating the power of liberal-capitalism to undermine freedom, it was Marx himself who made precisely this accusation against Hegel.

The study of civil society in the previous chapter has shown just how difficult it is to establish the kind of institutions that can cultivate freedom. The corporations, to which Hegel gives such importance, were swept aside by capitalism with almost breathless ease. This suggests that the corporation, the lynchpin of Hegel's claim that freedom can be cultivated in civil society and the fate of the Condition of Right avoided, was utterly incapable of fulfilling its role. Marxian writing on these topics makes the same kind of criticism of those who say today that liberal-capitalism can be reformed from within. This raises once more, as the saying goes, the spectre of Marx and socialism. The tide of euphoria that greeted the success of liberal-capitalism after the collapse of the Soviet Union is already dissipating and, indeed, is of little philosophical significance anyway. While I will argue below that the failures of Soviet state communism followed from contradictions of its own, we cannot assume that the empirical failure of the Soviet project implies that other more sophisticated forms of socialism will not turn out to be far more capable than either state communism or liberal-capitalism of cultivating freedom. The task of this chapter is to come face to face with this question: Does liberal-capitalism have within itself the institutional and philosophical resources to sustain the drive toward the full realization of democracy? I argue that neither liberal-capitalism nor state communism is capable of further cultivating the realization of freedom. This exploration will require the help of Marx.

Marx has already come up in this text at two key junctures. First, I have grappled with his claim that modes of production determine society, and concluded that since one cannot derive the fact of exploitation and domination from the technical means of transforming nature to meet human needs (productive forces), the subjugation of some people by others requires that an explanation be found in the conceptual and empirical dialectics of mutual recognition. Second, I showed why Hegel's concept of property is primordially *common* in a way that anticipates Marx's claim that the collectively produced surplus value of all labour belongs to the community that produces it. If this claim is implicit in Hegel, it is explicit in Marx. The same holds for Marx's explicit defence of democracy. Of course, there is no contradiction between the recognition of common property in principle and the collective decision that the best way to run an economy is in and through the free market and a regulating and interventionist state. It is precisely this theme, in the largest sense, to which I now turn.

There are, moreover, two additional reasons for exploring Marx's arguments. First, I claimed above that the state is charged with upholding and cultivating the universality of the system of mutual recognition. Marx, of course, claims that the state never represents a universal good, but generally a particular interest in disguise – namely, that of the economic class that exploits the rest of the society. The state in liberal-capitalism, Marx says, is "but a committee for managing the affairs of the whole of the bourgeoisie."[3] Marx, in effect, claims that a society predicated on private property generates what I have described in terms of the tyranny of the Condition of Right. Second, Hegel defends wage-labour, a claim that must come face to face with Marx's argument that wage-labour is exploitation. Indeed, Hegel has no theory of exploitation at all.

The broader goal of this chapter, then, is to articulate the dialectic of liberal-capitalism and in the process engage with the challenge of Marx's philosophy and socialist politics. More specifically, I seek to address four key themes. The first section defines liberal-capitalism within the terms of the conceptual dialectic I have been elaborating. The second section addresses the cultivation of freedom within civil society in light of both the failure of Hegel's corporations and developments in contemporary civil society. The third section focuses on explaining how the cultivation of freedom, understood within the Hegelian terms I have been developing, places a demand upon us to consider capitalist exploitation unjust. The fourth section, finally, claims that the cultivation of freedom also carries with it an imperative to cultivate democracy well beyond our contemporary forms of political representation and into the economy and other spheres of social life.

I LIBERAL-CAPITALISM AND THE CONCEPTUAL DIALECTIC OF FREEDOM

As stated in chapters 1 and 2, the goal of the conceptual dialectic of political life is not merely to determine the institutions of a fully free and just society but to articulate this just society as the result of the cultivation of freedom through failed and yet progressively more sophisticated realizations of freedom. I show in this chapter that liberal-capitalism does not live up to the demands of the free society, and that it can best be understood as a hybrid of the Condition of Right and the Society of Absolute Freedom.

The Society of Absolute Freedom is predicated on a commitment to the cultivation of abstract universality, modelled on Enlightenment notions of reason that are found in the philosophies of, for example, Rousseau and Kant. The political focus of *liberal-capitalism* is thus based on a vigilant application of the notion of universal human rights within a democratic constitutional structure. Even if the liberal state has been highly complicit in the flourishing of capitalism, there is no way that it can simply be reduced to "a committee for managing the affairs of the whole of the bourgeoisie," and it was not Marx's intention to make such a claim in a deterministic manner. Indeed, in his own careful study of the length of the working day, in the context of his study of capitalism's strategy for the maximization of the appropriation of surplus-value, Marx shows that the English state frequently did not side with the interests of capitalists and that its ultimate trajectory, at least on this point, was to shorten the working day, further protect children, and improve working conditions, all of which decrease the rate of exploitation – thus predictably raising the ire of capitalists.[4] This is to say that the commitment to rational freedom, especially in the notion of human rights, has sometimes trumped the interests of capitalists.

Indeed, the liberal state's commitment to universality has at times motivated opposition to the domination or exploitation of some particular groups or classes over others. It is sometimes in the name of the abstract universality of human rights that the civil rights movement challenges racism, that the feminist movement challenges sexism, that many ethnic groups address their exclusion, and that gays and lesbians claim equality with heterosexuals in the eyes of the law. In all these struggles, the philosophical principles of the universality of human rights have (to one degree or another, depending on the country and the situtation) facilitated progress in addressing exclusion. Similarly, the United Nations Declaration of Human Rights is animated by the same philosophical principles, all of which are predicated on – though not limited to – the universal yet abstract equality of persons. It goes without saying that the forces arising from within liberal-capitalist societies that oppose these struggles have often been formidable, violent, and backed by great wealth and political power.

Yet there is a key reason why liberal-capitalism is not merely an embodiment of the Society of Absolute Freedom. Recall that the goal of Absolute Freedom was to "determine the particular" such that it would not undermine the universal. Rousseau's participatory democracy and St Just's notion of equal property are examples of this concern. Contemporary liberalism does not uphold this aspect of the Society of Absolute Freedom. Indeed, it typically considers the development of certain particular inequalities to be the legitimate outcome of rightful action on the part of individuals. For example, if I choose to pursue the accumulation of great wealth and do so in a "legal" manner, then I am by and large entitled by law to that wealth – even if it creates great inequality and the factions that Rousseau and others so greatly feared.

In this sense, then, liberal-capitalism is not organized according to the concept of Absolute Freedom but according to the *Condition of Right*. In the Condition of Right, recall, individual persons pursue their own interests as they see fit. The Condition of Right, like liberal-capitalism, liberates the "arbitrary will," which simply follows its own desires and impulses and is protected under the law in its right to do so. Attempts to educate or cultivate the will are thus understood in the Condition of Right as potentially coercive of the free will. The "procedural republic," Sandel says, is characterized by the "neutral state" – a state that is neutral with respect to the particular ways individuals develop their freedom.[5]

Moreover, it is the very structure of capitalism to institutionalize the bad infinite of appetitive desire as precisely the motor of economic development. This is the secret of its success and the source of its greatest danger. Capitalism is an economic system predicated on private property and the accumulation of wealth *as an end in itself*. The means to this end is the exploitation of labour, a topic I study in detail below. As Marx concisely puts it, "The driving motive and determining purpose of capitalist production is the self-valorization of capital to the greatest possible extent, i.e., the greatest possible production of surplus value, hence the greatest possible exploitation of labour-power by the capitalist."[6] The motive force here is plainly what I have been calling, with Hegel, appetitive desire. "The magnitude of the profit" generated by capitalism "gives [the capitalist] an insatiable hunger for yet more profit."[7] The goal of a capitalist economic entity (a joint-stock company, for example) is not merely the production of commodities to meet needs (what Marx calls use-value), nor even just profit, but *perpetual growth*. This economic growth is necessitated by the demands of relentless competition and takes the form of insatiable capital accumulation. Non-capitalist economies produce "capital" in the broad sense of the term, understood as that portion of profit that can be used for investment. Typically, however, non-capitalist economies use capital as a means to more efficiently or abundantly meet the needs of those who produce it. In capitalist economies, capital is *not the means* to more efficient or abundant satisfaction of needs but that for the sake of which production happens in the first place.

When a company competes with others, it does so in order to achieve greater market share and in this way not only increase its revenue and profits but become stronger in its further claims on market share. The "lasting satisfaction" of more sophisticated forms of mutual recognition is anathema in capitalism. By nature, capitalist competition requires of capitalists that they be eternally *dissatisfied*. Yet it is precisely this eternal dissatisfaction that generates, in the Condition of Right, the accumulating wealth and power that lead to tyranny. If capitalism has harnessed appetitive desire more effectively than any other economic system in history, its momentum toward oligarchy and tyranny is potentially just as formidable.

Hegelian philosophy shows precisely why the character of liberal-capitalism poses a threat to freedom and why human beings will be motivated to create more sophisticated forms of society. Before proceeding to explore this, however, I will briefly establish some working definitions that will be of use in the remainder of this chapter and the next.

I call "social democracy" a society predicated on a free market which is based predominantly on private property, but one that understands the demands of the "cultivation of freedom." Such a society claims that the best means to develop the wealth and cultivate the freedom of singular selves and particular organs within the society is to allow them to function in a private property-based, free market. However, social democracy is also well aware of the problems that face it when it organizes civil society in this way, and thus it cultivates in its citizens a willingness to support state action that would inhibit the effects of individualism, mitigate the rate of exploitation, and channel the resources and creative energies of the society toward the universal – toward the common good. Above all, it would be aware that the key to this task is the promotion of participation in the universal conversation of political life, the narrowing of the gap between rich and poor, and the provision of high-quality public services that mitigate the alienating effects of capitalist civil society. To put this another way, social democracy holds the view that it is possible to harness the appetitive desire of capitalism to benefit the common good. It holds that it is possible to incarnate appetitive desire in civil society while still containing and thus limiting it within more sophisticated forms of recognition found in other sectors of civil society and in the state. Many Western democracies find themselves somewhere on a spectrum between traditional liberalism (which gives predominant political weight to the free will's capacity to do what it wants) and social democracy. In sum, a fully social democratic polity is one that observes the priority of the universal, of the community as a whole, but perceives that the best way to achieve this end is through a free market economy that is carefully regulated by the state. Many readings of the *Philosophy of Right* place Hegel in this camp.[8] However, I will argue that Hegelian philosophy, having learned from the history of capitalism since Hegel wrote, demands more comprehensive change.

I call "state socialism" a society that is predicated on common property and that is centrally administered and rationally planned. In any society based on common property, each citizen has a right to a share of the commonwealth, as we saw above, but the way in which economic production is organized and shares distributed in state socialism is decided by a central governing body. Nearly all twentieth-century communist nations were or remain state socialist in roughly this sense, notwithstanding the fact that many are opening up markets to a certain extent or in certain specific ways or contexts.

I call "socialist civil democracy" a society in which property is common but is organized in such as way as to be administered by economic co-operatives in the first instance and representative democratic bodies in the ultimate instance. Co-operatives compete with each other in a market, but capital is administered by the state. The state of Yugoslavia between 1945 and approximately the mid 1980s comes closest to having instantiated this form of socialism. I will also suggest that some new social movements, including and especially the Movement of Landless Rural Workers of Brazil, work in the name of this form of socialism.

I hope to have indicated in this opening section that the dialectic of freedom leads us to be critical of liberal-capitalism. The commitment to the abstract rationality of reason qua human rights is far too weak to inhibit the tendency for wealth and power to centralize in the competitive, market economy of capitalism. Liberal-capitalism, in short, follows the path of the Condition of Right. Perhaps, however, there are structures in civil society in liberal-capitalist societies that offset this tendency. Since Hegel postulated the corporation as the institution that would cultivate freedom in civil society, I turn to consider alternatives to the corporations that may have developed in liberal-capitalism.

2 ALTERNATIVES TO HEGEL'S CORPORATIONS

As the previous chapter has shown, Hegel thought that corporations, which are organs of workers and employers, could cultivate their members toward participation in the universal conversation of social life. They would do this by recognizing the dignity and honour of workers, which would dissuade them from seeking recognition through the endless and unsatisfying means of constantly increasing wealth and power. Moreover, since the corporations would provide education, a degree of security in bad times, and camaraderie across classes, they would function as an individual's "second family." Since corporations are made up of employers and workers, both understand themselves not as antagonistic to one another but as having a common stake in the society as a whole. Corporation members would engage in a particular conversation among themselves, presumably focused primarily on their collective well-being, but they would do so in a manner that was also institutionally linked, through their participation in the society at large and their representatives in the estates, to the rest of the society. The corporation, then, cultivates the *particular* conversation that allows corporation members to participate responsibly in the *universal* conversation. For all these reasons, Hegel thought that the corporations were ideally suited to cultivating a concern for the universal and, therefore, could offset the tendencies toward oligarchy and tyranny in civil society, including the formation of the rabbles of the wealthy and the poor.

Given the demise of corporations, the Hegelian questions for contemporary civil society are twofold. First, are there similar institutions or combinations of structures that can effectively play the role of cultivating freedom in civil society? Second, is the problem a more radical one, as Marx thought: Namely, can any civil society built on the capitalist free market hope to stem the tide of concentration of wealth and power and avoid the fate of the Condition of Right? A third key question will wait until the next section: Is exploitation just on Hegelian terms?

Does capitalist civil society, then, contain institutions or other structures that could play the role Hegel assigned to the corporations? A thorough answer to this question is beyond the scope of this text, but I will begin a few forays.

There are some key mid- to late twentieth-century developments in liberal-capitalism that are relevant to Hegel's argument. First, Hegel himself argued that the "universal estate," the bureaucracy, is oriented to the universal as its explicit mandate. The bureaucracy for Hegel is essentially the public service, which has expanded well beyond its status in Hegel's time to now include most people who work in the health care system (except in the United States), most people involved in education – from daycare providers to public school teachers to university professors – and many thousands of other public servants of many different types (again, with great variety represented in different countries, with the United States usually the least elaborated in this respect). That is to say, the so-called universal class has not only expanded in scope well beyond the early nineteenth century; it has descended into civil society and is spread across the length and breadth of most Western nations. A public high school teacher does not work for the institution of the state in the same sense as does an advisor in the Department of Foreign Affairs and she would never say she is a "bureaucrat." For these reasons her work is situated more within the realm of civil society than the state as such. But nonetheless she is paid by the state, is ultimately accountable to the state, and, most important of all, has as the explicit mandate of her job the universal education of all citizens. Her vocation is quite literally the cultivation of freedom (notwithstanding the degree to which the curricula of determinate educational systems play into the dynamic of the Condition of Right). Even if we adopt a skeptical attitude toward public education and claim that it is, for example, serving the interests of the capitalist class by training its employees, there is (in my view) an unavoidable sense in which universal literacy and a well-educated citizenship is an obviously necessary condition for what I have called the universal conversation. In sum, a key feature of late twentieth- and early twenty-first-century life is that the so-called universal estate has become a vital part of contemporary civil society.

Similarly, labour unions provide workers with an environment in which they can overcome the individualism of their workplace, co-operate together to meet their goals, mitigate the wealth and power of their employers, and decrease the degree of their own exploitation.[9] This strengthens their autonomy within the workplace and, when labour unions become strong enough, gives them a voice in local, regional, and national political debates. Of course, this is mitigated by the fact that unions are in an antagonistic relationship to their employers and are likely to find that the government will back their employers in serious labour disputes, especially since the beginning of the right-wing turn in Western nations in the 1980s. To make matters worse, the rate of unionization is in steady decline, especially as technological and service sector capitalism replaces industrial capitalism and as more and more companies are able to move their operations to Third World countries where workers are generally unorganized and far more vulnerable. Insofar as these developments decrease unionization, they decrease the sense in which workers perceive the state interest to be the common interest, and they are thus likely to consider the state merely as an appendage of the particular interest of their employers. This, in turn, makes labour unions themselves more likely to concern themselves with nothing other than their own particular good, such that they contribute to the decline into factional division. Workers and employers descend into more and more individualistic ways of seeking recognition. Of course, this trend is debatable and, if it does in fact exist, perhaps also reversible. Civil society is filled with many other organizations that play something of the role of corporations: social movements, churches, non-governmental organizations, charities, service clubs, and a host of other organizations provide forums for citizens to engage in the universal conversation in ways that might promote the cultivation of freedom.

Still, when civil society is organized on the basis of competitive units, there is a powerful motivation for many people to perceive society only in terms of particular interests. These forces may well be more powerful than the countervailing pressures of an extended universal class, unions, civil society organizations, social movements, and so on. While there is no way of determining this question in advance of historical developments, it remains the case that when civil society is predicated on private property and liberal values, the Condition of Right may well be the fate of Western nations. This situation also raises the question as to whether a different mode of organizing civil society, some kind of socialism, might better harmonize the vital contradiction of freedom.

However, if there is one feature of nineteenth- and twentieth-century Marxism that has been universally abandoned, it is the notion of the "necessity" of the demise of capitalism.[10] Philosophers and other theorists in the last two centuries have recognized that an essential feature of freedom is that we cannot say what will unfold in the future.[11] The goal of my argument, however (following upon Hegel and Marx), is that we can nonetheless point to contradictions that emerge in contemporary liberal-capitalism and discuss the ways in which the conflicts that arise therein can either motivate further deterioration *or* the cultivation of a more sophisticated set of alternatives. It is quite possible that trends toward something like the Condition of Right, even if very strong in late twentieth-century liberal-capitalism, can be reversed so that a sturdy form of social democracy will arise. It is also possible, however, that Western liberal-capitalism will collapse into the dystopian barbarism of the Condition of Right in a way that gives rise to no new form of freedom. It is further possible that new institutions will develop, such as those within what I have called socialist civil democracy, that are capable of carrying forward the project of the cultivation of freedom. As I will make clear in the remainder of this chapter and in the next, however, it is not necessary that we know the future in order to know what kind of philosophical and political engagement is called for in the present. I now turn to this form engagement in a discussion of wage-labour and exploitation.

3 THE HEGELIAN THEORY OF EXPLOITATION

Hegel has no theory of exploitation and he explicitly defends wage-labour. I argue here that this is a significant failure on Hegel's part and it is a failure, once again, *on his own terms*. This argument amounts to the claim that even if it is possible to posit ways in which capitalist civil society can avoid a collapse into outright oligarchy or tyranny, its structure is still impossible to justify because of the injustice of exploitation. Indeed, the fact that there is nothing within the juridical structures of the Society of Absolute Freedom or the Condition of Right to prevent exploitation is further evidence that each fails to cultivate concrete freedom. Thus, I will try to show that the Hegelian theory of freedom requires a theory of exploitation and to establish its basic principles. In order to build up such a theory, however, I begin with Marx's definitive theory of exploitation – arguably his most important contribution to the history of philosophy and indeed to human history itself.

For Marx, all value is created by labour.[12] Since the natural world prior to labour is unable to satisfy our needs, we must transform nature through labour, and since labour has the creative power to produce more than is necessary to meet the worker's basic needs, we can say that work can create a "surplus value." To put this point more technically, the quantity of surplus value produced by labour consists in the difference between the value of the final product and the value consumed by workers in the satisfaction of their needs (indeed, the cost of reproducing the working class itself). Considered from the point of view of a society as a whole, there is a "socially necessary" amount of labour needed to create the aggregate value that will satisfy the collective needs of the members of the society.[13] There is also, typically, a surplus value the destiny of which, as discussed in chapter 3, depends on the society. In theory, this excess can be used up in potlatch-like festivals, consumed as luxury, or used as capital for investment. Indeed, a society can decide to work less. Most often, of course, the surplus value is expropriated from the workers who produced it by an exploiting class.

Exploitation takes place, that is, when most or indeed all of the new value created by work is expropriated from the class that has produced it by a class that did not. The ratio of necessary labour (the labour time necessary to meet the needs of the workers) to surplus labour (the thus unpaid labour time that creates surplus value) determines the rate of exploitation. "The rate of surplus-value," Marx calculates, "is therefore an exact expression for the degree of exploitation of labour-power by capital, or the worker by the capitalist."[14] Ernest Mandel expresses the same thing in another way: surplus value in capitalism "is the monetary form of that part of the worker's production which he surrenders to the owner of the means of production without receiving anything in return."[15] Of course, even the raw materials and tools used in the production process are themselves the expropriated products of the work of others – the fruit of exploitation. "The means of production," Marx says, "with which the additional labour-power is incorporated, as well as the necessaries with which the workers are sustained, are nothing but component parts of the surplus product, parts of the tribute annually exacted from the working class by the capitalist class. Even if the latter uses a portion of that tribute to purchase the additional labour-power at its full price, so that equivalent is exchanged for equivalent, the whole thing still remains the age-old activity of the conqueror, who buys commodities from the conquered with the money he has stolen from them."[16]

There are three classic modes of exploitation. The product of the slave's labour is exploited not only because the master owns the means of producing new value (tools, land, etc.), but because the master owns the slave herself. Furthermore, all new value created by the slave goes to the master, though the rate of exploitation of a slave is not one hundred percent, since some of the slave's product must be devoted to keeping her alive. Serfdom is also exploitation, but in a considerably different way. Since the serf typically has effective control over his farmland and access to common lands, we can say that, in some strong sense at least, the serf has control over the means of producing the use-values he or she needs. However, the serf is also forced to work a determinate amount of time, say three days per week, on his noble's land. Since the new value created by the serf on those three days is expropriated by the noble, the serf is exploited to that specific extent – 100 per cent on those days. Wage-labour, finally, has the appearance of freedom since, unlike the slave or the serf, the wage-labourer is free to enter into contracts to sell his or her labour-power for a negotiated price. Marx shows, however, that this freedom is illusory. Since the worker does not own the means of production, she must sell her labour to a capitalist who does. "In order that a man be able to sell commodities other than his labour-power, he must of course possess means of production, such as raw materials, instruments of labour, etc."[17] Since the capitalist class has a virtual monopoly of the means of production, workers are "compelled" by bare economic necessity "to offer for sale as a commodity that very labour-power which exists only in his living body."[18] If the serf was exploited on those three days of the week in which he worked on his noble's land, the wage labourer is exploited for that part of the working day which produces value beyond what will pay her wages. In all three cases, the new value produced by workers is expropriated by a class that, by virtue of its power to exploit, does not have to work. In each case the determinate system of property right legalizes this relationship of domination, and this legal right is backed up by the fact that the exploiters generally assign themselves the unilateral right to violence.

It must be emphasized that capitalist exploitation involves a deception: Exploitation is hidden behind the screen of the free contractual labour market. The fact that wages are paid throughout the working day covers over the difference between necessary (paid) and surplus (unpaid) labour time. Under the feudal system, Marx observes, "The labour of the serf for himself, and his compulsory labour for the lord of the land, are demarcated very clearly both in space and time. In slave labour, even the part of the working day in which the slave is only replacing the value of his own means of subsistence, in which he therefore actually works for himself alone, appears as labour for the master. All his labour appears as unpaid labour. In wage-labour, on the contrary, even surplus labour, or unpaid labour, appears as paid. In the one case, the property-relation conceals the slave's labour for himself; in the other case the money-relation conceals the uncompensated labour of the wage-labourer."[19] Philosophy (though not necessarily academic philosophy) becomes a necessary condition for the liberation of exploited people since only theoretical self-consciousness is able to disclose the fact that capitalist labour is, to varying degrees, unpaid and thus exploited.

The starting point for a Hegelian engagement with the theory of exploitation was established in chapter 3, where I argued that Marx is unable to derive the fact of domination and exploitation from developments in productive forces. They arise, instead, from the dialectic of mutual recognition. Marx's theories are not wrong insofar as they explain the emergence, structure, and decline of determinate forms of domination, but they do not explain how and why domination arises in the human condition in the first place. A Hegelian analysis shows that domination and exploitation can develop when human beings in the Ethical Society reduce human relations to natural categories, and thus dominate and exploit their "inferiors." In the struggle for mutual recognition, submission and domination are always options in the vital contradiction that arises in and through our relations with each other. I analysed this most explicitly with the master and slave, but I also argued that the vital contradiction of human relations is always suspended between *vulnerability* and *power*. Since domination is always condemned on the basis of mutual recognition, and if exploitation really is a mode of domination, then the Hegelian philosophy of freedom is committed to identifying and criticizing it. I now turn, therefore, to the task of building a Hegelian theory of exploitation.

Hegel justifies wage-labour as follows: "I can *alienate individual* products of *my particular physical and mental skills* and active capabilities to someone else and allow him *to use them for a limited period*, because, provided they are subject to this limitation, they acquire an external relationship to my *totality* and *universality*."[20] In the abstract, there is nothing particularly problematic about this claim. It seems convincing that the sale of my labour-power in determinate amounts and determinate situations does not constitute the loss of my universal selfhood. One can imagine many situations, even in regimes of common property, where wages as such would be appropriate – from the boy hired to cut his neighbour's lawn to a consultant hired by a co-operative. Ultimately, the key here is that wages paid represent a reasonable judgment as to the surplus value produced by that worker such that there is no exploitation.

That is, in abstract terms, two persons can form a contract such that one pays wages to the other for a determinate amount of time and work. This kind of contract is just because it embodies the equality of mutual recognition and does not (necessarily) entail any exploitation. Hegel is right when he argues, at the abstract level, for the freedom of property right, alienation, and contract. As we have seen, the failure of the Ethical Society demonstrates that the universal recognition of singular freedom is a necessary (though insufficient) condition for a just society. However, Hegel is never satisfied with formal abstraction as a complete account of the rationality of society. This is why he is intrigued by Smith's "invisible hand" and why he posits the "cunning of reason" – rationality is at work "behind our backs." For this same reason, then, Hegelians must take into account the elaborate behind-the-scenes structure of capitalism. Hegel himself did this to an admirable extent, but Marx and the Marxist tradition are indispensible to a serious inquiry into this question.[21]

One of the key mechanisms by which Marx grounds the theory of exploitation is his now controversial labour theory of value, which he adapted from British political economists like Smith and Ricardo. Since Marx's theory of exploitation is premised on the labour theory of value, those wishing to refute it typically do so by refuting the theory of value that undergirds it.

Richard Dien Winfield gives precisely this kind of argument, and his attempt to refute Marx's theory of exploitation is explicitly grounded in

Hegelian arguments.[22] Winfield thinks that the labour theory of value can be refuted by demonstrating its failure adequately to respect formal right and to account for supposed non-labour values. He says, "What makes it possible for non-produced items, such as labor power and land, to be exchanged and bear exchange value as much as any product is precisely the reciprocal freedom in which every commodity exchange consists. No matter what origin a good may have, be it the fruit of nature or of manufacture, so long as some individual agrees to trade another commodity for it, that good acquires exchange value set by the transaction in which it figures. Once this is recognized, the exchange value of non-produced goods is no longer the puzzle it remains for advocates of a labour theory of value"[23]

I deal first with the notion of "reciprocal freedom" and then with "non-produced goods."

I have already affirmed that Hegelian political philosophy is founded on the universal mutual recognition of citizens – "reciprocal freedom" – and that this demands the mutual recognition of singular freedom. Moreover, modes of production do not determine forms of domination (since any technique for transforming nature could be employed co-operatively). That is, all work relations including relations of domination presuppose mutual recognition. Winfield is thus right to make this challenge: any theory of justice is grounded on the right of individuals in relations of mutual recognition and not, therefore, on abstract quanta of labour time (as in Marx). The first premise of a Hegelian theory of exploitation, therefore, is that the theory be grounded on the same terms of mutual recognition as any other mode of social and political justice.

Winfield also rejects the labour theory of value because it fails to account for "non-produced goods" and thus cannot explain concrete "exchange value." This is the familiar and important challenge to Marx's notion that labour value should be roughly equivalent to price, and that this equivalence fails because, in particular, Marx cannot account for the value of goods not produced by labour – like land and labour-power itself. Indeed, Marx says, "Price is the money-name of the labour objectified in a commodity. Hence the expression of the equivalence of a commodity with the quantity of money whose name is that commodity's price is a tautology."[24] Marx himself held that even if specific commodity prices differed from the quantity of value put into them in labour-time, there would be an overall, measurable equivalence of labour value and prices.

On this basis, measurements of the rate of exploitation of labour could be made by distinguishing the quantity of necessary and surplus labour-time that went into making a product. Marx's ambition to tightly link labour value and price has proved to be a total failure. Most commentators attribute the failure of the labour theory of value to this consideration,[25] and instead recognize some version of the theory of marginal utility.

Even granting this point (which I will not explain in detail) it is worth dwelling for a moment on so-called non-labour values – "non-produced goods" – in light of the concept of mutual recognition. Land, insofar as it is a commodity, still requires much labour organized within a system of mutual recognition in order to be considered private property and be bought and sold. This system includes surveying, the administration of legal title, legal oversight of contract, the administration of property and capital gains taxes, and so on. That is, the land qua pure piece of nature is produced not by labour but by the understanding – it is an abstraction. This is never what is at issue in a concrete economy. The land qua piece of property and qua commodity presupposes an elaborate system of mutual recognition like any other commodity – indeed, just like the newspaper considered above.

Labour-power itself is also produced by labour in an elaborate system of mutual recognition. Workers require food, shelter, clothing, healthcare, daycare, and education, and all these needs must be met by co-operative work. Parenting itself might be socially necessary labour in the broadest sense of the term, but it becomes relevant to the economy only when a) it is commodified as, for example, in the payment of daycare workers or b) it is time-consuming enough to withdraw potential workers from the economy such as to reduce both available workers and income (and thus also effective demand). A similar point could be made about housework.

I therefore posit something of a "mutual recognition theory of work and value." As we already saw in Hegel's theory of civil society, the aggregate demand for products to satisfy needs creates an elaborate web of co-operation in mutual recognition. These needs thus create a corresponding demand for an aggregate amount of labour to make the products that will satisfy that need. This total amount of labour answers, first, to the amount and character of aggregate need and, second, to developments in the technology of production which can both a) change (usually reduce) the total amount of necessary labour and/or b) change the character of need by creating a new need (with concomitant impacts on the amount of necessary labour). As a system of mutual recognition, citizens implicitly or explicitly consent to participation within it.

The key theoretical importance of this mutual recognition theory of work and value is not to explain, for example, the precise rate of exploitation of any given worker, nor to correlate a quantity of labour necessary to produce a determinate commodity with the price fetched by that commodity in a given contractual exchange. Its importance, rather, is that it posits the implicit structure of mutual recognition in an economic system that takes place "behind the backs" of its participants. That is, we can readily perceive the macroeconomic rationality of a structure by which a certain class, which owns the means of production (typically in stock portfolios) is juxtaposed to another class, which does not own the means of production and thus must sell its labour-power. The latter, the working class, produces wealth with its labour-power so that the former, the capitalist class, need not work at all to generate determinate income, or receives income vastly out of proportion to work performed. This is exploitation. Of course, we can qualify this by saying that there are degrees of exploitation that arise when the income of those who do actually work is grossly in excess of what it should be – the CEO, for example, who makes ten million dollars per year. At the other end of the spectrum, we will often find exploited workers who are very small-scale capitalists – like the Toyota worker who makes forays on the stock market with his or her savings.[26] Exploitation, especially when combined with inheritance and other similar structures, is necessarily a class structure – roughly, an exploited class and an exploiting class. The mutual recognition theory of exploitation, as I have begun to articulate it here, does not presuppose the labour theory of value and is thus compatible (with caveats explained below) with contemporary Marxist theories of exploitation. John Roemer, who holds such a theory, says, "Exploitation is said to exist if in a given economy some agents must work more time than is socially necessary (longer than the socially necessary labour time) to earn their consumption bundles and others work less time than is socially necessary to earn their consumption bundles." The theory of exploitation and other useful features of Marxist theory do not, he argues, "require reference to the labor theory of value, or to a specific Marxist theory of price determination."[27]

Of course, this does not yet prove that exploitation is unjust. One could lament these developments (say, because of large differences of wealth) and take positive action to mitigate their effects without ever claiming that wage-labour is an injustice. The next key step to a Hegelian theory of exploitation is thus the following. If the wealth created by a society is, in truth, a collective or common wealth produced by the co-operative action of everyone and if, in truth, this common wealth is the common property of all members of the society to which each has a right to a share, then workers who spend long hours in sometimes difficult conditions generating enormous wealth not for themselves but for others, and who face unemployment as a fact of day-to-day life, may well consider themselves to not be in receipt of their fair share of the common wealth and on that basis refuse to enter into unfair contracts to sell their labour-power. This is to say nothing of the segment of the population that is chronically shut out of work because of labour surpluses, or the millions upon millions of workers essential to liberal-capitalist production who work in countries where there is little or no protection for their rights, working conditions are unhealthy and dangerous, and wages are appallingly low. All the while, the work (or the unemployment) of these people is taking place within the most fantastically wealthy economic order in human history, in which a small minority enjoys great wealth as a result of no labour at all or earns incomes grossly out of proportion to their work That is, exploitation is the name, in Hegelian philosophy, for an unjust distribution of the common property of society. Workers are forced materially (insofar as they do not own the means of production) and ideologically (insofar as this whole system is institutionalized as "fair and just") to enter into this unjust distribution of common property. They, in fact, have a right to a share of that common property and can demand that this system of production and distribution be changed in order to provide them with their rightful share.

This point can be developed with the help of Winfield, who argues that "Marx's argument falls into the trap of all labor theories of value by not only assuming that every commodity is produced, but by contradicting the voluntary character of commodity exchange."[28] If by "voluntary exchange" Winfield is referring to a system of mutual recognition that governs the economy (which I think he is), what kind of "voluntary exchange" is the worker agreeing to? When a worker signs a contract to sell his labour for a wage, this contract does not stipulate that he receives a "share" of the wealth produced commensurate with the amount of work he did, or determined as a percentage of the total wealth divided by the total number of people who co-operated to make the product, or again by any other calculation of proportion. Indeed, he gets no *share* at all. He gets, instead, precisely the fixed sum that was determined in the contract which is itself subservient to the going rate of sale for the commodity "labour-power." Thus, there is no direct relationship between the amount a worker gets paid and the amount of wealth produced. Meanwhile, there is also no relationship of proportion between what the owner of the means of production gets paid and the amount of work he has done, including and especially if he did no work at all by virtue of being forced into unemployment. More broadly still, all these "free" transactions take place in the context in which workers do not own the means of production (even though it is rightfully theirs by virtue of the precedence of common property) and must therefore sell their labour-power on a labour market to buyers who have far more power than they do, despite whatever strength they may acquire by joining or forming a union. For, as Marx showed, even a union merely decreases the rate of exploitation.

In sum, given that the wealth of a society is in truth the common property to which each person has a rightful share, and given that by the mechanisms articulated above they receive in their wages no share at all (just a fixed sum determined by the labour market), then surely it is possible that workers can claim that they *should* have a right to a just share of what is, after all, *theirs* – the common property of the society as a whole. They also have a right to demand that others do their fair share of the work. Indeed, if workers were fully self-conscious of the character of exploitation, they may well refuse to voluntarily enter into wage-contracts. The Hegelian theory of exploitation would thus be articulated as follows: I am exploited if I am working to contribute to the common wealth of the society as a whole, but do not get a rightful share of this common property. Correspondingly, one is an exploiter if one gets far more than a just share, especially in the case in which one does not work at all to generate a determinate income. Moreover, since the exploitation has characterized the economy for centuries, most of the wealth invested by the capitalist class was itself unjustly earned. There are, of course, many ways in which one could determine what each citizen's rightful share should be, but the only court of appeal is the universal conversation of the society itself.[29] The key is that it be a *share* determined by negotiation, rather than a *wage* determined by the contingencies of the labour market.

I want to emphasize a key point, however – one that answers to Winfield's decisive Hegelian claim that the economy must be based on voluntary exchange. For wage-labour in liberal-capitalism to be unjust, for it to be exploitation, it *would have to be* the case that workers *lay a claim* to the effect that it is unjust. If freedom in systems of mutual recognition is something that is cultivated and, indeed, is something that cultivates *itself in history*, then there can be no standard outside of freedom by which issues like this can be decided. Freedom is its own judge and its own standard. But this means that the difference between the just and the unjust can be established only in and through the cultivation of freedom itself, which is to say, it can be established only *in history*.

In order to better understand how to make an argument that wage-labour is exploitation, I want to consider Hegel's stance on slavery. From the point of view of the liberation of all human persons, we can look back on periods in which slavery was just and condemn them from our own point of view. This is, of course, anachronistic, and therefore Hegel's criticism of slavery must be more subtle. He shows that it is usually the understanding (*Verstand*) that animates debates about slavery and thus, not surprisingly, an antinomy is formed. On the one hand, it is plainly the case that slavery is valid in certain historical moments by virtue of determinate historical notions of justice. On the other hand, from the standpoint of the fully developed concept of self-consciousness, "slavery is absolutely contrary to right." This antinomy between historical contextuality and context-free truth is an antinomy which, "like all antinomies, is based on formal thinking, which fixes upon and asserts the two moments of an Idea in separation from each other, so that both are lacking in truth and do not conform to the Idea." We must know how to say, along with Hegel, that even if slavery was never "right," it was nonetheless often "valid."[30]

The conceptual dialectic of societies studied earlier sheds light on this issue. Four different systems of mutual recognition have been examined, and all have their own claims to justice and injustice. In an Ethical Society like the Greek world, human beings are understood to be natural types – man, woman, slave – and these natures *differ*. A slave is, therefore, a slave *by nature*, and thus a slave fulfills his own nature only in obedient service to his master. Hegel says that slavery depends "on regarding the human being simply as a *natural being*."[31] For the same reason, a woman in this form of society is subordinate to a man. Citizens have authority over slaves just as men have authority over women. From the standpoint of their historically situated notion of justice, this exploitation is *not unjust*. Our contemporary judgment that slavery and sexism are indeed unjust plainly arose long after the Greek period and it is thus anachronistic if applied to the Greeks. Slavery and the subordination of women were, therefore, at that time, *just*.

They were just, that is, until human beings determined themselves to *be otherwise* – due, as we saw in chapters 1 and 4, to work and other forms of action that educate us as to the character of our freedom. Again, to reject all transcendent standards and thus take our cues only from the history of freedom itself means that slavery becomes unjust only when slaves and their allies make that claim of themselves. What was practically unthinkable in 400BCE became highly contested by 1840, the universal legal truth by 1885 (the year that slavery was made illegal in the last country to permit it, Brazil), and common sense in our time.

Does this open Hegel to the charge of relativism, such that if many people changed their minds, slavery might become just again? Certainly not, for freedom makes itself *more and more sophisticated* as it cultivates itself – more self-determining and less constrained by contingency and the forces of nature. It develops itself as that which allows us, to use Hegel's terms once more, to be "*at home* and *with* [ourselves] in ... *externality* as such,"[32] and to have done so in a way that cultivates us to develop our powers as much as possible. Once we human beings have claimed that we are all free by virtue of our universal capacity to doubt, reflect, and choose for ourselves, there is no going back. This freedom must be entrenched as a right, and children must be educated (cultivated) to lay claim to this right. Any turning back is a decay rather a merely contingent change in the dialectic of freedom. Such decay is possible, of course, and happens frequently in human history, but it happens precisely because of the failure to cultivate the conditions of freedom that have already been attained. From the point of view of the liberation of all human persons, we can look back on periods in which slavery was just and say, in Hegel's words, that even if slavery was not "right," it was nonetheless "valid."

So, on what grounds, if any, can it be said that wage-labour and its concomitant exploitation are unjust, if freedom itself must establish the criterion? Just as slavery became unjust only when slaves and their allies fought for their freedom, the same form of cultivation applies to wage-labour. Exploitation, in the way I have defined it above, has been taking place for millennia. However, it becomes unjust only when the freedom of workers has developed to a point that they come to think of it as unjust and lay a public claim to this effect. This would amount to a claim, on the part of the exploited, that the terms of the universal consensus be changed such that they participate fully in negotiations over what would count as a just share of a common property to which they have a right.

Has this already happened? Indeed, to an important extent, it has. The world's communist revolutions were predicated on Marxist philosophy and relied to a great extent on the claim that the worker must recover the alienated product of her labour. The communist revolutions were fought to some significant measure in order to establish the claim that the exploitation of wage-labour is unjust. Wage-exploitation was thus abolished and made illegal in these countries. For a considerable part of the twentieth century, a sizable proportion of the world's population lived in regimes that observed this philosophy, and many millions still do. Of course, it seems that the tide of communism has ebbed and the forces of liberal-capitalism are steadily rolling it back – either through regime change, as in the former Soviet Union, or through the gradual introduction of wage-labour within so-called communist societies, as in China. This trend may be reversed or it may continue. The point is that it seems unclear whether we can affirm the proposition that "workers have proclaimed exploitation by wage-labour to be unjust."

Can it be said, then, that wage-labour is unjust on the grounds that a movement opposed to it clearly emerged and, at least temporarily, won the day in large parts of the world? Or that these movements never actually succeeded in convincing humanity of their view and, since they are now palpably on the wane, the philosopher must say that wage-labour is just?

After he was arrested for assaulting the Moncada barracks in Havana in 1953, Fidel Castro confidently predicted that "History will absolve me," but since dialectical philosophers must reject teleological thought, Castro's (dubious) confidence in the future is of no philosophical value at all. The future will be the creation of freedom, and precisely because freedom *is* freedom, one cannot determine in advance how events will turn out.

Must the philosopher, then, at least throw his or her weight behind one or the other? Yet surely this would be an arbitrary decision – a non-philosophical decision. Should the philosopher wait it out, and let history decide the question? To abandon action, however, is itself an action, and will thus favour whichever side of the question is currently enjoying hegemony. Indeed, both arbitrary action and waiting it out are examples of Sartrean *bad faith* – they renounce open engagement with what Simone de Beauvoir calls the "ambiguity" of our freedom.

This impasse can be overcome through a proper understanding of what freedom is for Hegel and, in particular, what freedom is in the political realm. The fullest realization of freedom arises when we cultivate freedom in all its concreteness.[33] That is, we realize freedom when we encourage the flourishing of freedom through the cultivation of more and more sophisticated forms of mutual recognition. Marx and Hegel agree that freedom is not achieved when harmony arises from the curtailment of the development of human capacities. That is, neither Hegel nor Marx would be happy if the development of freedom stagnated at a certain point in its development, even if that created a kind of "harmonious" society.

When Descartes and others started systematically outlining the parameters of the infinite character of the mind, following of course on the heels of the Greek philosophers' studies of *nous*, it was hardly clear that these explorations would lead to a family of political philosophies based on the free, infinite will, much less that these political philosophies would in various ways be embodied in revolutions and come to inaugurate the era of universal human rights. Yet to have been a dialectical philosopher in Descartes' time would have been to hope for these developments, for they represented the cultivation of the powers of freedom. Since there was no reason in principle why Descartes' *cogito* argument could not carry forward into political philosophy and from there be embodied in political institutions, it would have been a refusal to cultivate freedom to have discouraged its political development. That is, the commitment to the cultivation of concrete freedom demands that we act in ways that expand and enrich the scope of freedom, even if we do not know whether our efforts will succeed. Indeed, this is arguably what Hegel himself did in the case of slavery, condemning it well before it was abolished in most nations. It is the same with the question of wage-labour and other similar phenomena involving the systematic exclusion of some people from the universal conversation of social life.

Property is primordially common since it is the entire community of mutual recognition that "puts its will in the thing." It is consistent with this argument that a worker could claim a share of this collective product that is in some strong sense commensurate with his contribution in work. A fortiori, it is consistent with this argument that people who labour for their whole lives only to create a vast wealth which is expropriated by others would protest and create movements not only to improve their standard of living, but to claim that they are being exploited. Indeed, to organize a society such as to guarantee a fair share of the collective, common property as a right would be perfectly consistent with the argument as so far developed, and not only would workers who did so enjoy greater freedom, but the society itself would be more democratic. This claim is all the stronger when it is put in the context of common property, in which a worker not only receives a share of the common wealth but has a direct voice in the governance of the community in which he works. Surely such participation is an expansion of the scope of freedom. To refuse to support such social movements is to deny the imperative of freedom. In short, the vocation of freedom has as its political imperative that philosophers side with the potential elaboration of freedom in *any way*, including the potential abolition of exploitation.

The dialectic of freedom, then, requires of us that we always side with those who are seeking to expand the parameters of their freedom and decrease their systematic exclusion and exploitation. A labour union working for nothing other than the pecuniary gain of its own workers and with no eye to the good of the rest of the society is to some degree engaged in a struggle whose logic we studied in the Condition of Right. This is not to say, however, that the effort of such a union does not address exploitation since in capitalism every improvement in workers' wages and living conditions diminishes the rate of exploitation. In feudalism, by contrast, it was easy to determine how much of a peasant's work was exploited by virtue of the fact that he worked specific days for the noble and others on his own land. The wealth produced every day that a peasant spent working for the lord was immediately and unambiguously expropriated. Thus, only a change in the working conditions on the lord's land changed the status of exploitation. In capitalism there is no such distinction. It is much less obvious in capitalist wage-labour which part of the productive day generates wealth for the worker and which part is exploited. Whereas a feudal peasant would have no illusions about his exploitation, the capitalist wage-labourer can much more easily be blinded to this. But since all profits earned by a capitalist (minus his own share if he did any work) are the result of exploitation, every issue of wages and working conditions is also an issue of exploitation and all gains by workers in these areas decrease the degree of exploitation. Thus in capitalism, as Ellen Meiksins Wood puts it, "The struggle over appropriation appears not as a political struggle but as a battle over the terms and conditions of work."[34] We might say, however, that this struggle is political *in itself* but not yet fully *for itself*, and this makes an enormous difference. Class conflict is seriously diminished if workers do not know that they are, in fact, always already engaged in it.

On the other hand, a social movement like Brazil's Movement of Landless Rural Workers (MST), which empowers impoverished and unemployed Brazilians to seize unused land from wealthy landowners and build farming communities on it, is cultivating freedom in a way that is attentive to its members' particular needs qua workers and to the common good of the society as a whole.[35] This is because the MST explicitly challenges the exploitation of all wage-labourers and is a highly politicized organization. They use their own struggle, the exploitation of mostly itinerant plantation workers and the alienation of those trapped in urban slums (most of whom are the children of rural workers who emigrated to the city), as a springboard for a political struggle in which they work in solidarity with all exploited and marginalized peoples for a just society. Thus, if Hegel's imperative to cultivate freedom calls upon us to support labour unions who address exploitation by improving wages and working conditions, a fortiori it calls upon us to support those who do so in a politicized way and who actively seize the means of production, such as the MST.

In sum, the justice of wage-labour is compromised when it is placed in the context of the systematic exploitation of workers within capitalism because the exploitation of workers is a transgression of concrete freedom, which Hegel's philosophical principles call upon us to challenge. Yet even if this argument is, in the abstract, convincing, it might lose its force when it is placed in a still wider context. To wit, it might well be that a regime of common property erected in the name of the abolition of exploitation proves itself less able to fulfill freedom in many *other* respects. If, in the name of freedom, a regime abolished wage exploitation but, in order to do so, also had to abolish civil liberties, curtail democracy in the society at large and in the workplace, and centrally organize itself such that only a tiny elite controlled governance (as in the state socialism of the Soviet bloc), then perhaps abolishing exploitation is not worth the price.

If abolishing exploitation were responsible for the abolition of other very important achievements of freedom, then exploitation would have to be accepted as a feature of the vital contradiction of social life, for more would be lost by eliminating it than is gained. Indeed, state socialist societies like the former Soviet Union, as defined above, actually seriously compromised the freedom of their citizens even as they liberated them from exploitation.[36] Few workers would prefer the regime of common property in the former Soviet Union to the regime of private property and wage-labour in Sweden or Canada. The latter enjoy far higher standards of living, vastly greater civil liberties, and, quite possibly, better public services like health care and education. A centrally planned structure has proved itself incapable of organizing a highly complex economy, creating shortages and greatly limiting productivity. If, in a capitalist economy, millions and millions of decisions are made everyday by millions of people sensitive to local conditions, these same millions of decisions in a centrally planned society must be made by a relative handful of managers who enjoy no such intimacy with local conditions. A centrally planned economy thus typically leads to stagnation. Worse still, the workers in such an economy must follow the directives of these planners, and are thus more remote from the practical power to determine their lives than they would be if they were engaged in wage-labour, where at least they can form unions, bargain collectively, go on strike, take other forms of job action, and lobby and elect politicians who will uphold their cause. The attempt to keep state socialist workers in line, finally, encourages managers to limit civil liberties and the right to protest. Immigration to wealthier capitalist nations is severely limited or prevented altogether. Common property, in short, when it is organized according to the centrally planned, state socialist model, seems to curtail rather than elaborate freedom.[37]

If this is so (and I believe it is), and there are no other forms of common property (a view I am *not* convinced of), then exploitation is only unjust when it is considered in the abstract. The bad effects of exploitation, so the story would continue, must be considered as among the many other contributions to our story of the vitality of contradiction. Thus a key demand for the claim that exploitation is ultimately unjust is that it be shown that freedom, on the whole, would be best served if conditions were created in which exploitation could be either eliminated or drastically reduced. It must be shown, in other words, that a concrete political and economic regime could be created which would, on the one hand, eliminate or greatly reduce exploitation while, on the other, not abridge and indeed promote freedom in many other respects. I make an argument for such a society, a socialist civil democracy, in the next chapter.

In the meantime, I have concluded that the imperative to cultivate freedom compels us to support workers who seek to challenge their exploitation. First, it is always possible that co-operatives be formed within a capitalist economy. Second, it is possible to diminish the rate of exploitation by all forms of policy that provide for the well-being of lower- and middle-income citizens. Since the wealth of the rich is derived from exploitation, any legislation that diminishes the gap between rich and poor, from progressive taxation to universal health care, decreases the rate of exploitation. Third, all improvements in wages and working conditions diminish exploitation. Suffice it to say for now that the imperative to cultivate concrete freedom requires that we always act in such a way as to increase the scope and sophistication of self-determination, especially in those who have been systematically marginalized, dominated, or, in this case, exploited. Workers who act to overcome the exploitation of wage-labour are certainly acting in a manner that enriches their freedom and that is consistent with the character of freedom itself. So far, however, the argument has shown only that the imperative of freedom requires that we support workers who seek to minimize exploitation by improving their wages and working conditions, that we support the formation of co-operatives, and that we support legislation that diminishes the gap between rich and poor. This amounts to demanding the democratization of the economy. It does not show that the regime of private property should be replaced *in toto* within a regime of common property. I address that issue in the next chapter.

4 ECONOMY AND THE CEILING ON DEMOCRACY

I argued above, with Hegel, that property is not fundamentally *things* but *rights to things*. As a right, property presupposes mutual recognition, and for this reason the truth of all property is common property. That is, property presupposes a collective participation in and a collective consent (even if implicit) to a certain regime of the distribution of goods. Each system of mutual recognition is a claim to the truth predicated on a certain notion of what it means to be human, and the specific structures of recognition, such as property right, follow from this determination. Thus, the motive cause of domination and exploitation has little to do with scarcity or modes of production and more to do with the degree to and the manner in which human beings have cultivated the capacity to negotiate the terms of their own community and thus their own freedom. Liberalism, as Marx argued in *On the Jewish Question,* might liberate the "abstract citizen," but it does not liberate the "man." Indeed, it transforms the human being into an "egoistic man" whose selfishness is falsely ennobled by the raiment of citizenship and state.[38] Marx, in an analysis consistent with Hegel's in the *Condition of Right*, goes on to observe that "Politics is in principle superior to the power of money, but in practice it has become its bondsman."[39] Indeed, if there is an inconsistency between the aspiration of freedom for the self qua *citizen* and the self qua *worker* in civil society, then we have a system of right that justifies the exploitation and exclusion of most human beings.

If for Marx, however, freedom turns on the question of exploitation, for Hegel it turns on a broader range of dynamics. The character of citizenship and labour in ancient Greece provides a useful case study with which to flesh out this point. Ancient Greece was a thriving slave society and yet was also predicated on a non-exploited citizenry. Citizen peasants generally enjoyed the privileges of political participation (at least at certain times and in certain ways). The peasant citizen occupied something of an upper-middle place in the hierarchy of social and political life. As a citizen, he had responsibilities and real power, though certainly not nearly as much in most cases as a member of the Athenian elite. As a worker, he was not exploited by anyone. He owned his means of production and did with the product of his labour what he wanted. Typically, he also did not make his living by exploiting others, except, perhaps, the labour of his wife.[40]

In her interesting and perceptive study of the Greek peasant worker, Ellen Meiksins Wood discusses the remarkable facts that Greek peasants were not exploited and that they had genuine political power.[41] These facts invite an interesting comparison between the Greek peasant worker and the contemporary worker in capitalism. Although the latter can take advantage of civil rights (no small gain, especially for women and those who would have been slaves), he or she is nonetheless exploited as a wage-labourer. The peasant citizen in ancient Greece is, at least in this sense, better off and more free, since he is not exploited. Thus, the key determination by which one is free for Wood (as a Marxist) is that one is a non-exploited producer – one owns the means of production and its product. One is free to develop oneself in and through productive labour.

Hegel's characterization of this society and the peasant citizen explains much more. As an example of an Ethical Society, the Hegelian interpretation of the Greek world is that it relies on "natural" categories to determine the political status of individuals. That is, the peasant citizen, like any other Greek, uses what he or she thinks of as natural categories, predetermined by the gods, to decide who does what and why. Citizens, women, and slaves have their status because they are understood to be metaphysical essences. The Athenian does not, as a Marxist might put it, seek to dominate slaves and then concoct an ideological claim as to their ontological inferiority to justify this.[42] On the contrary, wealthy Athenian citizens refuse to exploit their fellow peasant citizens only because they really believe that they are their ontological equals and, *together*, they are all naturally superior to slaves. And, of course, the peasant citizen believes exactly the same thing. This is an "ideology," and it favours the dominant classes (as Marx would say), but it is not simply concocted by the dominant classes in order to enslave the subordinate ones. Rather, it represents an example of what Hegel would call "religion" – the comprehensive self-understanding of a people that represents some stage in the historical development of freedom. Enslaving peasant citizens is completely out of the question, not because it would not maximize the efficiency of a certain mode of production but because it is contrary to nature and to the gods to enslave one's equal. Marxist theorists might use the term "free" to describe Greek peasant citizens, but freedom here means nothing other than "not exploited" and "holding the privileges of citizenship in their polis."

By Hegelian standards, however, Greek peasant citizens are a very long way from realizing their freedom – even if they are not exploited. They are still slaves to the divine law, to imperatives set down by the gods and nature. Even though they enjoy a privileged status within this divinely ordained, customary society and its hierarchy, they are hardly free and self-determining beings in Hegel's sense. They have yet to enjoy even the freedom of arbitrary will as persons (as in the Condition of Right), or the freedom of rational, moral agents (as in the Society of Absolute Freedom), or the freedom of being cultivators of their own concrete freedom (in the fully free society whose character I am seeking to determine). Moreover, the Hegelian claim is that this society is rife with domination precisely because all its members are slaves to the natural categories, mandated by the gods, that they, like Antigone, hold to be obviously and self-evidently true.

Yet, although Greek democracy is plainly inadequate to freedom, the same is not true of the fully realized concept of democracy. The question of how property is distributed has everything to do with how the members of the society conceive their own status in these systems of mutual recognition. Regimes of property presuppose regimes of mutual recognition. The character of this mutual recognition depends on the degree to which freedom has cultivated itself. Since all forms of mutual recognition, even those predicated on domination and exploitation, involve the implicit consent of their members, the fullest cultivation of one's self-determination would require that this consent become *explicit* rather than implicit. Once again, this is democracy. But to be the kind of person who could make such decisions, indeed, even to be the kind of person who considers herself to have the right to make such decisions, is already to have cultivated oneself into a more sophisticated ontological plane than those who are obedient to a property regime simply because they believe it to be natural or the will of the gods.

To put this another way, the person who gives her consent explicitly, in the fullest sense, is one who deliberates in the formation of the laws and customs that structure her life. The regime of mutual recognition that cultivates her capacity to so participate is, then, a *democracy*. Democracy, when it is understood as the cultivation of concrete freedom, is the most sophisticated form of decision-making within a system of mutual recognition for three reasons:

1 It acknowledges that the most sophisticated feature of human life (and, indeed, of reality as such) is the universal conversation.
2 It does so in a way that recognizes the fully developed singular self, with all its capacities to doubt, deliberate, choose, and act. In democracy, her consent and participation are no longer implicit.
3 It recognizes that this self is cultivated in particular communities and within the universal web of mutual recognition itself.

If democracy represents the most sophisticated form of mutual recognition within a community, what can be said about the concept of democracy in modern liberal-capitalism? Democracy emerges in the conceptual dialectic with the Society of Absolute Freedom. The singular self unites with the rational universal by directly participating in, as Rousseau would have it, the general will. While such a regime is impossible, it accomplishes not only the centrality of the cultivation to freedom, but in political terms, it is the first system that introduces a qualitatively superior form of democracy to that of the Greeks. Freedom is understood as the power of all singular selves qua rational to participate in the formation of the universal or common good of their society. The Greek concept of democracy, while monumental historically, is far inferior because it is not based on the universality of reason but on the natural contingency of birth in a class understood to be ontologically superior.

Economic entities in liberal-capitalist societies, meanwhile, are systems of mutual recognition, but they are not democratic. The fact that I might work for Toyota or for my local grocery store, and that I support myself and other members of my family with that income, does not entitle me to any participation in the character of those systems of mutual recognition. As a member of a union, I can attempt to influence their decisions by collective bargaining or job action, but this is *indirect influence* and not a *right* to participate in the decision-making that determines the life of this corporation – this system of mutual recognition. That is, there is a ceiling on democratic participation in liberal-capitalist societies such that comprehensive democratization of the economic sphere is ruled out.

Perhaps, however, there are good reasons that the economic sphere is not democratic. Indeed, there are other spheres within democratic polities, such as the supreme court (and all levels of the judiciary in many countries), that are not democratic for reasons that can be derived from the nature of democracy itself. If a logic similar to that which justifies the non-democratic appointment of supreme court justices applies also to the economic sphere, then the non-democratic character of the latter would be justified. Why, then, are judicial appointments not democratic?

A brief study of the family will help to construct the necessary line of argument. A family is a system of mutual recognition that is not, on the whole, democratic. It may be democratic in the relationship of the adult members, but children are not equal democratic participants. As I have argued already, children are not democratic participants precisely because their capacities for autonomous, responsible action have yet to be adequately cultivated. The role of the family could be understood as preparing a child for democracy, but precisely in way that could not itself be purely democratic. Children are given more responsibility and power as they get older, and in this way they are habituated (cultivated) in the direction of responsible participation in civil society and the state. This is another way of stating the vital contradiction between family and civil society identified earlier – the family must prepare the child for participation in a realm, civil society, that has a different constitutive logic, and thus the family succeeds in this task precisely by failing in some measure. It is by disclosing its own limits to the child that the family launches him into civil society. So, the family is not democratic, but for reasons that have everything to do with the cultivation of democracy.

The Supreme Court of Canada or the United States is democratic when it renders its judgments on the constitutionality of a given law insofar as each judge renders his or her opinion and casts a vote equal to the others, but citizens themselves do not have a say in or a vote on the constitutionality of a given law or indeed on the appointment of justices, despite the fact that the constitutionality of laws is of direct concern to them. Here, the justification for rejecting full democracy is essentially the same as that of the family. A child is not cultivated to the degree of autonomy necessary for democratic decision-making, and the same kind of claim is made about the everyday citizen vis-à-vis participation in the decisions of the Supreme Court. That is, the ability to make informed judgments as to the constitutionality of laws passed by the legislative and executive branches of government requires a highly cultivated understanding of constitutional law, its history and its philosophical principles. Only a small number of citizens are able to receive this education and, of these, an even smaller number will be qualified to sit on the court. Furthermore, the Supreme Court must itself be the right size such that, first, it is not so small that it is dependent on an excessively small number of opinions, but second, that it is not too large to prevent detailed debate among its members. It is possible to disagree about the correct number of justices, but suffice it to say that a tiny number of citizens will ultimately have this important responsibility – nine in Canada and the United States. Indeed, this is how it should be. That is, any citizen with enough education in the demands of democracy would consent to what is not actually a limitation to democracy but one of the conditions of its possibility – even though this means that each citizen does not have a direct say in determining the judgments before the court.

In short, if a specific sphere of mutual recognition is not to be organized according to the principles of democratic decision-making, it must be manifestly clear why this is in fact desirable on the basis of democracy itself. Or again, the principles of democracy, understood as the cultivation of concrete freedom, will themselves justify when decision-making procedures cannot themselves be democratic. Indeed, this makes a great deal of sense, for if democracy is not understood simply as an abstract right of participation but in terms of an achieved state of cultivation, then there will be situations in which individuals are insufficiently educated to participate responsibly in a determinate sphere of society. I could continue this analysis, discussing other institutions, such as the military, schools, universities, and so on, but I raise these issues in order to explore democracy in the economic realm. Is there a good reason, acceptable on the grounds of democratic freedom itself, why employees of economic units should not have the right to participate in their system of mutual recognition?

The most obvious argument to this effect is that, like the Supreme Court, the management of a large and sophisticated business requires certain specific technical and leadership capabilities that it is not possible for all workers to have. The company's accountant must be trained in accounting and the managers in managing. The managers must have a detailed knowledge of the dynamics within and without the company that require full-time concentration. Indeed, I take it that this kind of argument is convincing to most people who understand the demands of running a large business.

However, it is not an argument against the democracy of the corporation as a whole, but simply an argument supporting the wisdom of hiring trained managers and accountants. Of course, this is precisely how a common stock company works. The owners, the shareholders (most of whom do no work for the company at all), collectively hire a management team (a board of directors with a CEO) which is responsible to the shareholders. Shareholders have votes in annual general meetings, commensurate with the number of shares they own, and if they are not happy with the management team, a majority can vote to dismiss them. Day-to-day management, however, is not carried out in direct consultation with the owners but by the managers alone. In the broader sense of the answerability of management to its shareholders, a corporation is democratic, but there are three key points to note. First, it is not the owners who manage, but the managers. Second, there is an obvious reason for this: managing requires a sophisticated technical ability while ownership generally does not (at least not nearly as much). Third, in the corporation, it is the shareholders, and not the wage-earning employees, who have democratic powers. While it is quite possible that most employees would not be able to step into management positions without some preparation, this is a statement about their capacity *to manage* and not about their capacity *to own*.

Someone might argue, furthermore, that shareholders, people who have invested in a company and who thus have something at stake, will care for the company precisely because they have something to lose and something to gain. An employee, by contrast, can always get a job elsewhere if problems arise in the company and thus will not be sufficiently motivated to devote herself to its well-being. This is a very weak argument against democracy in the economic sphere for two reasons. First, if the worker was a shareholder, he or she would have every bit as much at stake as the shareholder who is not an employee. Second, the worker would arguably have a *greater stake*. After all, the corporation is not simply a place where he has invested some surplus capital in the hope of making a profit; it is also the place where half of his waking hours are spent. It is typically the site of the engagement of his creative powers and public participation. It is one of the key communities of mutual recognition in which he cultivates, or fails to cultivate, himself as a free, responsible member of his society. Moreover, the more one cultivates these abilities, the more one can contribute to the company, and thus the greater success the company is likely to have. And the decisions of management about pay, working conditions, and internal structure have potentially enormous impacts on the quality of his life. This is to say nothing of the fact that the worker depends on the existence of the company for his living, and it is frequently difficult to find work that is equally rewarding, secure, and well remunerated.

Surely, then, an employee potentially has a greater stake in a company than an absentee shareholder, and certainly has a greater stake if the employee is also a shareholder. It should not be surprising, then, that workers might want a say in the management of the company, or at least want to have the power to hold managers accountable for their decisions and behaviour. They might choose to have this to some limited degree, say, by simple attempts at persuasion or protest, or they may form a union. However, they may well decide that the best way for them to have a say is to have a share in the ownership of the company. And since they, as employees, have the most at stake in the company, they may well decide that they want a *determining share*. If they were to make these decisions and implement them, and if shares were distributed only among workers, then they would have formed a co-operative. A co-operative, of course, is nothing other than an economic entity that is run democratically. A co-operative can hire managers just like any other corporation can, the only difference being that the managers are accountable to all the employees (remembering, of course, that the managers themselves are also employees, and thus also necessarily shareholders). Thus, there is no reason why a workplace should be non-democratic like the family or the Supreme Court. The restriction on the democratization of the economic sphere in liberal-capitalism is not determined by the nature of freedom itself, but by the dynamics of exploitation embodied in wage-labour. Indeed, it answers not to the fully formed concept of freedom, but to the partially formed concept of freedom of the Society of Absolute Freedom.

A co-operative, moreover, seems to be the ideal institution to fulfill the role assigned to corporations by Hegel in his *Philosophy of Right*. A corporation, recall, accomplishes the task of providing recognition for workers, both management and employees, so that they feel honoured and respected for their work. Moreover, since the corporation takes responsibility for the well-being of its members and nominates representatives to the legislative assembly of the state, the corporation is the key to the promotion of its members' participation in the "universal conversation." Thus, the corporation cultivates participation in the universal without repressing the particular – because it is in and through one's particular place of work that one's freedom is cultivated – or the singular – because one's own deliberation and choice is recognized in one's participation.

A co-operative is arguably a far better institution to fulfill the tasks of Hegel's corporations than the corporations themselves. A co-operative would not be divided by a hierarchy of owner/employee as would Hegel's corporation, and the collective ownership of and responsibility for the co-operative would give workers a far greater sense of the importance of their participation in the universal conversation of public life.[43]

In a society committed to freedom, that is, committed to the cultivation of concrete freedom, there is therefore no reason in principle why economic production cannot be democratized. Indeed, the power to participate in and take responsibility for the total well-being of one's place of work is surely an example of the cultivation of freedom. A commitment to the cultivation of concrete freedom carries with it the imperative to encourage the amplification of the scope and complexity of freedom. Greater autonomy and responsibility of workers, culminating in self-management in co-operatives, is surely an example of this. At the very least, then, there is no reason why co-operatives, as sites of full democracy within the sphere of economic production, should be precluded. Moreover, if the imperative of freedom is to cultivate concrete freedom, then one should encourage oneself and others to cultivate the capacity to take more responsibility for their workplaces and, indeed, ultimately to democratize the economic realm.

In the preceding discussion I have shown only that the imperative of freedom requires us to encourage the formation of co-operatives. This does not mean that it is necessarily in the interest of all workers in all sectors to be organized in co-operatives, much less that the entire society should be. However, the co-operative is a nucleus of socialism, and its benefits for the cultivation of concrete freedom are so manifest that I now ask whether some form of socialism, based on co-operatives, stands the best chance of harmonizing the dynamic and vital contradictions of freedom.

11

Liberal-Capitalism and Socialist Civil Democracy

Hegel, in his *Philosophy of Right*, provided a detailed prescription for what he considered to be a free and just society, appropriate to early nineteenth-century Germany. He did this not only because he wanted to influence politicians who would conceivably write a new constitution for Prussia (politicians who were, in fact, defeated before they could do so), but also for the philosophical reason that the generalities of philosophy must be shown to be capable of determinate specification. That is, they must be shown to be rational by virtue of the power to be made actual. Hegel thus leaves few stones unturned in his text. This chapter is written in the same spirit, although I cannot go into as much detail as Hegel did. I articulate why utopian forms of social criticism must be rejected, and go into some detail about what a non-statist form of socialism – socialist civil democracy – would require. Following the mandate of Hegelian freedom itself, I answer to the demands of our own time.

In the previous chapter I argued that there are three reasons to hold the view that freedom requires a challenge to liberal-capitalism and the advocacy of co-operatives. First, modern liberal-capitalist civil society is incapable of cultivating a care for the universal, making it vulnerable to the aristocracy and tyranny of the Condition of Right. Second, the logic of freedom has as its imperative the encouragement of human beings to organize property right such as to repudiate exploitation. Third, this would best happen in the formation of democratic units of economic production – co-operatives. Co-operatives eradicate exploitation, extend the logic of democracy into the sphere of economic production, and, arguably, would provide for the cultivation of care for the universal *in and through partic-*

ularity. Given that co-operatives can form the basic structure of socialism, our next question (and the task of this chapter) is to explore whether freedom is best realized in some form of socialism. If it is not possible to institutionalize a society based on common property such as to cultivate concrete freedom, then exploitation and the limitation of democracy to the political realm may turn out to be irresolvable aspects of the vitality of contradiction.

This chapter is organized as follows. First, since the form of socialism must follow from the demands of the dialectic of freedom itself, no form of *utopian* socialism is to be advocated. This issue has already been raised in our general discussion of dialectic, but here I clarify the terms of a non-utopian criticism of society. This includes a very brief consideration of Hegel's and Marx's positions on this theme. With these sources as background, I suggest three fundamental criteria for non-utopian social criticism, each of which will constitute a section of this chapter. Briefly, it must (a) *identify contradictions* in forms of social life by means of an immanent critique; (b) *identify the solutions* that present themselves in the course of immanent critique, and, finally, (c) show how these contradictions and solutions are, or at least could be, embodied in social conflicts and the movements and organizations that emerge to resolve them. I then give an outline of this kind of non-utopian, immanent critique of liberal-capitalism in three steps corresponding to the criteria just introduced. I conclude that only the juridical institutions of what I call *socialist civil democracy* (which I introduce in skeletal form) provide the necessary conditions for the cultivation of freedom. Hegel's philosophy, in other words, shows how it is that freedom, at least at our own juncture of history, may best be fulfilled in a form of *worker-managed* or *market socialism*.[1] I briefly analyse four examples of societies or social movements which, to a significant degree, are characterized by the structures of socialist civil democracy that I defend. These are, first, the system of worker-managed communism in Yugoslavia that was in place from the 1950s to the 1970s; second, the Israeli kibbutz movement; third, the Basque Mondragon co-operative; and, finally, the Brazilian "Movement of Landless Rural Workers." On the basis of these arguments I conclude that a) socialist civil democracy provides the institutional means for political freedom and b) constitutes the basis of a non-utopian social criticism.

1 THE THREE CRITERIA OF NON-UTOPIAN CRITIQUE

Every system of mutual recognition, every society, casts a "horizon of possibility" ahead of itself. In general, the specific determinations of a given social form open up the possibility of a variety of futures while already eliminating others. The resolution of a contradiction between concrete-lived and juridical-imaginative recognition in a given society is but one possible future. I consider the criticism of a system of recognition *utopian*, however, when the alternative social arrangements it posits do not appear *concretely* on the horizon of possibility of that society.

Being dialectians, both Hegel and Marx make strong anti-utopian arguments. This can be seen as much in Hegel's famous claim that the "Owl of Minerva rises only at dusk"[2] as in Marx's even better known distinction between *utopian* and *scientific* socialism.[3] For Hegel, the role of philosophy is to clarify an already existing social form, with little or no commentary on the future. For Marx, the legitimacy of arguments in favour of socialism rests solely on a rigorous understanding of the contradictions of the present.

Hegel's most emphatic anti-utopian stance is taken in the preface to the *Philosophy of Right* in a famous passage which I quote in its entirety.

> This treatise, therefore, in so far as it deals with political science, shall be nothing other than an attempt to *comprehend and portray the state as an inherently rational entity*. As philosophical composition, it must distance itself as far as possible from the obligation to construct a state *as it ought to be*; such instruction as it may contain cannot be aimed at instructing the state on how it ought to be; but rather at showing how the state, as the ethical universe, should be recognized.
>
> 'Ιδοὺ 'Ρόδος, ἰδοὺ χαὶ τὸ πήδημα.
>
> *Hic* Rhodus, *hic* saltus.[4]
>
> To comprehend *what is* is the task of philosophy, for *what is* is reason. As far as the individual is concerned, each individual is a *child of his time*; thus philosophy too is *its own time comprehended in thoughts*. It is just as foolish to imagine that any philosophy can transcend its contemporary world as that an individual can overleap his own time or leap over Rhodes. If his theory does indeed transcend its own time, if it builds itself a world *as it ought to be*, then it cer-

> tainly has an existence, but only within his opinions, a pliant medium in which the imagination can construct anything it pleases.[5]

I hope my emphasis on Hegel's analysis of the three self-contradictory forms of society from the *Phenomenology of Spirit* demonstrates that Hegel should never be interpreted as an apologist for a given state of affairs on the grounds of nothing other than the fact of its existence. However, it is equally imperative that philosophy not be utopian.[6]

For Marx and Hegel, any talk of social orders revolves around the question of internal contradiction and the rejection of the creation of utopian scenarios that purport to resolve real problems. It is easy for the human imagination to design ideal worlds and criticize existing social orders on this basis. Such criticism, however, generally fails in two ways. First, it fails to acknowledge adequately the *rationality* of social life.[7] That is, it fails to acknowledge some of the necessary conditions for and the vital contradictions of freedom. It fails to appreciate the importance of structures that, even if flawed, perform a vital task in the cultivation of freedom. Accordingly, utopian critique usually ends by undermining practices that are actually necessary to freedom. That is, utopian projects typically undermine freedom in the name of freedom, precisely because they do not grasp the rationality of freedom itself. In this sense, the aspirations of the Society of Absolute Freedom analysed above were utopian.

Second, since utopian social criticism fails to understand the rationality of freedom, it also fails to grasp the immanent rationality of an alternative social order. A weakness in grasping the rationality of one will likely be reflected in a weakness in articulating the rationality of the other. This also means that utopian social criticism is likely to wrongly evaluate which social movements and sociopolitical conflicts work toward the realization of freedom and which actually undermine it. It thus generally fails to commit its energy toward those forms of political action that are most progressive.

In general, philosophy has the task of explicating the rationality of its own time, but part of this rationality is its horizon of possibility. Each determinate form of social life includes and excludes certain determinate eventualities and possibilities. A feudal economy is clearly not within the immediate horizon of possibility of liberal-capitalism, while, I will argue, socialist civil democracy clearly is. Indeed, the most trenchant forms of social struggle are often the battles fought between those who hold competing visions of the future, both of which can be said to be present in the horizon of possibility of a determinate society.

On the basis of these introductory remarks, I would like to develop the three essential criteria of non-utopian social theory – all founded upon our study of dialectic in chapters 1 and 2. First, non-utopian social criticism must identify contradictions between juridical-imaginative and concrete-lived recognition in a given social order on the basis of an immanent critique. Second, immanent critique must disclose not only a contradiction but also a *solution*. In this case, the demand of criterion 1 will consist of identifying the contradictions of liberal-capitalism and the demand of criterion 2 will consist of showing that socialist civil democracy presents itself as a solution. Third, non-utopian criticism must identify how conflict and social movements designed to resolve this conflict could, or preferably, *already have* emerged from within a self-contradictory society. In this case, the task of criterion 3 is to identify forms of social conflict in liberal-capitalism that motivate the emergence of social movements that prefigure socialist civil democracy.

2 THE CONTRADICTIONS OF LIBERAL-CAPITALISM

I begin with a brief review of the juridical-imaginative structure of liberal-capitalism, looking first at liberalism, and then at capitalism.

Liberalism has as its form of juridical recognition the institutional recognition of *individual right*. The classical liberal arguments begin with individual will, its self-possession and its right to private property, speech, and other forms of self-actualization. The right of each individual to think, say, do, and possess anything that does not infringe on the right of others is protected by the institutions of juridical recognition in the society, and is grounded in the universal capacity of all human wills to engage in these activities.[8] The universality of the will is best articulated in the Society of Absolute Freedom, which posits abstract rationality as that toward which the free will should cultivate itself. However, given the abstraction of the universal in liberal political philosophy, liberalism is faced with precisely the dilemma I articulated regarding the Society of Absolute Freedom. This leads to one of two eventualities within the conceptual dialectic. First, the Society of Absolute Freedom can hold its course and continuously pursue its attempt to repress the emergence of particularities, which always require that whatever particular faction gains power terrorize other particular factions. This struggle can carry on until one faction is dominant enough to control the society. But this is simply to lapse into a new version of the Condition of Right.

Second, the Society of Absolute Freedom can recognize its own contradiction, cease the repression of particulars and, therefore, plunge immediately back into the Condition of Right. In terms of liberal-capitalism, this predominantly takes the form of the concentration of wealth and power that characterizes a free-market economy. This is the process of *monopolization* or, as has turned out to be more frequently the case, *oligarchalization*, that is, the domination of the market by a handful of extremely large corporations, such as Coca Cola and Pepsi Cola. Either way, then, liberal political philosophy tends toward the tyranny of particulars. This is not to claim that this end awaits modern liberal democracies, but to name the contradiction with which it must cope. But the eventuality of such a tyranny is possible, even likely, and well under construction already.

Capitalism, meanwhile, is that form of economic life by which property owners appropriate the surplus value created by wage-labourers in the form of capital and have as their goal first and foremost not the satisfaction of needs, but growth as an end in itself. The appropriation of surplus-value is exploitation, but exploitation justified, according to liberal principles at least, by the fact that both employer and employee freely enter into contracts in which the latter sells labour-power to the former. The correlative to the juridical sphere of institutionalized individual right in *imaginative* recognition is the cultural ethos of the "free, choosing individual."[9]

The priority that liberal-capitalism gives to the free person and that person's right to private property is certainly not without importance. The study of the Ethical Society showed how the capacities of the singular self demand recognition. Private property, which is the right of each individual to exclude all others from the use of something, indeed follows from the character of the singular self. However, common property includes as well a guarantee of the rights of singular selves because common property is defined as the right of each singular to a share of the common property. Once, however, this share has been allocated it functions in much the same way as liberal private property. That is, once I have received my pay check as a share of the co-operative to which I belong, from that moment forward, I have a right to exclude others from it, and the attempt to take it from me is theft.

Moreover, liberal justifications of private property, by which individuals put their "labour" (Locke) or their "will" (Hegel) into a thing demonstrate their own failure. Thinking about the concrete experience of work reveals that it is always a collective labour and a collective will. Indeed, the entire system of mutual recognition, extending across the world and backward in time, puts its will in the thing, and thus property is primordially common.

This argument undermines the foundation of individualistic liberal justifications of private property, but it has a specific limit. That is, an advocate of capitalism could accept this argument as to the priority of common property and still argue that the capitalist free market is not only the most efficient means to distribute the communal goods but also the most productive and the most respectful of singular freedom.

Only the future will tell, but much will rest on the capacity of particular institutions within liberal-capitalism to cultivate freedom in the way that Hegel has mandated for the corporations. It is not hard to see why the prospects for this cultivation are doubtful, even dubious. Capitalist enterprises locked with each other in a life-and-death struggle to control market share are not likely to be sites that cultivate the universality of freedom. This tendency can be only partly ameliorated, it would seem, by the fact that the bureaucratic class (the "universal class") has extended itself into civil society and by the presence in civil society of other institutions that cultivate freedom. Moreover, in Hegel's own discussion of civil society, he anticipated problems frequently commented upon by Marx and Marxist inspired writers – chronic unemployment, boom and bust cycles of productivity and recession, unfulfilling and tedious labour, and so on. This is to say nothing of the profound threat to the environment posed by an economy whose necessary logic is the infinite expansion of capital and thus also infinite growth.[10] Liberal-capitalism, in its standard individualistic forms, has a dubious capacity to prevent the emergence of something like the Condition of Right.[11]

I also argued, on Hegelian grounds, that whatever the fate of contemporary liberal-capitalism, its system of exploitation is unjust. Capitalism creates not only great inequalities in wealth, but does so because one class can appropriate the surplus value created by another. As argued in the previous chapter, the philosopher in under an obligation to criticize exploitation and to encourage workers to resist it. Of course, in co-operatives workers are not exploited at all.

Furthermore, I argued that democracy, which is the most sophisticated form of decision-making in societies committed to freedom, has been excluded from the realm of economic productivity. By forming co-operatives based on common property, workers would not only institutionalize a structure that reflects the primordial truth of common property and eliminates exploitation; they would also democratize their workplaces. As it stands now, there is a ceiling on their participation in the system of recognition in which they work, for they have (as discussed in the previous chapter) no right to participate directly in decisions that profoundly affect their lives.[12] In a co-operative, however, they would not only work in a fully democratized environment but also in one that arguably cultivates a care for the universal in a far more sophisticated way than does a company predicated on private property and the exploitation of wage-labour. Since the imperative of freedom is to cultivate concrete freedom, those committed to freedom are responsible to encourage workers to form self-governing co-operatives.

In sum, liberal-capitalism tends to obfuscate the priority of common over private property, motivates a movement toward a tyrannical concentration of wealth and power, does so through the exploitation of workers' labour in a non-democratic work environment, and is probably incapable of counteracting this momentum precisely because it fails to cultivate a care for the universal. To put this another way, the vital contradictions of freedom are likely, within the structure of liberal-capitalism, to generate something like the worst-case scenarios outlined above: increasing concentration of wealth and power and decreasing democratic participation in society. While liberal-capitalism, in certain respects, has done much to promote certain categories of abstract freedom in the world (human rights, for example), its capacity to carry the burden of further stages in the cultivation of freedom is, I conclude, systematically impoverished.[13]

3 THE MOTIVATION OF A SOCIALIST SOLUTION

The second criterion of non-utopian social critique is that the vital contradictions of a given form of society must present a possible solution within its horizon of possibility. In this section I want to suggest that "socialist civil democracy" is the juridical-imaginative system of recognition that may best be able to cope with the vital contradictions of human society and to cultivate freedom.

I argue that socialism should no longer be understood, as in the Marxist tradition, simply as universal and co-operative control over the means of production (though this plays a key role). Socialism is here defined as the system of juridical recognition whose basic institutions cultivate the self toward maximum participation in the ongoing creation of his or society, within the constraints of the vital contradictions of freedom. Socialism is, I am arguing, the fulfillment of what Ernesto Laclau and Chantal Mouffe have called the *democratic imaginary* of free societies.[14]

Socialist democracy is not, however, simply *participatory democracy*. Dreams of participatory democracy, like those of Rousseau, are utopian. Nor is socialist civil democracy simply a *representative democracy* in the traditional liberal sense in which individuals vote for representatives on a regional basis. This form of democracy too easily contributes to the decay of society into the Condition of Right because it does not provide space for the participation of most particular sectors in the juridical apparatus of the state. Real democracy arises only when both the political and economic spheres are democratized. Socialist democracy is what I call *a civil democracy*, which is defined as a system of representative democracy that institutionalizes *worker-managed co-operatives* as the fundamental site of democratic participation and the cultivation of concrete freedom within the society. My argument implies that the key to democracy lies as much in the institutions of civil society – especially worker-managed co-operatives – as in the institutions of the state.

The following is nothing more than a skeletal introduction to the kinds of institutions that are necessary for the fulfillment of human freedom. I also give some indication of successful attempts to implement versions of socialist civil democracy in practice (criterion 3 of non-utopian critique),[15] and point to a small portion of the rich theoretical and practical literature on this topic. My general goals here, then, are two. First, in the *Philosophy of Right* I take Hegel to be making the claim that if singularity and particularity are of equal weight with universality in the concept, then it is insufficient to conclude a work of political philosophy with generalities. This work could have ended with chapter 9, with the articulation of the three necessary institutions of a free society (family, civil society, and state). Philosophy for Hegel, however, is as much about careful and detailed debate about how these generalities are articulated as it is about establishing them in the first place. Second, I make no claim to have provided a satisfactory argument for claims I will make below, but only to have indicated that the imperative to cultivate freedom is an imperative to enter into these kinds of debates and, ultimately, provide more comprehensive arguments.[16]

3i The Common Property of Socialist Civil Democracy

There is a large literature on worker-managed socialism that I draw on for my arguments. The most extensive single source of this literature emerged from Yugoslavia in the period from 1945 to1980 when, under Tito's leadership, Yugoslavia broke from the Soviet bloc and introduced a decentralized form of socialism based on the worker-managed co-operative.[17] There is also, however, a burgeoning new literature on this topic that responds to the serious attempt to learn from the mistakes of state socialism by articulating a notion of socialism worth struggling and hoping for.[18]

It is not an exaggeration to claim that Yugoslavia's break with the communism of the Soviet Union must be understood, in some large measure, in terms of property relations. Specifically, Yugoslavian socialists sought to institutionalize a form of common property that distinguished their socialism from, on the one hand, liberal-capitalist private property and, on the other hand, what they called Soviet-style "*etatist*"[19] property. As Branko Harvat explains, "Elaborating on Roman-bourgeois legal theory, the socialist tradition distinguished three types of property: private, cooperative and state. In this respect, the landmark was provided by the Soviet Civil Code of 1922. Its paragraph 52 enumerates the three types of property … The first type is characteristic of the capitalist system and, in a postrevolutionary society, is said to present vestiges of the past. As such, it ought to be destroyed as fast as possible. The second, higher form of property is unstable under both capitalism and socialism, and represents a traditional category. State property is considered to be the highest form of property and, as such, provides the foundations for socialist production relations."[20] This model of state property is clearly different from the definition of state property I articulated above. Here state property is the totality of property of the society – it is a version of common property.

The Yugoslavian tradition of socialism preserves the notion that all property is ultimately common, but rejects the idea of Soviet state property that the highest attainment of freedom is achieved in the centralized management of that common property by the state. In fact, Horvat identifies Soviet state property and capitalist private property with respect to one crucial determination. "There is no basic difference between private and [socialist] state property. True, the first can be considered a subjective right … Yet, this implies only that individual owners are replaced by functionaries. Consequently, private property generates capitalism, and state property generates etatism – both of which are class systems."[21] Horvat's point here is that, whatever the intentions of the common property structure of state socialist property, it is, in practice, reduced to a form of property in which all effective control resides in the class that manages the state apparatus.[22] This then produces a class structure that is arguably even more rigid and oppressive than capitalist class relations.

It is the democratization of *effective control* that is essential for the cultivation of freedom, where effective control is understood as the right to participate in decisions relevant to production, distribution, and working conditions. Soviet workers may have, en masse, owned the entire product of the Soviet Union, but they had even less effective control over that common property than does a worker in a British, Canadian, or American factory. This means that the working conditions of the Soviet worker did next to nothing to cultivate freedom since there was little opportunity for the worker to take on new responsibilities and thus no motivation to participate in a (universal) conversation about the prospects of her factory and the society at large. Soviet common property, in short, not only failed to cultivate freedom but arguably bred a worse form of passivity than does wage-labour.

A universalized form of effective control is possible only in a regime of *decentralized common property*, with the worker-managed co-operative as the key institution of civil society. This is because the cultivation of freedom in civil society has two necessary conditions, both of which are absent from state socialist property. First, workers must have effective control over production and working conditions. Second, this effective control must be exercised co-operatively. Without effective control, workers are denied the pedagogical benefits of taking responsibility for planning, working, and marketing their product. Moreover, with effective control, workers must take seriously the place of their co-operative within the regional and national economic and political scene. They are participants in the universal conversation of social life in and through their daily working lives. Without effective control exercised co-operatively, the pedagogical benefit is privatized and loses its character as an activity of fully mutual recognition.

Worker-managed socialism favours the effective and co-operative control of workers over their production process (as opposed to their exploitation by another class) and for that reason its defenders advocate the rejection of socialist state property. "In any hierarchically organized society, the ruling elite is in a position to extract and control the surplus labor.

The basic difference between a society based on capitalist wage labor and one based on etatist wage labor lies in the mode in which surplus labor is extracted: in the former case, private property, and in the latter, state property, determine this mode. The state not only ensures the reproduction of production relations but also, and first of all, the reproduction of relations of domination and hierarchy."[23] Private and state socialist property are both based, Horvat says, on "relations of domination and hierarchy." In other words, Horvat is saying that centrally planned systems of common property do not actually eliminate exploitation.

The Yugoslavian socialists defended a conception of common property that retains effective control co-operatively in the hands of workers. This "social property" is an example of what I have called common property because it does not exclude any individuals from sharing in it and, indeed, allocates rights to each individual to a share, in terms of both income and democratic participation. Horvat explains, "Socialism conceived as a self-governing society implies that there exists no particular class of owners of the means of production, either individual or collective. Everyone is equally an owner, which means that no one in particular is an owner ... If no one is excluded, then everyone has equal access to the means of production owned by the society. As a consequence property confers no special privileges."[24] Note here how Horvat articulates this notion of social property in a way that is compatible with the notion of the right associated with what I have called common property. We can say that everyone has a *right* to "equal access to the means of production."

Indeed, Horvat articulates the notion of social property into its *legal*, *social*, and *economic* determinations, each of which contributes to a delineation of the *rights* and *obligations* of membership in social (common) property. As a *legal structure*, social property is determined by the right to "use, change, or sell commodities" and to the usufruct of "productive assets." Yet, because the property is common and not private, there is a responsibility to the community that "the value of productive assets must not be diminished."[25]

The *social* determination of social property holds that it must not be based on exploitive relationships, such as those that constitute private property (the exploitation of wage-earners by property owners) and of state socialist property (the exploitation of wage-earners by the state apparatus). This requires the articulation of three rights. Each member of the society has "the right to work,"[26] the "right to compete for any job," and, most importantly, "the right to participate in management on equal terms" with other workers.[27] Finally, the economic determination of social property "implies the negation of the very essence of property in presocialist societies – the appropriation of income from property." The usufruct that corresponds to common property must, therefore, be constituted not only by a *right* to a portion of that product, but also an *obligation* on the part of the worker to "derive economic benefits exclusively from his work and none from his property."[28] This obligation to derive benefit from work and not property is essential because it is privately controlled property, in the form of either land or capital, that is the basis of class exploitation in a system of private property. While a liberal-capitalist worker can sell his or her labour-power for a wage and even be an entrepreneur, only capital allows for accumulation since it allows for continual reinvestment and infinite accumulation (just as land allows for rent).[29]

In worker-managed socialism, as in traditional communism, all property, means of production, capital, and so on, is social (common) property. Management of this property, however, is decentralized. As Bajt notes, even though capital is social property, "Work collectives themselves decide on the form of concrete means of production to be given to the capital which is social property. They freely buy and sell these means, whether in the country or abroad ... [This form of ownership] is significant because it does not make possible the appropriation of income on the basis of ownership as such, but only of the incomes of entrepreneurship, which in essence derive from capabilities of enterprises to transform undifferentiated social capital into such means of production and to direct it into those areas that yield satisfactory surpluses of income above costs."[30] Essentially, the society at large, which owns its common property, including its capital resources, engages in the decentralized management of these common resources. Horvat concludes "that social property represents a special type of property with distinct legal, social, and economic characteristics that make exploitation impossible. In this context, exploitation is defined as: a) command over the labor of others; and b) appropriation of nonlabor income. Alternatively, social property may be said still to be property in the legal sense (a bundle of appropriately defined rights and obligations) but no longer in the social or economic sense (no privileges accruing to persons on the basis of property). The latter implies that legal property cannot be turned into capital."[31]

We see in Horvat and Bajt an articulation of common property (social property) that is based on a series of rights and obligations with respect to its distribution and management. These rights and obligations are articulated to the individual, and ensure not only that the individual has the right to the goods and services he or she needs to consume, but also the right to participate fully in the system of recognition of which he or she is a part. There is no "ceiling" to participation in the system of recognition that is enforced by a set of private property limitations. In the system of social property the individual can realize him or herself by participating as a full and equal member in the system of mutual recognition – the self participates fully in the universal, rational structures of his or her community. Furthermore, this form of property allows for the co-operative exercise of responsibility that cultivates freedom.[32]

3ii The Structure of Worker-Managed Co-operatives

In this section I argue that worker-managed co-operatives within the context of a socialist market economy provide the institutional structure necessary for maximum participation in the system of mutual recognition and thus also for the cultivation of freedom.[33] I begin by defining what co-operatives are, and go on to articulate the role of co-operatives within the economy as a whole. This section is a synthetic appropriation of four sources – first, the Yugoslavian socialists to whom I have already referred, especially Branko Horvat, Mihailo Marković, and Jaroslav Vanek;[34] second, Alec Nove, whose text, *The Economics of Feasible Socialism*,[35] has become a *locus classicus* in this field; third, ongoing debates about market socialism;[36] and fourth, the largest worker-managed socialist movement in the world at this historical juncture, O Movimento dos Trabalhadores Rurais Sem Terra Do Brasil (The Movement of Landless Rural Workers of Brazil, or MST).[37] This account of the worker-managed co-operative in specific, and of socialist civil democracy in general, can be only skeletal. My goal is to indicate the basic structure and plausibility of these institutions within the concepts I have been defending (the cultivation of freedom, mutual recognition, etc.), and to refer readers interested in more detailed accounts to the relevant literature.[38]

The co-operative is, of course, a system of mutual recognition. It is organized in such a way as to maximize the participation of all its members in the ongoing decisions that are essential to its life. A worker-managed co-operative has an essential political and an essential economic role. First, as a political unit, it is the basic community of corporate representation in local, regional, and national government. Second, it is the basic unit of economic production in a socialist society. The internal structure of the co-operative that maximizes the cultivation of freedom has, I suggest, seven essential characteristics: collective ownership, equal participation in management, nesting of units, a distinction of legislative and professional roles, income from wages, provision for the accumulation of capital, voluntary membership, and provision for education.[39] I will briefly describe each of these features.

First, worker-managed co-operatives produce goods or provide services in which the means of production, other assets, and the products of production are the common property of the society as a whole. This means that workers do not own their co-operative but it is, nonetheless, worker-managed. There are three reasons why property must be both common to the society as a whole and yet worker-managed in co-operatives. First, if workers own their own co-operatives in market socialism (in what would be a system of corporate private property), the already problematic tendency of co-operatives to become purely self-interested would be exacerbated. Second, market socialism requires a strong central government to balance the fragmentation in decentralized market socialism. Third, full worker ownership of co-operatives creates a disincentive for investment for the following reason. In a capitalist corporation, capital investment generates a share of realized profit plus a return of the original capital investment upon the sale of shares. In a co-operative in which ownership is collective but not based on shares, there is no way to invest in this way. Worker-managed co-operatives, Saul Estrin says, "should not be owned by their workers": property should be social. Arrangements of this kind "eradicate the tendency of producer cooperatives to under invest. As far as the enterprise is concerned, all finance is external and the capital stock is hired at a market clearing rate. There is, therefore, a wedge driven between return on capital and the increases in earnings by a loss of principal; workers do not put up any of the funds themselves."[40] In worker-managed co-operatives, individuals have a right to a share of the benefits either generated by the community or to which he or she is entitled by other means (payment for services, grants, and so on). Moreover, each individual also has a right to participate in the decision-making processes in which the character and quantity of individual allocations are determined (I will say more about these procedures shortly). Membership in and income from the co-operative should not be based on the *ownership* of shares, but on an equal commitment to participation in the productive activity, management, and external relations of the co-operative (or, more simply, membership is based on work).[41] Jiroslav Vanek emphasizes the basis for this claim. "The philosophical and moral basis of this [policy] must always remain the work in common of a group of men and nothing else, in particular not, as was often the case with traditional producer cooperatives, some kind of ownership of shares or basic contributions. This is nothing but an expression of a fundamental humanist principle upon which any viable self-managed economy must be based."[42] In this way, the individual right to work, manage, and enjoy the benefits of membership in the community is recognized within the co-operative as deriving fundamentally from participation. However, these rights are also essential aspects of the juridical-imaginative system of recognition in the society as a whole.

Second, the co-operative is collectively managed in such way that each member has the same basic right to participate in the management process.[43] It is essential for the cultivation of freedom that the participation of each member of the co-operative in its democratic structures be maximized.[44] While it is not possible to prevent a vertical division of labour, one overwhelming benefit of co-operatives is that they make management as horizontal as possible and ensure that all management positions are open to members of the co-operative.[45] To the degree that it is practical to do so, positions of responsibility should be rotated among the membership, with adequate training provisions, including apprenticeships, assistanceships, and so on, which will allow members to move from position to position within the structure with minimal loss of effectiveness. Finally, the assembly of all members (the workers' council) must be a) the basic unit of legislative power for the co-operative and b) structured on a one member-one vote basis.

Third, in order to maximize democratic participation, the co-operative should be divided into *work units* that correspond to specific organic functions within the co-operative as a whole.[46] To whatever degree possible, work units should be collectively responsible for any decision-making and implementation that affects their own sphere of activity.[47] "Most of the decisions that affect the daily lives of workers," Horvat says, "can be made at the work unit level. These are the decisions concerning job assignment, work conditions, social priorities, distribution of the surplus, employment and dismissal, conflict resolution and so on."[48] Work units should range, based on the Yugoslav experience, from between ten and two hundred persons so that decisions can be made *in plenum*. Its chairperson represents the unit at higher levels of decision-making.[49] When decisions must be made that affect either other work units or the co-operative as a whole, the decision must be delegated up to the next higher level of the management structure. In large co-operatives this would comprise sectional committees made up of representatives of work units. In smaller co-operatives these decisions would go directly to the foundational democratic body of the co-operative, the *workers' council*.[50] The workers' council comprises the entire membership and is the body to which all other structures in the co-operative are responsible.[51] The worker's council elects, at certain regular intervals, an executive committee that takes care of day-to-day administration and implementation of the policies determined by the workers' council, including the overseeing of professional activity in the co-operative. The executive committee is chaired by a president and staffed by officers who are elected by the workers' council. The workers' council also appoints commissions to take care of specific functions – housing, investment, and so on.[52]

Horvat comments on the pedagogical potentiality of participation on these commissions. "An unskilled worker sitting on the income distribution commission for several years may, for all practical purposes, become an expert in the field." And, indeed, "A skilled mechanic sitting on the investment commission may prove to be a valuable source of practical information for investment planners."[53] Due to the fact that these procedures never would work perfectly smoothly, and there is always the possibility of abuse of power, corruption, and so on, the co-operative must institutionalize conflict resolution and sanction power and control mechanisms.[54]

Fourth, there must be a clear distinction between the legislative function of the co-operative and the professional positions that implement its legislation.[55] While it is the case that everyone in the co-operative is a member of equal standing with other members, it is essential that the structure have members who have professional skills that correspond to the division of labour in the co-operative. This includes various aspects of the division of labour in production or the provision of services, but also in management, accounting, marketing, and so on. The *president* of the co-operative is the most responsible position in the legislative branch while the *general manager* is the most responsible position in the professional branch.[56] In smaller co-operatives in which there are few important divisions of labour and a relatively equal level of skill, the distinction between legislative and professional activities need not be drawn so clearly, nor need there be both a president *and* a general manager.

Fifth, each member receives a share of the profit or income of the co-operative over which he or she then has exclusive control, within the legally constituted constraints of the society at large. Generally, however, wages in co-operatives are tied to the success of the co-operative.[57] Wages are assigned on the basis of work performed and vary according to the division of labour and the standards held by the co-operative and the society at large, as determined within its democratic structures.[58]

Sixth, each co-operative must commit a determinate amount of its profit to capital accumulation for the purpose of reinvestment.[59] In liberal-capitalist economies the society at large is vulnerable to the willingness of the owners of productive power to commit part of their profits to capital accumulation and investment rather than personal consumption. This leaves the character of economic growth in capitalist societies largely in the hands of its relatively small class of very wealthy citizens, who then determine both the quantity and character of growth (in their own interest).[60] A socialist civil democracy takes democratic control over issues of capital accumulation, reinvestment, and allocation of resources by, among other things, specifying the legitimate range for the ratio of wages to capital accumulation and reinvestment as a condition of incorporation. However, workers are very unlikely to have enough money on their own to capitalize their co-operatives. I will discuss capital investment below under "financial and administrative support for co-operatives."

Seven, membership in individual co-operatives must be essentially voluntary – although no worker in a co-operative is a non-member.[61] Civil society rests on the recognition of the freedom of the individual will to be its own measure in the world and to have a sphere of action and property that is exclusively its own. Moreover, as I will argue shortly, no socialist economy can run exclusively on the basis of co-operatives. In certain specific cases individuals who are inclined to work in privately owned enterprises must be permitted to pursue such employment, albeit with restrictions on the hiring of labour and the accumulation of wealth.[62]

Co-operatives, meanwhile, must be attractive to individuals on the basis of the quality of life they make possible, within the constraints of empirical economic and social conditions.

Having introduced these seven key features of the internal structure of worker-managed co-operatives, I would like to briefly outline the politico-economic context within which they are the basic unit. Drawing here on the same sources, I describe the six essential politico-economic features of socialist civil democracy as a whole: the typology of productive units, the structure of market relations, financial and administrative support for co-operatives, the importance of non-economic organizations in civil society, universal public education rooted in civil society, and representation of co-operatives and other sectors in democratic institutions. Once again, this introduction will be but a brief sketch of the most essential features of socialist civil democracy.

First, the economy of a socialist civil democracy is made up of a variety of forms of productive activity. It is both undesirable and impractical to insist that all economic activity be performed by co-operatives. There are certain industries that cannot be run co-operatively since the level of technical expertise needed and/or the dependence of the system of recognition on the organization is particularly large – the management of a nuclear power station, for example. Certain kinds of large-scale enterprises, like electricity, should be run by the state, but in a manner that is accountable to a democratically elected assembly. Also, there are certain fields that lend themselves to individual activity – the plumber or the artist. I concur with Alec Nove that the economy of a socialist civil democracy should have five different kinds of productive unit: (1) state enterprises, (2) publically owned but autonomously managed enterprises, (3) collectively owned and worker-managed co-operatives (the majority), (4) regulated but nonetheless private enterprises that have a limited number of employees, and (5) individuals.[63]

Second, socialist civil democracy has a market economy. Centrally planned economies have been incapable of responding to the specificity of consumer demand and the astronomical number of decisions that are necessary to run a complex economy. It is preferable, moreover, that the individual have the power to make choices about what goods and services to purchase from those produced by the community at large. Yet choice of goods and services implies the existence of alternatives, and thus also a competitive market. Indeed, the choice of an individual to produce a product of better quality or price than that which is currently available is also an essential part of this socialism. Vanek argues for market socialism as follows: "The optimal form of the self-managed economy or sector is one based on the market mechanism, in the sense that all firms act to the best advantage of their working collectivities and whoever else they may be concerned with, while using prices in all product and factor markets as objective signals in their decision-making."[64] Competition inevitably brings with it advertising, temptations for price-fixing, and momentum for concentration.

These features of market economies in general cannot be avoided altogether, and must be regulated by the co-operative structure of civil society and by the state. In Vanek's terms, "The authorities, planning institute or the shelter organization can and ought to exercise influence over the individual firms of the participatory sector by means of nondiscriminatory tools (tax policies of all kinds, price ceilings and other price controls)."[65] Once again, the inefficiencies or tendencies of market socialism to produce unfair advantage can be offset at least partially by a balance between decentralized and centralized authority.

Third, a key problem in all forms of socialism has been difficulty in attaining capital for investment. Co-operatives must be able to rely on a centralized institution for credit and other forms of support. Vanek calls this a "shelter organization." "It is imperative to establish a shelter organization or institution on the national level (which can be decentralized according to need), whose express function would be to fund and promote the self-managed sector of the economy. More specifically, this agency would be charged with the supervision but not the control of the capital market, the promotion and expansion of new firms or sectors according to national plans, the coordination and spreading of information regarding alternative investment projects, technical and other assistance to new groups desiring to form self-managing firms, and supervision designed to secure in the long run the equalization of income per worker."[66] Naturally, this "shelter organization" would have to be closely monitored by representative institutions in the society.[67]

John Roemer suggests the innovative possibility that each citizen would be given coupons good only for investment in companies. Investors would receive dividends for their investments in regular currency, but the coupons could not themselves be turned into regular currency or given away as gifts.

These coupons could also be traded on a stock market. Upon death all coupons return to the state and are then redistributed to other adults.[68] This proposal creates the problem that non-workers would profit from a corporation, but it has the benefit of taking exclusive control of capitalization away from (co-operative) banks while preventing the accumulation of large amounts of capital in private hands (over generations). Of course, Roemer's proposal does not base the economy on co-operatives, and thus loses the sociopolitical benefits of the co-operative that are so important to socialist civil democracy.

Fourth, the cultivation of freedom in civil society happens not only in co-operatives but in a host of sectoral organizations, associations, institutions, and alliances within civil society.[69] In the socialist tradition, the need for strong, pedagogically stimulating institutions in civil society has often been ignored, but that has not always been the case. In the years of the Nicaraguan revolution, for example, state and private co-operatives were supplemented by labour unions, popular organizations, sectoral organizations, and neighbourhood committees, which formed an elaborate series of consultative structures that mediated between individuals and the formal structures of the state.[70] In socialist civil democracy co-operatives prevent economic power from becoming concentrated, but they do nothing to represent racial and ethnic minorities, gays and lesbians, those of different religious beliefs, and so on. While the organizations that represent these groups cannot carry the load of cultivating freedom alone, and hence the necessity of socialism, they are nonetheless an essential complement to the co-operatives of socialist civil democracy.[71]

Fifth, a primarily self-managed economy requires individuals to have sophisticated skills not only in the sphere of production or activity in which they are employed but also in the kinds of communication, co-operation, and management skills required by each co-operative. A considerable part of this education can take place inside co-operatives themselves through various kinds of on-the-job training programs, apprenticeships, and so on. However, there must be a high-quality, universal, and fully public system of education. The most essential feature of such an educational institution is that it cultivate freedom in the broadest sense, but that, vis-à-vis the co-operative sector, it also ensure that those students who specialize in technical, scientific, administrative, and business skills are appropriately trained in the philosophical and relational skills necessary to participate as fully as possible within co-operatives and the society at large.[72]

Sixth, the structure of worker-managed economies does not in itself prevent the emergence of situations of sectoral or inter-institutional conflict over the distribution of goods and services. I have tried to show how a co-operative structure of socialist civil democracy provides the necessary institutional structure to educate desire, yet without a corresponding sphere of mutual negotiation in the society as a whole, the cultivation of freedom potentially remains stalled at the level of sectoral and institutional conflict. However, the key to the cultivation of freedom beyond sectoral allegiance is the state. If co-operatives and other institutions are not to become themselves the units of conflictual power struggle, these institutions and sectors must have formal responsibility for negotiating the character of the system of recognition within the structure of the state.[73]

I begin with a model of sectoral representation in a legislative assembly designed by Branko Horvat, who describes a bicameral structure made up of the House of Citizens and the House of Producers. "We can distinguish two different categories of interests: territorial and functional, or quality of life interests and productive interests. The latter correspond to producers' representation and the former to consumers' (and citizens') representation. Thus the Commonwealth Assembly will consist of at least two houses, a House of Citizens and a House of Producers. Members of the House of Citizens will represent their regions, while members of the House of Producers will represent their branches of production."[74] Accordingly, the legislative assemblies of socialist civil democracy should be made up of representatives of the key *sectors* and *institutions*,[75] especially the co-operatives, but also groups, such as racial and ethnic communities, that are essential to the functioning of the community at large. A contemporary scheme of such representation was developed in socialist Yugoslavia, where the Federal Chamber was divided into distinct Chambers of Nationalities, Economy, Education, and Culture.[76] Moreover, civil democracy requires that there be constitutionally enshrined means to ensure that these sectors are appropriately represented, and that new ones come to be represented just as old ones are withdrawn.

This form of representative government is plagued by a serious problem which must be understood in terms of vital contradiction. It is by no means easy to determine which institutions and sectors in the society deserve to be represented and which do not. While it seems possible that constitutional arrangements could be made on the basis of proportional representation for ethnic minorities and key sectors, and institutions of production (labour unions, co-operatives or blocs of co-operatives, and so on), it also is impossible that such arrangements would ever adequately represent the complexity of struggles for recognition in a society. Even so, a civil democratic constitutional structure would be vastly superior in this respect to simple representative democracy. Moreover, this form of civil democracy makes it clear that claims to sectoral and institutional representation are legitimate. Civil democracy must thus be equipped with reasonably effective means to make changes in the content of representation, perhaps at the judicial level, guided by determinate constitutional norms of representation.

3iii Summary

In the foregoing I have articulated a provisional defence of the claim that socialist civil democracy presents itself as the solution to the limitations of liberal-capitalism. These claims, then, suggest that a socialist critique of liberal-capitalism meets the first and second criteria (the identification of contradictions and the positing of their solution) for non-utopian social criticism. Socialist civil democracy can thus be said provisionally to stand within the horizon of possibility of liberal-capitalism. Correspondingly, social criticism animated by a socialist perspective is legitimized, again provisionally. My next task is to move to the third criterion for non-utopian social criticism. I must identify forms of social conflict that emerge in liberal-capitalism in response to its contradictions and whose potential resolution foreshadows the concrete possibility of the socialist solution.

4 SOCIAL CONFLICT AND THE FORESHADOWING OF SOCIALISM

I would like now to suggest how socialist civil democracy meets the third criterion of non-utopian social criticism. It must be possible to observe forms of social conflict characteristic of the contradictions demonstrated by the immanent critique and identify potential or already existing social movements that foreshadow socialist civil democracy. In this section, I first give a general critique of the state-oriented posture of the left in the twentieth century. This is followed by a brief exposition of four situations in which socialist civil democracy has been put into practice with varying degrees of sophistication and comprehensiveness. These examples are the

Israeli Kibbutzim, Yugoslavian worker-managed socialism, the Spanish Mondragon co-operative, and the Brazilian Movement of Landless Rural Workers (MST).[77]

4i Statist Socialism in the Twentieth Century

In Western countries, and indeed in many parts of the Third World, the liberal-capitalist system of *imaginative* recognition received a great boost from the failure of Eastern European communism. The failure of Soviet-led state communism, the dismal inability of the Chinese political model to represent anything desirable in the eyes of most Westerners, the defeat of revolutionary movements in Latin America, and the isolation of Cuba have encouraged a kind of liberal-capitalist triumphalism. According to the story generated therein, the new millennium, or at least the new century, will be one of the global consolidation of liberal-capitalism. In the popular mind, socialism failed when given the chance to prove itself. Given that imaginative recognition is a feature of any juridical system of recognition, this popular view is a matter of great importance, no matter how erroneous it may be in light of many other criteria. Nonetheless, twentieth-century socialism failed for intelligible reasons, and the contradictions that gave rise to these (failed) attempts to overthrow liberal-capitalism persist as motivators to the formation of social movements that anticipate a different future.

I have defined socialism as a *civil democracy* in which there are no juridical limitations on individuals and social sectors that would prevent them from seeking recognition in their society. Moreover, socialist civil democracy functions in terms of a family/civil society/state structure. The most important condition for the achievement of socialism is a sphere of civil society that is highly autonomous and that provides a forum for the cultivation of freedom. In civil society, the achievement of socialism in broad historical terms must be said to rest on the gradual accumulation of sophisticated skills of self-governance. Yet twentieth-century socialism has often sought ends very different from this ideal.

First, the great communist revolutions of the twentieth century took place in countries that had almost no civil societies. Instead, pre-revolutionary Russia and China were agricultural societies in which industrial communism was imposed by the state. Socialism in this context generally amounts to nothing less than authoritarianism, and guarantees an extraordinary amount of power to one social sector – those who have access to positions in the state apparatus.[78]

Second, twentieth-century socialist activists, both communist and social democratic, have been primarily concerned with the seizure of state power. Revolutionary movements in Latin America, for example, were preoccupied until quite recently with the military overthrow of the state apparatus.[79] This meant that infrastructural development within the revolutionary movements tended to be subordinated to military goals. Moreover, except in the case of Cuba and Nicaragua, these military attempts to overthrow the state were unsuccessful and were met with American-backed systems of repression that stopped at nothing to eliminate the guerrilla movements.

Similarly, social democratic political parties strove for, and often achieved, state power. In many cases, such as Guatemala in 1954 and Chile in 1973, among many others, they were overthrown by military coups. More generally, socialist goals were eviscerated in the search for electoral success[80] and, even more important, the capitalist market economy proved to be too powerful for socialist reform at the state level.[81] Far more destructive in the long term, however, was the prioritization of state-based solutions to the issues that prompted social conflict. Typically, social movements developed in response to inadequacies and contradictions in what I call their systems of recognition. As they organized themselves to fight for their goals, they often greatly accelerated the development of self-governance in civil society precisely because they provided a forum for the generation of sectoral self-consciousness and participation. However, most of the time the goal of these movements was state legislation that, once achieved, resulted in the dissipation of the social movements that had brought them about in the first place. The effect, then, was ultimately to weaken civil society by creating a bloated state apparatus that managed social life on behalf of the society.[82]

Socialism, as I have defined it, is precisely the opposite of this state-centred orientation to social change. It requires a highly autonomous civil society and a comparatively compact, though efficacious, state apparatus. In general, the state-centred strategies of communists and social democrats failed to address the fact that genuine socialism must be built from civil society upward.[83] The following are four examples of institutions and movements that have created the logical structures of socialist civil democracy based not on state structures but on strong institutions in civil society.

4ii Four Instantiations of Socialist Civil Democracy in the Making

The key to the development of a fully free society is the cultivation of freedom in civil society within sectors organized to make this possible. I have proposed that worker-managed co-operatives fulfill this role. The co-operative provides a forum for citizens to cultivate freedom in and through responsible participation in their community, and the institutions of the society itself encourage and enable their participation. Socialism requires the cultivation of freedom that takes place in and through responsible, co-operative life. In this section I provide examples of co-operatives from the past and present that, by their success, testify that social criticism from the point of view of socialist civil democracy meets the third criterion of non-utopian critique. While there are many hundreds of case studies that I could choose from, drawing from movements that emerged over the last three centuries on every continent and that enjoyed widely ranging degrees of success,[84] I have picked four, each of which has been successful in unique ways. Specifically, I focus on (a) the three-decade-long worker-managed economy of socialist Yugoslavia; (b) the eighty-year-old kibbutz movement in Palestine/Israel; (c) the enormous Mondragon co-operative of the Basque region of Spain; and (d) the Movement dos Trabalhadores Rurais Sem Terra do Brasil (The Movement of Landless Rural Workers of Brazil). My goal is to introduce these examples in minimal detail in order to show that a) they have a logical structure roughly congruent with what I have proposed for socialist civil democracy – indeed, I have drawn on their examples to articulate that logic; and b) to testify briefly to their success in practical implementation.

My first example is Yugoslavian worker-managed socialism.[85] Josep Broz Tito, the Yugoslavian Partisan war hero, led communist postwar Yugoslavia in an independent direction from the Soviet Union, then under the leadership of Joseph Stalin, and leading to an embargo of Yugoslavia by the other Cominform nations.[86] Starting in the early 1950s the Yugoslavian leadership gradually shifted from the centralized state planning that characterized the Soviet bloc nations to an economy of worker-managed co-operatives that functioned within a kind of market socialism.[87] This amounted to a dramatic shift in the power base of the society from the institutions of the state to the dispersed productive enterprises in civil society. This orientation ensured that Yugoslavia was very different from the other European communist nations – with greater intellectual freedom, civil liberties,[88] small-scale private enterprise and private farms,[89] a standard of living close to that of Western capitalist nations, education and health services that surpassed most Western nations, and an annual economic growth rate that was among the highest in the world.[90] The worker-managed enterprises suffered from the fact that Yugoslavia, like the other Eastern European communist nations, fell prey to a trend toward extremely large-scale heavy industry. When enormous production plants became managed by workers, they generally proved too large to maximize the benefits that follow from participation in smaller worker-managed enterprises.[91] All the same, worker-managed enterprises were the foundation of decades of impressive Yugoslavian economic growth.

The decline of Yugoslavian worker-managed socialism happened in pace with the collapse of the nation into antagonistic ethnic factions that would lead to the war of the 1990s. It proved impossible to hold together the enormous ethnic and economic differences in the country. The death of Tito in 1980 and the collapse of European communism a decade later undermined the ability of Yugoslavian socialism to retain its character as a beacon for civil society-centred socialism in the world. Moreover, the Yugoslavian experience of worker-management suffered from the fact that it was born out of a centralized, statist communism, rather than developing upward from civil society. While the coalescence of factors in the 1980s destroyed not only Yugoslavian socialism but Yugoslavia itself, these factors did not follow from worker-managed socialism, which proved itself economically viable for thirty years despite the inhospitable milieu.[92]

Decades before the emergence of socialism in Yugoslavia, the first of the kibbutzim emerged in Palestine – in 1910 to be precise.[93] The kibbutzim played an integral role not only in Zionism but also in the emergence of, in my terms, civil society-based socialism. For the first seven decades, the kibbutzim were strictly egalitarian. All property was held in common, no external labour was hired, everyone received the same wage, and a policy of strict equality in the distribution of goods and services was upheld – not only with respect to education and health care but also in the distribution of common clothing, a universal house for children, and common dining.[94] The observance of equality of wages was particularly important, along with the firm rejection of any monetary incentives. In 1971 Haim Barkai discussed this issue and the reliance on what I have called mutual recognition rather than wages and benefits for the kinds of motivation needed in the kibbutzim. "Differential material benefits, which are a major means for motivating individual performance in the nonkibbutz world, are ruled out by ideology and, for all purposes in practice. Nonmaterial benefits which are also relevant in the nonkibbutz world are, however, not excluded. Respect and esteem for a good day's work and for the success in managerial and entrepreneurial functions is undoubtedly an important factor in the attitude of individuals towards work and responsibility in the kibbutz environment. And *per contra,* the disfavor with which shirking is viewed is, in the closely knit communities which even the largest kibbutzim still are, a powerful sanction."[95]

The kibbutz movement grew quickly, with 230 founded by 1971 for a total membership of nearly 100,000. The movement also spread well beyond the agricultural sector, developing various forms of industrial production and other commercial activities. This rapid growth rate diminished and then actually started to decline, reaching a low point in 1985. Since then there has been a slow but steady increase in kibbutz membership. As of 1991 there were 270 kibbutzim in Israel with a total membership of 129,300[96] and in 2005 the membership was 116,000 in 266 kibbutzim.[97] In 2010 there are reportedly still around 270 kibbutzim, which produce 9 per cent or USD$8 billion of Israel's overall industrial output and 40 per cent or USD$1.7 billion of its agricultural output.[98]

The strict egalitarianism very gradually gave way to a greater recognition of individuality. First, women led the campaign that overcame the norm of standardized clothing, and an industrial boom on the kibbutzim in the 1950s led to the hiring of outside labour for the first time in order to alleviate serious labour shortages, especially at certain times of the agricultural calendar.[99] In the 1980s common meals were cut down, wages were differentiated on the basis of various criteria, and the common children's home was eliminated. While some have seen these reforms as a sign of the weakening of the idealism of kibbutzim, I understand them as the emergence from within the kibbutzim of far greater recognition for singular freedom and the family – both of which I take to be absolutely central to the long-term viability of co-operatives.[100]

Meanwhile, at roughly the same time that Yugoslavian worker-managed socialism was maturing, the most successful co-operative in history was born not far away. The Mondragon Co-operative Corporation is a network of some 150 co-operative companies based in the Basque region of Spain. It was formed in 1956 during the Franco dictatorship by a priest named Jose Arizmendiarrieta. By 2001 it had grown to be the largest economic entity in the Basque region and now the seventh largest in Spain as a whole. In 2009 Mondragon had 85,000 members, nearly double what it had in 2000 (43,000). It made nearly triple the annual sales in the same period (USD$19.4 billion and USD$6.6 billion respectively) and accumulated nearly four times the assets (USD$43 billion and USD$13 billion respectively). In 2010 Mondragon quadrupled its profit from 2009, to over USD$227 million, and increased its total membership by 1,378 – all despite the Spanish financial crisis.[101]

The Mondragon system of co-operatives is worker-managed and committed to manufacturing. In R. Oakeshott's words, "Historically cooperatives have been fairly successful in the retail trade and to some extent in agriculture. With the odd exception in France, cooperative manufacturing, where it exists at all, is usually confined to low technology activities like boot and shoe production. But production at Mondragon *is heavily concentrated on manufacturing and, within that, on capital-intensive, high-technology activities.*"[102]

From the beginning Mondragon avoided the strict equality of the kibbutzim, relying on the gradual purchase of capital shares of up to no more than 5 per cent of the total per member. It also instituted wage differentiation and weighted voting in general assemblies depending on one's position and seniority.[103] Certain sectors of the co-operative have even gone on short strikes, protesting wage rates and other benefits – prompting extraordinary meetings of the general assembly. The Mondragon co-operative network has developed an elaborate system of incentives. "The combination of participation in decision-making with respect of organisation of work and the distribution of earnings; narrow differences and fixed wages; of an extensive programme of education and on-the-job training; of a high degree of security of employment; and of a financial stake in the ownership of their own co-operative factory, adds up to a system of collective incentives which is not found in private enterprise, which partly explains why performance in the cooperatives has achieved such a high degree of efficiency."[104]

The Mondragon co-operative has demonstrated the capacity of an elaborate worker-managed enterprise to run itself democratically, to compete successfully in a capitalist market, to produce sophisticated manufactured goods, to evolve through five decades of dramatic political and economic change in Europe, and to maintain a structure of unity while recognizing individual difference. While economic efficiency is not the highest priority of socialist civil democracy, the Mondragon co-operative has shown that worker-managed enterprises can be at least as productive as hierarchically structured capitalist enterprises.[105]

I dwell on my fourth and final example, the Brazilian MST, in somewhat more detail than the previous three. I do this because the conditions created by capitalism in the Third World in general, and Latin America in particular, are especially ripe for the development of movements animated by principles similar to those I have posited for socialist civil democracy. Unlike the examples described above, then, the MST is a social and political movement whose goal is, in co-operation with other like-minded social movements, unions, and political parties, the establishment of a socialist society.

The Brazilian Movement of the Landless has become the largest and most well-organized social movement in Latin American history, already with up to 1.5 million people organized on thousands of settlements (*assentamentos*) – a remarkable achievement considering that the movement was only founded in 1984.[106] The MST shows a willingness to repudiate the law of the state (that is, it refuses to consent to the system of recognition) by forcibly and illegally occupying large tracts of underused land typically owned by wealthy Brazilians or by the state. This land is occupied by a group of families that have been trained to create a variety of co-operative agricultural communities. However, this is the extent of its extra-legal activity. The Movement then takes advantage of a constitution provision that says that land can be expropriated by the government if it is not being used to fulfill its "social function." After settling on the land, the MST then seeks title under the rubric of this clause of the constitution.

There is a long history of co-operatives in Latin America in general and in Brazil in particular. Often, however, co-operatives have been large and ultimately run by a small elite who become, effectively, capitalists. Workers, in turn, become employees. José Vicente Tavares dos Santos describe this situation as follows. "The fundamental motive that draws farm workers to associate themselves with cooperatives derives from the subordinate condition in which they find themselves in the process of market exchange, which is an expression of their subordination to the sector of industrial capitalism ... Given this, even if a cooperative functions juridically as associated property, it may become structurally an institution of the capitalist mode of production, an institution that follows the determinations of the ever-widening reproduction of capital ... [which generates] inherent social tensions ... The directors [of the cooperative] establish relations of exploitation over the workers ... We thus see here the crystallization of the directorate as a dominant group in the interior of cooperatives."[107] It was essential for the MST both to prioritize the formation of economically viable settlements, and also to ensure that they remain within the effective control of their members.

In the early 1990s the MST leadership attempted to collectivize all its settlements and, though there were many success stories, the strategy was, over all, a failure. The membership much preferred mixed forms of communal life and, since the settlements are fundamentally self-governing, the MST turned to more practical solutions. Nearly all MST settlements are the common property of the whole community and are administered by a "settlement association" of which everyone is a member. The settlement association determines the form of land distribution and usually they have chosen to divide the land into family-sized plots which are then farmed individually. It is essential to emphasize that these family plots remain the common property of the whole settlement and remain within the jurisdiction of the settlement association. That is, even when a settlement is not fully collectivized it still functions on the principle of common property. Typically, moreover, settlements still have a common land (*terra solta*) where, for example, animals are grazed in common. MST settlements also work co-operatively to provide education and health care facilities right on the settlement. In order to increase the sense of community, the settlement is often organized into villages (*agrovilas*) so that families are not too spread apart and can have easy access to the school, health care centre, and other shared buildings.

Moreover, there are many elaborate forms of formal and informal co-operation. Even if production co-operatives on communally farmed land are relatively uncommon, there is a variety of credit, seed, tool, storage, marketing, and shipping co-operatives. The MST has also been successful in the development of "agroindustries," co-operatives that produce goods for the market like jam, liquor, and other products made with crops grown on the settlement. MST settlements also constantly organize informal work-brigades – the *mutirão*. The MST has set up national and regional organizations in order to encourage the elaboration of co-operatives and train members in their successful operation.[108]

The MST also functions democratically beyond the boundaries of the settlement. Each settlement sends delegates to local, regional, and national assemblies, each of which is responsible for various sectors of the MST's work. The MST runs a wide range of local, regional, and state schools as well as the Florestan Fernandes National School, where members are trained in the philosophical, historical, and political ideas they need to be good activists. The other regional and state training centres, which are often linked to nearby universities, provide education in technical fields like agriculture and co-operative administration. The MST retains independence from political parties and above all from the Brazilian state. At the national level the MST has become a powerful political voice, which is strengthened still further by its active membership in international organizations like the Via Campesina.

The MST constitutes an emerging social movement in civil society that demonstrates why socialist criticism of liberal-capitalism is non-utopian. First, it clearly responds to the contradictions of liberal-capitalism by seeking to increase the self-determination of its members and by eliminating exploitation. Second, it does so in a way that establishes the Movement as an independent and self-governing institution of civil society. Moreover, it is run in a manner that explicitly rejects the liberal notion of private property without at the same time failing to recognize the individuals who are its members.

4iii Summary

It is very important to emphasize that the social movements and co-operatives I have used as examples do not signify that the emergence of a socialist world is imminent. Imminence is not a criterion for non-utopian social criticism because, in general, dramatic changes in human social organization typically take a long time to mature, and socialist civil democracy requires the development of sophisticated self-governing institutions in civil society rather than sudden and dramatic changes at the level of the state. Socialism, to use Gramsci's phrase, requires, rather, a protracted "war of positions."[109] The four contemporary examples I have identified above have all contributed to this struggle, building the kind of basis in civil society that is necessary for non-statist, genuinely democratic socialism to emerge.

The task of non-utopian socialist criticism is to engage in social discourse in such a way as to encourage self-consciousness about the character of social conflicts. I hope to have shown in this chapter that socialist criticism of liberal-capitalism is non-utopian by arguing that socialist civil democracy provides a solution to the contradictions of liberal-capitalism and that contemporary movements of worker-managed enterprises foreshadow its emergence. Socialist civil democracy, I claim, provides the juridical means to cultivate freedom. This amounts to arguing that socialist civil democracy provides the only juridical-imaginative structure of recognition that is in harmony with concrete-lived recognition.

Conclusion

As we have now seen in some detail, Hegel holds that "Contradiction in motion, instinctive urge, and the like, is masked for ordinary thinking."[1] Ordinary thinking is beguiled by what simply is, or better yet, is too anxious in face of difference to withstand contradiction. It lunges for the simple consolations of mere "identity," only to discover that this "is merely the determination of the simple immediate, of dead being."

On the other hand, "Instinctive urge in general ... is nothing else but the fact that something is, in one and the same respect, self-contained and deficient, the negative of itself." Contradiction, in other words, is not what restricts, limits, or forestalls. It is not an impasse, an impossibility, an antinomy, or an aporia. "Something is ... alive only in so far as it contains contradiction within it, and moreover is this power to hold and endure the contradiction within it." Indeed, all life, from the germinating seed to the springing fox to mass demonstrations against exploitation, are what they are insofar as they can "hold and endure the contradiction."

Thought also has this double character, this founding difference, this originary self-opposition. If "ordinary thought," governed by the understanding, masks and covers over the vitality of contradiction, and in the process fails to live up to movement and change, then what Hegel calls "speculative thought," governed by reason, allows the vital contradictions of being to animate its activity and its insight. It "holds fast contradiction." Indeed, speculative thought – dialectical philosophy – is the vital contradiction in its richest form. It lives the tension of the founding antagonism at the height of its vibrancy and at its greatest vitality.

The vital contradiction not only propels us to learn how to cultivate the institutions of a free society; it is that in and through which freedom has life. This life could never be satisfied purely and simply with what is, nor is this the kind of dissatisfaction that beguiles appetitive desire, with its insatiable thirst for yet more wealth or more power. This dissatisfaction does not have the logical structure of capitalism.

Rather, if speculative thought has the courage and the "power to hold and endure the contradiction within it," then it knows that there will always be people who are, relatively at least, marginalized, dominated, and excluded. Yet, animated by the vocation to cultivate freedom, it takes the side of those who respond to their domination and exclusion by struggling to overcome it. If they succeed, the world will still have others on margins of some kind, but it will be qualitatively more free. That is, even if anti-racist activism, feminism, movements of workers who refuse to be exploited, and other struggles for liberation are successful, there will still be others excluded in other ways. But the new world – the world with less racism, with equality between men and women, with workers who not only are not exploited but receive their rightful share of the commonwealth – is a qualitatively *better* world. Dialectical philosophy is an activist philosophy. It knows that it is both created by the vital contradiction of being and called by that same vitality not just to "interpret the world, but to change it."[2]

Although it could be claimed that Marx grasped the activist essence of dialectical philosophy better than Hegel, and that Marx's contribution to the criticism of capitalism has been the most powerful and influential in history, I have argued that it was Hegel who first recognized the vitality of contradiction that leads us not only to the most radical and insightful criticisms of liberal-capitalism, but also directly into the midst of the "strife of passions" that will cultivate a world that is more just and thus more free.

Notes

PREFACE

1 I refer to the English title for Denys Arcand, director, *Le Déclin de l'empire américain* (1986). The sequel, *Les Invasions barbares*, might have interested Hegel as well, since it posits a kind of individual salvation in the face of death not unlike Hegel's own characterization of early Christianity in the context of the Roman Empire.

2 Edward Gibbon, *Decline and Fall of the Roman Empire*, 6 vols. (New York: Everyman's Library, 2010).

3 *PH*, 21 / 26.

4 "Spirit is not an inert being but, on the contrary, absolutely restless being, pure activity, the negating or ideality of every fixed category." *PM*, §378A (translating "spirit" rather than "mind" for *Geist*). For interesting reflections on this theme, see Jean-Luc Nancy, *The Restlessness of the Negative*.

5 Immanuel Kant, "Second Proposition" of the "Idea for a Universal History with a Cosmopolitan Purpose" in Hans Reiss, *Kant: Political Writings*, 42–3.

INTRODUCTION

1 *SL*, 439 / 75.

2 *HP*, I, 279 / 320.

3 Heraclitus, Fragment 51, in Kirk and Raven, *The Presocratic Philosophers*, 193. For an interesting discussion of this fragment, see Russon, *Reading Hegel's Phenomenology*, 51–3.

4 Judith Butler, Ernesto Laclau, and Slavoj Žižek, *Contingency, Hegemony, Universality*, 24.

5 Slavoj Žižek, *The Sublime Object of Ideology*, 6–7.

6 Cf. Emmanuel Levinas, *Totality and Infinity.*

7 *SL*, 439 / 75.

8 *SL*, 435 / 69.

9 *SL*, 434 / 68.

10 *SL*, 440 / 76.

11 *PH*, 5 / 494. Although he does not speak of these issues specifically in the light of vital contradiction, Stephen Houlgate gives a good description of "letting go" in *An Introduction to Hegel*, 248–68.

12 Dialectics has roots not only in Plato's notion of eros but also in Christian conceptions of love. In a way, the mandate of dialectic was articulated by Jesus: "If you love those who love you, what credit is it to you? For even the sinners love those who love them … Love your enemies." Luke 6:32, 35. NRSV. That is, there is no possible characteristic of the other that would preclude the mandate that it be loved on its own terms.

13 *PRel*, 418 / 221–2.

14 For a fine study of the *Parmenides*, see Erik Sanday, *A Study of Dialectic in Plato's* Parmenides.

15 Catherine Malabou, *The Future of Hegel.*

16 On this note, see, for example, John Russon, "Reading: Derrida in Hegel's Understanding."

17 Kant, "Idea for a Universal History," "Fourth Proposition," in Hans Reiss, *Kant: Political Writings*, 44–5.

18 For an excellent study of antagonism and conflict in the political philosophies of Kant and Hegel, see Réal Fillion, *Multicultural Dynamics and the Ends of History*, parts 1 and 2.

19 "But it is just this necessity itself, or the *origination* of the new object, that presents itself to consciousness without its understanding how this happens, which proceeds for us, as it were, behind the back of consciousness." *PS*, M87 / 67–8.

20 *PH*, 19 / 32.

21 *PR*, 21 / 26.

22 *PH*, 456 / 539–40.

23 *PH*, 456 / 539–40, 452 / 535.

24 Frederick Neuhouser puts similar emphasis on these three fundamental institutions, but without reference to their vital contradiction. See his *Foundations of Hegel's Social Theory*.

CHAPTER ONE

1 *SL*, 439 / 75.

2 Plato, *Phaedo*, 75a.

3 Of course, in a broader sense the world of flora and fauna is also not determined in advance, insofar as random genetic mutations lead to the elaboration of different forms of life.

4 *PS*, M78 / 61.

5 *PS*, M11 / 10.

6 "This consciousness suffers this violence at its own hands: it spoils its own limited satisfaction." *PS*, M80 / 63.

7 John Russon gives a phenomenological account of learning as the encounter of familiar and unfamiliar in *Human Experience: Philosophy, Neurosis, and the Elements of Everyday Life*, for example, 65–7.

8 For an excellent account of the dialectics of interpersonal learning, see Kym MacLaren, "On Being Moved: A Phenomenological Account of Emotion and Transformation."

9 As we shall see in some detail shortly, cultivating the stance in which one can be *at home*, or *with oneself* in that which is most other to oneself is Hegel's definition of "freedom." Freedom, he says, "is the spirit *at home* and *with itself* in ... *externality* as such." *PR*, §187R.

10 Since dialectic is not a priori but is, rather, the structure of change itself, one cannot isolate a determinate structure of change (like thesis/antithesis/synthesis) and apply it willy-nilly to all forms of being. Hegel certainly never does this, as even a cursory familiarity with his texts shows.

11 Russon, *Human Experience,* especially chapter 5, "Neurosis."

12 H.S. Harris, in a discussion of the relation of Real Philosophy to the *Phenomenology of Spirit* and *The Science of Logic* calls Real Philosophy "the science of what is empirical and historical" (*Hegel's Ladder* 2:745. Harris discusses this issue in general from 744–6. See also 776–7.

13 On this topic, see John Burbidge, *Hegel's Systematic Contingency*, and Burbidge, "The Necessity of Contingency" in his *Hegel on Logic and Religion: The Reasonableness of Christianity*," 39–51.

14 This paragraph draws on insights from R.G. Collingwood's excellent work, *An Essay on Philosophical Method.*

15 Kant's "Table of Categories" articulates the twelve forms of synthesizing judgment. See the *Critique of Pure Reason*, A80 / B106. Hegel engages in a dialectical development of these and other categories in the *Science of Logic.*

16 Jay Lampert, "Husserl and Hegel on the Logic of Subjectivity," 366–7.

17 See *EL*, §147. As Slavoj Žižek puts it, "*It is only the subject's (free) act of 'dotting the i' which retroactively installs necessity*, so that the newer act by means of which the subject recognizes (and thus constitutes) necessity is the supreme act of freedom and as such the self-suppression of necessity." *Tarrying with the Negative: Kant, Hegel and the Critique of Ideology*, 150.

18 Aristotle, *Nichomachean Ethics*, 1099b34–1101b8.

19 Stephen Houlgate gives an informative discussion of what I am calling conceptual dialectic, at least as it pertains to the *Science of Logic*, in *An Introduction to Hegel: Freedom, Truth and History*, 38–43.

20 The dialectic of being, nothing, and becoming is in *SL*, 82–108 / 82–115. As an empirical dialectic of the history of ideas, it is studied in terms of the Eleatics, especially Parmenides and Heraclitus, in *HP* 1:239–98 / 275–343.

21 Robert Pippin makes a point not unlike mine in *Hegel's Practical Philosophy: Rational Agency as Ethical Life*, 126.

22 Houlgate uses the term "letting go" in his discussion of dialectic. See, for example *An Introduction to Hegel*, 41.

23 John Rawls, *A Theory of Justice*, especially 17–22.

24 In the *Encyclopedia Logic* Hegel articulates the conceptual dialectic of thought into three steps such that the term "dialectic" itself names only the second step. The steps go as follows. First, the "understanding stops short at the fixed determinacy and its distinctness vis-à-vis other determinacies." *EL*, §79. Second, "The *dialectical* moment is the self-sublation of these finite determinacies on their own part, and their passing into their opposites." *EL*, §81. Third, "The *speculative* or *positively rational* apprehends the unity of the determinacies in their opposition." *EL*, §82. For an excellent discussion of this, see John Burbidge, *The Logic of Hegel's Logic*, 40–1. See also his *On Hegel's Logic: Fragments of a Commentary*.

25 "But when, on the other hand, the result is conceived as it is in truth, namely, as a *determinate* negation, a new form has thereby immediately arisen." *PS*, M79/62.

26 Peter Simpson uses the term "transcendental induction" to describe Hegel's epistemology. See his *Hegel's Transcendental Induction*.

27 Most generally, Hegel thus defends a philosophy that is presuppositionless. This is a philosophy that presupposes no determinacy as first principle that is not itself "self-determined" – *free*. Richard Dien Winfield gives an excellent account of the demands of what he calls a philosophy "without foundations" in *Reason and Justice*, especially 14–17 and 117–50. See also

an excellent discussion in Houlgate, *An Introduction to Hegel*, chapter 2, "Thinking without Presuppositions.". Also Burbidge, *The Logic of Hegel's Logic*, 38–41.

28 *PS*, M808 / 530.

CHAPTER TWO

1 *PS*, M167 / 121.

2 Plato, *Symposium*, 200e–201b.

3 *PN*, §245A.

4 "Self-consciousness means I can be aware of myself, the identical knower and agent, as distinct from the objects I know. This is structurally different from the knowledge of objects, yet it includes knowledge of objects because the self knows itself as a different kind of being known in a different way, and so defines its self-awareness over against the knowledge of objects. Hegel claims, however, that human beings are not self-aware automatically and immediately from the start. Only in relation to other selves can the complex maneuver of self-awareness be possible. It is 'learned.'" Kolb, *Critique of Pure Modernity*, 23–4.

5 *PS*, M174 / 125. Hyppolite explores this issue well. "Self-consciousness ... claims to be independent of [the rest of life] and wishes to pose itself as absolutely for-itself. Nevertheless, it will encounter the resistance of its object. Thus the object of consciousness is as independent in-itself as consciousness is." Jean Hyppolite, *Genesis and Structure of Hegel's Phenomenology of Spirit*, 162.

6 *PS*, M186 / 129–30.

7 *PS*, M174 / 125.

8 So much so that William Wallace translates *Begierde* as "appetitive desire" and "appetite" in the *Philosophy of Mind*, *PM*, §426.

9 H.S. Harris, however, claims that it is really sexual desire that is at work in this dialectic. He says in his commentary on M171, for example, "By achieving its climactic satisfaction, by achieving this supreme feeling of unity with itself, the sexually distinct organism sublates its sexual antithesis with the other, which is what made it thus far something distinct on its own account. In the orgasm at the climax of copulation the differences dissolve into the more comprehensive fluidity of the Kind." There is evidence that Hegel also thinks along these lines. He says that without love "the natural [sexual] drive is reduced to the modality of a moment of nature which is

destined to be extinguished in its very satisfaction." *PR*, §163. However, I think that sexual desire always already involves a certain minimal degree of recognition of otherness that is not present in eating and, moreover, it is in eating and not sexual desire that the other is literally consumed and transformed into oneself. Even rape presupposes the minimal recognition of another will. Rape is much better understood as a gesture of domination than the satisfaction of a physical need. See Harris, *Hegel's Ladder*, 1: 326.

10 *PM*, §428.

11 *SL*, 137–50 / 149–66. As Harris puts it, "Self-realization through the struggle is a bad infinite; and when one becomes too old to fight one is left with the 'shame of not being dead.'" Harris, *Hegel's Ladder*, 1: 355.

12 *PS*, M187 / 130.

13 For an excellent discussion of the attitude of desire to be "determining centre," see John Russon, *Reading Hegel's Phenomenology of Spirit*, 158–60.

14 *PS*, M189 / 132.

15 I do not mean to suggest here that my account exhausts all of what Hegel means to show in this dialectic – far from it.

16 See once more Collingwood's transposition of dialectical categories into the terms of genus and species in his *An Essay on Philosophical Method.*

17 *PR*, §1; *EL*, §213; *SL*, 755–60 / 462–69

18 *A* I, 153 / 203.

19 Of course, this is true of all of Hegel's conceptual dialectics and we could thus carry out the same kind of comparisons using the terms of, say, the *Science of Logic.*

20 "There are still many [women] who take shelter in the shadow of men; they adopt without discussion the opinions and values recognized by their husband or their lover, and that allows them to develop childish qualities." Simone de Beauvoir, *The Ethics of Ambiguity*, 37–8.

21 "Work, on the other hand, is desire held in check, fleetingness staved off; in other words, work forms and shapes the thing." *PS*, M195 / 135.

22 *PS*, M195 / 135.

23 As Allen Wood puts it, "This result only points to the fact that the desiring self-consciousness is always dependent on a new object, whereas its aim was rather to establish its own independence and the nothingness of the object." *Hegel's Ethical Thought*, 85.

24 Houlgate perceives in contemporary philosophical and social movements, such as those that have a Nietzschean heritage of privileging Dionysian desire over Appollonian clarity, "[a] relapse back into the eternally unsatisfied

condition of natural desire, a condition which Western civilization deemed unworthy of humanity many centuries ago." He goes on to say that, "For Hegel, human beings are not ultimately at the mercy of restless desire because they have the power to transform their natural origin into genuine self-presence and genuine civility." *An Introduction to Hegel*, 228.

25 It is in and through the working service the slave performs for the master "that consciousness disciplines itself and detaches itself from natural Dasein." Hyppolite, *Genesis and Structure*, 175.

26 *PS*, M195 / 135.

27 *PS*, M196 / 135–6.

28 *PN*, §245A.

29 Ibid.

30 "The 'Ought' of practical feeling is the claim of its essential autonomy to control some existing mode of fact – which is assumed to be worth nothing save as adapted to that claim." Hegel, *PM*, §472.

31 It is important to note here that Hegel is not speaking of mere appetitive desire (*Begierde*) in this context. "Impulse [*Trieb*] must be distinguished from mere appetite [*Begierde*]. The latter belongs ... to *self-consciousness* and occupies, therefore, the standpoint where the opposition between subjectivity and objectivity is not as yet overcome. It is something *single*, and seeks only what is single for a single momentary satisfaction. Impulse, on the other hand, since it is a form of volitional intelligence, starts from the surmounted opposition of subjectivity and objectivity, and embraces a series of satisfactions, hence is a whole, a universal." *PM*, 473A. My interpretation here does not require the level of detail that would make this distinction significant. Suffice it to say that the experience of holding one's desire (*Begierde*) "in check" is precisely what is necessary for the formation of more universal forms of impulse.

32 *PM*, §469A, substituting here and elsewhere "Concept" for "Notion" as a translation of *Begriff*.

33 *PM*, §480.

34 *PM*, §481.

35 *PM*, §482.

36 Marx is more attentive to this theme than Hegel, but it is perfectly consistent with Hegel's philosophy of work *as a manifestation of mutual recognition*. Marx says, for example, that "the productive power of social labour ... arises from cooperation itself. When the worker cooperates in a planned way with others, he strips off the fetters of his individuality, and

develops the capabilities of his species." *Capital*, 1:447. We will see in chapter 8, however, that the "universal conversation" generated by work is decisive to Hegel's study of civil society.

37 *PM*, §472A.

38 "Through his own labor the slave's consciousness becomes for him an object in the element of being." Hyppolite, *Genesis and Structure*, 179.

39 "The concept of property requires that a person should place his will in a thing" *PR*, §51A.

40 "In his laboring as a destructive activity [the slave] expresses his own being-for-self consciously. Here the serving consciousness is aware that it is in and for itself." Harris, *Hegel's Ladder*, 1:367.

41 For an account of the slave's work that develops the implications of the slave's fear, see Houlgate, *An Introduction to Hegel*, 69–71. Harris calls into question the necessity of fear in the account of the slave's work in *Hegel's Ladder*, 1: 370.

42 *PS*, M197 / 137–8.

43 *PS*, M175 / 126.

44 Axel Honneth carries out a very interesting and thoughtful elaboration on the theme of recognition in his *The Struggle for Recognition: The Moral Grammar of Social Conflicts*. See also, *The I in We: Studies in the Theory of Recognition*. A classic essay on the relation of Hegel's concept to general discussions of Western society is Charles Taylor, "The Politics of Recognition," in *Philosophical Arguments*.

45 *PS*, M177 / 127.

46 Hyppolite argues that by the time of the *Phenomenology* Hegel rejects love as an embodiment of mutual recognition. "Love does not dwell sufficiently on the tragic nature of separation." *Genesis and Structure*, 164. He quotes a fragment of the following passage from Hegel's preface in support of this claim. The idea that God is "a disporting of love with itself ... sinks into mere edification, and even insipidity, if it lacks the seriousness, the suffering, the patience and the labour of the negative." *PS*, M19 / 14–15. But Hegel is not rejecting love here, only claiming that *if* love itself is understood insipidly then it does not do justice to the "labour of the negative." Even romantic love is full enough of suffering and the tragic to keep us preoccupied for a lifetime, much less the Christian demands of *agape* to which Hegel is probably referring in this passage.

47 John Russon explores the unconscious and habitual structures of mutual

recognition in his "The Ritual Basis of Self-Identity" in *Reading Hegel's Phenomenology*, 169–83.

48 There is some debate as to the importance of mutual recognition in Hegel's political philosophy. Houlgate says, "Fully developed self-consciousness, according to Hegel, is to be found only where such recognition is mutual ... as, for example, in the modern constitutional state." *An Introduction to Hegel*, 68. Paul Franco, on the other hand says, "What distinguishes Hegel's account of the struggle for recognition in the *Phenomenology* from his earlier accounts is the diminished political role that it plays. No longer does this struggle lead directly, as it did in Hegel's earlier writings, to the absolute ethical life of a people or to the legal relationships characteristic of civil society." *Hegel's Philosophy of Freedom*, 92. I think Franco is mistaken here for two reasons. First, he tends to emphasize the *struggle* for recognition rather than its achieved states – law, custom, society, state, language, and so on. Second, he understates the sense in which the struggles of civil society are struggles for recognition. We will see below that the entire success of the project of the cultivation of freedom depends on the struggle for recognition which the "Corporation" attempts to address. See chapters 8 and 9. Moreover, I will argue there that the vital contradiction which animates political life is essentially a struggle for recognition.

49 Isaiah Berlin, "Two Concepts of Liberty," in Sandel, *Liberalism and Its Critics*, 15–36.

50 *PR*, §187R. Hegel says the same thing at EL, §24A. "Freedom is: being at home with oneself in one's other."

51 This is already a very clear hint that the "being at home" in one's family is an inadequate experience of freedom, for the terms of this being at home, familial love, could never be recreated in the enormous world of strangers outside the family. As we shall see, one must learn a different and more sophisticated way of being at home in the civil and political realms.

52 *PS*, M69 / 51.

53 *EL*, §23R.

54 *PR*, §187R.

55 Karl Marx and Friedrich Engels, *Manifesto of the Communist Party*, in Tucker, *The Marx-Engels Reader*, 491.

56 Hegel himself uses this image in the preface to the *Phenomenology of Spirit*. "The individual has the right to demand that Science should at least provide him with the ladder to [the Absolute] standpoint, should show him this

standpoint within himself." *PS*, M26 / 20. Hegel links this dialectical ladder directly to education. "The task of leading the individual from his uneducated standpoint to knowledge had to be seen in its universal sense, just as it was the universal individual, self-conscious Spirit, whose formative education had to be studied." *PS*, M28 / 22.

57 "What is the real purpose of love? ... It is giving birth in beauty, whether in body or in soul." Plato, *Symposium*, 206b.

58 Ibid., 208e–211e. Of course, the highest stair in the *Symposium* is love of "Beauty itself," but, adopting a dialectical interpretation of Plato, this highest stair is but an empty abstraction of the general or universal *eidos* that animates all the specific stairs in the ladder of *eros*, but has no existence independent of them.

59 SL 439 / 74.

60 *SL*, 439 / 75.

61 For detailed discussion of contradiction in Hegel, see Burbidge, *The Logic of Hegel's Logic*, especially 12–13 and 84–94 for comparison with traditional logic, as well as two essays in Stewart, *The Hegel Myths and Legends*, namely "Hegel's Metaphysics and the Problem of Contradiction" by Robert Pippin and "From an Ontological Point of View: Hegel's Critique of the Common Logic" by Robert Hanna. See also Songsuk Susan Hahn, *Contradiction in Motion: Hegel's Organic Concept of Life and Value.*

62 Hahn gives a good account of this issue with respect to organic growth in her work *Contradiction in Motion*, especially 40–1.

63 Aristotle, *Metaphysics*, in Barnes, *The Complete Works of Aristotle,* vol. 2, 4.4.

64 Cf. *SL*, 413–16, 431–43, 447, 452 / VI, 41–5, 64–79, 84, 91. Hahn is very helpful. See *Contradiction in Motion*, especially chapter 3, "Formal and Natural Contradictions."

68 Heraclitus, Fragment 51, in Kirk and Raven, *The Presocratic Philosophers*, 193.

66 Žižek, *The Sublime Object of Ideology*, 6–7. See also *Less Than Nothing: Hegel and the Shadow of Dialectical Materialism*. For an interesting debate about these and related issues, see Judith Butler, Ernesto Laclau, and Slavoj Žižek, *Contingency, Hegemony, and Universality: Contemporary Dialogues on the Left.*

67 Žižek's Lacanian Hegel, which quite brilliantly integrates the Imaginary, Symbolic, and Real into Hegel's philosophy, is an exciting intellectual breakthrough. However, vital contradiction is not best conceived as radical loss.

CHAPTER THREE

1 "The road can therefore be regarded as the pathway of *doubt*, or more precisely as the way of despair." *PS*, M78 / 61.

2 *PH*, 21 / 26. The "wrecks confusedly hurled" is likely taken from Quintus Smyrnaeus (Kointos Smyrnaios), *Posthomerica*, 14 – the storm that devastates the Achaean fleet as it leaves Troy.

3 Houlgate, in his chapter "History and Truth" in *An Introduction to Hegel*, gives a particularly good introduction to these issues. See also a very interesting and insightful discussion, in particular of the "Cunning of Reason" and the "Reason-ability" of history, in Fillion, *Multicultural Dynamics*, 87–103.

4 *PS*, M11 / 9–10.

5 Susan Buck-Morss makes the interesting and provocative claim that Hegel models the master-slave dialectic in the *Phenomenology of Spirit* on the Haitian Revolution, the only politically successful slave revolution in Western history, which culminated in the Declaration of Independence in 1804. See her *Hegel, Haiti and Universal History*. The key issue in my reading of Hegel is not to what degree Hegel in fact was thinking about the Haitian revolution when he wrote the master-slave dialectic, but whether Hegel's text and the historical events are mutually illuminating, and the answer to that question is clearly yes.

6 Marx, *Capital*, 1:102–3.

7 Marx, *Grundrisse*, 88–100.

8 Karl Marx and Friedrich Engels, *The German Ideology*, in *The Marx-Engels Reader*, 157–8.

9 I will give a more detailed analysis and a Hegelian version of the theory of exploitation in chapter 10, section 3, "The Hegelian Theory of Exploitation."

10 I have used G.A. Cohen's exhaustive account here as a guide to productive forces and the mode of production. *Karl Marx's Theory of History*, 28–55, 79–84. An excellent consideration of issues of "determination" is found in the five chapters that make up section 1, "Historical Materialism and the Specificity of Capitalism," in Ellen Meiksens Wood, *Democracy against Capitalism*.

11 See Marx, preface to *A Contribution to the Critique of Political Economy*, in Tucker, *The Marx-Engels Reader*, especially 4–5. The most important and systematic defence of this claim is made by Cohen in *Karl Marx's Theory of*

History. It is very ably summarized and alternative Marxist accounts discussed in Roemer, *Free to Lose*, 108–24.

12 Marx and Engels, *The Manifesto of the Communist Party*, in Tucker, *The Marx-Engels Reader*, 473.

13 This premise is not necessarily secure. It is possible to conceive of a class society in which, though everyone works, one class is forced to carry out the most tedious, arduous, undervalued, or dangerous labour.

14 As Jan Elster puts it, referring to a passage from G. A. Cohen, "It is misleading, therefore, to say that 'as long as there is some surplus class society is possible.' Rather, it is the possibility of a surplus that makes class society possible." *Making Sense of Marx*, 169. The Cohen passage is from *Karl Marx's Theory of History*, 198.

15 Cf. Georges Bataille, *The Accursed Share*, 63–77.

16 See, for example, David Schweickart, *After Capitalism*, especially 58–73.

17 Marx, *Capital*, 3:958–9.

18 See Wood, "History or Technological Determinism," in *Democracy against Capitalism*, 108–45.

19 This account of Marx is an adaptation of a reading of various texts of Marx given by Cohen, *Karl Marx's Theory of History*, 214.

20 Engels proposes in *Anti-Dührung* that an administrative class is formed on the basis of surplus product, and this administrative class composes the proto-exploiting class. Engels' account is plausible as a description of an emerging division of labour, but it does not explain why this division of labour would become one predicated on domination. Cited in Cohen, *Karl Marx's Theory of History*, 209–11.

21 Marx, *Capital*, 3:928.

22 Cohen and Elster do the same thing. Elster says, "I have discussed … the world historical importance of surplus labour that makes possible the advance of civilization by creating free time for a small class of non-producers. I insist on the word 'possible' in the preceding sentence." *Making Sense of Marx*, 168–9. Cohen says, "We may envisage a complete material description of a society – a 'socio-neutral' description – from which we cannot deduce its social form." *Karl Marx's Theory of History*, 94.

23 Ernest Mandel, *Marxist Economic Theory*, 1:39–40.

24 Ibid., 7.

25 Of course, Hegel himself cannot be relied upon as a guide on all these points. He very likely held non-European peoples to be inferior, at least culturally. He certainly held women to be inferior to men and, on that basis, unsuited to fully realized freedom.

26 There is a debate in Marxist literature based on Robert Brennar's claim that it was class conflict that created the conditions for change from the feudal to the capitalist mode of production rather than changes in productive forces. He argued that the struggle of lords to recuperate losses after the Black Death and peasant resistance thereto created the conditions for the evolution of capitalism. Such a claim is perfectly consistent with the Hegelian argument I have been developing, though obviously not with Hegel's *Lectures on the Philosophy of History*. See Brennar's "Agrarian Class Structure and Economic Development in Pre-Industrial Europe," and a series of articles devoted to the debate around this issue in T.H. Ashton and C.H.E. Philpin, *The Brennar Debate*.

27 *PS*, M25 / 19.

28 David Kolb notes the distinction between the recognition of free individuality in "modernity," which develops later in the conceptual dialectic, and the Ethical Society. "What is new about modernity is that this process of freedom as withdrawal and self-determination is institutionalized in a more complete way. In earlier societies there was no separation between a person's identity and his or her definite social role. It is true that a person could have drawn such a separation in his or her own thought, but there was no institution in which one could live a life based on that separation." *Critique of Pure Modernity*, 29.

29 Aristotle, *Politics*, in *The Complete Works of Aristotle*, 2:1254b39–1255a2.

30 There is ample precedence for this reading of Hegel in the literature. Charles Taylor argues for the importance of *Sittlichkeit* for all of human moral life in *Hegel*, 365–88. John Burbidge makes the comparable point that the "unhappy consciousness" cannot be reduced to medieval Christianity in "'Unhappy Consciousness' in Hegel." John Russon claims, in *The Self and Its Body in Hegel's Phenomenology of Spirit*, chapter 4, that chapter 6 of the *Phenomenology* cannot be reduced to its examples, but refers to general forms of social life. For another study of this kind of theme, see Andrej Warminksi, "Reading For Example."

CHAPTER FOUR

1 *PS*, M419–37 / 277–87.

2 I do not intend here a summary of Hegel's argument but merely to indicate its plausibility. For an insightful and more detailed discussion of this argument, see H.S. Harris, *Hegel's Ladder*, 2:149–50, 164; Jean Hyppolite, *Genesis and Structure*, 315–18; John Russon, *The Self and Its Body*, 47–8.

3 In Charles Taylor's words, "'*Sittlichkeit*' refers to the moral obligations I have to an ongoing community, of which I am a part. These obligations are based on established norms and uses, and that is why the etymological root in '*Sitten*' is important for Hegel's use. The crucial characteristic of *Sittlichkeit* is that it enjoins us to bring about what already is. This is a paradoxical way of putting it, but in fact the common life which is the basis of my *sittlich* obligation is already there in existence. It is in virtue of its being an ongoing affair that I have these obligations; and my fulfillment of these obligations is what sustains it and keeps it in being. Hence in *Sittlichkeit*, there is no gap between what ought to be and what is, between *Sollen* and *Sein*." Taylor, *Hegel*, 376.

4 For a good general study of Hegel's views on ancient Greece, see Dominique Janicaud, *Hegel et le destin de la Grèce*.

5 Sophocles, *Antigone*, 19.

6 In Harris's words, "As Antigone insists, the consciousness of God's law is *ageless*. It becomes a moment of self-conscious spirit when it comes into conflict with real human law-giving. It is important that Antigone's 'ageless' law is the bond of natural feeling ... The sense of something as *sittlich* is a feeling of having *no choice*. The obligation of *Sittlichkeit* is the sense of what it means to be a member of this community." Harris, *Hegel's Ladder*, 2:198–9.

7 *PS*, H465 / 305.

8 *PH*, 252 / 308.

9 *PS*, H448–9 / 293.

10 These terms are taken from *PS* H449, 450 and 455 / 293–4, 298.

11 *PH*, 251–2 / 308.

12 *PR*, §355.

13 *PR*, §356.

14 *PH*, 225–6 / 277–8.

15 Obviously this does not amount to a vote of confidence in Hegel's empirical claims about either, but especially not the Oriental world.

16 See Harris, *Hegel's Ladder*, 2:157 and 175–7, and Russon, *Human Experience*, 63–4.

17 For example, Telemachus meets with the council before his departure to see Menelaus at the beginning of book 2 of Homer's *Odyssey*, and the Phaeacians have a town council in book 6. Odysseus is also concerned, as the *Odyssey* closes, to placate the rest of the families from which the dead suitors have come.

18 Aristotle, *Politics*, 1252b30–1, 1252b22 and 1253a19–20.

19 *PS*, H462 / 303.

20 *PS*, H455 / 298.

21 Harris, *Hegel's Ladder*, 2:173.

22 Aristotle points out that early forms of the polis are monarchies precisely because of their roots in the family. "Every family is ruled by the eldest, and therefore in the colonies of the family the kingly form of government prevailed because they were of the same blood." *Politics*, 1252b20–2.

23 *PS*, H451 / 294–5.

24 *PS*, H457–9 / 299–301. There is no evidence this brother/sister mutuality existed in the Greek world, and it seems likely to be an attempt by Hegel to read too much meaning into Antigone's claim that she has a special relationship with her brother.

25 *PS*, H451 / 294.

26 *PS*, H452 / 295–6. Hegel would have been aware that it was not a woman's role to carry out funeral rites and other such rituals, but they would be supervised by the male head of the household. Antigone's action to bury her brother was thus a provocative political act. Ismene represents what must be considered a more typical response.

27 *PS*, H453 / 297.

28 *PS*, H463 / 303. See also *PS*, H460 / 302.

29 *PS*, H455 / 298.

30 Indeed, this kind of organic totality, when idealized, is Hegel's definition of beauty. *A* 1:91–115 / 99–120. The fall of the beautiful Greek harmony thus marks not only the end of the Ethical Society but the end of art focused on beauty (the "classical" art of ancient Greek sculpture and literature) and the inauguration of the non-beautiful art of interiority (the "romantic" art of Christian and then secular Europe). For an excellent discussion of this issue as it relates to fine art, see Houlgate, *An Introduction to Hegel*, chapter 9, "Art and Human Wholeness."

31 *PH*, 223 / 275.

32 *PS*, M437 / 286.

33 Sophocles, *Antigone*, 15.

34 Ibid., 16.

35 Cf. *PN*, §245A.

36 Simone de Beauvoir, *The Second Sex*, 66–81.

37 *PS*, H447–8 / 292–3. Hegel is no feminist, but his (sexist) views about women cannot be drawn from this section of the *Phenomenology*, which is an explication of a specific conceptual and historical context and not a statement about women in general..

38 *PS*, H468 / 308.

39 Ibid.

40 Hegel reads Plato's *Republic* and its condemnation of private property as conservative in a related way to his reading of the *Antigone*. Both Plato and Sophocles are understood to have perceived the threat of singular self-consciousness and then written texts whose task was to address this threat. *PR*, §46R.

41 Sophocles, *Antigone*, 19.

42 Ibid., 20.

43 *PS*, H466 / 306.

44 Hegel uses *Tat, Tun*, and also sometimes *Handlung* for words translated as *deed*, *act*, and *action*.

45 *PS*, H464 / 304.

46 *PS*, H444 / 291.

47 *PS*, H468 / 308.

48 *PS*, H475 / 314.

49 Ibid.

50 *PH*, 260, 255, 260 / 317–18, 312, 309 respectively.

51 *PH*, 253, 253, 268 / 309, 309, 327 respectively.

52 *PH*, 269–70 / 329.

53 *PH*, 267 / 326.

54 *PS*, M437 / 286–7.

55 The person of The Condition of Right supersedes the Ethical Society. Hegel correspondingly and explicitly links the Condition of Right to stoicism and the Ethical Society to mastery and slavery. "Just as stoicism emerged from lordship and bondage, which is the immediate determinate being of *self-consciousness*, so too personality has issued from the immediate *spirit*, which is the universally sovereign will of all, and equally their subservient obedience." *PS*, H479 / 317.

56 *PS*, H455 / 297–8.

57 *PS*, M194 / 134 and H455 / 297–8 respectively. Harris unconvincingly argues that it is the tyrannical emperor of the Condition of Right that corresponds to the master (and slave), and not the Ethical Society. Harris thus says, "So it is in the Roman world, not in True Spirit, that we can see the *universal* shape of Lordship and Bondage." *Hegel's Ladder*, 2:224. Harris's argument is flawed for three reasons. First, Hegel explicitly states at H479 that the progression from mastery and slavery to stoicism is repeated in the transition from ethical life to the Condition of Right. The chaos of the

Condition of Right is then, second, explicitly linked not to mastery and slavery but to skepticism. To interpret the argument as Harris does is to invert the direction of the dialectic completely. Third, Hegel considers all three forms of flawed society to either consist in or collapse into forms of domination: the mastery of the divine authority in ethical life, the tyranny of the emperor in the Condition of Right (*PS*, H482 / 319), and the Terror of the Society of Absolute Freedom (see *PS*, H590 / 389–90). Each is its own new form of domination, and thus not a continual repetition of the same logic as the lord and bondsman.

58 *PH*, 268 / 327.

59 *PS*, M199 / 138.

60 Russon, *The Self and Its Body*, 16.

CHAPTER FIVE

1 *PS*, H464 / 304.

2 Ibid. *Rechtszustand* has been translated into English as *Legal Status* (by Baillie and Miller) and the *Condition of Right* (by the Hegel Translation Group). Although *Rechtszustand* has long been called *Legal Status* in the literature, I will use the Hegel Translation Group's rendering, both because the term "Right" (*Recht*) is decisive in this discussion and because the Hegel Translation Group's translation of the "Spirit" chapter should certainly now become the standard scholarly text.

3 For a study of the link between the Condition of Right and its Roman example, see Patricia Fagan, "Philosophical History and the Roman Empire."

4 *PS*, H478 / 316.

5 *PS*, H477 / 316.

6 *PS*, H 480 / 317–18

7 *PS*, H 477 / 316.

8 *PS*, H 478 / 316.

9 David Kolb makes a related point with respect to the character of recognition of modern subjectivity. "Mutual recognition (in the modern world) does not depend on any particular content. My identity as free is primary; what I choose is secondary. Even my needs and desires are a content with which I am not fully identical." *Critique of Pure Modernity*, 27.

10 *PS*, H479 / 317.

11 In this text Hegel does not discuss the Condition of Right in terms of "civil society." But note Kolb's characterization of civil society and its

isomorphism with the Condition of Right. "Civil society's members should feel no pressure to care for the whole except the formal requirements of procedural justice and the external requirements of trade and exchange ... What is distinctive about civil society is not that it does away with structures of mutual recognition but that it renders those structures empty and formal." *Critique of Pure Modernity*, 28.

12 Of course, specific forms of stoic action would not, strictly speaking, meet this definition. If one should, as a good stoic, act such as to be concerned only with what one *can* do and control and not bother with what one cannot control, then one can of course judge others for not living up to this standard. But this standard amounts to very little because, cast in terms of what Hegel calls *arbitrary will*, the imperative of stoicism is equivalent to the much more mundane "Do what you want and pay no attention to what you cannot bend to your own will." See Epictetus, *The Handbook*.

13 *PS*, H480 / 318.

14 Ibid.

15 *PH*, 317 / 384.

16 *PR*, §357.

17 *PR*, §15R.

18 *PS*, H480 / 317–18.

19 Ibid.

20 As Kolb says, "To demand freedom from all particular content is, in the end, to put yourself all the more thoroughly under the domination of contingent and arbitrary content ... The emptiness of his freedom and his domination by impulse are among the roots of the endless drive for *more*." *Critique of Pure Modernity*, 35–6.

21 *PR*, §357.

22 Ibid.

23 Hegel likely draws on Plato's dialectic of cities in books 8 and 9 of the *Republic*. For an excellent discussion of these themes which concludes in a Socratic *defence* of democracy, see Gregory Recco, *Athens Victorious*. See also Russon, *The Self and Its Body*, 80.

24 *PS*, H 484 / 320–1.

25 Russon says that the power of choice in the Condition of Right "turned out to be its own worst enemy ... since what it ended up proving was precisely that everything substantial is open to the destructive negative power of the singular will ... [W]hat we really see here is the absolute vulnerability of all selves to the stronger singular." *The Self and Its Body*, 92.

26 *PS*, M484 / 321.

27 "Anarchy reigns, and the world goes mad. The system is supposed to keep the legalized world safe from the 'barbarians' beyond its frontier, but the raging of the rival armies inside the Empire is the same tumult of natural passions that exist outside it." Harris, *Hegel: Phenomenology and System*, 65.

28 *PR*, §357. Hegel has much to say about the "rabble" in his discussion of capitalist civil society. See chapter 9 below.

29 Alexis de Tocqueville, *Democracy in America*, 2:317–18. See Löwith, *From Hegel to Nietzsche*, 253–7.

30 The Condition of Right appears in the same subsection of chapter 6, "Spirit," as the Ethical Society because both are societies of immediacy: Ethical Society immediately unites particular and universal and the Condition of Right unites singular and universal.

31 There seems to be another form of immediate identity that we have not considered. If the Ethical Society immediately identifies universal and particular, and the Condition of Right unites universal and singular, what of the immediate unity of singular and particular? But we have considered this above, for such a "society" would not be a society at all, but a Hobbesian state of nature in which singular selves purely and simply do whatever they want. There is no form of community, no universal, no recognition whatever. Hegel studies this kind of phenomenon, as we have seen in chapter 1, in the "Struggle to the Death" of chapter 4 of the *Phenomenology*. It leads eventually, as we saw, to the recognition of the necessity of the community of mutual recognition – a society. Since the immediate identity of singularity and particularity is not a society, it cannot appear in the dialectic of society but instead in the dialectic of self-consciousness.

32 If the Condition of Right corresponds to the stoicism of self-consciousness, its deterioration corresponds to stoicism's collapse into "the babble of the negative" of skepticism. *PS*, H480 / 317.

CHAPTER SIX

1 Rebecca Comay gives an insightful and very readable study of Hegel's views on the French Revolution in her *Mourning Sickness: Hegel and the French Revolution.*

2 Kant, *Grounding for the Metaphysics of Morals*, 14 / 402.

3 Kant, *On Education.*

4 Rousseau, *The Social Contract*, 1.6.

5 Kant, *Grounding*, 40 / 433.
6 *PS*, H584 / 386.
7 *PR*, §27.
8 Richard Dien Winfield, in an excellent technical study of this issue, says, "[T]he will must will itself." But for this self-willing not to be merely "empty solipsism ... the will must will new particular character for itself ... Consequently, for the will to be free, it must will its relation to other free wills as part of its own self-determination ... The conclusion is unequivocal: free willing is not the action of a single will alone, but rather a self-determination of one agent that is inextricably bound up with the self-determination of others ... what Hegel has termed 'reciprocal recognition.'" *Reason and Justice*, 163–4. See also Houlgate, *An Introduction to Hegel*, 182–5.
9 For particularly good studies of Hegelian criticisms of this form of rationality as it pertains to ethics and politics, see Winfield, *Reason and Justice*, 73–116 and Russon, *Reading Hegel's Phenomenology*, chapter 10, "The Contradictions of Moral Life: Hegel's Critique of Kant."
10 *PS*, H500–26 / 331–48.
11 *PS*, H513 / 339.
12 Note, in Charles Taylor's words, how Absolute Freedom and other forms of Culture are the direct opposite of *Sittlichkeit*. "Societies refer to theoretical 'value' formulations as their norms rather than to practices, when they are trying to make themselves over to meet an unrealized standard; e.g. they are trying to 'build socialism,' or become 'fully democratic.'" Taylor, *Hegel*, 383.
13 Paul Franco and Frederick Neuhouser analyse the importance of Rousseau to Hegel in Franco, *Hegel's Philosophy of Freedom*, especially 3–11, and Neuhouser, *Foundations of Hegel's Social Theory*, especially chapter 2, "Rousseau: Freedom, Dependence, and the General Will."
14 Rousseau, *The Social Contract*, 1.6.
15 Rousseau, *The Social Contract*, 3.15. Note a similar claim by de Tocqueville. "But this system of people shake off their state of dependence just long enough to select their master and then relapse into it again." Alexis de Tocqueville, *Democracy in America*, 2:319.
16 *PS*, H588 / 389.
17 *PS*, H585 / 387.
18 *PS*, H587 / 388.
19 Rousseau, *The Social Contract*, 2.3.
20 There is a sense in which Marxist thought overlaps with certain features of

the Society of Absolute Freedom. Traditional Marxism understands class conflict to be the ultimate form of factionalism and understands these particularities to be abolished in a rationally organized society of abundance. In a society in which everyone has what he needs and there is no competition for scarce resources, the particularity of private property no longer skews the universal: material possession is a particularity that makes no difference. For a criticism of this Marxist ideal that uses the notion of opportunity cost, see Alec Nove, *The Economics of Feasible Socialism Revisited*, 30.

21 "To be a self, then, *universally* and *necessarily* means to insist on one's alienation from others, that is, not to *be able* simply to identify oneself with the rest of humanity. Consequently, just by virtue of existing as a self, every self is an enemy of the revolution, since every self is a set of vested interests that *cannot* fulfill themselves without in some measure denying to others the right to fulfill their own needs." Russon, *The Self and Its Body*, 98.

22 *PS*, H591 / 390.

23 "Nothing guarantees that it will embody the general will. It is therefore a matter of principle to suspect it. It cannot act, since any positive action, inasmuch as it is its own work, excludes from itself the activity of others." Hyppolite, *Studies on Marx and Hegel*, 57.

24 *PR*, §5A.

25 On this topic, see Sandel, *Democracy's Discontents: America in Search of a Public Philosophy*, and Arendt, *On Revolution*, especially chapter 6, "The Revolutionary Tradition and Its Lost Treasure."

CHAPTER SEVEN

1 Kant, *Critique of Pure Reason*, A443 / B473–A447 / B473.

2 Since freedom is continually self-surpassing, to be conservative is to cling to and defend a shape of freedom that has been surpassed or that is in the process of being surpassed in favour of a new and more sophisticated form of freedom.

3 *PS*, H594 / 321.

4 "Culture posits human identity as realizable only through culture – through cultivation." Russon, *Reading Hegel's Phenomenology*, 141.

5 My analysis here is influenced by Russon, *Human Experience*, especially 61–8 and *Bearing Witness to Epiphany*, especially 53–9; and Ciavatta, *Spirit, the Family, and the Unconscious*.

6 *PS*, M441 / 290.

7 *PR*, §158.

8 *PR*, §175.
9 *PR*, §174.
10 *PR*, §174A.
11 *PR*, §175R and §175A.
12 For a good discussion of this, see Winfield, *Reason and Justice*, chapter 9, "The Family as an Institution of Freedom." See also Winfield, *The Just Family*, Ciavatta, *Spirit, the Family and the Unconscious*, and Russon, *Human Experience*.
13 In the *Philosophy of Right*, part C of section 1, "The Family" is entitled, "The Upbringing of Children and the Dissolution of the Family." The family is said to "disintegrate" in *PR* §179 and 181.
14 *PR*, §182.
15 Ibid.
16 *PR*, §189.
17 *PR*, §157.
18 *PR*, §183.
19 Ciavatta explores this issue with insight in *Spirit, the Family, and the Unconscious*, especially 92–3.
20 *PR*, §184.
21 *PR*, §261R.
22 *PR*, §§209–56.
23 *PR*, §258R. Here and in other citations from Nisbet's translation, I have changed the translation of *der Einzelnen* and its cognates to "singular selves" or "singular" in order to preserve Hegel's explicit reference to the quantitative concept (singularity, particularity, and universality) which is so decisive to his thinking here. Here I follow the lead of the Hegel Translation Group.
24 *PR*, §258R.
25 *PR*, §258A.
26 See, for example, Kolb, *Critique of Pure Modernity* and Henrich, "Logical Form and Real Totality."
27 Hegel articulates these universal, particular, and singular characteristics of the concept of the state at *EL*, §198.
28 *PS*, M177 / 127.
29 *SL*, 439 / 75.
30 In chapter 2, I outlined three forms of contradiction, but the first was the classical form articulated by the understanding (*Verstand*) which was first named by Plato and Aristotle. This form of contradiction is not "vital," as opposed to the two forms of vital contradiction that animate reason (*Vernunft*).

31 Heraclitus, Fragment 51, Kirk and Raven, *The Presocratic Philosophers*, 193.
32 Of course, Freud is decisive in this line of argumentation. See, for example, *Civilization and Its Discontents*.
33 De Beauvoir, *The Ethics of Ambiguity*, 37.

CHAPTER EIGHT

1 Shlomo Avineri was decisive in revealing these aspects of Hegel's social theory in *Hegel's Theory of the Modern State*, especially 87–98. Hegel indeed foreshadows Marx on this point, though his failure to develop a theory of exploitation and to draw the conclusion that capitalism will thwart the common good are the key weaknesses of his political philosophy, as we shall see.
2 Houlgate, *An Introduction to Hegel*, chapter 8, "Freedom, Rights and Civility."
3 Georg Lukacs, *History and Class Consciousness*, "Preface to the New Edition," xxiii.
4 Avineri, *Hegel's Theory of the Modern State*, 94n32.
5 Harris, "The Social Ideal of Hegel's Economic Theory," 190.
6 For example, in the "Spiritual Animal Kingdom" in the *Phenomenology*, "The work *is*, i.e., it exists for other individualities, and is for them an alien reality, which they must replace by their own in order to obtain by *their* action the consciousness of *their* unity with reality; in other words, *their* interest in the work which stems from *their* original nature, is something different from this work's *own* particular interest, which is thereby converted into something different. Thus the work is, in general, something perishable, which is obliterated by the counter-action of other forces and interests, and really exhibits the reality of the individuality as vanishing rather than as achieved." *PS* M405 / 267.
7 *PR*, §182A.
8 Ibid.
9 *PR*, §185.
10 *PR*, §191A.
11 Adam Smith, *An Inquiry into the Nature and Causes of the Wealth of Nations*.
12 For an excellent discussion of this issue, see Harris, "The Social Ideal of Hegel's Economic Theory," 187–212.
13 *VPR* 1819, 194 / *PR*, 453.
14 *PR*, §245.

15 Recall that Hegel also used the term rabble to describe the fate of the Condition of Right qua "Roman Realm" in the *Philosophy of Right*, §357.
16 *PR*, §245. For an engaging and original exploration of the rabble, see Frank Ruda, *Hegel's Rabble: An Investigation into Hegel's Philosophy of Right*.
17 *PR*, §244.
18 "The actuality preserves its determinate being through self-consciousnesses' *own* externalization [*Entäusserung*] and abandonment of essence, which in the devastation which rules in the world of Right, appears to self-consciousness to be brought about from the external violence of the elements let loose." *PS*, H484 / 321.
19 *VPR*19, 194–6 / *PR*, 453–4. Of course, Marx makes much of this alien force, which is both the product of human activity and its persecutor. It is the key to his notion of alienated labour and the fetishism of commodities. See, respectively, *Economic and Philosophic Manuscripts of 1844*, in Tucker, *The Marx-Engels* Reader, 70–81 and *Capital*, 1:163–77.
20 *A*, 260 / 337.
21 *PR*, §187R. The whole sentence reads, "Only in this way is the spirit *at home* and *with itself* in ... *externality* as such."
22 *PR*, §185.
23 *A*, 260 / 337.
24 *VPR* 1819, 196 / *PR* 454.
25 *PR*, §194.
26 *PR*, §194.
27 *PR*, §197.
28 Ibid.
29 *PR*, §194.
30 *PR*, §192.
31 *PR*, §192A.
32 *PS*, M69 / 51.
33 *PS*, M177 / 127.
34 *PR*, §203.
35 I will give a more detailed study of the Movement of Landless Workers in Brazil in chapter 11.
36 *PR*, §205.
37 *PR*, §§298–315.
38 *PR*, §204.
39 *PR*, §238.
40 *PR*, §239.

41 *PR*, §229A.
42 *PR*, §239.
43 *PR*, §242–9.
44 *PR*, §228R.
45 *PR*, §244.
46 *PR*, 1819 194–6/ 453.
47 There is a lively and important debate on Hegel's racism. See, for example, Robert Bernasconi's "Will the Real Kant Please Stand Up," and the exchange between Bernasconi and Joseph McCarney, "Exchange: Hegel's Racism?" 32–7. See also Sandra Bonetto's detailed review of Hegel's texts on the issue, "Race and Racism in Hegel – An Analysis." In my view, Hegel was undoubtedly racist in the sense that he held naive and condescending views of non-European peoples, but that he does not hold any systematic views about the relationship of biological race and the capacity for human freedom. Indeed, his philosophical system, as we have seen, insists that mind learns to transcend its natural immediacy.
48 *PR*, §242R.
49 *VPR* 1817, 125 / *PR* 452.
50 *PR*, §198.
51 *JR*, 444 / 232.
52 *PR*, 253R.
53 *VPR* 1817, 143 / *PR*, 455.
54 Ibid.
55 *PR*, §253.
56 *PR*, §185A.
57 *PR*, §185.
58 Žižek insightfully articulates the relations of desire and capitalist consumption in, for example, *The Fragile Absolute*, especially 11–40.
59 *PR*, §253R.
60 *PR*, §252.
61 *PR*, §255.
62 See *PR*, §273R and *NR*, §135R.
63 *NR*, §135R.
64 *PR*, §290A.
65 For a good discussion of this issue, see David MacGregor, *Hegel and Marx: After the Fall of Communism*, 182–5.
66 *PR*, 21 / 26.

CHAPTER NINE

1 See, for example, Robert Nozick, *Anarchy, State and Utopia*.
2 *PR*, §35A.
3 *PR*, §35R.
4 *PR*, §35A.
5 *PR*, §57.
6 *PR*, §44.
7 *PR*, §51A.
8 *PR*, §§54–8.
9 *PR*, §46.
10 For an excellent discussion of Hegel's theory of property, see Jay Lampert, "Locke, Fichte, and Hegel on the Right to Property," especially 57–73.
11 *PR*, §127A.
12 *PR*, §49.
13 *PR*, §324.
14 *PR*, §46A.
15 *PS*, H477 / 316.
16 *PS*, H 480 / 317–18.
17 *PS*, H 480 / 318.
18 *PH*, 317 / 384.
19 "Whatsoever then he removes he removes out of the state that nature hath provided, and left it in, he hath mixed labour with, and joined to it something that is his own, and thereby makes it his property." Locke, *Second Treatise on Government*, chapter 5, §27.
20 See Russon on property right in *Bearing Witness to Epiphany*, 95–105.
21 C.B. Macpherson, *Property*, 2.
22 Ibid.
23 See, for example, Macpherson, *Property: Mainstream and Critical Positions*, 10.
24 Ibid.
25 Ibid., 5.
26 Ibid.
27 *PR*, §46A.
28 See Alexander Bajt, "Social Ownership," in Horvat et al., 151–3 for an articulation of this distinction.
29 Ibid., 159. It is absolutely necessary to point out, however, that this redistribution cannot be complete, for this would be tantamount to reducing the rate of profit to zero.

30 *PR*, §44.

31 "Even primitive societies make" the "distinction between property and mere physical possession ... This holds for land or flocks or the produce of the hunt which were held in common, and for such individual property as there was." Macpherson, *Property,* 3.

32 Marx, "Critique of the Gotha Program," in Tucker, *The Marx-Engels Readers*, 531.

33 David Kolb seems to be on the verge of drawing the same conclusion as I have when he says, "Being capable of property is not a quality an individual can possess by himself. Individuals in civil society recognize one another as people capable of putting their freedom into objects they own. My recognition of you as capable of owning property, which I respect as you respect mine – that structure of mutual recognition is carried by a whole system of contract and exchange." *Critique of Pure Modernity,* 26–7.

34 Indeed, we could go on to discuss the participation of nature in the substance of Spirit.

35 In fact, I take this to be close to Hegel's own conclusion. I see little evidence, however, that Hegel had a hidden political ideal of something that might correspond to Marx's notion of communism, especially because there is no textual evidence for it and, moreover, Hegel has no objection to wage-labour. See David MacGregor, *The Communist Ideal in Hegel and Marx*. See also John McCumber, "Contradictions and Resolution in the State: Hegel's Covert View."

36 I submit the arguments I propose here and in the rest of this text as a legitimate reading of Marx's famous claim that "*Communsim* is the *positive* abolition of *private property*, or *human self-alienation*, and thus the real *appropriation* of *human* nature through and for man." *Economic and Philosophic Manuscripts of 1844,* in Bottomore, 155. I concur with the commentators who insist that Marx has no intention of eliminating "private property" altogether. Richard Schacht, for example, states that Marx "is commonly thought to have advocated the complete abolition of private property. This is a profoundly mistaken interpretation of his position as he sets it forth in the 'Manuscripts.'" Schacht, *Alienation*, 85. Schacht argues that Marx readily adopts the Hegelian account of property and individual will (personality). "Marx even retains," Schacht continues, "the Hegelian emphasis upon the importance of property" and "accepts Hegel's contention that property is essential to the realization of personality and urges instead its 'genuine appropriation.'" (This term is taken from the *1844 Manuscripts,* 153). Schacht, moreover, contends that the "crude communism" of Proudhon

and others criticized by Marx is that form of *flawed communism* that rejects all private property. (See *Manuscripts,* 152–5). However, Schacht draws our attention to a key issue. Marx claims, once again, that "The supersession [*Aufhebung*] of private property is, therefore, the complete emancipation of all the human qualities and senses." *Manuscripts,* 160. This passage might be interpreted to mean that private property, in the terms I am proposing in this section, is compatible with his notion of communism.

37 Bajt gives the Marxist version of the same claim I am making here. "Relations of distribution are the reflection of property relations, says Marx. Hence we can determine property relations only if we know the distribution relations." Property involves the question of "how the national product must be allocated." Bajt, "Social Ownership," 155.

38 *PS*, M26 / 20.

39 It is worth noting Hegel's notion of the "cunning of reason" at this point, for it may well be taken as evidence that Hegel's philosophy of emerging self-consciousness is not meant to be applied to the political realm. He says, after all, "This may be called the *cunning of reason*, – that it sets the passions to work for itself, while that which develops its existence through such impulsion pays the penalty and suffers loss." *PH* 33 / 49. Yet Hegel's supposed view that it is mere passion, rather than self-conscious action, that determines action is exaggerated, if not altogether wrong. Robespierre and Jefferson were no doubt motivated by their passion, but by a passionate commitment to an idea whose time had come. The juxtaposition of passion and self-conscious purposefulness is an antinomy of the understanding. Reason allows for no such dualism. For an excellent interpretation of Hegel's philosophy of history as "reasonable," see Réal Fillion, *Multicultural Dynamics and the Ends of History*.

40 Marx, *Contribution to the Critique of Hegel's Philosophy of Right*, http://www. marxists.org/archive/marx/works/download/Marx_Critique_of_Hegels_Philosophy_of_Right.pdf.

41 Noam Chomsky and Edward S. Herman, *Manufacturing Consent*.

CHAPTER TEN

1 For a detailed exploration of this journey, see Taylor, *Sources of the Self*.

2 Sandel not only skilfully traces the political and philosophical themes but demonstrates an intimate familiarity with and understanding of American history in general and American judicial history in particular.

3 Marx and Engels, *Manifesto*, in *The Marx-Engels Reader*, 475.

4 See Marx, *Capital*, 1: 340–416. Marx's statement about the "committee" of the "bourgeoisie" from the *Manifesto* should be read as generally true enough to be an effective slogan in political exhortation, but certainly not true enough to be a rigorous theoretical claim. Hence the far more nuanced stance in *Capital*.

5 Sandel, *Democracy's Discontents*, especially chapter 2, "Rights and the Neutral State."

6 Marx, *Capital*, 1: 449.

7 Marx, *Capital*, 1: 530.

8 See, for example, Taylor, *Hegel and Modern Society*; Winfield, *Reason and Justice*; and Kolb, *The Critique of Pure Modernity*.

9 I will defend the notion that capitalist wage-labour is exploitation in the next section.

10 Ernesto Laclau and Chantal Mouffe's work *Hegemony and Socialist Strategy* is a tightly argued refutation of this form of Marxist argumentation.

11 I do not intend to claim that Marx himself adhered to a deterministic notion of the fall of capitalism and the communist revolution. Sometimes he writes with great confidence about this, but there are many other respects, such as his refusal to articulate the character of communist society, in which he steadfastly refuses to participate in what will be the business of future generations to decide.

12 Marx's articulation of the theory of exploitation is most thoroughly stated in *Capital*, 1: 247–339. It is also neatly summarized in sections 6 to 14 of his lecture "Value, Price and Profit" which is oddly not included in many standard Marx anthologies. See Marx, *Value, Price and Profit*. Excerpts are in *The Portable Karl Marx* and available at http://www.marxists.org/archive/marx/works/1865/value-price-profit/.

13 "Socially necessary labour-time is the labour-time required to produce any use-value under the conditions of production normal for a given society and with the average degree of skill and intensity of labour prevalent in that society." *Value, Price and Profit*, 129. For a good discussion of this concept, see Mandel, *An Introduction to Marxist Economic Theory*, 32–6.

14 Marx, *Capital*, 1: 326.

15 Mandel, *An Introduction to Marxist Economic Theory*, 36.

16 Marx, *Capital*, 1: 728.

17 Ibid., 272.

18 Ibid.

19 Ibid., 680.
20 *PR*, §67.
21 Winfield thinks that these issues are complicated by the fact that Hegel's system is prescriptive whereas Marx's is descriptive. *Reason and Justice*, 211. I think that there is no doubt that Marx tries to evade this complicated problem by siding with the latter – resulting in familiar problems of justice and normativity in Marxist theory. Winfield is wrong, however, to place Hegel in the prescriptive camp because the distinction itself is undialectical – it is an antinomy of the understanding. That is, it is the understanding that divides theoretical discourse into the descriptive and prescriptive. *Vernunft* is phenomenological and thus recognizes the imperatives that lurk in any and all putatively empirical description.
22 Winfield, *Reason and Justice*, especially 80–2 and 116–19.
23 Ibid., 216–17.
24 Marx, *Capital*, 1:195–6.
25 For a solid version of this argument, see Roemer, *Free to Lose*, 47–51. For a detailed examination, see Ian Steedman, ed., *The Value Controversy*.
26 This does not apply to pension plan investments, which are not made up of surplus income but of deferred income to cover the needs of the worker between retirement and death.
27 Roemer, *Free to Lose*, 20, 51. See also Roemer, *A General Theory of Exploitation and Class*. Jan Elster and G.A. Cohen also argue for theories of exploitation that do not rest on the labour theory of value. See Elster, *Making Sense of Marx*, and Cohen, *Karl Marx's Theory of History*.
28 Winfield, *Reason and Justice*, 218.
29 There are many important and complex issues that arise with respect to exploitation. For example, should "innate" talents, hard work, risk-taking, entrepreneurial ability, and so on merit greater shares, and if so to what degree? For discussions of these issues by Marxist writers, see Elster, *Making Sense of Marx*, 216–33; Roemer, *Free to Lose* and *A General Theory of Exploitation and Class*; and Schweickart, *After Capitalism*.
30 *PR*, §57R and A. For a good discussion of this, see Wood, *Hegel's Ethical Thought*, 97–9.
31 *PR*, §57R.
32 *PR*, §187R
33 Once again, this is not a teleological claim. As I will argue in more detail in chapter 11, dialectics posits a future, a horizon of possibility, by which it

recognizes and addresses its contradictions. However, this future is immanent in the present and does not refer to a non-temporal or a priori standard.

34 Wood, *Democracy against Capitalism*, 44.

35 I will study the MST in much more detail in the next chapter.

36 Indeed, arguably it sometimes did not liberate them from exploitation. It is possible to argue that the Soviet elite received income disproportionate to their contribution, and that workers laboured to support this elite. See Roemer's analysis of exploitation in state socialist societies in *Free to Lose*, 139–43.

37 For a detailed argument to this effect, see "Socialism and the Soviet Experience" in Nove, *The Economics of Feasible Socialism Revisited*. See also Roemer, *A Future for Socialism*, 37–45. Also, Schweickart, *After Capitalism*.

38 Marx, *On the Jewish Question*, in Tucker, *The Marx-Engels Reader*, 46.

39 Ibid., 50.

40 From the point of view of modern human rights, societies that are sexist and patriarchal are, ipso facto, societies of domination, but they do not necessarily practise the *exploitation* of women (in Marx's sense of the word).

41 See Wood, "The Demos Versus 'We, the People': From Ancient to Modern Conceptions of Citizenship," in *Democracy against Capitalism*, 204–37.

42 Since Marx and Marxists tend to neglect the cultivation of freedom, they must overemphasize the role of ideology. For them it is the dominant class's ideology, in addition to its means of physical coercion, that cements a system of exploitation. The emphasis on ideology becomes even stronger in the twentieth century, when Marxists, such as those in the Frankfurt School, had to explain the failure of revolution to spread beyond the Soviet Union.

43 For a good discussion of the corporations in a similar vein to the one I am developing here, see MacGregor, *Hegel and Marx after the Fall of Communism*, 112–40.

CHAPTER ELEVEN

1 MacGregor comes to a similar conclusion in *Hegel and Marx*, 175–81.

2 *PR*, 23.

3 Marx, *Manifesto*, in *The Marx-Engels Reader*, 497–500.

4 "Here is Rhodes, jump here," from Aesop's Fables.

5 *PR*, 21–2 / 26.

6 It may be that Hegel is particularly emphatic about this point in the preface to the *PR* precisely in order to reassure the conservative censors of his day (whose superiors had already dismissed some faculty for subversion). However, Hegel is systematically anti-utopian. See, for example, his discussion of the "ought" in the *SL*, 131–5 / 144–8 and his condemnation of "Law of the Heart and the Frenzy of Self-Conceit" in the *PS*, M367–80 / 244–51. Of course, it was also the anti-teleological premises of Hegel's dialectic that so strongly motivated Marx to condemn utopian socialism, notwithstanding Marx's somewhat overconfident claims about the future in some texts. See the *Manifest of the Communist Party* on both counts.

7 One of Hegel's key philosophical goals is to "reconcile" human beings with their society by demonstrating its inherent rationality. For an excellent text on this theme that avoids turning Hegel into a conservative, see Michael O. Hardimon, *Hegel's Social Philosophy*.

8 This is commonly determined as the priority of right over good. The classic expositor of right-based political philosophy is Kant. See, for example, "On the Common Saying: 'This May Be True in Theory, but It Does Not Apply in Practice" in Reiss, *Kant: Political Writings*, 67–72. John Rawls's formulation is the basic contemporary text. *A Theory of Justice*, 27–33. For an excellent critique of this position from within the liberal tradition, see Sandel, *Liberalism and the Limits of Justice*, especially 184–218.

9 For an interesting immanent critique of the free, choosing self, see Charles Taylor's call for the "retrieval " of the "authenticity" of the individual will in *The Malaise of Modernity*, chapter 1.

10 For a detailed discussion of these failings of capitalism, see David Schweikart, *After Capitalism*, especially chapters 4 and 5.

11 From a more mainstream position, Michael Sandel responds, as we have seen, to the same kind of preoccupation. "From the standpoint of the republican tradition, the demise of the political economy of citizenship constituted a concession, a deflation of American ideals, a loss of liberty. Republican political theory teaches that to be free is to share in governing a political community that controls its own fate. Self-government in this sense requires political communities that control their destinies, and citizens who identify sufficiently with those communities to think and act with a view to the common good. Cultivating in citizens the virtue, independence, and shared understandings such civil engagement requires is a central aim of republican politics. To abandon the formative ambition is thus to abandon the project of liberty as the republican tradition conceives it." *Democracy's Discontent*, 274.

12 Adam Przeworksi argues that the acceptance of what I have called the "ceiling" was a compromise made by organized labour and its political parties with capital. Labour restrains itself from seeking control over the means of production in return for the commitment of capital to reinvest for the sake of economic growth and the provision of always improving wages and working conditions. See *Capitalism and Social Democracy*, 29–38, 172–82. See also Antonio Negri and Michael Hardt, *Labor of Dionysus: A Critique of the State Form*, especially chapter 3, "Labor in the Constitution." For an excellent account of the changes wrought in the compromise between labour and capital in the "new capitalism," see Marta Harnecker, *Tornar Possível o Impossível*, 274–85.

13 For good accounts of this concentration of power, see Horvat, *The Political Economy of Socialism*, 11–20; and Przeworski, *Capitalism and Social Democracy*, 277–81.

14 Laclau and Mouffe, *Hegemony and Socialist Strategy*, 155ff. It will also be evident from my text that, even if I agree with Laclau and Mouffe on the notion of a democratic imaginary, I do not consider their views on capitalism, on the dialectic in general, or on Hegel's dialectic to be convincing.

15 Arguably, the closest a nation has come to implementing the kind of socialism of which I am about to speak is Yugoslavia prior to the collapse of Eastern European communism.

16 The major contemporary alternative to worker-managed, market socialism on the left is anarchist economics, in particular the "parecon" of Michael Albert (available on-line at http://www.zcommunications.org/zparecon/pareconlac.htm). Parecon involves the radical democratization of the economy with consultation of all citizens on need and production. This proposal strikes me as overwhelmingly complex and thus impossible to implement, even in small communities, much less in entire nations. For a detailed debate about Parecon between Albert and David Shweickhart, see http://www.zcommunications.org/znet/zdebatealbertvsschweickart.htm. See also Daniel Guérin, *Anarchism* and Chris Spanos, ed., *Real Utopia*.

17 See, for example, Branko Horvat, *The Yugoslav Economic System* and *The Political Economy of Socialism*; M. Marković, *From Affluence to Praxis*; J. Vanek, *Self-Management*, *The General Theory of Labour-Managed Market Economies* , *The Participatory Economy*, and *The Labor-Managed Economy*; B. Horvat, M. Marković, R. Supek, and H. Kramer, *Self-Governing Socialism*. See also W. Brus, *The Economics and Politics of Socialism*.

18 See, for example, Alec Nove, *The Economics of Feasible Socialism Revisited*;

Schweikart, *After Capitalism*; David P. Ellerman, *Property and Contract Economics*.

19 Horvat distinguishes three socioeconomic systems, "capitalism," the "etatism" of Soviet and Chinese communism, and the "worker-managed" socialism of Yugoslavia. See his *The Political Economy of Socialism*, part one, "A Critique of Contemporary Socioeconomic Systems."

20 Horvat, *The Political Economy of Socialism*, 235.

21 Ibid., 235–6.

22 For a detailed examination of the concentration of power in state-socialist societies, see Nove, *The Economics of Feasible Socialism Revisited*, chapter 2, "Socialism and the Soviet Experience," 73–126.

23 Horvat, *The Political Economy of Socialism*, 48.

24 Ibid., 236.

25 Ibid., 237.

26 The right to work cannot be easily assured. There is a relationship between worker-managed socialism and unemployment that Nove demonstrates formally. "Compare a capitalist, or a Soviet manager, with a workers' council, assuming that the council is interested in maximizing net revenue per worker. Income of workers according to the model is based upon the sum arrived at by dividing net revenue by the numbers employed. There is no material interest in taking on extra labour if the effect is to diminish this figure. It is easy to visualize that in an otherwise identical situation a capitalist concerned with profit, or a Soviet manager anxious to fulfil plans, would employ additional labour." Nove, *The Economics of Feasible Socialism*, 147.

27 Horvat, *The Political Economy of Socialism*, 237.

28 Ibid.

29 Alexander Bajt says (once again), "private ownership of productive forces, which makes possible the appropriation of incomes by their owners in accordance with the prices that the factors obtain in the corresponding economy, implies the exploitation of the owners of less productive factors by the owners of more productive factors. Nevertheless, there is an essential difference here between the owners of land and capital, on the one hand, and the owners of work capabilities, on the other. The point is not so much that some obtain products without any real contribution to production (in the sense of effort), while others obtain products on the basis of it. What is more significant is that the accumulation of work capabilities in one person, even when it is a matter of entrepreneurship, is clearly limited by the impor-

tance of these factors themselves, while the accumulation of land and capital is not limited in this way. Hence private ownership of land and capital allows the concentration of power over owners of other factors, which is the basis of class social orders. Accordingly, private ownership of land and capital, insofar as they are not limited by exogenous factors, constantly *give rise to class exploitation.*" Bajt, "Social Ownership – Collective and Personal," in Horvat et al., *Self-Governing Socialism,* 2:157–8.

30 Ibid., 162–3.

31 Horvat, *The Political Economy of Socialism*, 239.

32 Horvat on this point: "The organizational/political goal of a socialist enterprise is to maximize democracy in decision making together with the efficiency of implementation. Traditional organizational theory considers this double goal to be inherently contradictory. It is considered equally contradictory as a coupling of market and planning. A socialist organizational theory will treat the two goals as complementary. This has to be shown." Horvat, *The Political Economy of Socialism*, 239.

33 Worker-managed co-operatives have a long history, dating back especially to the early years of the nineteenth century as inspired by, for example, Saint-Simon, Fourier, Proudhon, and Owen. For summaries of this history, see Horvat, *The Political Economy of Socialism,* 109–73; Vanek, "Introduction" to *Self-Management*, especially 16–21; and Julian Le Grand and Saul Estrin, *Market Socialism*, 26–9, 168–9. For a selection of classic texts, manifestos, and constitutions in the history of worker management, see Horvat et al., *Self-Governing Socialism* 1, part one, "Historical Development."

34 See note 16 above for a list of texts by these authors.

35 Nove, *The Economics of Feasible Socialism.*

36 For an excellent collection of essays that propose a variety of forms of market socialism, see Pranab Bardhan and John Roemer, eds., *Market Socialism.* See also John Roemer, *Free to Lose, A Future for Socialism*, and *Equal Shares.*

37 The very high unemployment and poverty rates that have plagued Brazil for centuries have spawned a large and highly organized co-operative movement under the umbrella of the Movimento dos Trabalhadores Rurais Sem Terras do Brasil. In English, see Sue Branford and Jan Rocha, *Cutting the Wire*, and Wendy Wolford and Angus Wright, *To Inherit the Earth.* In Portuguese, see João Pedro Stedile and Bernardo Mançano Fernandes, *Brava Gente*, and Bernardo Mançano Fernandes, *A Formação do MST no Brasil.*

38 Winfield argues, on essentially Hegelian grounds, that all configurations of

worker-managed co-operatives will compromise "personal freedom." Winfield does not, however, consider worker-managed co-operatives within a configuration of socialist civil democracy as I have articulated it here. Individuals herein all still choose their career and so on, and have far more personal freedom in their workplaces. See *Reason and Justice*, 128–9.

39 I construct this list on the basis of the following five sources: Jaroslav Vanek, introduction to Vanek, *Self-Mangement*, especially 26–36; Vanek, *The Economics of Worker's management*, chapter 4, "The Worker-Managed Enterprise as an Institution"; Branko Horvat, *The Political Economy of Socialism*, 239–50; and Nove, *The Economics of Feasible Socialism*, part 5, "Feasible Socialism."

40 Saul Estrin, "Workers' Cooperatives: Their Merits and Their Limitations," 186, also 180–2. See also Peter Abell, "An Equitarian Market Socialism," 95. Both essays are in Le Grand and Estrin, *Market Socialism.* I return to the issue of investment in the discussion of the "shelter organization" below.

41 Some worker-managed co-operatives are established on a share basis, including Mondragron (see below). For a discussion of this issue, see Estrin, "Workers' Cooperatives" in Le Grand and Estrin, *Market Socialism*, 172–4.

42 Vanek, "Introduction" to Vanek, *Self-Management*, 34.

43 The size of worker-managed co-operatives plays a key role in the degree to which democratic participation is realistically possible. Within the confines of economies of scale, then, the general rule is that economic units be as small as possible.

44 The benefits of participation can easily be exaggerated. Nove comments, "Yugoslavia's experience suggests that the desire to participate is by no means universal. Many workers and other staffs are not keen to sit on committees, to acquire the detailed knowledge that would enable them to be in any significant sense co-managers. It is for this reason above all else that the management has very considerable power. It is tempting, but misleading, to attribute this lack of interest to faults in the system. A man or woman who works conscientiously may have other interests." Nove, *The Economics of Feasible Socialism*, 145–6. Indeed, I have argued that human beings are fundamentally preoccupied by their struggles for recognition. The character of workplace relations is but one part of the totality of one's social relations and there is no inherent reason to think it should be given priority over one's relations with friends, lovers, and children, and other pursuits.

45 Nove, 230–8.

46 "The basic organizational unit is not the enterprise but the work group ... I shall call it the *work unit.* A work unit is not only a group of workers but also a definite subsystem in the production system known as the enterprise." Horvat, 240–1.

47 The decentralization of power in worker-managed socialism presents many problems that must be dealt with at regional and federal levels of government, and thus decentralization should not be exaggerated. For a discussion of problems arising in Yugoslavia, see Nove, *The Economics of Feasible Socialism*, 149.

48 Horvat, 242.

49 Ibid., 242–3.

50 "Whenever the decisions of a work unit affect substantially the interests of other work units, the right of decision making ought to be delegated to the next higher level. This is the justification for establishing a *workers' council* as the second level decision-making body." Ibid., 241.

51 D.D. Milenkovitch, for his part, calls the combination of work units and work councils, as well as any other bodies of worker management, the "workers' collective." *The Worker Managed Enterprise*, 187–91. This is also essentially the structure of MST co-operatives, where work units are responsible for tasks that range from basic agricultural work to running the schools and health care centres. The Israeli kibbutzim operate on the basis of committees that are responsible to a "general assembly." See H. Barkai, "The Kibbutz: An Experiment in Microsocialism," in Vanek, *Self-Management*, 213–26.

52 Horvat identifies the following auxiliary "commissions" of most large co-operatives: the commissions of grievances, work responsibility, employment, income distribution, research and development, investment, housing, and social welfare. *The Political Economy of Socialism*, 243.

53 Ibid., 244.

54 Ibid., 241. For a detailed account of the conflicts and problems that typically emerged in Yugoslav co-operatives, and the means by which resolution procedures developed, see Horvat, 250–62.

55 Horvat says that there must be a "separation of two different spheres of activity; the interest sphere and the professional sphere. The former consists of policy decisions, the latter of professional work and administrative routine. Policy decisions are legitimized by political authority; executive and administrative work, by professional authority. The former represent value judgments;

the latter, technical implementation. In the interest sphere, the rule of one man, one vote applies; in the professional sphere, vote is weighted by professional competence." *The Political Economy of Socialism*, 241.

56 Ibid., 244–5.

57 "Since each worker now has a stake in the profit of the firm, material incentives can act to reinforce a fundamental change in attitude toward work. The consequence of this reduced alienation and increased involvement may therefore be substantial gains in the productive efficiency of the organization." Estrin, "Worker's Cooperatives," in Le Grand and Estrin, *Market Socialism*, 171. The problems with tying wages to the performance of one's co-operative, however desirable, are many. Nove summarizes this issue as follows: "If the notion of self-management is to have any meaning, then success or failure must affect income. Income will then vary significantly according to whether the enterprise is or is not commercially successful. But this depends on a variety of causes, many of them quite outside the control of the workers: market fluctuations, imposition of a tariff by a foreign country, and so on. It may indeed have little to do with effort, or with productivity ... Yet there is among workers the not unreasonable feeling that work of the same quality and intensity deserves the same reward, whatever may be the commercial result of the given enterprise's operations." *The Economics of Feasible Socialism*, 143–4.

58 "Although inequalities may remain between workers in sectors of low and high profitability, the replacement at the economy-wide level of a small owning group by the labour force as a whole will act to equalize the distribution of income. In addition, the distribution of income between people of different skills within each enterprise becomes a matter for internal debate and vote under self-management, rather than being imposed from above by management. While the outcome will still reflect to some extent the market position of those with special skills, it is likely to be more egalitarian than pertains in capitalist firms." Estrin, "Workers' Cooperatives," in *Market Socialism*, 171.

59 "The returns on capital and land should in their entirety or at least predominantly be earmarked for accumulation – that is, creation of new capital assets – and not for individual consumption of any kind. In this way the fundamental problem of accumulation facing especially the developing economies is resolved, while at the same time the objection to personal capital income (non-labour income) on distributional grounds is eliminated. It can be shown that rates of accumulation attainable through this method are

quite considerable." Vanek, introduction to Vanek, *Self-Management*, 34–5.

60 See Przeworksi, *Capitalism and Social Democracy*, chapter 1.

61 The hiring of external labour is often necessary at times of higher work volume, but this opens up the possibility of discrimination between wage rights for members and non-members and seems to run counter to co-operative principles. See Estrin, "Workers' Cooperatives" in Le Grand and Estrin, *Market Socialism*, 174–84.

62 The goal of a society of common property is not to radically equalize income but to ensure that, to the highest degree possible, income arises from labour rather than other sources, and that inheritance does not create a class structure.

63 Nove, *The Economics of Feasible Socialism Revisited*, 213.

64 Vanek, introduction, *Self-Management*, 36.

65 Ibid.

66 While the co-operative, and not the shelter organization, has control of the capital, the shelter organization "is entitled to adequate remuneration at a rate reflecting the relative scarcity of that factor in the economy." The same conditions apply to productive land. Vanek, introduction, *Self-Management*, 34–5.

67 Due to the disincentives to investment in worker-managed co-operatives relative to capitalist corporations (see above), most financing in worker-managed socialism would be borrowed. Estrin proposes instead of the single shelter organization, a multitude of holding companies regulated by the state authority. See Estrin, "Workers' Cooperatives," in Le Grand and Estrin, *Market Socialism*, 181, 187–92.

68 Roemer, *A Future for Socialism*, especially 48–51 and 61–90; and Roemer, *Equal Shares*.

69 Vanek, introduction, *Self-Management*, 36.

70 See, for example, Centro de Investigaciones y Estudos de la Reforma Agraria, *Participatory Democracy in Nicaragua*, 1985.

71 There is a wide literature on this topic from within the liberal perspective. Michael Oakshott, "Political Education," in Sandel, *Liberalism and Its Critics*, and Sandel, *Democracy's Discontents*. Once again, Hannah Arendt discusses the isomorphism of American town-hall democracy and the original aspirations of the *soviets* in the Russian Revolution in the final chapter, "The Revolutionary Tradition and Its Lost Treasure," of *On Revolution*, 217–85. Of course, her observations require abstracting from the rather significant difference that the *soviets* were predicated on the elimination of

liberal-capitalist private property. In my view, the forces that motivate the centralization of power in capitalism overwhelm the non-economic institutions in civil society that promote democratization.

72 Recognizing this need, the MST founded its own university in São Paulo State, called the Escola Nacional Florestan Fernandes. It has five basic objectives: To "a) Elaborate an intellectual and political praxis that generates to the highest degree possible the scientific understanding necessary for the transformation of society; b) Stimulate social, political and economic organization in order to overcome internal challenges in the areas of agrarian reform; c) Develop leaders who can contribute to the construction of a just, fraternal, democratic and egalitarian society; d) Provide for the interchange of knowledge and experience with other worker organizations, both rural and urban; e) Develop the technical capacities of agrarian reform activists in the areas of greatest need to the Movement." The university's areas of study include everything from philosophy and politics to agricultural science and co-operative management. *Campanha: Escola Nacional Florestan Fernandes* (São Paulo: Publicações do Movimento dos Trabalhadores Rurais Sem Terra Do Brasil, 2001) my translation. The institutions of popular education in Brazil have as their founding theoretical basis the enormously influential texts of Brazilian educational philosopher Paulo Freire. See especially his *Pedagogy of the Oppressed.*

73 For much more detailed analyses of democratic structures in non-statist socialism than those I am about to give, see W. Brus, *Socialist Ownership and Political Systems*, 134–47; Horvat, *The Political Economy of Socialism,* 292–327; C.B. Macpherson, *Democratic Theory*; Mihailo Marković, "Self-Government and Planning," in Horvat et al., *Self-Governing Socialism* 1; and David Schweickart, *After Capitalism.*

74 Horvat, *The Political Economy of Socialism,* 293.

75 This idea has its formal roots in Hegel's claim that three estates must be represented in the assembly – the agricultural, the commercial, and the bureaucratic – which corresponded in logical form to the immediate unity of the family, the multiplicity of civil society, and the universal or mediated unity of the state respectively. See Hegel, *PR,* §§300–1.

76 John R. Lampe, *Yugoslavia as History*, 280.

77 With the exception of Yugoslavian socialism, the examples I cite refer to worker-managed co-operatives that exist within the context of capitalist competition. This presents all kinds of problems to co-operatives, including the effects of direct competition with capitalist corporations, retention of workers during periods of economic boom, retention of highly skilled workers,

and so on. These issues have serious ramifications for whether worker-managed socialism can emerge from within a capitalist society gradually or whether revolutionary action is ultimately necessary. I will not address this difficult issue here, but for excellent discussions of it see Estrin, "Workers' Cooperatives" in Le Grand and Estrin, *Market Socialism*, 174–92 and, above all, Horvat, *The Political Economy of Socialism*, part four, "The Period of Transition." Horvat develops separate theories of transition for developed capitalist countries, etatist socialist countries, and undeveloped capitalist societies.

78 The emergence of communism in pre-capitalist societies was, to say the least, a great surprise for orthodox Marxist theoreticians, for whom it was axiomatic that capitalist alienation is the necessary condition for the possibility of any viable communism. The need to develop Soviet industry and national power, in the face of enormous pressure from the West and ongoing civil war, made it imperative to centralize authority. It was assumed that this state of affairs would be temporary, pending the development of the Soviet Union and the achievement of revolutionary victories in Western Europe, especially in Germany. For interesting analyses of this phenomenon, see Maurice Merleau-Ponty, *Humanism and Terror*, and Ernesto Laclau and Chantal Mouffe, *Hegemony and Socialist Strategy*.

79 The authoritative account of the Latin American revolutionary left in the second half of the twentieth century is Jorge Castañeda, *Utopia Unarmed*. See also Walter LaFeber, *Inevitable Revolutions*.

80 For an excellent analysis of this problem see Przeworski, *Capitalism and Social Democracy*, 23–34.

81 The exemplar of this failure is Salvador Allende's socialist government of Chile, which found it impossible to implement socialist reform within the constraints of capitalist commodity markets and private capital accumulation and investment. For analysis of the failure of the economic program of Allende's government, see Alec Nove, *Socialism, Economics and Development*, 3–29, and Marta Harnecker, *Tornar Possível o Impossível*, 63–70.

82 In the past decade the electoral success of erstwhile socialist presidents in Venezuela and Bolivia has reopened the possibility of a state-centred solution. However, these efforts, even if partly successful, must always rely on co-operative action that builds from civil society upward.

83 See Andrew Arato and Jean L. Cohen's notion of "self-limitation" in *Civil Society and Political Theory*, 32, 57–8, 63.

84 See Vanek, *Self-Management*, and Horvat et al., *Self-Governing Socialism*, for an abundance of case studies.

85 This brief account draws on the following sources: John B. Allcock, *Explaining Yugoslavia*; Branko Horvat, *The Yugoslav Economic System*; John R. Lampe, *Yugoslavia as History*; Jan Vanek, *The Economics of Workers' Management*.

86 Accordingly, Tito was instrumental, along with Indian prime minister Jawaharwal Nehru and Egyptian president Gamal Abdel Nasser in the formation of the Non-Aligned Movement in the 1950s. The Non-Aligned Movement provided an excellent forum for the international promotion of worker-managed socialism.

87 This began with the new constitution of 1953, which shifted substantial powers to the workers' councils.

88 Of course, one should not be too sanguine about Yugoslavia's record here. There is certainly a history of political and cultural persecution.

89 Tito's government attempted to regulate small private enterprises in 1963. This led to many of these enterprises disappearing, but public protest forced Tito to repeal this policy.

90 Note the account of the first period of worker-management: "Yugoslavia's economy grew at a faster pace from 1953 until 1961 than most others in the world, including those of the Soviet bloc. The indicators ... are impressive indeed. The value of industrial production led the way with an average annual increase of 12.7 percent by official statistics, reduced only to 11.2 by ... critical recalculation ... Employment in the 'social sector' (industry and services plus state farms) grew from 1.8 to 3.2 million workers. Despite a modest increase in labor productivity that averaged only 3.9 percent, industrial wages rose by 6.2 percent a year and controlled prices just 3 percent." Per capita GDP grew (in 1966 prices) from 216 in 1950, to 333 in 1960 and 520 in 1970. Lampe, *Yugoslavia as History*, 272 and 289.

91 Enterprises with "more than 4,000 workers employed 62 percent of the labor force and those with over 125 workers employed 97 percent." The ten largest manufacturing and mining firms employed more than 30,000 workers each, and most of the largest 130 firms employed more than 10,000. The government tried to deal with this by allowing workers' councils to divide themselves. Lampe, *Yugoslavia as History*, 277, 310–12.

92 Of course, it is not hard to find examples of writers anxious to blame the ethnic conflict in Yugoslavia, at least in part, on socialism. "In the wake of the disintegration of the Yugoslav federation, and perhaps understandably so in view of the seriousness of the accompanying armed conflict, the attempt to provide an explanation has dwelt quite disproportionately upon

the factor of ethnic diversity. Nevertheless, I contend that no explanation which does not place at its heart economic factors deserves to be taken seriously." Allcock, *Explaining Yugoslavia,* 89.

93 My sources here are H. Barkai, "The Kibbutz: An Experiment in Microsocialism" in Vanek, *Self-Management.* This article is itself an adaptation of a chapter of *Israel and Arabs*; Eliezer Ben-Rafael, *Crisis and Transformation*; Daniel Gavron, *The Kibbutz*; Henry Near, *The Kibbutz Movement.*

94 Barkai, "The Kibbutz," 216.

95 Ibid., 218.

96 Near, *The Kibbutz Movement*, 2:343.

97 Avrahim Pavin, *The Kibbutz Movement.*

98 Editorial, "Kibbutz Reinvents Itself after 100 Years of History," *Taipai Times*, 16 November 2010, 9.

99 Barkai, "The Kibbutz," 222–5.

100 See Near, *The Kibbutz Movement*, 2:351–8. Certain kibbutzim have all but abandoned co-operation; others have seriously weakened it. Accordingly, in 1999 a movement of kibbutzim called the "Common Trend" was formed in an attempt to protect the following traditional kibbutz values: "joint ownership of the productive assets of the kibbutz; avoidance of any differentials in allowances or incomes, unless based on family size, seniority or special needs; comprehensive mutual assistance among members of the kibbutz; and cooperative and democratic management." Gavron, *The Kibbutz,* 276.

101 Cited from Mondragon's website: www.mondragon.mcc.es.

102 R. Oakeshott, "Mondragon: Spain's Oasis of Democracy," in Vanek, *Self-Management,* 290. This article originally appeared in the *Observer* colour supplement, 21 January 1973.

103 Oakshott, 292. The wage differential has been determined democratically at 3:1. Estrin, "Workers' Cooperatives," in Le Grand and Estrin, *Market Socialism*, 171–2.

104 H. Thomas and C. Logan, *Mondragon*, 161.

105 For a detailed yet brief study of Mondragon, see Schweickart, *After Capitalism*, especially 66–73.

106 In addition to the texts on the MST I have cited above, the information in this section is taken from a wide assortment of articles in *Revista Sem Terra*, São Paulo, and my own visits to MST settlements in Brazil.

107 José Vicente Tavares dos Santos, *Colonos do Vinho*,119–20 (my translation).

108 For a more detailed exposition of the structure of MST co-operatives, see

Aldiva Sales Diniz and Bruce Gilbert, "'Socialist Values' and Cooperation in Brazil's Movement of Landless Rural Workers," *Latin American Perspectives* 140, no. 4 (July 2013): 19–34; and Bernardo Mançao Fernandes, *A Formação do* MST *no Brasil,* 228–34.

109 Gramsci, *Prison Notebooks*, 108–10.

CONCLUSION

1 All the quotations from the *Science of Logic* in this conclusion are from *SL* 439–41 / 75–7.

2 Derived, of course, from Marx's eleventh thesis on Feuerbach: "The philosophers have only interpreted the world in various ways, the point, however, is to change it." Marx, *Theses on Feuerbach*, in *Marx-Engels Reader*, 145.

Bibliography

WORKS OF HEGEL

Aesthetics: Lectures on Fine Arts. 2 vols. Translated by T.M. Knox. Oxford: Clarendon Press, 1975/*Werke* 13–15

Die Philosophie des Rechts: Die Mitschriften Wannenmann, Heidelberg 1817–1818, und Homeyer, Berlin 1818–1819. Edited by K.-H. Itling. Stuttgart: Klett-Cotta Verlag 1983

Early Theological Writings. Translated by T.M. Knox and Richard Kroner. Philadelphia: University of Pennsylvania Press, 1971/*Theologische Jugendschriften*. Edited by Hermann Nohl. Tübingen: Mohr 1907

Elements of the Philosophy of Right. Translated by H.B. Nisbet. Edited by Allen W. Wood. Cambridge: Cambridge University Press 1991/*Werke* 7

Encyclopedia Logic. Translated by T.F. Geraets, W.A. Suchting, and H.S. Harris. Indianapolis: Hackett Publishing Company 1991/*Werke* 8

Hegel: Werke: Theorie Werkausgabe. Frankfurt: Suhrkamp Verlag 1970

Jenaer Realphilosophie (1805–1806). In *Hegel and the Human Spirit*. Translated by Leo Rauch. Detroit: Wayne State University Press 1983/Edited by J. Hoffmeister. Hamburg: Felix Meiner Verlag 1969

Lectures on the History of Philosophy. 3 vols. Translated by E.S. Haldane. Lincoln: University of Nebraska Press, 1995/*Werke* 18–20

Lectures on Natural Right and Political Science: The First Philosophy of Right. Translated by J. Michael Stewart and Peter C. Hodgson. Edited by the Staff of Hegel Archives. Berkeley: University of California Press 1995/*Vorlesungen über Naturrecht und Staatswissenschaft*. Volume 1, *Vorlesungen: Ausgewählte Nachschriften und Manuskripte*. Edited by C. Becker et al. Hamburg: Felix Meiner Verlag GmbH 1983

Lectures on the Philosophy of Religion. Edited by Peter C. Hodgson. Berkeley: University of California Press 1988/*Werke* 11–12

Phenomenology of Spirit. Translated by A.V. Miller. Oxford: Oxford University Press 1977/

Phänomenologie des Geistes. Hamburg: Felix Meiner Verlag 1988

Philosophie des Rechts: Die Vorlesung von 1819–1820. Edited by Dieter Henrich. Frankfurt: Suhrkamp Verlag 1983

Philosophy of History. Translated by J. Sibree. Buffalo: Prometheus Books 1991/*Werke* 12

Philosophy of Mind. Translated by A.V. Miller. Oxford: Oxford University Press 1971/*Werke* 10

Philosophy of Nature. Translated by A.V. Miller. Oxford: Oxford University Press, 1970/*Werke* 9

Political Writings. Edited by Laurence Dickey and H. B. Nisbet. Translated by H.B. Nisbet. Cambridge: Cambridge University Press 1999

Science of Logic. Translated by A.V. Miller. Atlantic Highlands: Humanities Press 1989/*Werke* 5–11

Spirit: Chapter Six of Hegel's Phenomenology of Spirit. Translated by The Hegel Translation Group, Trinity College, University of Toronto. Edited by Daniel E. Shannon. Indianapolis: Hackett Publishing Company 2001

System of Ethical Life and First Philosophy of Spirit. Edited and translated by H.S. Harris and T.M. Knox. Albany: State University of New York Press 1979/*System der Sittlichkeit*. Edited by George Lasson. 2nd ed. Hamburg: Felix Meiner Verlag1923. Reprinted in 1967 as vol. 144a, *Philosophische Bibliotek*, and *Jaenauer Systementwerfe* 1. Hamburg: Felix Meiner Verlag 1975

OTHER WORKS

Abell, Peter "An Equitarian Market Socialism." In Le Grand and Estrin, *Market Socialism*, 78–99

Adorno, Theodor. *The Culture Industry: Selected Essays on Mass Culture*. Edited by J. Bernstein. London: Routledge 1991

– *The Jargon of Authenticity*. Translated by Knut Tarnowski and Frederic Will. Evanston: Northwestern University Press 1973/*Jargon der Eigentlichkeit: Zur Deutschen Ideologie*. Frankfurt am Main: Suhrkamp Verlag 1964

– *Minima Moralia: Reflections from Damaged Life*. Translated by E.F.N. Jeffcott. London: Verso 1978/*Minima Moralia*. Frankfurt am Main: Suhrkamp Verlag 1951

– *Negative Dialectics*. Translated by E.B. Ashton. New York: Continuum 1990/ *Negative Dialektik*. Frankfurt am Main: Suhrkamp Verlag 1966
– *Prisms*. Translated by Samuel Weber and Shierry Weber. Cambridge: Massachusetts Institute of Technology Press 1981
– *Three Essays on Hegel*. Translated by Shierry Weber Nicholsen. Cambridge: Massachusetts Institute of Technology Press 1994/*Drei Studien zu Hegel*. Frankfurt am Main: Suhrkamp Verlag 1963
Adorno, Theodor, and Max Horkheimer. *Dialectic of Enlightenment*. Translated by John Cumming. New York: Continuum 1987/*Dialelektik der Aufklärung*. Frankfurt am Main: S. Fischer Verlag GmbH 1969 (1944)
Albert, Michael. *Parecon*. London: Verso 2003
Allcock, John B. *Explaining Yugoslavia*. New York: Columbia University Press 2000
Althusser, Louis. *Essays in Self-Criticism*. Translated by Graham Lock. London: NLB 1976
Althusser, Louis, and Étienne Balibar. *Reading Capital*. Translated by Ben Brewster. London: Verso 1997/*Lire le Capital*. Paris: François Maspero 1968
Arato, Andrew, and Jean L. Cohen. *Civil Society and Political Theory*. Cambridge: Massachusetts Institute of Technology Press 1992
Arato, Andrew, and Eike Gebhardt, eds. *The Frankfurt School Reader*. New York: Continuum 1982
Arendt, Hannah. *The Human Condition*. Chicago: University of Chicago Press 1968
– *The Origins of Totalitarianism*. New York: Harcourt, Brace, Jovanovich 1951
– *On Revolution*. New York: The Viking Press 1962
Aristotle. *Basic Works*. Edited by Richard McKeon. New York: Random House 1941
– *The Complete Works of Aristotle*. Edited by Jonathan Barnes. Princeton: Princeton University Press 1984
– *Nichomachean Ethics*. Translated by Martin Oswald. Upper Saddle River: Prentice Hall 1999
Aron, Raymond. *Marxism and the Existentialists*. Translated by Helen Weaver, Robert Addis, and John Weightman. New York: Simon and Schuster 1970
Ashton, T.H., and C.H.E. Philpin, eds. *The Brennar Debate*. Cambridge: Cambridge University Press 1985
Avineri, Shlomo. *Hegel's Theory of the Modern State*. Cambridge: Cambridge University Press 1972
– *Karl Marx: Social and Political Thought*. Cambridge: Cambridge University Press 1968

Bajt, Alexander. "Social Ownership – Collective and Individual." In Horvat et al., *Self-Governing Socialism* 2: 151–63

Bardhan, Pranab, and John Roemer, eds. *Market Socialism: The Current Debate*. Oxford: Oxford University Press 1993

Barkai, H. *Israel and Arabs: Views from the Left*. New York: Bantam Books 1972

– "The Kibbutz: An Experiment in Microsocialism." In Vanek, *Self-Management*, 213–26

Bataille, Georges. *The Accursed Share: An Essay on General Economy*. Vol. 1. Translated by Robert Hurley. New York: Zone Books 1991

– *L'Érotisme*. Paris: Les Éditions de Minuit 1957/*Erotism: Death and Sensuality*. San Francisco: City Lights Books 1986

Baur, Michael, and John Russon. *Hegel and the Tradition: Essays in Honour of H.S. Harris*. Toronto: University of Toronto Press 1997

Beauvoir, Simone de. *The Ethics of Ambiguity*. Translated by Bernard Frechtman. New York: The Citadel Press 1968

– *The Second Sex*. New York: Vintage Books 1989

Benhabib, Seyla. *Critique, Norm and Utopia: A Study of the Foundations of Critical Theory*. New York: Columbia University Press 1986

Benjamin, Jessica. *The Bonds of Love: Psychoanalysis, Feminism, and the Problem of Domination*. New York: Pantheon Books 1988

Ben-Rafael, Eliezer. *Crisis and Transformation: The Kibbutz at Century's End*. Albany: State University of New York Press 1996

Berlin, Isaiah. *Four Essays on Liberty*. New York: Oxford University Press 1970

Bernasconi, Robert. "Will the Real Kant Please Stand Up? The Challenge of Enlightenment Racism to the Study of the History of Philosophy." *Radical Philosophy* 117 (January/February 2003): 13–22

Bernasconi Robert, and Joseph McCarney. "Exchange: Hegel's Racism?" *Radical Philosophy* 119 (May/June 2003): 32–7

Bonetto, Sandra. "Race and Racism in Hegel – An Analysis." *Minerva – An Internet Journal of Philosophy* 10 (2006)

Bradley, F.H. *Ethical Studies*. Oxford: Clarendon Press 1927

Branford, Sue, and Jan Rocha. *Cutting the Wire: The Story of the Landless Movement in Brazil*. London: Latin America Bureau 2002

Braudel, Fernand. *Civilization and Capitalism: Fifteenth to Eighteenth Century*. Vol. 1, *The Structures of Everyday Life*. Vol. 2, *The Wheels of Commerce*. Vol. 3. *The Perspective of the World*. Translated by Siân Reynolds. Berkeley: University of California Press 1984

Brennar, Robert. "Agrarian Class Structure and Economic Development in Pre-Industrial Europe." *Past and Present* 97 (1982): 16–113

Brus, Włodzimierz. *The Economics and Politics of Socialism: Collected Essays*. London: Routledge and Kegan Paul 1973

– *The Market in a Socialist Economy*. Translated by Angus Walker. London: Routledge and Kegan Paul 1972

– *Socialist Ownership and Political Systems*. Translated by R.A. Clarke. London: Routledge and Kegan Paul 1975

Buck-Morss, Susan. *Hegel, Haiti and Universal History*. Pittsburgh: University of Pittsburgh Press 2009

Burbidge, John. *Hegel on Logic and Religion: The Reasonableness of Christianity*. Albany: State University of New York Press 1992

– *On Hegel's Logic: Fragments of a Commentary*. Atlantic Highlands: Humanities Press 1981

– *Hegel's Systematic Contingency*. New York: Palgrave 2007

– *The Logic of Hegel's Logic*. Peterborough: Broadview Press 2006

– "'Unhappy Consciousness' in Hegel: An Analysis of Medieval Christianity?" *Mosaic* 11, no. 4 (Summer 1978): 67–80

Burke, Edmund. *Reflections on the Revolution in France*. London: Penguin 1968

Butler, Judith. *Subjects of Desire: Hegelian Reflections in Twentieth-Century France*. New York: Columbia University Press 1987

Butler, Judith, Ernesto Laclau, and Slavoj Žižek. *Contingency, Hegemony, Universality: Contemporary Dialogues on the Left*. London and New York: Verso 2000

Carens, Joseph H. *Democracy and Possessive Individualism: The Intellectual Legacy of C.B. MacPherson*. Albany: State University of NewYork Press 1983

Castañeda, Jorge. *Compañero: The Life and Times of Che Guevara*. Translated by Marina Castañeda. NewYork: Vintage Books 1998

– *Utopia Unarmed: The Latin American Left after the Cold War*. New York: Vintage Books 1994

Chapman, John W., and J. Roland Pennock. *Nomos XXII: Property*. New York: New York University Press 1980

Chomsky, Noam. *Turning the Tide: The U.S. in Latin America*. Montreal: Black Rose 1987

Chomsky, Noam, and Edward S. Herman. *Manufacturing Consent*. New York: Pantheon Books 1988

Ciavatta, David. *Spirit, the Family and the Unconscious in Hegel's Philosophy*. Albany: State University of New York Press 2009

Cohen, G.A. *Karl Marx's Theory of History: A Defense*. Ex. ed. Princeton: Princeton University Press 2000

– *Why not Socialism?* Princeton: Princeton University Press 2009

Collier, George A., with Elizabeth Lowery Quaratiello. *Basta! Land and the Zapatista Rebellion in Chiapas*. Oakland: The Institute for Food and Development Policy 1994

Collingwood, R.G. *An Essay on Philosophical Method*. Oxford: Clarendon Press 2005

Comay, Rebecca. *Mourning Sickness: Hegel and the French Revolution*. Stanford: Standford University Press 2011

Conway, Daniel. *Nietszche and the Political*. London: Routledge 1997

Coutinho, Carlos Nelson. *Contra a Corrente: Ensaios sobre Democracia e Socialismo*. São Paulo: Cortez Editora 2000

– *Gramsci: Um Estudo Sobre Seu Pensamento Político*. 2nd ed. Rio de Janeiro: Civilização Brasileira 1999

Cullen, Bernard. *Hegel's Social and Political Thought: An Introduction*. New York: St Martin's Press 1979

Deleuze, Gilles, and Félix Guattari. *Anti-Oedipus: Capitalism and Schizophrenia*. Translated by Robert Hurley, Mark Seem, and Helen R. Lane. Minneapolis: University of Minnesota Press 1983

Diniz, Aldiva Sales, and Bruce Gilbert. "'Socialist Values' and Cooperation in Brazil's Movement of Landless Rural Workers." *Latin American Perspectives* 140, no. 4 (July 2013): 19–34

Duplessis, Robert S. *Transitions to Capitalism in Early Modern Europe*. Cambridge: Cambridge University Press 1997

Dussel, Enrique. "The Four Drafts of Capital: Toward a New Interpretation of the Dialectical Thought of Marx." *Rethinking Marxism* 13, no.1 (Spring 2001): 10–26

Eagleton, Terry. *Marx and Freedom*. London: Phoenix 1997

Ellerman, David P. *Property and Contract Economics: The Case for Economic Democracy*. Cambridge: Blackwell Publishers 1992

Elliott, Anthony. *Social Theory and Psychoanalysis in Transition: Self and Society from Freud to Kristeva*. Oxford: Basil Blackwell 1992

Elster, Jon. *Making Sense of Marx*. Cambridge: Cambridge University Press 1985

Epictetus. *The Handbook*. Hackett Publishing Company 1983

Estrin, Saul. "Workers' Cooperatives: Their Merits and Their Limitations." In Le Grand and Estrin, *Market Socialism*, 165–92

Fagan, Patricia. "Philosophical History and the Roman Empire." In Baur and Russon, *Hegel and the Tradition*, 17–39

Fernandes, Bernardo Mançano. *A Formaçao do MST no Brasil*. Petropolis: Editora Voces 2000

Fillion, Réal. *Multicultural Dynamics and the Ends of History: Exploring Kant, Hegel, and Marx*. Ottawa: University of Ottawa Press 2008

Findlay, J.N. *Hegel: A Re-examination*. New York: Collier Books 1962

Franco, Paul. *Hegel's Philosophy of Freedom*. New Haven: Yale University Press 1999

Freire, Paulo. *Pedagogy of the Oppressed*. Translated by Myra Bergman. New York: Continuum 2000

Freud, Sigmund. *Civilization and Its Discontents*. Translated by James Strachey. New York: W.W. Norton and Company 1961

Fromm, Erich. *The Anatomy of Human Destructiveness*. Greenwich: Fawcett Publications 1973

– *The Art of Loving*. New York: Harper and Row 1956

– *Escape from Freedom*. New York: Discus Books 1965

– *To Have or to Be*. New York: Harper and Row 1976

– *Marx's Concept of Man*. New York: Frederick Ungar Publishing Co. 1974

– *The Sane Society*. New York: Holt, Rinehardt and Winston 1955

Gadamer, Hans-Georg. *Hegel's Dialectic*. Translated by P. Christopher Smith. New Haven: Yale University Press 1976

Galleano, Eduardo. *Las Venas Abiertas de América Latina*. México: Siglo Veintiuno 1980

Gauvin, Joseph. "Entfremdung et Entäusserung dans la *Phénoménologie de l'Esprit* de Hegel." *Archives de philosophie* 25 (1962): 555–71

Gavron, Daniel. *The Kibbutz: Awakening from Utopia*. Lanham: Rowman and Littlefield Publishers, Inc. 2000

Goldman, Emma. *Anarchism and Other Essays*. New York: Dover Publications 1969

Gramsci, Antonio. *Selections from the Prison Notebooks*. Edited and translated by Quintin Hoare and Geoffrey Nowell Smith. New York: International Publishers 1971

Guérin, Daniel. *Anarchism: From Theory to Practice*. New York: Monthly Review Press 1970

Guess, Raymond. *The Idea of a Critical Theory: Habermas and the Frankfurt School*. Cambridge: Cambridge University Press 1981

Habermas, Jürgen. *Legitimation Crisis*. Translated by Thomas McCarthy. Boston: Beacon Press 1975

– *The Philosophical Discourse of Modernity: Twelve Lectures*. Translated by Frederick Lawrence. Cambridge: Massachusetts Institute of Technology Press 1987

– *The Theory of Communicative Action*. Vol. 1, *Reason and the Rationalization of Society*. Vol. 2, *Lifeworld and System: A Critique of Functionalist Reason*. Translated by Thomas McCarthy. Boston: Beacon Press 1987

– *Theory and Praxis*. Translated by John Viertel. Boston: Beacon Press 1973

Hahn, Songsuk Susan. *Contradiction in Motion: Hegel's Organic Concept of Life and Value*. Ithaca: Cornell University Press 2007

Hanna, Robert. "From an Ontological Point of View: Hegel's Critique of the Common Logic." In Stewart, *The Hegel Myths and Legends*, 253–82

Hardimon, Michael. *Hegel's Social Philosophy: The Project of Reconciliation*. Cambridge: Cambridge University Press 1994

Hardt, Michael, and Antonio Negri. *Empire*. Cambridge: Harvard University Press 2000

– *Labor of Dionysus: A Critique of the State-Form*. Minneapolis: University of Minnesota Press 1994

– *Multitudes: War and Democracy in the Age of Empire*. New York: Penguin Books 2004

Harnecker, Marta. *Tornar Possível o Impossível: A Esquerda no Limiar do Seculo XXI*. Translated (from Spanish to Portuguese) by José Colaça Barreiros. São Paulo: Editora Paz e Terra S/A 2000

Harris, H.S. *Hegel: Phenomenology and System*. Indianapolis: Hackett Publishing Company 1995

– *Hegel's Ladder*. 2 vols. Indianapolis: Hackett Publishing Company 1997

– "The Social Ideal of Hegel's Economic Theory." In *Selected Essays on G.W.F. Hegel*, edited by Lawrence Stepelevich, 187–212. Atlantic Highlands, NJ: Humanities Press 1993

Haug, Wolfgang Fritz. "From Marx to Gramsci, from Gramsci to Marx: Historical Materialism and the Philosophy of Praxis." *Rethinking Marxism* 13, no.1 (Spring 2001): 69–82

Hayek, F.A. *The Collected Works of F. A. Hayek*. Chicago: University of Chicago Press 1989

Heller, Agnes. *The Theory of Need in Marx*. London: Allison and Busby Limited, 1976

Henrich, Dieter. *Between Kant and Hegel: Lectures on German Idealism*. Edited by David S. Pacini. Cambridge and London: Harvard University Press 2003

– "Französische Revolution und klassische deutsche Philosophie." In *Eine Republik Deutschland*, edited by D. Heinrich, 71–101. Frankfurt am Main: Suhrkamp 1990

– "Logical Form and Real Totality: The Authentic Conceptual Form of Hegel's Concept of the State." In Pippin and Höffe, *Hegel on Ethics and Politics*, 241–67

Hilton, Rodney, ed. *The Transition from Feudalism to Capitalism*. London: Verso 1978

Hobbes, Thomas. *Leviathan*. London: Penguin Books 1985

Hölderlin, F. *Hyperion*. Translated by Eric L. Santner. New York: Continuum 1990

Honneth, Axel. *The I in We: Studies in the Theory of Recognition*. Translated by Joseph Ganahl. Cambridge: Polity Press 2012

– *The Pathologies of Individual Freedom: Hegel's Social Theory*. Translated by Ladislaus Löb. Princeton: Princeton University Press 2001

– *The Struggle for Recognition: The Moral Grammar of Social Conflicts*. Translated by Joel Anderson. Cambridge: MIT Press 1996

Hook, Sidney. *From Hegel to Marx: Studies in the Intellectual Development of Karl Marx*. Ann Arbor: University of Michigan Press 1971

Horkheimer, Max. *Critical Theory*. Translated by Matthew J. O'Connell et al. New York: Continuum 1986

– *Critique of Instrumental Reason*. Translated by Matthew J. O'Connell et al. New York: Continuum 1974

Horvat, Branko. *The Political Economy of Socialism: A Marxist Social Theory*. Armonk, NY: M.E. Sharpe 1982

– *The Yugoslav Economic System: The First Labor-Managed Economy in the Making*. White Plains, NY: International Arts and Science Press 1976

Horvat, Branko, Mihailo Marković, Rudi Supek, and H. Kramer. *Self-Governing Socialism: A Reader*. 3 vols. White Plains, NY: International Arts and Sciences Press 1975

Houlgate, Stephen. *An Introduction to Hegel: Freedom, Truth and History*. 2nd ed. London: Blackwell 2005

– *The Opening of Hegel's Logic: From Being to Infinity*. West Lafayette: Perdue University Press 2006

Hyppolite, Jean. *Genesis and Structure of Hegel's Phenomenology of Spirit*.

Translated by Samuel Herniak and John Heckman. Evanston: Northwestern University Press 1974

– *Studies on Marx and Hegel*. Translated by John O'Neill. New York: Basic Books 1969

Independent Commission on International Development Issues, Willy Brandt, Chair. *North-South: A Program for Survival*. Cambridge: Massachusetts Institute of Technology Press 1980

Inwood, Michael. *A Hegel Dictionary*. London: Blackwell Publishers 1992

Jameson, Frederic. *The Hegel Variations: On the Phenomenology of Spirit*. London: Verso 2010

– *Representing Capital: A Reading of Volume One*. London: Verso 2011

– *Valences of the Dialectic*. London: Verso 2009

Janicaud, Dominique. *Hegel et le destin de la Grèce*. Paris: Presses universitaires de France 1975

Jay, Martin. *The Dialectical Imagination: A History of the Frankfurt School and the Institute of Social Research, 1923–1950*. Boston: Little, Brown and Company 1973

Kanoussi, Dora. *Una Introducción a Los Cuadernos de la Cárcel de Antonio Gramsci*. México: Plaza y Valdéz 2000

Kant, Immanuel. *Critique of Pure Reason*. Translated by Norman Kemp Smith. London: MacMillan 1929

– *On Education*. New York: Dover Publications 2003

– *Grounding for the Metaphysics of Morals*. Translated by James W. Ellington. Indianapolis: Hackett Publishing Company 1981

– *Kant: Political Writings*. Edited by Hans Reiss. Translated by H.B. Nisbet. Cambridge: Cambridge University Press 1991

– *Metaphysics of Morals*. Translated by Mary Gregor. Cambridge: Cambridge University Press 1996

Kirk, G.S., and J.E. Raven, eds. *The Presocratic Philosophers: A Critical History with a Selection of Texts*. Cambridge: Cambridge University Press 1957

Kojève, Alexandre. *Introduction to the Reading of Hegel: Lectures on the Phenomenology of Spirit*. Edited by Allan Bloom. Translated by James H. Nichols, Jr. Ithaca: Cornell University Press 1969

Kołakowski, Leszek. *Main Currents of Marxism*. 2nd ed. Translated by P.S. Falla. New York: W.W. Norton and Company 2005

Kolb, David. *The Critique of Pure Modernity: Hegel, Heidegger and After*. Chicago: University of Chicago Press 1986

Konder, Leandro. *Fourier, O Socialismo e o Prazer*. Rio de Janeiro: Civilização Brasileiro 1998

Kymlicka, Will. *Liberalism, Community and Culture*. Oxford: Oxford University Press 1989

Laclau, Ernesto. *Emancipations*. London: Verso 1996

– *On Populist Reason*. London: Verso 2005

Laclau, Ernesto, and Chantal Mouffe. *Hegemony and Socialist Strategy*. London: Verso 1996

LaFeber, Walter. *Inevitable Revolutions: The United States in Central America*. New York: W.W. Norton 1984

Laing, R.D. *The Divided Self*. London: Penguin 1990

Lakshmanna, C., R.C. Sarikwal, and S.P. Srivastava. *Workers' Participation and Industrial Democracy – Global Perspectives*. Delhi: Ajanta Publications 1990

Lampe, John R. *Yugoslavia as History: Twice There Was a Country*. Cambridge: Cambridge University Press 1996

Lampert, Jay. "Husserl and Hegel on the Logic of Subjectivity." *Man and World* 21 (1988): 363–93

– "Locke, Fichte and Hegel on the Right to Property." In Baur and Russon, *Hegel and the Tradition*, 40–73

Le Grand, Julian, and Saul Estrin, eds. *Market Socialism*. Oxford: Clarendon Press 1989

Leiss, William. *The Domination of Nature*. Boston: Beacon Press 1974

Levinas, Immanuel. *Totality and Infinity: An Essay on Exteriority*. Translated by Alphonso Lingis. Pittsburgh: Duquesne University Press 1969

Locke, John. *The Second Treatise of Government*. Indianapolis: Hackett Publishing Company 1980

Losurdo, Domenico. *Hegel and the Freedom of Moderns*. Translated by Marella Morris and Jon Morris. Durham: Duke University Press 2004

Löwith, Karl. *From Hegel to Nietzsche: The Revolution in Nineteenth-Century Thought*. Translated by David E. Green. New York: Holt, Rinehart and Winston 1964

Lukacs, Georg. *History and Class Consciousness*. Translated by Rodney Livingstone. London: Merlin Press 1990

– *The Ontology of Social Being*. Vol. 3, *Labour*. Translated by David Fernbach. London: Merlin Press 1978

– *The Young Hegel*. Translated by Rodney Livingstone. London: The Merlin Press 1975

MacDonald, Bradley J. "Marx and the Figure of Desire." *Rethinking Marxism* 11, no. 4 (Winter 1999): 21–37

MacGregor, David. *The Communist Ideal in Hegel and Marx*. Toronto: University of Toronto Press 1984

– *Hegel and Marx: After the Fall of Communism*. Cardiff: University of Wales Press 1998

Machiavelli, Niccolò. *The Prince*. Translated by Robert Adams. New York: W.W. Norton 1977

MacIntyre, Alasdair. *After Virtue*. South Bend: Notre Dame University Press 1981

MacLaren, Kym. "On Being Moved: A Phenomenological Account of Emotion and Transformation." PhD diss., Pennsylvania StateUniversity, 2004

Macpherson, C.B. *Democratic Theory: Essays in Retrieval*. Oxford: Clarendon Press 1973

– *The Life and Times of Liberal Democracy*. Oxford: Oxford University Press 1977

– *Property: Mainstream and Critical Positions*. Toronto: University of Toronto Press 1978

Maker, William. "Does Hegel Have a 'Dialectical Method'?" *Southern Journal of Philosophy* 20 (1982): 75–96

Malabou, Catherine. *The Future of Hegel: Plasticity, Temporality and Dialectic*. Translated by Lisabeth During. London and New York: Routledge 2005

Mandel, Ernest. *An Introduction to Marxist Economic Theory*. New York: Pathfinder Press 1969

– *Marxist Economic Theory*. 2 vols. Translated by Brian Pearce. London: The Merlin Press 1968

Mandel, Ernest, and George Novack. *The Marxist Theory of Alienation*. New York: Pathfinder Press 1970

Marcuse, Herbert. *Eros and Civilization*. Boston: Beacon Press 1966

– *An Essay on Liberation*. London: Penguin 1969

– *One Dimensional Man: Studies in the Ideology of Advanced Industrial Society*. London: Ark Paperbacks 1986

– *Reason and Revolution: Hegel and the Rise of Social Theory*. Boston: Beacon Press 1960

– *Soviet Marxism: A Critical Analysis*. New York: Vintage Books 1958

Marković, M. *From Affluence to Praxis*. Ann Arbor: University of Michigan Press 1974

Marx, Karl. *Capital: A Critique of Political Economy*. Vol. 1, translated by Ben

Fowkes, 1990. Vol. 2, translated by David Fernbach, 1992. Vol. 3, translated by David Fernbach, 1991. London: Penguin Books

– *Grundrisse*. Translated by Martin Nicolaus. London: Penguin Books 1993

– *Karl Marx: Early Writings*. Edited and translated by Tom Bottomore. New York: McGraw Hill Books 1963

– *The Portable Karl Marx*. Edited by Eugene Kamenka. London: Penguin 1983

– *Value, Price and Profit*. New York: International Co., Inc. 1969

Marx, Karl, and Friedrich Engels. *German Ideology*. Amherst, NY: Prometheus Books 1998

– *The Marx-Engels Reader*. 2nd ed. Edited by Robert C. Tucker. New York: W.W. Norton and Company 1978

McCumber, John. *The Company of Words: Hegel, Language, and Systematic Philosophy*. Evanston: Northwestern University Press 1993

– "Contradictions and Resolution in the State: Hegel's Covert View." *Clio* 15 (1986): 379–90

Merleau-Ponty, Maurice. *Adventures of the Dialectic*. Translated by Joseph Bien. Evanston: Northwestern University Press 1973

– *Humanism and Terror*. Translated by John O'Neill. Boston: Beacon Press 1969

– *Phenomenology of Perception*. Translated by Colin Smith. London: Routledge 1994

– *Sense and Non-Sense*. Translated by Hubert L. Dreyfus and Patricia Allen Dreyfus. Evanston: Northwestern University Press 1964

Milenkovitch, D.D. *The Worker-Managed Enterprise*. Princeton: Yale University Press 1971

Mill, John Stuart. *On Liberty*. Buffalo: Prometheus Books 1966

– *Utilitarianism*. Indianapolis: Hackett Publishing Company 1979

Mills, Patricia J. *Woman, Nature and Psyche*. New Haven: Yale University Press 1987

Montesquieu, Charles de Secondat, baron de. *The Spirit of the Laws*. Translated by Anne M. Cohlher, Basia Carolyn Miller, and Harold Samuel Stone. Cambridge: Cambridge University Press 1989

Nancy, Jean-Luc. *The Restlessness of the Negative*. Translated by Jason Smith and Steven Miller. Minneapolis: University of Minnesota Press 2002

Near, Henry. *The Kibbutz Movement: A History*. 2 vols. London: The Littman Library of Jewish Civilization 1992 and 1997

Neuhouser, Frederick. *Foundations of Hegel's Social Theory: Actualizing Freedom*. Cambridge. Harvard University Press 2000

Nove, Alec. *The Economics of Feasible Socialism Revisited*. London: Harper Collins Academic 1991

– *Socialism, Economics and Development*. London: Allen and Unwin 1986

Nove, Alec, and D.M. Nuti. *Socialist Economics*. London: Penguin Books 1972

Nozick, Robert. *Anarchy, State and Utopia*. New York: Basic Books 1974

Oakeshott, R. "Mondragon: Spain's Oasis of Democracy." In Vanek, *Self-Management: The Economic Liberation of Man*, 290–6

– "Political Education." In Sandel, *Liberalism and Its Critics*, 219–38

Offe, Claus. *Contradictions of the Welfare State*. Edited by John Keane. Cambridge: Massachusetts Institute of Technology Press 1984

Ollman, Bertell. *Alienation: Marx's Concept of Man in Capitalist Society*. Cambridge: Cambridge University Press 1971

Panitch, Leo. *Renewing Socialism: Democracy, Strategy and Imagination*. Pontypool: Merlin Press 2008

Pavin, Avrahim. *The Kibbutz Movement: Facts and Figures*. Yad Tabenkin: Research and Documentation Centre of the Kibbutz Movement 2005

Pelczynski, Z., ed. *Hegel's Political Philosophy: Problems and Perspectives*. Cambridge: Cambridge University Press 1971

– ed. *The State and Civil Society: Studies in Hegel's Political Philosophy*. Cambridge: Cambridge University Press 1984

Pinkard, Terry. "Freedom and Social Categories in Hegel's Ethics." *Philosophy and Phenomenological Research* 47 (1986–87): 209–32

– *Hegel's Dialectic: The Explanation of Possibility*. Philadelphia: Temple University Press 1988

Pippin, Robert B. *Hegel's Idealism: The Satisfactions of Self-Consciousness*. Cambridge: Cambridge University Press 1996

– "Hegel's Metaphysics and the Problem of Contradiction." In Stewart, *The Hegel Myths and Legends*, 239–52

– *Hegel's Practical Philosophy: Rational Agency as Ethical Life*. Cambridge: Cambridge University Press 2008

Pippin, Robert, and Otfried Höffe, eds. *Hegel on Ethics and Politics*. Translated by Nicholas Walker. Cambridge: Cambridge University Press 2004

Plamenatz, J.P. *Karl Marx's Philosophy of Man*. Oxford: Oxford University Press 1975

– *Man and Society*. 2 vols. London: Longman's 1963

Plato. *Complete Works*. Edited by John M. Cooper. Indianapolis: Hackett Publishing Company 1997

Proudhon, J.-P. *What Is Property? An Inquiry into the Principle of Right and Governance*. Translated by Benjamin R. Tucker. New York: Dover Publications Inc. 1970

Przeworski, Adam. *Capitalism and Social Democracy*. Cambridge: Cambridge University Press 1985

Rawls, John. *Political Liberalism*. New York: Columbia University Press 1993

– *A Theory of Justice*. Cambridge: Harvard University Press 1971

Recco, Gregory. *Athens Victorious: Democracy in Plato's Republic*. Lanham: Lexington Books 2007

Riedel, Manfred. *Between Tradition and Revolution*. Cambridge: Cambridge University Press 1984

– *Bürgerliche Gesellschaft und Staat bei Hegel*. Neuwied: Luchterhand Verlag 1970

– *System und Geschichte*. Frankfurt: Suhrkamp Verlag 1973

Ripstein, Arthur. "Universal and General Wills: Hegel and Rousseau." *Political Theory* 22 (1994): 444–67

Ritter, Joachim. *Hegel and the French Revolution*. Translated by Richard Dien Winfield. Cambridge: Massachusetts Institute of Technology Press 1982

Roemer, John. *Equal Shares: Making Market Socialism Work*. Edited by Erik Olin Wright. London: Verso 1996

– *Free to Lose: An Introduction to Marxist Economic Philosophy*. Cambridge: Harvard University Press 1988

– *A Future for Socialism*. Cambridge: Harvard University Press 1994

– *A General Theory of Exploitation and Class*. Cambridge: Harvard University Press 1982

Rosen, Stanley. *G.W.F. Hegel: An Introduction to the Science of Wisdom*. New Haven: Yale University Press 1974

Rousseau, Jean-Jacques. *Émile*. Translated by Allan Bloom. New York: Basic Books 1979

– *The Social Contract*. Translated by Maurice Cranston. London: Penguin 1968

Ruda, Frank. *Hegel's Rabble: An Investigation into Hegel's Philosophy of Right*. New York: Continuum Publishing Company 2011

Russon, John. *Bearing Witness to Epiphany: Persons, Things and the Nature of Erotic Life*. Albany: State University of New York Press 2009

– *Human Experience: Philosophy, Neurosis, and the Elements of Everyday Life*. Albany: State University of New York Press 2003

– "Reading: Derrida in Hegel's Understanding." *Research in Phenomenology* 36 (2006): 181–200

– *Reading Hegel's Phenomenology of Spirit*. Indianapolis: Indiana University Press 2004

– *The Self and Its Body in Hegel's Phenomenology of Spirit*. Toronto: University of Toronto Press 1997

Ryan, Alan. *Property and Political Theory*. London: Basil Blackwell 1984

Sanday, Erik. *A Study of Dialectic in Plato's* Parmenides. Evanston: Northwestern University Press, forthcoming

Sandel, Michael. *Democracy's Discontent: America in Search of a Public Philosophy*. Cambridge: Harvard University Press 1996

– *Liberalism and the Limits of Justice*. 2nd ed. Cambridge: Cambridge University Press 1998

– ed. *Liberalism and Its Critics*. New York: New York University Press 1984

Schacht, Richard. *Alienation*. Lanham: University Press of America 1984

Schiller, Frederich. *On the Aesthetic Education of Man: In a Series of Letters*. Translated by Elizabeth M. Wilkinson and L.A. Willoughby. Oxford: Oxford University Press 1982

Schmidt, Alfred. *The Concept of Nature in Marx*. Translated by Ben Fowkes. London: NLB 1971

Schmitz, Kenneth. "Hegel on Kant: Being-in-Itself and the Thing-in-Itself." In *Studies in Philosophy and the History of Philosophy*, edited by Richard Kennington, 12: 229–51. Washington: Catholic University of America Press 1985

Schweickart, David. *After Capitalism*. 2nd ed. Lanham: Rowman and Littlefield 2011

Selucky, Radoslav. *Marxism, Socialism, Freedom: Towards a General Democratic Theory of Labour-Managed Systems*. London: MacMillan Press 1979

Shklar, Judith. *Freedom and Independence: A Study of the Political Ideas in Hegel's Phenomenology of Mind*. Cambridge: Cambridge University Press 1976

Siep, Ludwig. "Zur Dialektik der Anerkennung bei Hegel." *Hegel-Jarbuch* (1974): 388–95

Simpson, Peter. *Hegel's Transcendental Induction*. Albany: State University of New York Press 1998

Smith, Adam. *An Inquiry into the Nature and Causes of the Wealth of Nations*. New York: Random House 1937

So, Alvin Y. *Social Change and Development: Modernization, Dependency, and World-System Theories*. Newbury Park, CA: Sage Publications 1990

Sophocles. *Antigone*. Translated by Paul Woodruff. Indianapolis: Hackett Publishing Company 2001

Spanos, Chris, ed. *Real Utopia: Participatory Society for the 21st Century*. Oakland and Edinburgh: A.K. Press 2008

Stedile, João Pedro, and Bernardo Mançano Fernandes. *Brava Gente: A Trajetória do MST e a Luta Pela Terra no Brasil*. São Paulo: Editora Fundação Perseu Abramo 1999

Steedman, Ian, ed. *The Value Controversy*. London: Verso 1987

Stepelevich, Lawrence S., ed. *Selected Essays on G.W.F. Hegel*. Atlantic Highlands: Humanities Press 1993

Stewart, Jon, ed. *The Hegel Myths and Legends*. Evanston: Northwestern University Press 1996

Tavares dos Santos, José Vicente. *Colonos do Vinho*. São Paulo: Hucitec 1984

Taylor, Charles. *Hegel*. Cambridge: Cambridge University Press 1975

– *Hegel and Modern Society*. Cambridge: Cambridge University Press 1979

– *The Malaise of Modernity*. Toronto: House of Anansi Press 1993

– *Philosophical Arguments*. Cambridge: Harvard University Press 1995

– *Sources of the Self: The Making of Modern Identity*. Cambridge: Harvard University Press 1989

Teichgraeber, Richard. "Hegel on Property and Poverty." *Journal of the History of Ideas* 38 (1977): 47–64

Thomas, H., and C. Logan. *Mondragon*. London: Allen and Unwin 1982

Thompson, E.P. *The Making of the English Working Class*. London: Harmondsworth 1968

Toqueville, Alexis de. *Democracy in America*. 2 vols. Translated by Henry Reeve. Revised by Francis Bowen and Phillips Bradley. New York: Vintage Books 1990

Tunick, Mark. *Hegel's Political Philosophy: Interpreting the Practice of Legal Punishment*. Princeton: Princeton University Press 1992

Vanek, Jaroslav. *The Economics of Workers' Management: A Yugoslav Case Study*. London: George Allen and Unwin 1972

– *The General Theory of Labor-Managed Economies*. Ithaca: Cornell University Press 1970

– *The Labor-Managed Economy*. Ithaca: Cornell University Press 1977

– *The Participatory Economy: An Evolutionary Hypothesis and Strategy for Development*. Ithaca: Cornell University Press 1971

– ed. *Self-Management: The Economic Liberation of Man*. London: Penguin Books 1975

Wallerstein, Immanuel. *Historical Capitalism*. London: Verso 1993

Walzer, Michael. "The Idea of Civil Society: A Path to Social Reconstruction." *Dissent* 38 (1991): 293–304

Warminski, Andrzej. "Reading for Example 'Sense Certainty' in Hegel's *Phenomenology of Spirit.*" *Diacritics* 11 (1981): 83–96

Weber, Max. *The Protestant Ethic and the Spirit of Capitalism.* Translated by Talcott Parsons. New York: Charles Scribner and Sons 1976

Weil, Eric. *Hegel and the State.* Translated by Marc Cohen. Baltimore: John's Hopkins University Press 1998

Westphal, Merold. *History and Truth in Hegel's Phenomenology.* 3rd ed. Bloomington: Indiana University Press 1998

Wilde, Lawrence. *Modern European Socialism.* Aldershot: Dartmouth 1944

Winfield, Richard Dien. *The Just Economy.* New York and London: Routledge 1988

– *The Just Family.* Albany: State University of New York Press 1998

– *Reason and Justice.* Albany: State University of New York Press 1988

Wolford, Wendy, and Angus Wright. *To Inherit the Earth: The Landless Movement and the Struggle for a New Brazil.* Oakland: Food First Books 2003

Wood, Allen. *Hegel's Ethical Thought.* Cambridge: Cambridge University Press 1990

– *Karl Marx.* London: Routledge and Kegan Paul 1981

Wood, Ellen Meiksins. *Democracy against Capitalism: Renewing Historical Materialism.* Cambridge: Cambridge University Press 1994

Žižek, Slavoj. *The Sublime Object of Ideology.* London: Verso 1989

– *Tarrying with the Negative: Kant, Hegel and the Critique of Ideology.* Durham: Duke University Press 1993

– *The Fragile Absolute – or Why the Christian Legacy Is Worth Fighting For.* London: Verso 2000

– *Less than Nothing: Hegel and the Shadow of Dialectical Materialism.* London: Verso 2012

Index